Making Love in the Twelfth Century

THE MIDDLE AGES SERIES

Ruth Mazo Karras, Series Editor
Edward Peters, Founding Editor

A complete list of books in the series is available from the publisher.

Making Love in the Twelfth Century

Letters of Two Lovers in Context

A new translation with commentary by
Barbara Newman

PENN

UNIVERSITY OF PENNSYLVANIA PRESS

PHILADELPHIA

Published by
University of Pennsylvania Press
Philadelphia, Pennsylvania 19104–4112
www.upenn.edu/pennpress

Printed in the United States of America on acid-free paper
10 9 8 7 6 5 4 3 2 1

Library of Congress Cataloging-in-Publication Data

Names: Newman, Barbara, author, translator. | Epistolae duorum
    amantium. Commentary on (work): | Tegernseer Briefsammlung des
    12. Jahrhgunderts. Selections. Commentary on (work): |Carmina
    Ratisponensia. Selections. Commentary on (work):
Title: Making love in the twelfth century : letters of two lovers in context
    / a new translation with commentary by Barbara Newman.
Other titles: Middle Ages series.
Description: Philadelphia : University of Pennsylvania Press. [2016] |
    Series: The Middle Ages series | Contains translations from Latin or
    German. | Includes bibliographical references and index.
Identifiers: LCCN 2015038849 | ISBN 9780812248098 (alk. paper)
Subjects: LCSH: Love-letters—Europe—History—To 1500. | Latin
    letters, Medieval and Modern—History and criticism. | Letter
    writing—Europe—History—To 1500. | Love—Europe—History—To
    1500. | Abelard, Peter, 1079–1142. | Héloïse, approximately 1095–1163
    or 1164. | Epistolae duorum amantium | Tegernseer Briefsammlung
    des 12. Jahrhunderts. Selections. | Carmina Ratisponensia. Selections.
Classification: LCC PN6140.L7 N49 2016 | DDC 876'.03—dc23
LC record available at http://lccn.loc.gov/2015038849

R. dilectissimo suo,

magistro virtutibus, magistro moribus,

viventium carissimo

et super vitam diligendo

Contents

Preface

Nine hundred years ago in the north of France, a man and a woman fell in love and began to exchange letters. The man was a philosopher, a famous teacher who, to the delight of his beloved, had also "drunk from the fountain of poetry." The woman, his student, was in her lover's eyes a great beauty. She was also eloquent, passionately devoted to her teacher, and morally earnest to the nth degree, inspiring him to call her "the only disciple of philosophy among all the girls of our age." Teaching must have been a competitive sport in their milieu, for one of her letters is a victory ode, congratulating her lover on his academic triumph over a rival. The couple's letters reveal little beyond this about their identity or individual circumstances, for they come down to us only in a single late, painfully abridged manuscript. We know the name of its compiler and scribe, but the lovers themselves remain anonymous, without even initials to hint at their names.

By reading these fragmentary letters in their historical context, we can glean a few more details. For instance, the woman had obviously been educated in a convent. She could have acquired her excellent Latin and her familiarity with classical authors, along with her deep knowledge of Scripture and liturgy, in no other milieu. Yet she was not a nun, far less a princess or lady of high rank—a fact that makes her unique among the handful of female correspondents known from this period. The discourse of virtue flows readily from her stylus, but one particular virtue—chastity—is nowhere mentioned. The only "vows" she acknowledges are those of love. She speaks constantly of *amicitia* (friendship) and *dilectio* (personal love), but also of *amor* (erotic love) and *desiderium* (desire) with its "flames." Her teacher, though certainly a cleric, seems not to be a monk or priest. His biblical allusions are fewer than hers, but his citations of Ovid more frequent. The themes of the correspondence are those of lovers everywhere (praise of each other's beauty and brilliance, cries of passion, fear of abandonment, professions of fidelity and eternal love), with a strong mix of period motifs (the duties of friendship, the danger of envious foes, the fear of scandal).

Despite the lovers' florid mutual compliments, the course of their affair was anything but smooth. Judging from a poem the man composed to celebrate their first anniversary, which falls about two-thirds of the way through the correspondence, they remained together for about a year and a half, though for much of that time they were separated and unable to meet. The woman seems to have found this long-distance relationship more troubling than her partner did, for she alternates between protesting her changeless constancy and accusing him of faithlessness—by which she means not loving another, but forgetting her and reneging on his promised visits. He defends himself fervently, insisting that his love has not changed except to grow even stronger—yet he admits to becoming more cautious as he tries to stifle dangerous rumors. After at least two bitter quarrels and hard-won reconciliations, the correspondence simply ends. We do not know how or why, for the exchange as we have it is maddeningly oblique. The sequence of letters in the manuscript does not preserve the order in which they were sent. Some are almost certainly missing, and a great many have been deliberately abridged, for the scribe makes it clear that his interest lies in fine specimens of epistolary style, not in the lovers' story. They were probably just as anonymous for him as they are for us. The manuscript from which he copied their letters, as any novelist could predict, has disappeared.

What happened to these lovers when their affair came to an end? Could some crime of passion have parted them? Did they marry each other? Or could they have entered religious life? One true, simple, and infuriating answer to such questions is "we don't know." A different answer—possibly true, not at all simple, satisfying to some but infuriating to others—is "yes" to all of the above.

Were the mysterious lovers, in fact, Abelard and Heloise?

Epistolae duorum amantium and the Second Authenticity Debate

The reader will guess that I am not the first to pose that question.

These letters are known to the scholarly world as *Epistolae duorum amantium* (EDA or *Letters of Two Lovers*) from the title given them by their scribe, one Johannes de Vepria or Jean de Voivre.[1] A young humanist monk and librarian at the Abbey of Clairvaux, de Vepria copied the letters in 1471, having discovered their presumably much older exemplars while cataloguing the library for his abbot. The anthology he produced (Troyes, Médiathèque municipale MS 1452) is a *summa dictaminis*, a collection of model letters assembled to illustrate the fine art of letter writing, with samples ranging from late antiquity to his own day. Among his models, the EDA are the only ones that constitute an ongoing correspondence between two individuals, as opposed to the collected letters of a single writer. In the absence of identifying names or initials, de Vepria designated these correspondents with marginal notes: M for *Mulier* (Woman) and V for *Vir* (Man). The approximate date of the letters, along with the separate identities of *Mulier* and *Vir*, were established by their editor, Ewald Könsgen, in 1974. On stylistic grounds (to be explored below), Könsgen showed that the EDA could not have been the work of a single author, such as a *dictator* (teacher of letter writing) with interests like those of Johannes de Vepria himself. If we accept his conclusion that the writers were in fact two distinct historical persons, the EDA are extraordinary even if they must remain anonymous, because they represent by far the longest correspondence between *any* two individuals to survive from the Middle Ages.[2]

Könsgen and his publisher may have aimed to tantalize readers by giving his edition the subtitle *Briefe Abaelards und Heloises*? But this was an honest question, for he concluded that the anonymous writers must have been a couple "like" Abelard and Heloise without presenting their authorship as fact.[3] That would hardly have been prudent in 1974, even if he had been more confident of the ascription than he was, because medievalists at the time were embroiled in a bitter controversy over the authenticity of what I shall call the monastic or canonical letters of Abelard and Heloise.[4] This debate grew indirectly out of a long-standing romantic fascination with the lovers. The *editio princeps* of their letters, published by François d'Amboise and André Duchesne in 1616, inspired numerous French adaptations, many of them more fanciful than accurate.[5] Alexander Pope's "Eloisa to Abelard" (1717), an Ovidian heroic epistle—composed in the same genre that so deeply influenced the real Heloise—is but the most famous of the innumerable poems, songs, novels, plays, paintings, and more recently, operas and films inspired by the couple. In 1817, Josephine Bonaparte had their bodies transferred to the new Père Lachaise Cemetery in Paris, where their tomb rapidly became a shrine. It was only natural that such a romantic legend should drive historians, fired by the new spirit of positivism, to take a more skeptical look at their Latin letters.

From the early nineteenth century onward, rumblings of doubt were heard from time to time, mostly from historians who suspected that Abelard had composed the entire correspondence as an exemplary fiction to illustrate the "conversion" of Heloise. At a time when the authenticity of virtually all writing by medieval women was being challenged, skepticism was fueled by disbelief that any twelfth-century woman could write such learned, eloquent Latin.[6] In Heloise's case, another factor weighed at least as heavily: the conviction that no abbess as successful as she could possibly have committed such sensual, even blasphemous thoughts to parchment.[7] The historian John Benton provoked a *cause célèbre* when, at a 1972 conference at Cluny, he proposed an elaborate forg-ery theory involving not one but two forgers working across two centuries.[8] In the same year, the influential critic D. W. Robertson, Jr., published a book sup-porting the thesis of an Abelardian fiction.[9] Heated controversy raged for more than two decades.

In addition to Robertson and Benton (who retracted his controversial view in 1979),[10] Hubert Silvestre, Deborah Fraioli, and others argued against authen-ticity from a variety of positions,[11] while other medievalists including Paul Zumthor, Georges Duby, and Peter von Moos adopted a stance of cautious but skeptical agnosticism.[12] If positivist history had fueled doubts of one kind, post-structuralist thought now encouraged another—a belief that "the text carries its own meaning," as Zumthor put it, in some "utopic place" of pure textuality. Thus "it matters little whether it is a fictional narrative or an autobiographical account."[13] The resurgence of feminism, on the other hand, made it possible to take historical women seriously again and sparked new interest in Heloise as both writer and abbess. From the 1970s through the '90s, medievalists such as Peter Dronke, David Luscombe, and I argued for authenticity, bringing new historical evidence and a wide range of methodologies to bear on the question.[14] M. T. Clanchy made a decisive intervention by treating the letters as authentic in his 1997 biography of Abelard.[15]

By the turn of the century, the First Authenticity Debate had subsided, with most participants either persuaded by argument or swayed by consensus—just in time to begin a Second Authenticity Debate over the *Epistolae duorum amantium.* This was provoked not by Könsgen's edition, which scandalously received only seven reviews (none of them in English),[16] but rather by Constant J. Mews's boldly titled 1999 volume, *The Lost Love Letters of Heloise and Abelard.*[17] Equipped with an English translation and a reprint of Könsgen's text, the book makes a forceful case for ascribing the EDA to Abelard and Heloise. But even if the First Authen-ticity Debate, with some of its heat and rancor, seems to merge seamlessly into the Second, the two are not really parallel. In the first case, the burden of proof lay squarely on the skeptics, given a strong manuscript tradition attributing the letters to the famous couple, many other medieval texts (literary as well as documentary) confirming their story, a lengthy tradition of interpretation and commentary, and not least, a work rich in historical particulars that could be checked against known facts. With the *Epistolae,* on the other hand, we have an unsigned, fragmentary text in a single manuscript written more than 350 years after the letters' presumed composition. That text was carefully edited by its scribe to remove any factual de-tails it might once have contained, and there is no history of engagement, skeptical or otherwise, with these previously unknown letters. So now, as Jan Ziolkowski has rightly said, the burden of proof must rest on those who would support the attribution.[18] Moreover, as von Moos points out, the second debate only pretends to be about "authenticity." While a genuine authenticity debate asks a yes-or-no question ("Did Peter Abelard actually write the *Historia calamitatum*, which bears his name?"), the attribution of an anonymous text confronts us with a garden of forking paths. The EDA themselves make no claim to be the work of Heloise and Abelard or anyone else, so if the ascription cannot be sustained, they simply remain anonymous. Questions of "forgery" cannot arise.[19]

It is now more than forty years since Könsgen first published the *Epistolae*, and more than fifteen since Mews threw down the gauntlet with his title. In the interim, an initial rush to judgment on both sides has been followed by thoughtful debate and steadily accumulating knowledge, but a fair-minded observer would have to say that the question remains open.[20] Among Könsgen's earliest readers, the philologists Karl Langosch and Walther Bulst accepted the authorship of Heloise and Abelard, while Bernhard Bischoff and André Vernet were skeptical.[21] Mews has continued to support and strengthen the attribution in a steady stream of articles,[22] as well as a revised and expanded edition of his book. In 1999, the same year that *The Lost Love Letters* appeared, C. Stephen Jaeger published *Ennobling Love: In Search of a Lost Sensibility*, arguing independently in favor of Heloise and Abelard as the authors.[23] He too has published additional articles on the *Epistolae*.[24] Further support comes from Sylvain Piron, the French translator of the letters, both in his translation and elsewhere.[25] The German and Italian translators take no stand on the ascription.[26]

On the other side, Peter Dronke, one of the staunchest champions of the authenticity of the canonical letters, accepts Könsgen's early twelfth-century date for the EDA, but not the attribution to Heloise and Abelard.[27] Jan Ziolkowski, Giovanni Orlandi, and Francesco Stella have presented stylometric analyses that arrive at various conclusions, but none support the ascription.[28] Giles Constable makes a case for moderate skepticism,[29] while von Moos has argued strenuously against the attribution, denouncing it as "the eternal return of hermeneutic naïveté."[30] Elsewhere he offers a wide-ranging contextual interpretation of the *Epistolae* as a work of late medieval literary fiction.[31] Considering the evidence more dispassionately, Anne-Marie Turcan-Verkerk and Jean-Yves Tilliette find the arguments so equally balanced that, in the absence of new discoveries, they can only justify an agnostic stance.[32] Many others have joined what they take to be a growing consensus on one side or the other, but without expressly weighing the arguments.

A New Approach: The *Epistolae*, the Ascription, and the History of Emotions

My purpose in this book is not just to take sides (though I will do so) but still more to advance interpretation of the letters from three standpoints. First, while the pioneering English translation by Mews and his student Neville Chiavaroli has served scholarship well thus far, it is time now to correct its several inaccuracies and infelicities in the light of subsequent research. There is room for a translation with greater literary ambitions, especially with respect to the thirteen poems that nestle among the prose letters. In preparing my version, I have carefully studied Könsgen's text and the Mews-Chiavaroli translation, as well as the excellent French version by Sylvain Piron. I have also consulted the German of Eva Cescutti and Philipp Steger, the Italian of Graziella Ballanti, the partial French version of Étienne Wolff, and a superb partial English version by William Levitan.[33] Since all four complete translations reproduce Könsgen's text, which has even been posted on the Internet,[34] I have reluctantly declined to include it here. This omission makes room for a detailed, letter-by-letter commentary that aims to be at once narrative, interpretive, and textual, citing the Latin extensively.

In the second place, I have done my best to situate the *Epistolae* more precisely in their intellectual and rhetorical milieu. Thus my comment on each letter ends with a list of citations, allusions, and parallels. Like any such apparatus, this is a collaborative project; I have added my own discoveries to the extensive work already done by Könsgen, Mews, Piron, von Moos,[35] and others. Electronic databases now constitute an invaluable tool for such research. I have made ample use of the online Latin Library, the *Patrologia Latina* database by Chadwyck-Healey, and the extensive BREPOLiS database, which includes the complete *Monumenta Germaniae Historica*—not to mention Google Books. Nevertheless, identifying allusions remains an art, not a science, and this is truer than ever in the digital age. Not every coincidence of two or three words denotes a deliberate allusion; my list could easily have been expanded with more generous criteria, or reduced with more rigorous ones. As von Moos remarks, a computer can only be a blunt instrument for intertextual studies "because computers work, as concordances once did, with the letter rather than the spirit."[36] Whittling down a massive list of possibilities, Stella restricted his parallels to those involving "the exact coincidence of at least two terms, except for case endings—and possibly, if it's a question of poetry, in the same metrical position."[37] Users of the apparatus should bear in mind that an "allusion" can range from the pointed, self-conscious citation of a biblical or classical text to the use of a familiar tag just because it comes readily to mind, to an elegant phrase tossed in for stylistic flair, to subliminal memories of some work studied long ago. In addition to identifying sources, I have noted parallels with other relevant letter collections from the twelfth century, mainly the Tegernsee love letters, the Regensburg Songs (*Carmina Ratisponensia*), and the letters of Abelard and Heloise. In these and many other cases, the parallels delineate not quotations but a shared intellectual or stylistic environment. Appendix B presents a summary of my results, which should be taken as one scholar's appraisal of the intertextual research to date. It makes no claim to be definitive.

Finally and most crucially, I want to ask what the *Epistolae* can tell us about the history of emotions, for which they are a uniquely valuable source. Here alone do we have a substantial dossier of letters exchanged in real time between two lovers, a man and a woman. None of the twelfth century's many fictional letters, verse epistles, troubadour and trouvère lyrics, goliardic songs, lais, or romances offer us a comparable opportunity to observe a real love relationship between two historical persons as it waxes and wanes, passing through every emotional phase from enchantment to disillusionment. The canonical letters of Abelard and Heloise come closest, but even though they are often called "love letters," that label is misleading. Exchanged between priest and nun, abbot and abbess, they dissect an affair that had long since ended, analyzing it within a context of spiritual formation and monastic direction. Whether or not the famous couple also wrote the *Epistolae duorum amantium*, the two exchanges are very different.

But the *Epistolae* cannot yield much insight if they are read naively as expressions of raw emotion, neglecting their status—especially on the Woman's side—as intensely rhetorical productions. So I will begin by situating them within a history of their genre. To accomplish this, I necessarily cross the often indeterminate boundary between models and genuine letters, that is, those that were actually exchanged. Dronke noted as early as 1976 that the EDA share a great deal stylistically with the so-called Tegernsee love letters.[38] These are ten letters (divided into groups of seven and three) incorporated into the larger Tegernsee Letter Collection from the Bavarian abbey.[39] The manuscript dates from 1160–86, but like other formularies (model letter collections), it contains older materials. In fact, the *ars dictaminis*, or art of letter writing, was an inherently conservative genre.[40] *Dictatores* or teachers of the art theorized existing practice, rather than innovating, and they frequently recycled models that were decades or even centuries old, as did Johannes de Vepria. The ten Tegernsee letters, eight of which have female authors, were written and received by nuns (or perhaps canonesses) and later given to the monks of Tegernsee to include in their massive letter collection.[41] Two of these letters end with passages in Middle High German, so they could not have circulated in France. But the Woman of the EDA might have known a similar collection, a formulary of letters by and for nuns, that does not survive. Given the intrinsic interest of the Tegernsee letters and their close relationship to the EDA, I have included a full translation along with a commentary on them. I have also translated a selection from the Regensburg Songs, a set of epigrams and verse letters exchanged between a teacher and his convent students in the early twelfth century. These straddle the boundary between school exercises and "genuine" exchanges, for they were both—illustrating a discourse of love and friendship quite different from what we find in the EDA.

Gerald Bond, C. Stephen Jaeger, Constant Mews, and Peter Dronke have all discussed the delicate flowering of love poetry exchanged between clerics and learned nuns in the late eleventh and early twelfth centuries.[42] We have surviving evidence from only two centers, Bavaria and the Loire Valley. But our knowledge of this subculture, even in those centers, rests on a manuscript basis so thin that we can reasonably assume much more has been lost. The same Ovidian revival might have flourished in other places where (like much literary production by nuns) it has left no trace.[43] Aside from the general paucity of early manuscripts and the brevity of that cultural moment, it is likely that much of this Ovidian poetry, seen as immoral and frivolous, was suppressed by monastic reformers of the next generation. We do, however, still have a small number of poems by nuns, novices, and convent students, though the supposed author of only one is known to us by name: Lady Constance, a nun of Le Ronceray in Angers. Together with the verse of their male friends, such as Baudri of Bourgueil and Marbod of Rennes, this poetry opens a unique window onto the state of Latin letters at the dawn of vernacular *fin'amor*.

I will consider such poetry as the artifact of an emotional community, one in which learning Latin, imitating Ovid, and cultivating a kind of high-minded but flirtatious cross-gender friendship went hand in hand.[44] This emotional community was a fragile one, not sustainable over the long term, because it made such outrageously high demands. Its elite members were required to maintain their vowed chastity or virginity, devote their lives to the service of God, attest to the disinterested purity of their friendships, and at the same time engage in a playful and competitive literary game whose very essence was the composition of amorous verse. This was hard enough for young and middle-aged clerics. Many of them were rhetorically bisexual, addressing love poems to boys as well as women, and if self-discipline failed them, they could break their vows of chastity without getting caught. But for girls and young women—cloistered, at risk of pregnancy, and at even greater risk of damaging their vitally important *fama*, their reputation for virtue—the game was an emotional high-wire act that may have had more casualties than we know. From the *Epistolae* we learn that the two lovers were products of such a textual and emotional community, although they were not in religious vows at the time of their affair. Their letters reveal what could happen when the ground rules failed: an intense literary friendship, pursued in both prose and verse, gets out of hand and evolves into a sexually engaged, passionate, life-or-death love affair.

If the lovers were Abelard and Heloise, these early letters show how they reached the point where we meet them in the *Historia calamitatum*. If we should decide the lovers were only a couple "like" Heloise and Abelard, as Könsgen proposed, their relationship can still yield much insight into the dilemma faced by their more famous contemporaries.

Making Love in the Twelfth Century

PROLEGOMENA

Making Love in the Twelfth Century

An Essay in the History of Emotions

"IT IS NOT pleasant to make love in the presence of a third person," wrote Anthony Trollope, "even when that love is all fair and above board."[1] Trollope's theme was not sexual voyeurism, but declaring love—the dominant meaning of "make love" from about 1600 to the 1920s.[2] Love letters, like suitors' declarations, guard their privacy. Nine hundred years ago, they already warn against the gaze of a "third eye." But perhaps, after so many centuries, our literary eavesdropping can be pardoned. Let me tempt you then, dear reader, to share my offense, for this book will be about making love in the twelfth century. It asks what Latin lovers (of the original kind) thought about love, in that age so deeply obsessed with it, and how they declared their passions in prose and verse.

The twelfth century has been called an *aetas Ovidiana*, an age of Ovid.[3] But *aetas amoris* would be even more apt, for love was the century's grand philosophical problem as well as its great literary theme.[4] Among the many discourses that explore it, we find the lyrics of numerous troubadours and trouvères; Latin love poetry such as the *Carmina burana*; spiritual treatises by William of Saint-Thierry, Bernard of Clairvaux, Aelred of Rievaulx, and Hugh and Richard of Saint-Victor; Song of Songs commentaries by Honorius Augustodunensis, Rupert of Deutz, and many more; the great Cistercian cycle of *Sermones in Cantica canticorum*, begun by St. Bernard but continued by Gilbert of Hoyland and John of Ford; the lais of Marie de France; the Arthurian romances of Chrétien de Troyes; romances of male friendship like *Amicus et Amelius*; and the neo-Ovidian *De amore* of Andreas Capellanus. Lyric love, fictional love, and spiritual love have all received their scholarly due. When we turn to "real" love—relationships between actual men and women—the evidence is thinner. Court cases testify to marriages gone bad, while other documents record scandals like the pregnancy of the nun of Watton. We even have saints' lives such as the *vita* of Christina of Markyate, itself half romance, whose heroine escaped her unwanted husband to become a chaste lover of Christ—and a parade of clerics.

But what about love letters? Though this was also a great age of Latin epistolography, we have fewer than we might expect. One reason is that the persons
most capable of writing them—priests, monks, and nuns—could not ethically do
so. Another is that the great bulk of women's writings have perished. When a medieval woman's letters do come down to us, it is almost always because she preserved them herself, having literary or spiritual ambitions exalted enough to
withstand the universal Law of Female Loss. Women of the caliber of Heloise,
Hildegard of Bingen, Hadewijch, Catherine of Siena, and Christine de Pizan assembled their own letter collections, or had their secretaries do so.[5] It is interesting
that three of these dossiers preserve the letters of their interlocutors. Hildegard
corresponded with abbesses, prioresses, and nuns at some thirty-five German
communities, a clear proof of religious women's widespread Latin literacy. As a
prophet, she herself ignored the rules of the *ars dictaminis*, but her correspondents
faithfully observed them.[6] Male letter collections, while vastly more popular, almost never include both sides of an exchange. Even the collections of monks who
corresponded extensively with women, such as St. Jerome and St. Anselm, rarely
preserve letters from the female friends whose learning and virtue they extolled.[7]
In the case of love letters—usually ephemeral by design and damaging to women's
honor—it is little wonder if their survival is rare.[8]

The Evidence

This very rarity invites scholars to question the authenticity of the few collections
we do have. In the following chapter on "Frequently Asked Questions," I will discuss the long-contested correspondence of Abelard and Heloise (1130s). But of the
many documents in that collection, only two letters by Heloise are arguably "love
letters," and the love they mourn is long past. The recently discovered *Epistolae
duorum amantium* (EDA) are more obviously love letters. Whether or not their
attribution to the same famous couple can be sustained, the EDA constitute a fascinating source for our topic. Even less familiar, at least to the anglophone world,
are the so-called Tegernsee love letters. Given that eight of these ten letters are
from women, they were most likely preserved by a community of Bavarian nuns
before their incorporation into the massive Tegernsee letter book. Two of the ten
are effusive letters to male friends and relatives, while three express intimate love
between women. Two more are seduction attempts by importunate male teachers,
which the young nuns shyly or fiercely refuse. Before these exchanges passed into
the hands of the Tegernsee monks to become literary texts, they could have been

retained to provide future nuns with models of their genre. Majority opinion (with some dissent) holds both the EDA and the Tegernsee letters to be "authentic" in the sense that they were actually sent, although they have come down to us anonymously.[9]

Composed chiefly in prose, these letters supplement two late eleventh-century collections of verse epistles by named poets, Marbod of Rennes (ca. 1035–1123) and Baudri of Bourgueil (1046–1130). With several contemporaries—Hildebert of Lavardin (ca. 1055–1133),[10] Hilary of Orléans, Godfrey of Reims (d. 1095)—these poets constitute the so-called Loire Valley school. (As with "school of Chartres," the Loire Valley is more a synecdoche than an accurate designation, for the same poetic movement is attested throughout northern France.) This elite coterie of highly educated churchmen produced some remarkable, classicizing letter-poems of love and friendship, addressed to boys, men, and women. But many of their poems are lost, while others just barely survive. Hilary's extant poems include four lyrics to religious women, four erotic poems to boys, and a lament on the exile of his teacher, Peter Abelard. These all survive in one manuscript (Paris, BNF lat. 11331).[11] Baudri's amorous verse, far more extensive, is likewise collected in a single manuscript of around 1100 (Vatican, Reg. lat. 1351), authorized by the poet himself.[12] When he left his abbacy at Bourgueil to become bishop of Dol in 1107, Baudri decisively renounced Ovidian verse. Another poet in this circle, Fulcoius of Beauvais, claims to have burned the "vain" poetry of his youth; the manuscript that contained it is visibly damaged.[13]

Marbod's case is more complicated.[14] Like Hildebert, he was elevated to a bishopric in 1096 and had to leave his long-term position as master of the cathedral school at Angers. While much of his work, especially his famous lapidary, continued to be read, he apparently suppressed the erotica. In his old age he explicitly recanted his earlier "frivolous" verse (*materies inhonesta levisque*), changing both his subject matter and his style.[15] Marbod's collected poems were published at Rennes, the diocese he had ruled, in an *editio princeps* of 1524, but only two exemplars remain. When the monk Antoine Beaugendre reprinted that work in 1708, he suppressed seventeen erotic poems, which thus remained unknown for centuries. Only a few of these survive in manuscript; twelve were first edited by Walther Bulst in 1950, in a Festschrift that had little impact.[16] Given that our knowledge of this whole poetic movement hangs by such a slender thread, it seems possible and even likely that more in the same vein has disappeared altogether. Nor is there any reason to think the Loire Valley was the sole region to foster such poetry. Gerald of Wales, for example, wrote at least one love letter-poem to a girl.[17] In late eleventh-century Alsace, the daughters of the master Manegold of Lautenbach taught literary students of their own.[18]

The abbot Guibert of Nogent, famed for his autobiography, was educated at the Abbey of Saint-Germer-de-Fly (Oise, Picardy), not otherwise known as a center of learning. His early training in the liberal arts centered on poetic composition, specifically the writing of verse epistles in imitation of Ovid's *Heroïdes*. At a ripe age he wrote in a rueful, Augustinian vein of these youthful studies, which he must have pursued in the 1070s:

> Meanwhile, I had immersed my mind beyond all measure in the study of verse composition, so that I laid aside all serious studies of holy Scripture for such ridiculous vanity. Led on by my own frivolity, I had already come to the point where I presumed to compose Ovidian and pastoral poetry; and I developed a taste for elegant love letters with a differentiation of roles, and epistles paired with responses [*lepores amatorios in specierum distributionibus epistolisque nexilibus affectarem*].[19] Forgetting the rigor appropriate to monastic vows, my mind had cast shame aside, delighting in the allurements of this infectious sexual liberty, considering only whether the verse I was composing in a courtly style [*curialiter*] could be ascribed to some poet.[20]

Guibert confesses, not surprisingly, that these verse experiments caused lascivious stirrings of his flesh (*carnis meae titillatione*). Despite his old tutor's dismay and even a visionary warning, he continued to write indecent poems in secret and recite them, to the delight of his peers, until divine chastisement in the form of illness brought him to repent. Needless to say, no verse epistles or love poems by Guibert survive.

If such poets as Guibert, Baudri, and Marbod felt compelled to retract their Ovidian verse as incompatible with high office in the church, later monastic generations had little interest in preserving or disseminating it. As bishop of Rennes, Marbod wrote an acerbic letter to the reformer Robert of Arbrissel around 1098, criticizing his intimacy with women. Baudri, as bishop of Dol, was more sympathetic to Robert's project—but he praised him precisely for segregating men and women and "sentencing" the latter to strict claustration.[21] Just a few years after these men attained their episcopal thrones, St. Bernard founded the Abbey of Clairvaux (1115). Like Baudri at Bourgueil, though with vastly more impact, the young abbot pioneered a passionate new literature of love. But his was based on the Song of Songs, not Ovid; and if Bernard's rhetoric is even more fervent, his ascetic devotion could scarcely be further from Baudri's playful, flirtatious, insolubly ambiguous professions of love to boys and women. Monks like Bernard and his friend William of Saint-Thierry had received a rhetorical education much like Baudri's, but they rejected its Ovidian ethos out of hand. In his treatise *On the Nature and Dignity of Love*, written within a few years of the *Epistolae duorum amantium*, William explicitly set out to provide a Christian *ars amatoria* to counter the corrupt Ovidian art. With remarkable swiftness, the Cistercians and other monastic reformers swept through northern France, putting a decisive end to the Loire Valley school's experiments with Ovid in the cloister.[22] The other habitat of Ovidian verse, the cathedral school's arts curriculum devoted to the *auctores*, was just as rapidly being displaced by a fascination with dialectic and a new aura of professionalism in the schools, much to the dismay of twelfth-century humanists like John of Salisbury.[23]

To be sure, the nascent Ovidian revival that we see in Baudri and Marbod—and the *Epistolae*—would have a rich future; but it would lie in the vernacular. So in dating and assessing the EDA, it is vital to recall the brevity of their cultural moment. Latin love letters (as opposed to later, fictive models in formularies) could flourish only during this space of two or three generations when literary "coeducation" was possible. As Dieter Schaller puts it, they emerged only in places "where religious men and women engaged as teachers and students in acquiring a liberal education (thus, in the realm of monastic and cathedral schools) and dealt with emerging erotic tensions in playful exchanges, taking pleasure in artistic language."[24] Only a self-conscious literariness allowed such texts to rise above the typically pragmatic, ephemeral purpose of love letters, and so to survive at all. Yet "pleasure in artistic language" need not imply that the "erotic tensions" expressed in these exchanges were not real.

The verse collections of Baudri and Marbod each preserve a single poetic reply from a woman: an anonymous *puella* in Marbod's circle and the young nun Constance of Angers among Baudri's friends. Not surprisingly, the authorship of both women's poems is contested. Constance's verse epistle is highly accomplished—and close stylistic kin to Baudri, which is what we should expect of a poetic exchange between teacher and student. Such fine scholars as Peter Dronke, Gerald Bond, and Jane Stevenson have accepted her authorship.[25] But much to my own dismay, I am persuaded by Jean-Yves Tilliette's philological arguments that this letter-poem is Baudri's superbly skillful impersonation of a female voice, modelled on the *Heroïdes*.[26] Tilliette, the editor of Baudri's collected works, points out that Constance's reply not only mirrors the form and structure of his letter exactly, as a gifted student might do, but imitates even his prosodic quirks and borrows numerous phrases from throughout his poetic oeuvre, which no one but he could have known so intimately. Moreover, her letter is the only one of the 256 poems in his manuscript to be ascribed to anyone but Baudri—except for two other fictional exchanges: a pair of letters between Paris and Helen and another between Ovid and his imaginary friend Florus. Thus, with chagrin, I relinquish its authorship to Baudri. But Tilliette does not ask whether he might have polished or improved on an actual letter from Constance, for medieval writers (including Baudri himself) often asked readers to correct any faults they found in their work. In a teacher-student relationship, this might well have been the norm. So I will follow Katherine Kong's lead in citing the poem *as if* it were Constance's.[27] The Woman of the EDA twice cites Baudri's letter to the young nun. Constance's reply can stand as a model of what chaste, but playfully literate women in this circle were *perceived* to be, and thus what the more ambitious might actually have aspired to be.

Where even the verse of eminent men barely survived, almost all of the women's has (as usual) perished. But "absence of evidence," Jane Stevenson writes, "is not the same as evidence of absence."[28] Three of Marbod's love poems have the title "Rescriptum," indicating that they formed half of a dialogue; one is even called "Rescriptum rescripto eiusdem" (a reply to her reply). We also know several nun-poets from this circle by name, although their works are lost.[29] Baudri, Hildebert, and Serlo of Bayeux all addressed verse letters to Muriel, a nun of Wilton, who was lauded in an epitaph as *inclyta versificatrix* (eminent poetess) and enjoyed such fame that visitors came to see her tomb.[30] Baudri recalled that when she recited her verse, her words had the sound of a man's, though the voice was a woman's.[31] Among his other female correspondents, along with Constance we find Emma, a *grammatica* or literary teacher, and the younger nuns Agnes and Beatrice, all from Le Ronceray in Angers. Hilary of Orléans corresponded with the next generation at the same community: Abbess Tiburga, Superba, Bona, and the English pupil Rosa.[32] The same Hilary wrote a short *vita* of Eve of Wilton, the learned nun for whom Goscelin of Saint-Bertin had composed his *Liber confortatorius* when she left Wilton to become a recluse at Le Ronceray. Fulcoius, a married cleric, sent two letter-poems to the "matron" Ida as part of a poetic exchange.[33] Hildebert and Baudri both addressed verse epistles to Cecilia, abbess of La Trinité in Caen (d. 1126), a daughter of William the Conqueror. Her sister Countess Adela of Blois was a noted literary patron and herself a poet.[34] Hence, despite the losses, there can be no doubt that religious men and women in northern France, at the time of the EDA, engaged in flirtatious literary correspondence.

One of the few unmistakably female-authored poems to survive is a lament for the end of this era. "Laudis honor," a neglected poem of almost sixty lines, rages against the forcible eviction of women from what had until recently been a shared literary culture.[35] The speaker, a nun, tellingly casts herself as a female Ovid. Like the Augustan poet, she has been charged with *error* and *grande crimen* (a great crime), even banished (*pellimur*)—for no offense other than writing and literary study (*littera*). Once, she complains, the Roman emperors used to revere "the Muses' grace, the fount of Pegasus," but in her own day "new princes" despise poetry and persecute poets, moved by nothing but envy and ignorance. Behind this classical facade lurk the religious reformers of the early twelfth century, who think nuns should devote themselves to prayer and not bother their little heads about philosophy, poetry, or rhetoric. Caesar punished Ovid himself less harshly than these superiors assault learned women:

> O new religious life, holy discernment!
>   Now if only I could discern why learning should be a crime.
> That monk or nun is "good" whose eyes are always downcast,
>   Who thinks that he is good because he knows nothing.
> Yet is that a holy life—in which meditation on nothing,
>   Knowledge of nothing, has led to being nothing?
> If God is grasped by understanding, grasped by reason,
>   Then a more rational person will grasp more of him.
> Much learning will not keep me from being good;
>   Learning does not forbid, but gives me knowledge of God.
> By reason, I believe and know that God exists,
>   And reason tells me God does not forbid what I do.
> If he forbids what I do, I will forbid what you men do!
>   Clio, faithful companion, depart! I am banished.[36]

The speaker claims that her chief "error" lay in producing historical poetry (*carminibus recitare nouis bene uel male gesta*). If only she had known that Hrotsvit, a religious woman who lived a century and a half before, was commissioned by the niece of Emperor Otto I himself to write his *gesta*! But the "new princes" of her day had their own ideas about monastic women:

> It is not for holy women to fashion verses,
>   Not ours to ask who Aristotle might be.
> That was laudable of old, but in your time, poems mean nothing;
>   Genus or species, nothing; the colors of rhetoric, nothing.
> What use is it to write correct meters, to note down proofs?
>   Clio, faithful companion, depart! I am banished.[37]

We are used to seeing "the reformation of the twelfth century" (in Giles Constable's phrase) through its own eyes, celebrating the fervor of the Cistercians and other new orders.[38] But in this poem we hear the voice of an old-order humanist, bitterly lamenting her exile from the antihumanist—and antifeminist—"new world." *Pellimur orbe nouo,* she writes, *studium quia littera nostrum*: "I am banished from the new world because literature is my passion."[39] We do not know which monastery harbored this poet, but I suspect that her enemy was someone not unlike "the cowled chief of the cowled populace" (*cucullatus populi Primas cucullati*), who figures as Abelard's foe in the "Metamorphosis Goliae."[40] In fact, "Laudis honor" could be read as a female pendant to that famous poem, which is itself a lament for the persecution of poetry and philosophy by a new, more austere religion. Be that as it may, the anonymous nun's plaint marks the closing of a brief window of opportunity for women. It was only during that window that the Woman of the *Epistolae,* and others like her, were able to flourish.

The Fine Art of the Love Letter

During that brief but privileged cultural moment, women began to double the established roles of young men as objects of desire and instruction. That may be one reason such poets as Baudri, Marbod, and Hildebert wrote verses for religious women as well as love poems to boys.[41] What interests us here is less their private sexuality than the opening of the charmed circle of literacy to both sexes. For elite women such as Constance, Muriel, and the author of "Laudis honor," advanced Latinity was the passport to a high-stakes, high-status emotional community, formerly open only to men. That community prized what C. Stephen Jaeger has called "ennobling love,"[42] and its presence sets the EDA and related works apart from the fictional love letters composed by *dictatores,* or teachers of letter writing. In ennobling love, an erotic attachment to a person of either sex is bound up with classicizing ideals of virtue, friendship, and self-improvement. The beloved is admired for moral excellence as well as beauty, spurring the lover on toward new heights of ethical or spiritual attainment. The *dictatores,* on the other hand, wrote model love letters in a more Ovidian vein, providing templates for seduction. Intended for the amusement and instruction of young professional men, such models first appear in *artes dictandi* by Bernardinus of Bologna and Bernard de Meung (ca. 1150–1200). They culminate in the amusingly cynical *Rota Veneris* (*Wheel of Venus*), composed around 1215 by a Tuscan professor of rhetoric, Boncompagno da Signa.[43]

Significantly, all the authentic love letters we know—the EDA, the Regensburg Songs, the love letters from Tegernsee, and the Loire Valley poems—probably predate these fictive models. The Tegernsee letters are the hardest to date; we can say only that they were written before the manuscript itself, which was the work of twelve scribes over two generations (1160–86).[44] Geographically distant in their origins, the EDA and the Tegernsee corpus share an extensive stylistic repertoire, which they probably owe to their writers' shared biblical, liturgical, and Ovidian formation. Along with the Loire Valley schools, Tegernsee and its environs were a major center of education, and specifically of the Ovidian revival, in the late eleventh and early twelfth centuries.[45] The Bavarian abbey certainly had some French connections, so the German nuns and the Woman of the EDA may have had other common sources, now lost.[46] In any case, neither the "two lovers" nor the Tegernsee writers could have known the formularies that survive. Nor did the *dictatores* know the deeply private EDA or the Bavarian nuns' letters. All our witnesses, then, are independent—except that the northern French lovers of the EDA were well versed in the poems of Baudri and Marbod. In short, we are dealing with the scattered remnants of what was once a much wider epistolary culture based in monasteries, well-heeled convents, and cathedral schools. What kinds of textual and emotional communities flourished in these environments? And how did such chaste habitats encourage the making of literary love?

In Robert d'Orbigny's romance of *Floire et Blanchefleur* (ca. 1150), the young hero and heroine are raised as brother and sister, though not actually kin. Sent to school from the age of five, they study Latin and love together:

Livres lisoient paienors	There they were reading pagan books
u ooient parler d'amors.	from which they learned to speak of love.
En çou forment se delitoient,	In these they took special delight
es engiens d'amor qu'il trovoient.	in love's ruses which they found there.
Cius lires les fist molt haster	This reading soon caused them to feel
en autre sens d'aus entramer	mutual love—of a different kind
que de l'amor de noureture	from the fond brother-sister love
qui lor avoit esté a cure.	in which they had been brought up.
. . . .	. . . .
Et quant a l'escole venoient,	And when they arrived at school,
lor tables d'yvoire prenoient.	they took up their ivory tablets.
Adont lor veïssiés escrire	Ah, if you had seen them carving
letres et vers d'amours en cire!	letters and poems of love in wax!
Lor graffes sont d'or et d'argent	With gold and silver styluses,

dont il escrisent soutiument.	they can skillfully compose
Letres et salus font d'amours....	love letters and lovers' greetings....
....	....
En seul cinc ans et quinze dis	In just five years and fifteen days,
furent andoi si bien apris	they were both so well instructed
que bien sorent parler latin	that they could speak perfect Latin
et bien escrire en parkemin,	and write very well on parchment,
et consillier oiant la gent	and talk in Latin secretly;
en latin, que nus nes entent.[47]	no one who heard could understand.

This charming passage is doubtless idealized. Few schoolchildren could afford ivory tablets or golden styluses, and few would have finished their studies—and fallen in love!—by the age of ten. Details aside, however, the lines are informative. We find here a coeducational grammar school, taught by an esteemed *mestre des ars*, where learning to read, write, and speak Latin is coterminous with acquiring the art of love. The children are reading "pagan books"—surely those of Ovid, the *magister amoris*, who could teach them "to speak of love" and was especially famed for his *engiens d'amor*, the clever stratagems he taught both sexes. (The hero's name "Floire" might even derive from "Florus," a friend of Ovid, invented in Baudri's verse epistles.)[48] Like the wax on their tablets, the children's impressionable minds quickly absorb the stamp of their reading. They learn composition in prose and verse by drafting *letres et vers d'amours*, as did a great many boys and perhaps not a few girls. Before long the children graduate from wax tablets to parchment. Having mastered Latin, the child lovers find that they have acquired a valuable code. From now on they can *consillier en latin*, or hold secret conversations, within earshot of others who know only the vernacular. Perhaps most important, even at their precocious age, reading about love teaches them to *feel* love, transforming their childish affection (*amor de noureture*) into a tender erotic passion.

A different kind of classroom, this time in the real world, shows a similar convergence between acquiring Latin and learning the art of love. In the *Carmina Ratisponensia* (Regensburg Songs, ca. 1106), chance has preserved some remarkable evidence of the literary and pedagogical culture that shaped the lovers of the EDA. At a convent in the Bavarian city of Regensburg, aristocratic girls, many of them future nuns, studied grammar with a master brought in from distant Liège, testifying to the pan-European character of this educational system. Some time after the teacher's death, a scribe for some reason was asked to copy his disorganized jumble of papers into one manuscript. Thus, nestled among classical commentaries, proverbs, mnemonic verses, patristic fragments, and other random texts, we find sixty-eight love poems and epigrams in leonine verse, scattered helter-skelter throughout the manuscript. The more polished poems are the teacher's, but almost half were composed by students, whose sometimes awkward verse and bizarre syntax show that they were still learning Latin. I have translated thirty-seven representative pieces, which voice a range of girlish infatuations, jealousies, playful teasing, and high-minded moralizing.[49] The teacher's contributions include a full-fledged Ovidian love poem (no. 3), an expression of ennobling love and friendship (no. 34), a poem insisting that his student now outshines him in composing verse (no. 37), and a number of playful epigrams in which—purely for the purpose of instruction, let us hope—he tries to seduce his charges (nos. 16, 27, 33, 61). But he also warns them against illicit love (nos. 2, 4). The students in turn give their master affectionate gifts (nos. 15, 24, 60), send him verses for correction (nos. 7, 46), defend their virtue against his real or (more likely) feigned advances (nos. 28, 31), and skillfully fend off extravagant compliments (nos. 44, 53). One even calls him a monkey because of his ugly face and tousled hair (no. 5). Young as they are, the girls are keenly aware of their high social standing. They welcome their new teacher, granting him the "right" to govern them (*dominandi jura*)—but only so long as he respects their virtue (no. 6). They are at an age where romantic rivalry is still tied up with envy of the teacher's pet (nos. 7, 29, 49, 50). In the remarkable no. 22, the girls enact the role of courtly *domnas*, declaring that only the most refined and polished gentlemen are worthy of admission to their fellowship. Like the lovers of the *Epistolae*, they often speak of making a "pact" (*fedus*, nos. 28, 31, 33) or "pledge" (*pignus*, nos. 27, 34) of love and friendship. But the play-acting character of these lyrics becomes clear in no. 32, where the teacher tells those who have just been veiled as nuns to "sanctify yourselves to the Lord." From now on it is time for them "to be wise and lay frivolity aside" (*sapiant et opus levitatis omittant*).

Like the nuns of Regensburg and the romance heroine Blanchefleur, aristocratic ladies of this era were often well educated. Aside from convents, we have little evidence about their schooling. But Shulamith Shahar writes that some noble daughters were educated at home by a *magister* or *magistra*, while others studied with an anchoress or else attended "a private school for children of the nobility (sometimes in the company of those boys who were not raised in the courts of seigneurs)."[50] This neatly describes the situation in *Floire et Blanchefleur*. We cannot doubt that children actually studied the *ars amatoria*, for a disputed question from the circle of Peter the Chanter (1190s) asks whether such a dangerous art should in fact be taught in schools.[51] The *magister* argues that all knowledge, including knowledge of the art of love, comes from God and is therefore good.[52] In response to an objection that actual *use* of this art is evil, he concedes that any good thing can be abused. But the art should still be taught *ad cautelam*, much as Andreas Capellanus tells his student Walter: one should know the art of love in order to guard against it, or to gain greater merit by resisting a sin one is capable of committing.[53] While these arguments (like most connected with the *ars amatoria*) have a specious ring, they justify Ovid's continuing place among the *auctores*, indispensable for the study of grammar and composition.

The disputing master was, of course, thinking of boys. By the end of the twelfth century, fewer girls would have had the opportunities for study that were still open to them a century earlier. Not a few misogynists opposed teaching even noble girls to read and write, for the very reason that they might use that knowledge to exchange love letters.[54] Around 1150 the *dictator* Bernardinus of Bologna published a textbook of letter writing, *Introductiones prosaici dictaminis* (Introduction to prose composition). His students, presumably all boys, began by learning the *salut d'amours* or lover's greeting, a genre mentioned in *Floire et Blanchefleur*.[55] Readers of the EDA will recognize some of his formulas, which were already timeworn:

> Nobili domine et amice karissime indissolubili dilectionis sibi dulcedine conjuncte; *vel:* inextricabili sibi amore copulate B.: se ipsum totum et quicquid habere videtur, quod Paris Helene, quod Thisbe Piramus, omnium delectabilium statum incomparabilem, summe dulcedinis unionem, intimam dilectionem *vel* amorem, intimi amoris copulam.[56]

> To his noble lady and dearest friend, joined to him with the sweetness of indissoluble love, *or:* coupled to him with inextricable love, B. [offers] his whole self and whatever he seems to possess; what Paris wished for Helen, what Pyramus wished for Thisbe; the incomparable condition of every delight; the union of supreme sweetness; intimate love; the bond of intimate love.

Having mastered greetings, the student could move on to write letters geared to specific love situations. A school manuscript from Tegernsee includes a section on *salutationes epistolarum* along with no fewer than three *accessus* (introductions) to Ovid's *Heroïdes*, the beloved text that pioneered the genre of love letter-poems.[57]

Another *dictator*, Bernard de Meung, supplies numerous love scenarios in his *Flores dictaminum* (Flowers of letter writing, late twelfth century).[58] One is a marriage proposal: a young man has heard that his mistress is betrothed to another, so he reminds her that when they were first joined with the help of Venus, they promised to marry as soon as possible. The woman happily replies that, since he has proven his constancy, she will spurn the rich man her father had chosen and marry him instead. In other examples, Pyramus outlines his fateful plan for a tryst with Thisbe, and Cydippe complains to Acontius that his love for her has cooled because he has been seduced by prostitutes. In a set of paired letters, a man exhorts his mistress to constancy. She replies, obscenely, that in her lover's absence she could not live without the sweet music of his mallets, so she has tried the skills of many men. But finding none to equal him, she will henceforth be faithful. This kind of bawdy humor made Bernard's textbook quite a success (nearly forty copies survive);[59] but I doubt very much that it was used for the instruction of women.

The *Rota Veneris* goes further in the same direction. Boncompagno da Signa gives the literary Don Juan what Andreas Capellanus offers the conversational one—an endless supply of specious, flattering arguments to beguile a lady's ear. None of the ladies in Andreas's dialogues capitulate to their suitors, but all of Boncompagno's do; every woman has her rhetorical price. After supplying the usual array of florid greetings, the *dictator* notes that a woman should be addressed in one vein *ante factum* and another *post factum*, while religious women should always be called "ladies" because addressing them as "nuns" would be counterproductive.[60] Men should realize that any woman will at first say no, but this should not be taken seriously. A miniature epistolary novel in nine letters carries one seducer from his initial plea through his lady's refusal to their eventual consummation. Another seduction campaign vanquishes a nun's scruples. In a set of letters related to breakups, a pregnant woman begs her seducer to return and do the right thing, but he responds, in effect, "Tough luck, baby! Now that I have such a lovely, distinguished bride, how can I possibly do what you ask? Anyhow, it was surely some other man who steered your boat into the harbor of shame."[61] Meant more for entertainment than serious study, this little compendium pushes the boundary between *ars dictaminis* and literary fiction. Even more than Bernard de Meung's work, it savors of a male homosocial world where women are desired, but hardly respected.[62] The emotional climate of all these *dictatores* is very far from the schoolroom of *Floire et Blanchefleur*, much less the EDA or the Tegernsee letters. In both those collections, the women are active, even dominant partners in a shared epistolary culture. In the *artes dictandi*, they are objects of seduction, and the letters ascribed to them patently the work of male hands.

Our authentic love letters, then, resonate very little with the professional *ars dictaminis*, which grew out of Italian notarial culture in the late eleventh century.[63] Significantly, none of the *dictatores* who incorporate fictional love letters eroticize the teacher-student relationship, which is central to all the authentic letter collections: the Loire Valley poems, the Regensburg Songs, the *Epistolae duorum amantium*, Abelard and Heloise, and the Tegernsee letters.[64] Conversely, the *Epistolae* lack any exemplars of the most common type of model letter, that of the opportunistic male seducer.[65] Yet monastic culture had its own, considerably older traditions of letter writing, grounded in biblical and liturgical rhetoric, classical *amicitia*, and Carolingian humanism. Such avid reformers as Peter Damian and Anselm of Canterbury used letters to consolidate their friendship networks, often couching political alliances in deeply emotional, even visceral language.[66] Women had long been part of this culture, not excluding its political side. Queen Matilda (aka Edith) of England, educated at Wilton, wrote fervently to both Anselm and Pope Paschal II, mediating between king and archbishop in the investiture controversy. Sally Vaughn judges the queen's letters (ca. 1103–6) to be "flowery, fawningly flattering, [and] frivolous," at least at first glance. Yet she surmises that they might represent "a contemporary epistolary style for educated aristocratic women," though little evidence of it survives.[67] This is surely the case. As we have seen, the celebrated poet Muriel was a nun at Wilton, and Eve, Goscelin's protégée, was trained there. Its school may have been one of several where highborn ladies could acquire a florid, ostentatiously learned Latin style.[68]

Not all letters of friendship had an instrumental character. For instance, an enigmatic capitulary of Charlemagne (789) insists that abbesses must forbid their nuns to compose or send *winileodas*.[69] We don't know exactly what *winileodas* were—prose or verse? Latin or vernacular?—but the term meant something like "love songs" or "love letters." Later nuns may have had their own formularies and *artes dictandi*, with a rhetorical shading subtly different from those written for notaries and courtiers. In a letter that survives by sheer chance, a nun at Lippoldsberg writes to the abbot of Reinhardsbrunn, requesting "two little books on the precepts of *dictamen*."[70] Within this monastic *ars dictaminis*, we can identify several subgenres akin to love letters, all cast in highly affective prose. These include letters extolling friendship, expressions of gratitude to patrons, pleas for visits or letters from absent friends, congratulations to a newly elected abbess or bishop, requests for advice and prayers, consolation to the bereaved, and appeals concerning children or other kin.

Significantly, one subgenre is the letter of reproach, which heaps recriminations on a "faithless" friend or kinsman who has neglected promises to write, visit, or perhaps enter religious life. Here is an example from the twelfth-century nuns of Admont, which I cite in full because it is so revealing, despite our complete ignorance of its context.

> To her beloved kinsman N. from his relative B.: not the fidelity and love that are his due, but only such as he deserves.
>
> I know—and it grieves me to know—that I do not have a faithful kinsman in you, but rather a reedy staff, useless and worthless; if a person leans on it, it will pierce his hand [Isa. 36:6]. For you have utterly forgotten the fidelity you owe me. Even though you yourself could not bear to remain in exile and hastened to return to your own people, you handed me over to oblivion in a foreign land, as if I were dead [Psalm 30:13]. Nor did you take pity on me, whom you well knew to be deprived of the comfort of all my friends. Where are the good words, the comforting words [Zech. 1:13] with which you said farewell to me—but took no care to back up with deeds? Because you have made your fidelity void and refused to fulfill your promises, I grieve more for you than for myself. For you have lost the favor and love of the whole congregation, whom you promised when you left that you would soon return and remain with them.
>
> Blush, therefore, for your unstable faith and do worthy penance, mindful that no faithless person has any share in heaven.[71]

Alison Beach, who edited this letter, speculates on the circumstances that might have prompted it. Was N. the writer's brother, who had promised to enter religious life with her but reneged? Had the two been partners in a failed marriage? Perhaps their union was dissolved on the ground of consanguinity?[72] We would hardly think of calling this angry missive a "love letter." Yet the second Tegernsee letter, with its rubric *amico amica derelicta* (an abandoned friend to her friend), sounds much like it:

> My soul will be consumed with grief and filled with sorrow because I seem to have been utterly blotted out of your remembrance—I, who always hoped to receive trust and love from you until the end of my life. What is my strength that I should bear this patiently and not weep now and forever? Is my flesh bronze or my mind a rock, are my eyes made of stone, that I should not grieve my bitter misfortune? (Job 6:11–12). What have I done? What have I done? Was I the first to reject you? How have I been found guilty? Truly, I have been cast off through no fault of my own. If you seek a fault it is you, *you* who are to

blame! For time and again I have sent you messages, yet never received the comfort of your words in the greatest affair or the least. So let all mortals depart and seek trust and love from me no longer!

Once again, context is lacking. The "friend" who provokes this torrent of rebukes could have been an ex-lover who seduced and abandoned the writer, forcing her to take refuge in a convent. Alternatively, he could have been merely a cousin who was slow to set quill to parchment—or, for that matter, one whose letters had been "lost in the mail." Now consider this passage from the Woman in the EDA (no. 69):

> With every surge of blood, my heart is stung by as many stabs of pain as there are letters in these words. O prize of my heart, what have you done? No matter what force drives you from me, I marvel how you could be so suddenly changed, you whom I sealed within my heart with a firm anchor of love. For this reason I have taken to sackcloth and ashes (Matt. 11:21), and day and night tears spill from my eyes (Jer. 14:17). What more? Above all, the sharpest arrow of pain is piercing me (Psalm 44:6), and harder than diamond will be the man who remains unmoved by my sighs of misery.

This time we do have some context, for the letter comes in the midst of a long romantic relationship. Separated by "envious" foes, the lovers have recently quarreled, and the Woman is feeling embittered and neglected. If we were to read her letter in a vacuum, we might think the Man had been sexually unfaithful. But the parallels from Admont and Tegernsee give us pause, for many circumstances could prompt such passionate reproaches. Although the Woman of the EDA no longer lived in a convent, she had been educated in one. An overarching textual community united her with the Bavarian and Austrian nuns. That community, grounded in Scripture and the Divine Office, acquired its canons of style and emotional expression from those sacred texts. In the three brief passages I have examined, the reproachful nun at Admont cites Isaiah, Zechariah, and the Psalms; the "abandoned friend" from Tegernsee quotes the lamentation of Job; and the Woman of the EDA alludes to Jeremiah, Matthew, and again the Psalms. Biblical writers, unlike Stoics, had no interest in suppressing emotions; their range of expression is rich, varied, and intense. This is true especially of the Psalms and prophetic writings, while the book of Job is unsurpassed for voicing anguish, and the Song of Songs for amorous yearning. Medieval Benedictines, chanting the liturgy of the hours, recited the entire Psalter every week; many doubtless knew it by heart. The lectionary, preaching, saints' lives, and commentaries offered still more occasions for immersion in Scripture. Intimate familiarity with its style produced habits so deeply ingrained that, when a monk or nun sat down to produce a letter, the Bible supplied a ready stock of phrases and metaphors for any emotion whatsoever—love, anger, joy, crushing disappointment, impatient longing. These allusions are not necessarily "religious"; they are simply the natural idiom of a textual community.

Biblical rhetoric pervades the *Epistolae* from beginning to end. It is a rhetoric of hyperbole: the beloved is sweeter than honey and the honeycomb (nos. 11, 39, 102), more precious than gold and topaz (nos. 45, 79). In absence the lover feeds on sighs, with only tears for drink (no. 108), while a letter from the beloved ravishes the reader to the third heaven (no. 112). The Woman's biblical language is untouched by any hint of irony, though the Man is occasionally mischievous; Christ's new commandment to "love one another" justifies their affair (no. 52). Both lovers call on God as witness of their sincerity (nos. 11, 23, 44, 53). As in most love letters, sincerity is a pervasive concern: the lovers must constantly avow that their devotion is true, loyal, pure, and unfeigned. This rhetoric is no less characteristic of the Tegernsee letters and, for that matter, the troubadours, who are forever swearing that their *fin'amor* is unlike the lying, deceptive love of their rivals, though its outward show is the same.

Rhetoric and sincerity have always had a stormy relationship.[73] Medieval *dictatores* presumably took this for granted, but their successors may need to address the issue more directly. Here is the modern *dictator* Verlyn Klinkenborg instructing young writers:

In writing, it's impossible to express sincerity sincerely.

That is, just by being sincere.

You really mean what you mean to say.

You feel an intense sincerity burning inside you.

And yet your sentences feel choked or formulaic. . . .

If you want the reader to feel your sincerity, your sentences have to enact sincerity—
verbally, syntactically, even rhythmically. . . .

Sincerity is a dramatic role for you and your sentences.

That makes it sound insincere.

But the apparently insincere manipulation of language is the tool that persuades us of
your sincerity.[74]

Some readers, even medievalists, might find it hard to believe that anyone truly in love could write as artificially as the lovers of the EDA. Klinkenborg's paradox warns against any such misplaced belief in spontaneity. To borrow his terms, the dramatic roles enacted by the two lovers' sentences hardly prove that their letters are "mere school exercises," though they probably do prove that their writers had practiced such exercises. So why, after acquiring proficiency in the art of rhetoric, should they abandon it in their hour of need? Though we should not assume that all the emotions performed on the page were identical to those actually felt, neither should we posit a complete disconnect.

The paradox of sincerity is not always expressed sincerely, as it were, but it seems to be a sine qua non of the genre. Baudri, the author of so many poetic love letters, defends himself against critics by protesting that he is *not* sincere: "Crede michi, non uera loquor, magis omnia fingo" (Believe me, I don't tell the truth, I make it all up). That sly *crede michi* makes the line into a version of the liar's paradox.[75] In another apologia, he claims that if he really felt ardent desire, his verse would say nothing about it: "Nam si quid uellem, *si quid uehementer amarem*, / Esset amoris tunc nescia carta mei."[76] Yet to Constance he swears, "*Te uehementer amo*, te totam totus amabo" (I love you ardently, all of me will love all of you).[77] Marbod, writing to one of his epistolary girlfriends, tweaks the paradox differently:

> Me non ex libris, sed totis dilige fibris,
> Qua te mente colo, me cole, digna polo.[78]

> Love me not out of books, but with every fiber of your heart.
> Adore me, my goddess, in the same spirit I adore you.

This is much like Sir Philip Sidney's famous sonnet from *Astrophil and Stella*. After the Renaissance poet has vainly spent himself "turning others' leaves" in search of inspiration for a love song, the Muse of sincerity intervenes: "'Fool,' said my Muse to me, 'look in thy heart and write.'"[79] The bookish poet-lover does not want to love (or be loved) out of books. Yet where else has his heart learned to love in the first place?

Today, anyone sufficiently *retardataire* to write a love letter might worry that it sounded false—too studied, too rhetorical, too stilted. The Woman of the EDA suffers from the opposite fear: she frets that her words are not "artful" (*litteratorie*) enough for her awesome teacher (no. 49), so her grateful spirit dares not send him "all the greetings it would like . . . lest it spoil them all by heaping up too many" (no. 13). In one letter she stages an allegorical debate between Affect and Defect, the first representing "the fervent affection of my mind" and the other, "the defection of my arid talent" (no. 23). Affect spurs her on to write, but Defect reins her in: "I had the will but not the power; I began and faltered, I struggled and fell, my shoulders crushed by the burden." This astonishing performance is more than a humility topos, more even than a backhanded plea for praise (although it is both of those things). Above all, it signifies the immense value the Woman set on this correspondence, the emotional capital she invested in letter writing. The Man's letters, with a few exceptions, are more casual, less elaborately wrought. For him, the correspondence had a more instrumental purpose. He seems to have begun the affair with an Ovidian letter-poem in Baudri's mode (no. 113), and later, when absence or the "envious" made it difficult to arrange trysts, he used letters to sustain the relationship. But if he ever expressed concerns about writing, it was only to downplay the importance of words (*verba*) in comparison with deeds (*res* or *facta*), a frequent motif in his letters (nos. 22, 54, 74, 75, 85, 105). This may have been his way of calming the Woman's anxieties, as well as offsetting a diet of constant hyperbole.

One note that we rarely hear in the EDA is Ovidian playfulness, so typical of the Loire Valley poets and the later Tegernsee letters (nos. 8–10). We do catch a few glimpses in the Man's letters, especially his poems:

> May your night be lucid, lacking nothing but me,
> And lacking me, my lovely, think that you lack all.
> See me in your dreams, dream of me when you wake,
> And just as I am yours, be mine, my spirit. (no. 111)

Erotic desire is heightened by the lover's absence. In other literary exchanges, such playfulness serves a purpose: its role is to mediate the gap between style and substance. As humanists and connoisseurs of Latin poetry, correspondents of this era could not help loving Ovid. But as Christians and (in most cases) vowed religious, they could not afford to have love affairs. Hence we find passages like this one in Constance's letter-poem:

> I have been chaste, I am chaste now, I want to live chaste;
> Oh, if only I could live as a bride of God.
> Yet not for this do I myself detest your love;
> The bride of God should love God's servants.[80]

The courtly triangle of God, his bride, and her devoted servant was current in this milieu. Hildebert of Lavardin tells the widowed Adela of Blois that "the bride of my Lord is my lady," and Abelard uses the same rationale with Heloise.[81] This conceit both permits intimate friendship and defines its limits. For Baudri and his Constance, chastity is an enabling condition. It is the preemptive "no" that permits a delicious toying with "yes," an imagined game of might-have-beens. If there were any danger of real seduction in the flesh, she would not dare to play the games she plays with her absent beloved—to caress his naked parchment with her naked hand, even to sleep with it next to her heart, a virtual embrace that results in "torrid" dreams.

A similar teasing drama unfolds in the last three Tegernsee letters. A young woman professes what sounds like passionate love for her teacher: "I have enclosed [you] in the marrow of my heart, deserving all the praise that human reason can give. For, from the day I first saw you, I began to love you. You mightily penetrated the inner depths of my heart and there (this is marvelous to say!) you prepared yourself a seat.... You alone have been chosen from thousands, you alone have been received into the inmost sanctuary of my mind, you alone are sufficient for me in all things—but only if, as I hope, you do not fall away from my love. As you have done, I have done; I have cast aside all pleasures for the sake of your love" (Tegernsee 8). But this is not what it seems to be, for the woman adds that her teacher set his throne in her heart with his "delightful conversation" and confirmed it with "epistolary speech." At the end of her original letter, which has been altered by the Tegernsee scribe, she must have gone on to refuse his sexual pleas, for he responds by reinforcing them with specious arguments: "If faith without works is dead [James 2:20] and the fulfillment of love is shown in deeds, you caught yourself in a contradiction when you did not fulfill your good beginning with a suitable ending, nor bring your sweet eloquence to a fitting close. Rather, contrary to the law of friendship, you opposed your *nolle* (I won't) to my *velle* (I will). So the first part of your letter should utterly reject its harsh epilogue, contrary to friendship—and what you have magnificently expressed in words, you ought to fulfill in friendly deeds" (Tegernsee 9). Perhaps the teacher was genuinely unscrupulous, or perhaps he was deliberately testing—and teasing—an attractive student. In either case, she responds to his casuistry in no uncertain terms: "To tell the truth, I wrote you a more intimate letter than any man before you could ever wrench from me. But you men are sly, or to put it better, deceitful. It is your habit to ensnare us simple young girls in talk because so often, as we proceed with you in our simplicity of mind onto the battlefield of words, you stab us with the sound reasoning (as you imagine) of your darts.... For with a wildly irreverent, unbridled spirit exceeding measure, you imprudently loosed the reins of your hasty speech ... because you think that, after our tender words, you should proceed to acts. But that is not so, nor will it be" (Tegernsee 10). Rhetoric in such letters is the cement of friendship. It is also the weapon of both seduction and embattled chastity.

This kind of playful flirting—the Baudriesque *iocus amoris* or merry game of love—is missing in the EDA, especially on the Woman's side. Not once does she protest or protect her chastity, and when she expresses anger (which is often), it is never because of the Man's sexual advances. Even though the *Epistolae* were abridged by their scribe, Johannes de Vepria, what he omitted seems to have been their mundane, matter-of-fact details, rather than emotional or rhetorical flights. So I think it safe to say that if, in the course of 116 letters and fragments, we find neither flirtatious coyness nor outraged modesty, it is because these two lovers were engaged in a flesh-and-blood affair. They were, in that respect, more like Abelard and Heloise than like Baudri and Constance or the Bavarian nuns and their teachers. Unlike the literary nuns, the Woman of the EDA never assumes the stance of resisting a too-importunate lover.

There is nonetheless an edginess in the exchange, a competitive spirit, that plays out on another plane. This has no analogue in the Tegernsee letters, but we catch a hint of it in Marbod's lyric "Ad amicam gementem" (To a sighing girlfriend):

> Woe is me if you only imitate the sighs of lovers
>   And what you speak does not come from your heart.
> When I read what you say, I'm inflamed by your loving words;
>   When I read that you weep, I too shed tears.
> From your wild laments, I know the burning in your breast;
>   A mouth that voices such pain betrays the heart's violence.
> I feel what you feel, chosen prize of my mind,
>   O dear to my heart; whatever you suffer, I suffer.
> So don't say this painful wound is yours alone,
>   Say rather that it hurts still more for me.
> I burn unjustly since I burn even more than you:
>   Either no love is yours, or mine is greater.[82]

Marbod stakes his claim to love on his empathy. Whatever his lovesick friend feels, he feels the same and more: he too weeps tears of love, feels its burning, endures its wounds. But all this potent affect is the fruit of her rhetoric. It is not when he sees his friend but when he reads her letters (*Cum lego*, he says twice) that her words move him so deeply. Then, because she is after all absent, he worries that she is not sincere, not speaking "from the heart," but merely imitating lovers' sighs. And if that is the case, because he knows that *his* emotion is real—*he* truly weeps and burns, whereas she may only claim to—he "burns even more" than she (*ardeo plus te*). This in turn means that he loves more. Thus, in a bizarre turn, what began as sympathy ("my poor dear, how I suffer because of your pain!") ends in erotic one-upmanship ("I'm the one who's really in love, you're probably faking it"). This perverse twist of the sincerity topos betrays a psychological dynamic that could easily exist in real love relationships, as well as literary or imagined ones.

The lovers of the *Epistolae*, who both seem to be high-spirited, strong-willed people, constantly strive to outdo each other in their declarations of love. Finally the Man proposes a brilliant, unusual way of dealing with this situation: "This is how our love will become immortal: if each of us strives to surpass the other in a friendly, joyful competition; and let neither of us consent to be outdone by the other. It may happen that a friend will grow weary of loving if he sees himself less loved by his friend than he deserves. So I would never want to have said that I love you more than I feel loved; such a remark is silly and breeds discord. Rather, I think it is much better to say that in our mutual love, I do not want to be the lesser, and I have no idea which of us surpasses the other" (no. 72). The *concertatio* or competition in virtue was a topos of classical friendship. As Jaeger demonstrates, it plays a key role in Augustine's *Confessions*.[83] But this theme is by no means conventional in the new literature of heterosexual love. Its prominence in the EDA constitutes a distinctive mark of that correspondence and the relationship that gave it birth.[84] Given the nature of literary love, a competition in loving inevitably becomes a competition in writing. That is one reason the Woman worries so much about the inadequacies of her style and polishes it to such a pitch of intensity. It is a triumph of self-conscious, competitive love when she can write—biblically, rhetorically, hyperbolically: "in all Latinity, I have found no word that can plainly say how intent is my mind upon you, for with God as my witness, I love you with a sublime and exceptional love. Hence there neither is nor shall be anything or any fate that can separate me from your love, save death alone" (no. 53).

The Emotional Dynamics of the *Epistolae duorum amantium*

The *Epistolae* can be connected with three different emotional communities, overlapping but not identical. First, there would have been the masculine world of the cathedral school where the Man began his studies. The subject he eventually taught was philosophy or dialectic, as the letters indicate, but he would have started with the standard curriculum in grammar and rhetoric. His letters, especially his poems, are steeped in the same Ovidian ethos that characterizes the work of Marbod and Baudri. The difference between his frame of reference and the Woman's is encapsulated by their initial choice of words for love itself.[85] For the Man, it is consistently *amor*, the Ovidian term, with a broad semantic range that extends from warm friendship through sheer carnal lust. In many letters, the Man presents himself as a straightforward Ovidian lover like the ones we meet in troubadour lyrics, romances, and the dialogues of Andreas Capellanus. By *amor*, he means yielding to the god of love because he has been vanquished by his lady's beauty (no. 113)—and not only her beauty, but also her brilliance (*ingenium*), eloquence, and virtue. Such love entails a passionate desire that verges on adoration of the beloved. The lure of sexual attraction is strong; though often playfully expressed, it is not concealed by euphemisms. The beloved is characterized with a lexicon of light and radiance (*lux, candor, fulgor, claritas, splendor*). She is sun, moon, and stars to her lover, who stresses his dependence as he becomes ever more obsessed with her. Love itself is an experience of blazing heat (*ardor, fervor, flamma*). In his definition of *amor* (no. 24), the Man emphasizes its unitive nature. Love continually pours itself into another "with a kind of appetite and desire" (*cum quodam appetitu et desiderio*) until the two become one.

While the Woman too appreciated Ovid, only one of her lyrics (no. 82) has a mildly Ovidian flavor. Her poetry, with its leonine rhymes and formal panegyrics, is more indebted to the Carolingians. Unlike the Man's, her rhetorical training came from a first-class convent school, which accounts for the affinity between her letters and the Tegernsee corpus. Despite geographical distance, the northern French nunnery where she was educated must have taught a feminine version of the *ars dictandi* similar to that of the Bavarian nuns, and immersion in this textual tradition shaped a subtly different emotional community. We know little about this monastic epistolary art, since most writing by nuns has perished, but it surely differed from the treatises on *dictamen* that grew out of Italian notarial culture. Like that of the Tegernsee writers, the Woman's emotional tone is less flirtatious than the Man's, but more intense and, if we can allow the word without prejudice, more sentimental. Of all the Tegernsee letters, those that express love between women (nos. 5–7) display the greatest parallels in phrasing and feeling with hers. This female emotional community privileged earnest assurances of *fides* (loyalty, fidelity, trust), whose role was partly to offset lamentations about the writer's misery in the absence of her

beloved. Ovidian rhetoric, though present, is overshadowed by biblical phrase-
ology. Lofty discussions of virtue and friendship, indebted to Cicero's *Laelius*,
mark both the longest Tegernsee letter (no. 8) and two of the Woman's most
exalted missives (nos. 25, 49).

Like the Bavarian nuns, the Woman at least initially preferred a more biblical term for love, *dilectio*, to the Ovidian *amor*. As Christine Mohrmann explains, *dilectio* was most likely a Christian coinage from *diligere*, to esteem or
cherish. Early translators used both *caritas* and *dilectio* to express the Greek
agape, but not *amor* (*eros*), whose connotations evoked either sensuality or a
pagan philosophical view of love.[86] Although St. Augustine used these terms
interchangeably, he observed that others made a distinction: "Many say that *dilectio* should be understood in a good sense, *amor* in a bad."[87] *Dilectio* occurs
frequently in the Tegernsee letters, where it is closely bound up with friendship
and kinship. For the Woman of the *Epistolae*, it denotes a species of love that
does not succumb helplessly to passion, but arises from rational choice and commitment of the will (no. 84).

Although they began from different starting points, the lovers converged to
form a private emotional community of two, with their own pet names and intimate quirks. Secrecy is a leitmotif of their correspondence. Jaeger notes astutely
that "the scaffolding of the Tristan romance" is already in place, several decades
before the earliest version known to us.[88] Although there is no adultery, "the envious" lie in wait for the lovers, keeping them apart and forcing them to stay out of
the public eye (nos. 28, 54, 85). These shadowy, unidentified figures recall the *lauzengiers* of troubadour lyric, always scheming to betray lovers' secrets and destroy
their lives.[89] Putting on a brave front against this threat, the couple take refuge in
the awareness of their sublime love, which they represent as wholly exceptional:
unicus, singularis, specialis, immortalis. In all the world, they are "those who love
each other uniquely" (*unice amantes*, no. 63). It is no wonder, the Man claims, that
the less fortunate should envy a friendship "so distinguished and so fitting" as
theirs (no. 28). God is their friend, they are quite certain, because their love is
grounded in virtue—a claim they maintain despite their refusal, for obvious reasons, to describe it as *spiritualis* or *non carnalis*.[90] As the fear of discovery looms
larger, their mutual dependence becomes plainer but also more fragile, for they respond differently to that threat: the Woman with increasing desperation and
neediness, the Man with cautious distancing and avoidance. But that is to anticipate an ending that is not predictable at the outset.

The love begins from two directions at once, so to speak, reflecting the different textual and emotional communities in which the lovers were raised.

Having first come to know the Woman as his student, the Man sends her a seduction poem that marks him as a full-fledged initiate of the Loire Valley
school.[91] It contains thirteen allusions to five different works of Ovid, as well as
two echoes of Fulcoius of Beauvais and one each of Baudri, Marbod, and Hildebert of Lavardin. A few lines will indicate its flavor:

> Forgive me: Love dictates what I'm forced to write.
>   Forgive me, I confess: I love not patiently.
> You have vanquished me, whom none could vanquish,
>   And so I burn the brighter, for this is my first love:
> Never before has the flame pierced to my marrow.
>   If ever I loved before, I was but lukewarm.
> You alone make me eloquent; none but you
>   Has won this glory—to deserve my song. (no. 113)

The Woman, unbound by vows, replies with neither the flirtatious ambivalence of Constance nor the determined chastity of the Tegernsee nuns. Instead,
she is thrilled, for even before the teacher makes his move, she has already fallen
in love. She responds in the earnest, hyperbolic, self-deprecating tone so characteristic of her: "It has pleased your nobility to send my lowly self a letter, and
by ... promising the solace of your love, you have ravished me up to the third
heaven with a kind of mental lightness stemming, it seemed to me, from too
great a joy. ... No language, no facility with words, is sufficient to express the joy
I feel on reaching the haven of your love—confident, yet not ungrateful. Though
I am utterly incapable of repaying so great a favor, I long with great longing to
devote myself unfailingly to you" (no. 112).

The Woman's reply includes six biblical allusions and one to Boethius, but
not a single Ovidian tag. Thus, although these first two items express the couple's mutual love, they also reveal radically different frames of reference, which
entail contrasting emotional tones.

The Woman is even more enamored of the Ciceronian ideal of *amicitia*, a
friendship that remains pure and disinterested because it "stems from integrity,
virtue, and intimate love" (no. 49). *Fides et amicitia*, fidelity and friendship, were
the staple currency of monastic letter writing and ennobling love. As one of the
Bavarian nuns puts it, "Our first, last, and central theme has always been friendship—true friendship, than which there is nothing better, nothing more joyful,
nothing more lovely" (Tegernsee 8). Her teacher responds, "Having read your intimate letter most diligently, I was delighted by your extravagant praise of fidelity

and friendship" (Tegernsee 9). At the beginning of their correspondence, the Woman of the *Epistolae* might have expected a similar exchange. Having declared their mutual affection, she and her lover would henceforth be intimate friends: they would study philosophy together, exchange quotations from their favorite poets, admire each other's virtues, write rhetorically brilliant letters, and grow steadily in *dilectio, fides,* and *amicitia.* For all her intensity, it is not clear that she desired or anticipated a sexual relationship at the outset.

For some time, the correspondence continues as a rhapsodic exchange of greetings and compliments, while the lovers vie with each other in mutual praise. The Man, however, is not content with this. Neither monastic vows nor physical distance hold his passions in check, and with proximity, the Woman's desire is growing too. "Just as fire is unquenchable and nothing can conquer it except water, its naturally powerful antidote," she writes, "so my love is incurable by any means; it is treatable by you alone" (no. 21). Catching the Ovidian scent once more, the Man closes in for the capture. In a witty astronomical conceit, he compares himself to the moon set ablaze by the light of the Woman's sun: "when I am with you I become altogether fire; I burn down to the marrow of my bones" (no. 22). That letter ends with a carpe diem plea: "Envious time threatens our love, yet you delay as if we had leisure." Perhaps to prolong this tantalizing delay, the Woman responds (unless there is some break in the sequence) with a bravura performance of humility topoi. But she slips in a double entendre that melds eros and intellect in the characteristic way of these lovers: "I often come with parched throat, desiring to be refreshed with the sweet nectar of your mouth and to drink thirstily of the riches [of philosophy] poured out in your heart" (no. 23). This letter opens onto the couple's first philosophical discussion of love (nos. 24–25), which the Man ends with the unmistakably sexual pleading of no. 26. He appeals to his beloved as his *summum bonum,* "whom he does not yet know but longs to know more intimately," while he "burns within himself to seek out the knowledge of so great a good."

A mildly prurient pastime for students of the *Epistolae* has been trying to pinpoint the exact moment when the love was consummated.[92] For instance, the Man will confess in no. 59, "I am the guilty one—I who compelled you to sin," and in the next letter, the Woman tries to end the relationship. Constant Mews has suggested that she was reacting to a forced sexual encounter.[93] But I would place the moment earlier—after the Man (channeling Terence, Lucan, and Ovid) begs his beloved to "let all your love release its riches upon me, conceal nothing at all from your most devoted servant—for I think nothing has been done as long as I see anything left undone" (no. 26). At this point I would guess that he took what he wanted. But he may have met some resistance from the Woman, for the tone changes abruptly. We next see a remarkably opaque greeting from her (no. 27); an exultant letter from the Man in which, for the first time, he defies the "crooked jealousy" that lies in wait for them (no. 28); then a deeply sorrowful message from the Woman (no. 29). It reads in its entirety, "Having given up everything, I take refuge beneath your wings; I submit myself to your authority, resolutely following you in all things. I can scarcely speak these sad words. Farewell." The note of submission is new and striking, an almost "wifely" moment that may be linked to her sexual surrender. Certainly the courtly *domna* of troubadour lyric did not submit to her lover—rather the reverse. Even in the Regensburg Songs, the young and still girlish correspondents retain a claim to moral authority over their teacher; they, not he, will be the arbiters of courteous mores.[94] But the EDA are different. After the Woman's "sad words" we see an impasse, in which each hopes the other will find some way to cope with their changed situation. The Man falls sick and recovers; the Woman reminds him that "prudent delay is better than reckless haste" (no. 34); then they quarrel. We come to a sequence of eleven straight letters from the Man (nos. 35–44), broken by only a few lines of lofty verse from the Woman (no. 38b). Sexual consummation, in short, seems to have provoked the first major crisis in this storm-tossed relationship.

Gender plays a complex, contradictory role in the exchange. Once the lovers have embarked on a sexual affair, yet without abandoning their claim to *amicitia* and ennobling love, they enter uncharted territory. Writing beyond Baudri's tongue-in-cheek love play and well before Chrétien de Troyes, Marie de France, or Andreas Capellanus, they no longer have any precedent for the relationship they have developed. Neither before nor after them do we find such a sustained correspondence between any pair of lovers, while for a woman to have an articulate voice in such an affair is unprecedented. Indeed, it is a significant "first" in literary history—and a major reason the EDA, even as anonymous letters, deserve our careful study. This lack of precedent is also a reason for the Woman's epistolary nervousness. Often she reverts to her role as the timid student, convinced that neither she nor her writing can be worthy of her exalted teacher (nos. 112, 23, 49, 79). Repeatedly she promises obedience and submission, which she may owe either qua student or qua mistress (nos. 25, 29, 71). As long as their relationship had been chaste, her role as *amica* was simply that of "friend" in the feminine. But from now on the term cannot cease to be ambiguous, for an *amica* (like a vernacular *amie*) is also a girlfriend or paramour. Qua friend, however, the Woman remains equal to her beloved; Ciceronian friendship was nothing if not a relationship between equals. So in no. 18 she greets him as *par pari*, "an equal to an equal," and in no. 83 she claims with odd formality to love him *condicione pari*, "on equal terms" or "on the same condition." But that is not all, for her gendered submission is further offset by an implied superiority. For all her professed obedience, the Woman readily assumes a dominant role in the art of love, retaining the *domna*'s rights to correct aberrant behavior, withdraw her favor, or lapse into sulky silence when her lover has displeased her. In fact, he often calls her *domina*, much like a courtly beloved (nos. 6, 8, 36, 61, 87, 108). She never calls him *dominus*.

We do not know how the lovers' crisis over consummation was resolved because, after an apparent gap in the sequence, their correspondence resumes on a completely different note. The Man has been out of town and the Woman joyfully awaits his return (no. 45). But when he does return, things quickly go wrong again. Soon we find the Man deploring his "hateful slumber" and "cursed idleness" (no. 47), while the Woman—though still head over heels in love—remarks frostily that "no one should live . . . if he does not know how to love and control his passions" (no. 48). Next in the sequence, if not in real time, come two lengthy philosophical letters on the nature of love (nos. 49–50). This dialogue and a similar one earlier in the exchange (nos. 24–25) explore some ideas about love that are both emotionally and philosophically challenging. Constant Mews has written at length about the philosophical issues,[95] so I will concentrate on the emotional dynamics they entail. Three themes in particular stand out: the ideal of coinherence, or exchange of self; the ethical demand to renounce all possessiveness; and the concept of love as permanent, unpayable debt.

In no. 24 the Man, at the Woman's urging, offers a formal definition of love. It is "a certain power of the soul, neither existing through itself nor self-contained, but always pouring itself into another with a kind of appetite and desire, willing to become identical [*idem*] with the other so that, from two different wills, one single thing [*unum quid*] may be produced without difference." The idea that love seeks union, fusion, or identification with the beloved was a commonplace, though this particular formulation is unique. But the question was discussed mainly in spiritual treatises where the Beloved is God, making the "union of wills" a very different matter from what obtains in a human relationship.[96] Neither Plato's *Symposium* nor Aristotle's *Nicomachean Ethics* was known to the West at this time, so the classical basis for philosophical reflection on love and friendship was slim. For Sallust, its chief quality was *idem velle atque idem nolle*—having a common will, wanting and not wanting the same things as the other.[97] For Cicero, whose definition was constantly cited, friendship is "agreement in all things divine and human, together with charity and good will" (cf. Tegernsee 8).[98] Early in their affair, the Man exults that he and his beloved have attained that ideal: "we affirm and deny the same things, we have the same views about everything. This can easily be proven, for you often anticipate my thoughts: what I intend to write, you write first, and if I remember well, you have said the same about yourself" (no. 24).

It takes no great wisdom, however, to realize that even the most loving, virtuous individuals will never agree on *all* things human (let alone divine). Pragmatically, it would seem that the only way to achieve such a goal is for one friend always to yield promptly to the other's will. In marriage, an unequal relationship and therefore not a friendship, wifely submission was in fact the requisite means to harmony. But the Man of the EDA took a different path, interpreting this union of wills as a metaphysical reality. The lovers' ideal mode of existence was to be coinherence, on the model of the Trinity: "in that day you will know that I am in my Father, and you in me, and I in you" (John 14:20). Hence the Man tells his beloved, "I am wholly with you, and to speak more truly, I am wholly in you" (no. 16). Later he invents a memorable gothic metaphor for their indwelling: "You are immortally buried in my heart; from this tomb you shall never emerge while I live" (no. 22). And in the fullest extension of the topos, the claim "I am *in* you" shades into "I am you," as the lovers proceed to a full exchange of the self: "That we may do our best to care for each other, you are I and I am you" (no. 77).

The sentence "I am you" turns out to have a long history, which Karl Morrison explores in his illuminating study of the hermeneutics of empathy.[99] An "I" and a "you" can become one by many means—imitation, sacramental union, mystical indwelling, extreme empathy, erotic bonding. But "I am you" always entails a positive as well as a negative content; it requires, at the same time, an emptying of the self and an appropriation of the other. Such appropriation can be dangerous because, unless the relationship is one of absolute equality, "I am you" can entail the corollary, "therefore *you* are nothing at all." That is why Morrison speaks of the formula as having both an "amorous" and a "malevolent" pole. The coercive dimensions of such an ostensibly loving appropriation were intensively studied by feminist and postcolonial critics, among others, in the late twentieth century.[100] When the Man in the flush of reciprocated love wrote that "you are I and I am you," he surely had no sinister project in mind. Yet the lovers lived in a patriarchal society where no heterosexual relationship, even outside marriage, could remain a genuine friendship of equals. So their attempt at lived coinherence must have caused at least subliminal tension, accounting in part for the Woman's tendency to veer between submissiveness and *hauteur*. And when she felt that the Man had appropriated her actual labor (no. 71), she did not take it lightly.

Central to Ciceronian ethics is a distinction between opportunistic friendship (what we now call "networking") and "true" friendship, which can be recognized by its disinterested character. The Woman eloquently voices this opposition:

> In my judgment, the friendship of those who seem to love each other for the
> sake of riches or pleasures will by no means endure, since the very things on
> whose account they love seem not at all enduring. Thus it happens that, when
> riches or pleasures fail them, their love also fails, because they did not love
> those goods for each other's sake, but each other for the sake of the goods.
> My love, however, is joined to you by a very different pact. For it was not the
> idle weight of riches that compelled me to love you. . . . No, it was virtue
> alone, the sole excellence, the source of all that is honorable, all that is
> prosperous. . . . I have indeed found in you this supreme good, the most
> outstanding of all, and that is why I love you. Because this good is agreed to
> be eternal, beyond doubt I shall love you eternally. Believe me then, O you
> whom I long for: neither wealth, nor honors, nor all that the partisans of this
> world desire, could separate me from the love of you. (no. 49)

Convinced that she loves in this pure, disinterested way, the Woman lays down a relentlessly high-minded ideal to which she will hold both herself and her partner. Quite early in the relationship, she boasts that "nothing will ever be so burdensome for my body, nothing so perilous for my soul" that she would not gladly do it for her beloved (no. 9). No self-seeking is to taint the purity of their friendship. Although the Man warmly applauds these sentiments, he does not himself pretend to such selfless love. To be sure, he disavows any profit motive; he is not seeking to marry the Woman for her dowry. Yet he does desire emotional benefits, as he admits: "I chose you among many thousands for your countless virtues, truly seeking no other benefit save that I might rest in you, that you might lighten all my woes, and that among all earthly goods, your charm alone might refresh me and make me forget all sorrows" (no. 50). That might sound like a reasonable expectation for any friendship, but it would in fact cause trouble between the pair. Apparently the Man made such a habit of "lament[ing his] miseries and troubles" in hope of comfort (no. 61) that the Woman grew weary of it, asking to see more virile fortitude: "I do not want any more tears to burst from your eyes, for it is improper for a man to weep when he should maintain the severity of strict honor" (no. 62).

Like the ideal of coinherence, that of disinterested love is easier to maintain in theory than in practice. It is traditionally a mark of male friendship, which the two lovers are among the first—though perhaps not the very first—to apply between the sexes. A girl in Marbod's circle (if not some male poet impersonating a girl) wrote a light-hearted poem, almost a sonnet, reproaching a lover who promised rich gifts but delivered nothing.[101]

> All the joys of maidens: violets and rose blossoms,
> Lilies of dazzling white, along with delicious fruits,
> A pair of doves—and throw in their mother too;
> A purple gown—if I wore it, I could outshine the nymphs
> As much, you say, as my face surpasses theirs—
> Plus silver, jewels, and gold: all this you promise.
> You promise everything, yet you send me nothing.
> If you loved me and really had what you promise,
> The gifts would have gone before, the words come after.
> So either it's all a lie, you don't know love's wounds,
> Or else you're rich in idle words and poor in goods.
> But even if you had abundant riches,
> You're a boor to think I love your goods—and not yourself.[102]

The girl, or whoever voiced her complaint, calls her lover's bluff on two counts. First there are his false promises, the gifts given in words alone; but a more serious problem is his *rusticitas*. Only a *rusticus*, a boor, could think her so mercenary as to be enamored of *tua, non te*—his goods and not himself. These words anticipate Heloise's insistence on the purity of her love for Abelard: "Nihil unquam, Deus scit, in te nisi te requisiui, *te pure non tua* concupiscens" (God knows I never sought anything in you except yourself; I wanted simply you, nothing of yours).[103] Taking this ideal to its logical extreme, Heloise would renounce marriage because it endows a wife with her husband's goods, thus compromising the purity of her love.

The Woman too anticipates Heloise when she declares in a poem, "If all that Caesar ever possessed were mine, / Riches so great would profit me nothing" (no. 82).[104] Nothing can be of value to her unless it is her lover's gift—and then she prizes the gift for the giver's sake, not vice versa. But as the relationship sours, her will to renounce possessions gives way to a sickening sense that she herself has become one. Possession, as both metaphor and reality, becomes a touchstone for the Woman's emotional state. When she fears that her lover's affection is waning, she accuses him of holding her cheap (*vile*, no. 69). "My prayers profit me nothing," she laments, "because I and what is mine have become worthless to you" (*tibi vilescunt*, no. 98). Finally, with withering contempt, she complains that "a possession, possessed by its possessor" (*possessio, que possidetur a possessore*) "should be attentively cultivated" and not "become worthless" (*vilescat*) in the owner's heart (no. 100). While the Man protests that these charges are false, he does seem to have distanced himself from the Woman for fear of scandal.

A third, baffling component of this philosophical conversation on love is the Woman's sense of limitless obligation. True lovers, she believes, are bound by a never-payable debt, owing infinite gratitude as well as infinite service: "The duties [*officia*] of true love are rightly fulfilled only when they are owed without ceasing [*sine intermissione debentur*], so that we do everything in our strength for the beloved, yet do not cease to will beyond our strength" (no. 25). Although *officium* is a Ciceronian concept, this idea of unending debt is neither biblical nor classical. But it resonates curiously with St. Anselm's reasoning in *Cur Deus homo* (Why God became man), a work of the 1090s. According to Anselm, man owes God a debt of obedience on which he defaults because of sin, necessitating a Redeemer whose capacity to pay will be as infinite as the debt itself. Obedience and debt are just as closely linked in the Woman's thought. Even when she sets out to draft a greeting or thank her beloved for a favor, she often feels overwhelmed. It is not just that she worries about her rhetorical skills; she also feels that the Man's "honeyed love" has conferred on her a joy and honor so great that she owes him infinite gratitude (nos. 23, 25, 81). But being herself finite, she cannot sufficiently pay. Hence "I am wholly inadequate in body and mind alike," she confesses, "to render thanks for each and every one of your favors" (no. 79). Trained in a convent, she writes as if she had projected the emotional dynamics of a relationship with God onto her lover. Such a transference may have been facilitated by the prominence of biblical diction in the *ars dictaminis*. But that alone cannot account for the Woman's straining after the infinite, her insistence that a love like hers can only be eternal (nos. 49, 84).

About halfway through the correspondence, if not sooner, we find the lovers living apart, seldom able to meet because of "envy" and the fear of scandal (no. 62). Subsequent letters often refer to their separation and longing for visits. The Woman, rhapsodic in her cries of desire and extravagant praise, never ceases to assure her lover of her constancy, while at the same time accusing him bitterly of neglect. For his part, he vacillates between ardent professions of love and casual messages that make her fear he is losing interest. Frequent quarrels and reconciliations mark this long-distance relationship. The Woman surprisingly proposes a breakup in no. 60, but by no. 64 they have made peace. Another quarrel, or else a resumption of the same one, erupts in nos. 69–75. This time it revolves around some thoughtless remarks the Man had uttered or written. The strained, quarrelsome tone disappears for a while as the lovers once again proclaim their affection and devotion (nos. 77–89), perhaps revitalized by the Man's proposal of a competition in love (no. 72). In the midst of this idyll he sends his beloved a long poem, celebrating their first anniversary and promising to turn over a new leaf. "Love must be harmed no more with bitterness," he writes. "Only the sweet henceforth, my life, I'll give you" (no. 87). They compare their secret love to a banked fire that burns all the more vigorously when concealed by ashes (nos. 55, 75, 88), hoping that secrecy and distance will intensify their flame. But the respite does not last, for the scandal the lovers dreaded has evidently come upon them. By no. 90 the Woman complains that she can scarcely write any more because "so many cares impede me, pulling my mind in different ways," and the Man responds, "No one is unhappier than we, who are pulled by love and shame in two directions at once" (no. 93). Ready to give up on him, she goes so far as to regret that she had ever committed herself to their love (no. 95). The Man wryly acknowledges her grievances when he writes, "Farewell, my martyr" (no. 96).

A few brief, carefree letters (nos. 102–5 and 109–11) interrupt this painful sequence with notes of joy. But their style and sentiments so closely echo letters 1–15 that they should probably be assigned to the same early phase of the relationship. (As I will argue in the next chapter, the sequence of letters in the manuscript is unlikely to be that of the actual exchange.) In what may have been his last letter, the Man berates himself as a "fortunate fool," utterly unworthy of the "good thing" he had once enjoyed, but did not know how to retain. Now, he says, "it is flying elsewhere, it is forsaking me, for it knows I am unworthy to possess it" (no. 106). The Woman in response offers a Boethian allegory that the scribe, sadly, has eviscerated. But she seems to imagine Lady Philosophy standing before her, full of reproach, charging that she suffers because she has failed to recognize a profound spiritual truth: "neither noble birth, nor an attractive figure, nor a beautiful face helps anyone unless the grace of the Holy Spirit comes first," teaching that person how to "resist worldly cunning" (no. 107). Whatever happened to the lovers, their correspondence soon afterward breaks off abruptly. Urgently as they had tried to outface a world bent on condemning a love like theirs, in the end they succumb. By imagining that they could somehow prevail against society, as Jaeger observes, "the 'two lovers' of the letters experience the same conceptual blindness as Madame Bovary and Anna Karenina."[105]

The Place of Sexuality

Jaeger's analogies still hold because Western attitudes toward extramarital sex have probably changed more in the last century than they did between 1100 and

1900. For this reason it is hard for us to grasp the very real danger faced by these lovers—not to mention the daring feat they attempted. "Taking sexuality into the idealism of ennobling love meant forcing a union of eros and agapé,"[106] a feat that to most contemporaries would have seemed less a sublime paradox than an absurd (and sinful) delusion. So the two lovers, while hardly restrained in their rhetoric, are discreet when it comes to sexuality. Kissing is mentioned just twice, innocently enough—the Woman kisses a letter from the Man (no. 49) and salutes him with a kiss of peace (no. 71)—while the *opus amoris* is never named. Jean Leclercq and Peter Dronke express doubt that the relationship was consummated at all.[107] But the lovers' ardor and sensuality seem to me unmistakable. In his initial poem the Man asks, "What is hidden beneath your clothes?—My restless mind!"[108] The Woman recites an Ovidian litany: "I can no more deny myself to you than Byblis could to Caunus, Oenone to Paris, or Briseis to Achilles. . . . I send you as many joys as Antiphila had when she welcomed her Clinia. Do not delay your coming; the sooner you come, the sooner you will find cause for joy" (no. 45). The Man responds by setting her love as his *summum bonum*: she is "his fiercely desired hope, a good so great that, once it is possessed, nothing more could be desired." And he adds, "would that I might deserve to be incorporated in that good, which I desire with such impatience that it can scarcely be believed or uttered" (no. 46). There is much more in that vein. Surely this is carnal love—yet it is also a passionately high-minded love, as the two philosophical dialogues clearly show.

I suggested earlier that the Woman, as a learned, idealistic, convent-educated virgin, did not necessarily enter into this friendship with the expectation of sleeping with her teacher. We are in no position to discuss the statistical frequency of love affairs; but as a general rule, epistolary love was not carnal, and carnal love was not literary. Like the nuns of Le Ronceray or Bavaria, the Woman could easily have embarked on such a correspondence without fearing any threat to her virginity. So I return to the Man's striking and unexpected confession, "I am the guilty one—I who compelled you to sin" (no. 59). We have almost no context for this statement except the Woman's response, surprising to say the least: she tries to end the relationship at once. "Your wisdom and knowledge have deceived me," she charges (no. 60). Since she was certainly no pushover, it is hard to see how he could have "compelled [her] to sin" except sexually. From this exchange, taken in isolation, it sounds very much as if he had forced her into unwanted sex. Although I have proposed that the consummation took place quite a bit earlier (after no. 26), causing the first major rift between the lovers, the Woman seems on the whole to have been more than willing. But even the most passionate woman may at times demur. It is possible that the Man had used force on this particular occasion, perhaps insisting on sex at a canonically forbidden time, such as when the Woman was menstruating, or else during Lent or another fasting season. Even married couples were expected to abstain during much of the liturgical year.[109] In any case, rape can occur even within a consensual relationship. We learn from Abelard that he sometimes forced sex on a resistant Heloise—something we could never have guessed from her own letters.[110]

If the Man had begun their relationship with rape, we might expect the Woman to have broken off all contact. Given the exchange that opens the correspondence (nos. 113, 112), seduction seems much more likely. But even that distinction may be more salient to modern than to medieval eyes. Rape victims in classical literature often fall in love with their rapists, and the story of Dinah (Genesis 34) presents an arguably similar case in the Bible. Marjorie Curry Woods has shown, in a disquieting article, that rape is ubiquitous in medieval school texts, including Ovid's *Metamorphoses*. In fact, many texts that were censored as problematic for adult (monastic) readers could be freely studied in the classroom.[111] As in *Floire et Blanchefleur*, learning Latin often *was* coterminous with learning the art of love, including its darker sides. Conversely, however, schoolboys were taught to identify with the raped or seduced-and-abandoned woman through the rhetorical exercise of *ethopoeia*, the speech in character. The point of this first-person exercise was to evoke the feelings of a mythological character in a specific situation, usually a painful one. Women, stereotypically linked with strong emotions, figured more often than not as subjects: What did Andromache say as she grieved for Hector? How did Niobe mourn her children? Augustine himself tells in the *Confessions* how he won a school prize for the best speech evoking Juno's grief and anger as she watched Aeneas sailing for Italy.[112] With the Loire Valley school's promotion of the *Heroïdes*, a plethora of new models for this exercise emerged. So, as Woods remarks, "sympathizing with hurt and angry women . . . was a surprisingly common experience for premodern schoolboys."[113]

Ethopoeia doubtless enhanced the popularity of a genre that we might call the "seduced and abandoned poem." A well-known lyric of this type is *Carmina burana* 126, "Huc usque, me miseram," in which a pregnant girl laments her parents' beatings and her lover's flight. It begins:

Huc usque, me miseram!	Until now, poor wretched me,
rem bene celaveram	I'd concealed things well,
et amavi callide.	and loved cunningly.
Res mea tandem patuit,	Finally, my secret's out,
nam venter intumuit,	for my belly's swollen up,
partus instat gravide.	showing I'm pregnant and soon due.

Hinc mater me verberat,	On one side my mother beats me,
hinc pater improperat,	on the other my father yells at me,
ambo tractant aspere.[114]	both of them are hard on me.

Much as we might like to enlarge the corpus of medieval Latin poems by women, lyrics like this do not qualify. As Stevenson writes, any poem "in which a female speaking voice presents herself as a dramatic spectacle" is unlikely to be autobiographical, especially if (as here) the woman's speech coincides with a misogynist cliché.[115] Juanita Feros Ruys's attempt to assign this poem to Heloise is doubly unpersuasive.[116] Heloise, unlike the speaker, rejoiced in her pregnancy,[117] and at the end of this poem the girl's lover goes back to France (*recessit in Franciam*), which Abelard could not have done because he was already there.

I have translated a less familiar lyric in this genre, "To a Fugitive Lover," at the end of this volume. From a late twelfth-century manuscript in Zurich, this poem is stylistically closer to the lovers of the EDA. Written in one of their favorite meters, leonine hexameter (shifting into elegiacs), it is a verse epistle like those of Baudri and could well date from the late eleventh or early twelfth century. Its editor thought the manuscript anthology could have been compiled by a German cleric during his studies in Paris or Orléans. Like the girl in "Huc usque," the speaker of this poem has been seduced and abandoned, probably with a child on the way. She waxes eloquent on the difference between her lover's attitudes *ante factum* and *post factum* (as the *Rota Veneris* would put it):

> I thought the Rhine would pour its golden streams
>   Into the Danube, before you'd refuse a private talk!
> Why should I now cause you greater shame
>   Than I did before? I am quite unable to say.
> Whatever in me displeases you . . . came from you!
>   Did you not test what was mine? Why now do you carp?
> *Then* I was a gem, a flower, a lily of the field—
>   *Then* no woman in the world was my equal!
> I am no different now, though I'm no longer virgin,
>   Nor can I ever be again—as I lament without end.
> I weep day and night that the Fates did not take
>   My life along with my tender maidenhood.[118]

Whether the poet was a man or a woman, this is an exercise in *ethopoeia*. Its author had a fine sense of moral outrage and knew the rhetoric of seduction. The

Man of the EDA also calls his beloved a gem (nos. 10, 22, 89) and a lily (no. 43, 52) and tells her no woman in the world is her equal (nos. 50, 113).[119] Aside from its function as speech in character, the poem could also have served as a rhetorical *dissuasio*. Regardless of its authorship, it captures the speaker's pathos so empathetically, without ridicule, that one can easily imagine women like Constance, the Woman of the *Epistolae*, or the Bavarian nuns reading it as a warning against the blandishments of seducers.

As Lawrence Lipking shows in *Abandoned Women and Poetic Tradition*, this is not merely a medieval genre; it is an archetypal theme of poetry throughout the world. The main lines of the Western heroic epistle run from Sappho to Ovid to Heloise to Pope ("Eloisa to Abelard"), but the genre is as modern as Rainer Maria Rilke or Marina Tsvetayeva.[120] Its twelfth-century shape, like the model letters in Bernard de Meung and the *Rota Veneris*, gives us some idea of the "normal" scenario for seduction. Men are opportunistic cads, so a seducer can be expected to walk away unscathed, leaving his victim alone and suicidal. Abandoned by her lover, beaten by her parents, ostracized by all, she suffers torments in pregnancy and expects nothing better than to die in childbirth. No longer virgin, she cannot hope for marriage; she will be lucky if some nunnery takes her in as a penitent. In light of such alarming prospects, the outcome of the two lovers' affair may seem less dismal than it first appears. The Woman does feel abandoned; as this essay shows, many of her letters complain of this. But the Man does not in fact abandon her. Although his visits are less frequent than she would have wished, he continues to write and to profess his love: "I am who I was. As for my passion for you, nothing in me has changed—except the flame of love for you springs higher every day. This change alone I must confess, this alone I rightly concede: my love for you constantly increases. But I now address you more cautiously, if you will take note; I approach more cautiously. Shame tempers love and modesty restrains it, lest it burst out to infinity. In this way we can both satisfy our sweet desires and gradually stifle the rumor that has arisen about us. Farewell" (no. 101). Whatever came of this probably futile hope, it appears from letters 106 and 107 that it was the Woman, not the Man, who finally broke off the affair. But here we are on dangerous grounds of conjecture, for as I have said, the chronological order of letters is uncertain, especially toward the end of the manuscript. The relationship itself did not necessarily end where the letters do.

Once again, the two lovers break with all literary precedent. Let me return to the models I sketched of two different textual and emotional communities, one grounded in Ovidian love poetry (as studied in cathedral schools like Marbod's at Angers), the other in ennobling love (as filtered through a convent version of the *ars dictaminis*). These models stand in vivid contrast at the start of the *Epistolae*, with the Man's seduction poem (no. 113) a typical product of the first, the Woman's effusive response (no. 112) a classic instance of the second. But neither model by itself would enable us to predict the outcome. On the first, Ovidian scenario, (a) either the Man should have proved no more serious in his passion than the sly Baudri of Bourgueil, (b) or if he truly aimed at seduction, he should have shrugged and walked off as soon as it was accomplished, leaving the Woman to mourn like the girl in "To a Fugitive Lover." On the second model, that of ennobling love, (c) the two friends should have remained triumphantly chaste, (d) or if the Man could not contain himself, the Woman should have deftly fended him off, like the writers of Tegernsee letters 3 and 10. Although the *Epistolae* do not reveal the couple's ultimate fate, it was clearly none of those four possibilities. Rather than following a known literary model, the lovers muddle through as best they can—two deeply devoted, flawed human beings in the midst of a real relationship, with all its contingencies.

How can we summarize the emotional portraits that emerge from this correspondence, unprecedented in both its length and its distance from available models? Both lovers come across as passionate, fiercely intelligent, strong-willed, and competitive, though also prone to self-pity. Schooled in the hyperbolic rhetoric of their day, each vigorously idealizes the other. The Man, not surprisingly, expresses greater sexual urgency (nos. 113, 22, 26) as well as greater self-confidence (nos. 28, 72, 78). He is inclined to take rash, impulsive actions (nos. 6, 17, 37, 46, 74, 75), a trait for which the Woman sometimes reproaches him (nos. 34, 48).[121] Yet he also expresses an overwhelming sense of dependence on her. We see this especially in his choice of metaphors—seal and sealing wax, sun and moon, soul and flesh—in which he always assigns his partner the active, "masculine" role and takes the passive or feminine on himself (nos. 16, 22, 24). It is she who will lighten all his sorrows and relieve his never-ending cares (nos. 28, 50, 61). In the first flush of sexual triumph, he defiantly challenges all who envy the lovers and strive to part them (no. 28). Yet when scandal does force a separation, he is apparently too concerned about his own reputation to visit his beloved or attend to her needs (nos. 101, 106)—or so at least she claims (nos. 90, 94, 95, 100).

The Woman represents herself above all as an idealist, fascinated with demanding ethical imperatives: Ciceronian friendship, disinterested love, limitless debt, unbounded gratitude. Though hardly pious (if she were, she would never have pursued a love affair), she writes epistles steeped in biblical rhetoric. It may have been her early religious training that inclined her to project something akin to divinity onto her teacher and lover. She may also have been seriously trying to win their amorous competition (no. 72) by praising her beloved ever more fervently, exalting her own love to the point of ineffability (no. 53). But she is also quite youthful (the Man in no. 50 calls her a *puella*). Like any young person who has yet to test her ideals against the daily grind, she is easily disappointed when the people she trusts fall short of her expectations. This perhaps explains why she is so quick to take offense, for she is just as passionate in her anger as in her devotion. Her lover is impressed by her intensity, but alarmed by her fits of sudden coldness and bewildered by their cause, which at times seems as opaque to him as it does to the reader (nos. 42, 61). In short, she is a high-maintenance girlfriend. In the second half of the correspondence, where quarreling dominates, readers might even be tempted to take sides. Is the Man a clueless jerk, making outrageous promises that he cannot keep (no. 75) while failing to appreciate all the sacrifices his beloved has made for him (nos. 71, 94)? Or is the Woman so determined to claim the moral high ground that she holds her lover to an impossible standard (nos. 84, 88), then blames him when he proves to be merely human?

Whoever the two lovers were, they were extraordinary people engaged in an extraordinary project. It fell to their lot to explore fresh terrain, not only in the field of letters but in the human heart. Yet pioneers need not be famous, nor does the incontestable novelty of the *Epistolae duorum amantium* prove that the lovers were Abelard and Heloise. If my interpretation is convincing, it may already have encouraged some readers to answer that question one way or another. But the debate over attribution cannot be resolved on these grounds alone. It requires that we look closely at the manuscript, the interests of its scribe, and more technical matters of style, such as vocabulary, salutation formulas, meter, rhymed prose, and *cursus* rhythms. It is to those questions that I turn in the next chapter.

Abelard and Heloise?
Some Frequently Asked Questions

BEFORE PRESENTING MY TRANSLATION and commentary, I will clarify my stance on the disputed authorship of the *Epistolae* by laying the relevant facts and conjectures on the table, weighing evidence for and against the attribution to Abelard and Heloise. I try to consider all serious contributions to the debate thus far, though I do not cite book reviews or writers who have simply weighed in on one side or the other without stating their arguments. I present the issues as a series of frequently asked questions about dating, style, provenance, and the like, summarizing the arguments to date while adding my own contributions.

How Many Letters Does the Collection Include?

Ewald Könsgen's edition includes 113 numbered letters, but he designated certain items as 38b, 38c, and 112a, so there are actually 116 letters and fragments. Of these, 67 are by the Man and 49 by the Woman. But hers tend to be longer, so their contributions are of roughly equal proportions—about 5,500 words apiece.[1] Seven of the Man's letters and four of the Woman's consist entirely or primarily of verse. In addition, her letter no. 69 begins with a poem but continues in prose, while her no. 49 is a long prose letter that concludes with three lines of verse.

Johannes de Vepria transmitted 75 of the letters in their entirety but abridged 41, slightly more than a third, signaling his omissions with double slashes. (These are indicated by the mark [. . .] in my translation.) Many of his excerpts are brief and fragmentary, consisting of little more than a salutation, but as he is drawn further in, he copies lengthier extracts and several nearly complete letters. Of the longer items, 15 are quite substantial (more than 200 words)—7 from the Man and 8 from the Woman. There is no way to know if de Vepria omitted any letters entirely.

When Were the Letters Written? How Can We Know?

Könsgen dated the letters to the first half of the twelfth century, while Jean Leclercq assigned a precise but unexplained date "between 1183 and 1185," possibly thinking of Andreas Capellanus.[2] Most scholars have been content with a broad designation of "twelfth century," with the exception of Peter von Moos who prefers a much later date, to be discussed below. Proponents of the ascription to Abelard and Heloise would require that the EDA be dated to the period ca. 1115–17, give or take a year on either side.[3]

Because de Vepria's editing removed all traces of the concrete and particular, the excerpts no longer refer to any datable events or contemporary persons, if they ever did. The dating, therefore, must rely partly on the writers' range of citations, partly on style, and partly (if more problematically) on their intellectual context. In both the Man's and the Woman's letters, Ovid is cited far more than any other classical writer—in fact, more than Cicero, Virgil, and Horace (the next-ranking authors) combined (see appendix B). Some sixty allusions cover the full range of the poet's works: *Metamorphoses* (cited twenty times), followed by the *Heroïdes, Amores*, and *Epistulae ex Ponto* (eleven or twelve times each), then the *Tristia, Ars amatoria, Fasti*, and *Remedia amoris*. These references range from direct citation to merely glancing allusions that indicate a deep study of the poet, not just acquaintance with florilegia.[4] This penchant for Ovid meshes well with the immense favor he enjoyed in the late eleventh and early twelfth centuries, the dawn of the *aetas Ovidiana*—especially in northern France, where Baudri of Bourgueil helped to popularize him. After the ubiquitous *Metamorphoses*, widely used as a school text, the EDA privilege the same Ovidian works most favored by other writers of the time, namely the epistolary poems (*Heroïdes* and *Epistulae ex Ponto*).[5] In no. 75, the Man names Ovid almost proverbially as the greatest poet, along with Cicero as the most eloquent speaker.

The lovers allude a few times to miscellaneous works of Cicero (*De oratore, De officiis, Tusculan Disputations*), but they make at least ten references to his *Laelius* (*De amicitia*). This lofty dialogue on friendship was then at the height of its popularity; it is similarly cited in the Loire Valley poets and the Tegernsee love letters. The ethics of friendship constitutes a core theme of the *Epistolae*, so the absence of Aelred of Rievaulx's *De spirituali amicitia* (1164–67), a Christianized adaptation of Cicero, may argue for a date before the last third of the century.[6] If Peter von Moos were correct in proposing a fourteenth- or fifteenth-century date, it would be hard to explain the lack of any reference to Aristotle's

Nicomachean Ethics, translated by Robert Grosseteste in the mid-thirteenth century and thenceforth central to ethical discussion on friendship.[7]

Other classical authors well known to the lovers include Virgil, Horace, and the comic playwright Terence. The Man alludes three times apiece to the epics of Lucan and Statius, and once each (distantly) to Plautus and Sallust. The Woman has one allusion apiece to the rare Catullus and Persius, the latter probably by way of Quintilian's *Institutio Oratoria*. The lovers' citations from these classics indicate an easy familiarity and appreciation for stylistic flair, though without the same deep engagement with ideas that we find in the case of Ovid and Cicero. Neither of the pair shows a taste for satire, while the Woman's exalted tone all but excludes humor. Patristic allusions are rarer, but the Woman is fond of Jerome's *Epistulae* and Boethius's *Consolation of Philosophy*. Only a handful of citations evoke Augustine, Gregory, Isidore, and a few others. All this is consistent with the range of reference we would expect in a learned, but resolutely secular correspondence of the late eleventh or early twelfth century.[8] At the same time, nothing in this context would exclude a later date.

A more useful index lies in the couple's acquaintance with contemporary poets. Both lovers, especially the Woman, cite the Loire Valley poets Marbod of Rennes (ten times) and Baudri of Bourgueil (seventeen times). They also knew works by Hildebert of Lavardin and Fulcoius of Beauvais. The verse epistles of Baudri and Marbod enjoyed a fragile, primarily local popularity in their lifetimes, but their literary reputations did not long outlive them.[9] Although Marbod died only in 1123 and Baudri in 1130, they had composed their teasing amorous poetry in the late eleventh century. Later in life, when they became bishops, they renounced and may even have suppressed the circulation of this early work.[10] So the couple's thorough familiarity with these poets constitutes a strong argument for situating the *Epistolae* quite early in the twelfth century, and in northern France. The Woman cites more Carolingian poetry (Alcuin, Walahfrid Strabo) as well as the contemporary comedy known as *Ovidius puellarum*. Of the century's later philosophical poets, such as Bernard Silvestris and Alan of Lille, we find no trace, though the lovers could have been expected to admire them if they had known their works. Unlike the Loire Valley poets, those writers were widely imitated by later generations as masters of verse and prose, making their absence all the more telling.[11] I have sought but failed to find any allusions to Hilary of Orléans, Abelard's student, who composed poetry and drama in the 1120s. His absence proves nothing, of course, but his clear presence would make the letters too late to be those of Abelard and Heloise.

Since an accurate assessment of the writers' citations is indispensable for dating, a word should be said here about Peter von Moos's approach to the question. Alone among those who have written about the *Epistolae* (on either side of the attribution controversy), von Moos argues that they belong not to the twelfth century, but to the age of early humanism, much closer to the date of the manuscript itself. The letters could have been produced in France or Italy, he suggests, as "either the reworking of stylistic exercises . . . from a school of the late *ars dictaminis*, or a bravura literary performance of early humanistic epistolary art."[12] In his lengthy register of citations, however, he fails to identify a single echo of any humanists, such as Petrarch, whom he names as relevant to their intellectual context.[13] In fact, his only citations postdating Abelard derive from other twelfth-century writers—Bernard of Clairvaux, Aelred of Rievaulx, Richard of Saint-Victor, and Peter of Blois—who were all discussing love or friendship, drawing on the same biblical, classical, and patristic authorities as the two lovers. All these passages display affinities in thought, but no exact parallels.

More tendentiously, von Moos's register excludes every reference to Baudri, Marbod, Fulcoius of Beauvais, and even Hildebert, who continued to be widely read long after his lifetime, because these would strengthen a dating in the era of Heloise and Abelard. Recognizing that frequent allusions to Baudri and Marbod would be especially damaging to his thesis, he tries to explain away thirteen of them, arguing that the *loci* are either commonplaces or explicable on the grounds of earlier or later sources.[14] But in most cases, the passages in question are verbally closer to the Loire Valley poets than to any proposed alternatives. The lovers knew Baudri's letter poems to Muriel (see no. 113) and Constance (nos. 25, 73), as well as his fictive exchange between Ovid and Florus (no. 38a, 82); and the Woman's concept of a "special" as opposed to a general or universal friendship (nos. 25, 76) offers a close parallel to his usage. Three of her poems also allude to Marbod's: there is an exact quotation in no. 73 and a pointed allusion to his epitaph for Anselm of Laon in no. 66. An extravagant gesture in no. 82—weighing the value of all Caesar's riches as nothing in comparison with the beloved—echoes one of Marbod's love poems, and is in turn echoed by Heloise. Baudri's lack of a posthumous audience, strongly emphasized by von Moos,[15] is all the more reason to think the two lovers must have been his contemporaries. He was a coterie poet, circulating his verse epistles among a small group of appreciative friends, so either the Man or the Woman must have belonged to that circle or known others who did. In fact, their personal connections may have been quite direct. One of Baudri's friends was the preacher and reformer Robert of Arbrissel (d. 1116), whose *vita* he later wrote. Baudri probably also knew

Robert's spiritual companion Hersende (d. 1113), the co-founder and first prioress of Fontevraud—an abbey only nineteen kilometers from Bourgueil.[16] Recent research has identified the same Hersende, who entered Fontevraud as a
widow, as the probable mother of Heloise.[17] So, if Heloise was the Woman of the
Epistolae, it is not hard to guess how she might have come upon Baudri's poems.

I will discuss style in detail below, but here I briefly summarize its bearing on
the date of the correspondence. The Man is a plain, even colloquial stylist, so his
prose is less useful for dating than the Woman's because she was more attuned to
rhetorical trends. Her letters rely heavily on rhymed prose, in which clauses are
paired through the repetition of endings. This stylistic ornament reached the
height of its popularity circa 1050–1150, after which it began to fall rapidly from
favor.[18] She also makes some use of *cursus*, or rhythmic cadences to mark the ends
of *clausulae*, but that technique is less consistently employed. The deliberate cultivation of *cursus* was introduced into French manuals of letter writing only in the
1180s, though some authors were already using it extensively in the eleventh century.[19] There has been some quantitative research on *cursus* types in the *Epistolae*,
but results thus far have been inconclusive.[20] Certainty is hard to attain with a
statistically small corpus, because chance instances are produced by the very structure of the Latin language. Yet von Moos's statistics demonstrate that *cursus velox*
is by far the least favored cadence in the EDA, although in Latin prose circa 1150–
1300, it was the most favored among writers who used the ornament at all.[21] For
him, this anomaly supports a late dating (after 1300), but of course it could just as
easily support an early one (before 1150), as I am arguing here. As I shall demonstrate below, the Woman's thoroughgoing use of rhymed prose *combined* with the
selective incidence of *cursus* is unusual and positions her among a rather small
group of writers of the early twelfth century.

The poems of both lovers employ leonine distichs and leonine hexameter,
meters that diverge from their classical antecedents by introducing internal
rhyme between the two hemistichs of each line. This form, already popular in
the Carolingian and Ottonian eras, remained in use throughout the twelfth
century and was especially favored in inscriptions. But some of the most important poets of the mid-twelfth century and later—Bernard Silvestris, Walter
of Châtillon, Matthew of Vendôme, Alan of Lille, the *Ysengrimus* poet—
rebelled against it.[22] Metrical evidence, therefore, also favors a probable date in
the earlier twelfth century.

Von Moos, reading the letters as a sophisticated literary fiction, argues that
they could not have been written before the *ars dictaminis* attained its highest
pitch of refinement—enabling the author(s) even to characterize the two lovers by

differing Latin styles, seen as more appropriate for men and women respectively. If he were right about the fictionality of the letters, a late date would necessarily follow, for such a sustained work of epistolary fiction (as opposed to an individual piece of impersonation, like Constance's letter-poem) would not have been possible in the early twelfth century. Yet he fails to explain why a fourteenth- or fifteenth-century *dictator* ambitious enough to conceive such a work would have chosen the archaic, unfashionable media of rhymed prose and leonine verse. Was he trying to characterize the lovers by period as well as gender? Humanists did write some letters in the personas of classical and mythological characters, but not anonymous figures from the earlier Middle Ages—and it should go without saying that, if some *dictator* had been trying to forge pseudoletters of Abelard and Heloise, he would have included their names and allusions to their story. Moreover, von Moos scarcely touches on the epistolary poems in the EDA, except to suggest that a few were "perhaps student productions inserted later" from some other source.[23] This strikes me as special pleading to eliminate some inconvenient evidence. So, while von Moos's interpretation includes a great deal of interest and value, I remain unconvinced by his principal (and closely intertwined) arguments for a late medieval date and a genre of epistolary fiction.

Where Were the Letters Written?

All indications point to northern France, almost certainly Paris. In addition to the couple's familiarity with the Loire Valley poets, whose fame was only regional, the Man calls his beloved *gemma tocius Gallie* or "gem of all France" (no. 89). *Gallia* is more or less synonymous with *Francia*, the Île-de-France. In no. 49, the Woman boasts that *francigena cervicositas* or "French stubbornness" has been forced to yield to her lover's philosophical prowess. This indicates, first, that he was teaching somewhere in France, but second, that he was not himself French—a stipulation that would fit the career of Abelard, native to Brittany (not part of medieval *Francia*).[24] The Man also indicates in no. 113 that he and his beloved live in the same city (*urbi nostre*). Among the northern French cities known for their schools in the early twelfth century were Paris, Angers, Orléans, Reims, and Chartres. But all except Paris specialized in the classical *auctores*, whereas the Man's subject was philosophy or dialectic. Only Paris at this time was especially famed for instruction in that field. Finally, the competitive teaching milieu betrayed by the Woman's ode on her lover's victory over a rival (no. 66) points strongly toward Paris. While rivalry between masters was not unknown elsewhere, it normally ended in victory for the incumbent and disgrace for the upstart. Only in Paris, so far as we know, could a combative young teacher like Abelard attract such throngs of students that he could force a predecessor to retire in disgrace.[25]

What Subject Was the Woman Studying?

The Man was instructing his beloved in philosophy. In no. 50 he calls her "the only disciple of philosophy among all the girls of our age," and in no. 23 she tells him that, even though she has received great joy "from the riches of your philosophy," she thirsts for still more. In no. 5 she prays for skill in the *ars philosophie*. What is probably her first letter, no. 112, indicates that she already knew her teacher to be "nurtured at the hearth of philosophy." But she had only then learned (from the verses he sent her) that he had "drunk from the fountain of poetry." Although the Man's letters can hardly be called philosophical texts, he employs a playful syllogism in no. 16 and offers a philosophical definition of love in no. 24. The Woman too likes to flaunt the technical terms she is learning. In no. 53 she mock-humbly throws in a state-of-the-art term in epistemology (*scibilitas*, knowability), not because the context requires it, but to show off what she has learned. Another of her rare technical terms is *equipolenter* (equivalently) in no. 21. Both terms point to the era around 1100. *Scibilitas* is an Abelardian coinage, not used subsequently until Ramon Llull, and *equipolenter* is associated with two late eleventh-century masters: Lanfranc of Canterbury (d. 1089) and Bruno the Carthusian (d. 1101), who was master of the cathedral school at Reims until 1079.[26]

This point is worth stressing because some have argued that the Man was teaching the Woman rhetoric, or specifically the *ars dictaminis*. Thus, in their essay on "The Young Heloise and Latin Rhetoric," John Ward and Neville Chiavaroli maintain that the lovers' "mutual reading and 'exercises' clearly fell ... within the field of 'grammar,' sensitive reading and imitation of the prescribed *auctores*, exploration of the literary dimensions of *amicitia*," and so forth.[27] Further in this vein, Juanita Feros Ruys asserts that Abelard was training Heloise "in the rhetorical ideals of the new scholasticism," a process that would entail replacing her florid style with his plainer one.[28] Hence in no. 71 she sends him an "unadorned letter to prove how devotedly I submit myself to your commands in all things," and in no. 63 he praises her success in the plain style: "The letter you sent was marked by mature judgment and a rational, orderly composition. I have certainly never seen one more aptly arranged." On that view, some letters can even be read as homework assignments. Thus William Levitan takes the praise I just quoted to mean that the bitter quarrel running through letters 58–62, during which the Woman seeks to end the relationship, is not a real fight but a rhetorical exercise.[29] Similarly, in no. 41 the Man writes, "I have no command for you; do what you will. Write me any-thing—two words at least—if you can." This note comes near the end of a sequence in which the Woman, apparently angry, has left a long series of letters unanswered. Each partner seemingly expects the other to resolve their crisis. But on this inter-pretation, no. 41 is not the Man's desperate plea for even a brief response; it is a free-form writing assignment.[30]

I find such interpretations problematic for several reasons. Aside from specific references to the Woman as a student of philosophy, it is counterintuitive to think that she, the more accomplished stylist, would be studying rhetoric with one who was *less* proficient. True, the Woman is not yet a mature writer: she can be too mannered for her own good, and her literary ambition sometimes gets the better of her syntax. But she is clearly a gifted stylist, and I see no evidence that she is aiming for a *sermo humilior* as the correspondence proceeds. In fact, the letter that Ruys singles out as her deliberate attempt at "unpolished style" (no. 49) is among the most highly wrought (not to say overwrought) of them all. Be that as it may, rheto-ricians and *dictatores* in the early twelfth century were simply not in the business of teaching plain style. Since Ward and Ruys both accept the ascription to Abelard and Heloise, it is even more peculiar that they would read the letters in this way.

Abelard had studied rhetoric with William of Champeaux and wrote two early treatises on rhetoric and grammar, one of them lost. But his extant com-mentary on Boethius's *De differentiis topicis* deals with modes of judicial argu-ment; it has nothing to do with epistolary style.[31] While Abelard notes in *Historia calamitatum* 17 that Fulbert was eager "to further his niece's education in letters" (*doctrinam litteratoriam*), he and others clearly indicate that Heloise had earned her reputation for literary skill before the two ever met.[32]

How Can We Tell if the Letters Were Real Love Letters or Rhetorical Models?

Most scholars, except for von Moos, have argued that the EDA are either real love letters (perhaps those of Heloise and Abelard) or rhetorical models. No question matters more for their interpretation, because learning to express love or anger in polished prose is very different from expressing actual love or anger—even if the first might, in the long run, shade into the second.

Rhetorical models survive in much greater numbers than genuine love letters. But that does not mean that few were actually sent. In fact, it could mean the opposite; there would be little point in providing models to imitate if there were no demand for the real thing. Although the late *ars dictaminis* could at times attain the status of "art for art's sake," as von Moos suggests, this was certainly not the case in the twelfth century.[33] Even today, online *artes dictandi* offer sample letters of numerous real-world types: job applications, thank-you notes, apologies, complaints, recommendations, authors' letters to publishers, and yes, love letters. (One site recommends sending these "on nice stationery" sealed with a dab of perfume.)

Some scholars have been skeptical about the *Epistolae* as genuine letters because of their very survival. Giles Constable, for example, observes that most letters, even those that were actually sent, were redacted to some degree before they were copied into collections: "Medieval love letters are extremely rare, and private letters . . . hardly existed."[34] The originals, sent on scraps of parchment or (in the case of the EDA) wax tablets, had little or no chance of preservation. If letters were to survive at all, they had to be incorporated into collections maintained by enduring institutions: monasteries, cathedrals, royal or papal chanceries, universities, and the like.[35] Important officials had secretaries to copy their outgoing letters into codices to provide a permanent record—and supply future writers with models. But love letters were by definition private, even secret; no institution would have a stake in preserving them. Moreover, very few persons in the twelfth century other than clerics, monks and nuns, and canonesses would have been literate enough to compose Latin love letters. Clerics certainly did so, if only as rhetorical exercises, yet their vocation made even the exercise morally problematic. As we have seen, such accomplished writers as Guibert of Nogent, Fulcoius of Beauvais, and even Marbod of Rennes suppressed or destroyed the love letter-poems they had written in their youth. Clerics who had been carrying on actual affairs would hardly have copied their love letters in the scriptorium for all to see.

In a fascinating study, Mary Garrison has examined medieval archaeological sites where letters were *inadvertently* preserved. These include hundreds of messages found on inscribed rune-sticks in the harbor of Bergen (Norway), and hundreds more scraps of incised birch bark discovered beneath the corduroy sidewalks of Novgorod. These informal messages, never meant to be saved, have little in common with letters that were deliberately copied and preserved. The great medieval collections deal overwhelmingly with matters of religion, government, and belles lettres; they are filled with "the ubiquitous topoi of *amicitia*, requests for reciprocal prayers, long discussions of theology and politics."[36] Private messages sent by the laity say nothing of these topics. Instead they might contain charms, children's drawings, a marriage proposal, obscene tavern messages, "ephemeral business notes... and love letters."[37] The *Epistolae duorum amantium* occupy a rare middle ground because they are obviously Latinate and learned, yet also deeply private. Their (partial) survival may be a lucky fluke, but it is not just that. It testifies to the highly unusual determination of at least one lover to preserve these letters—and to their literary merit, which so impressed Johannes de Vepria that he copied them into his formulary.

The Woman of the EDA had clearly studied rhetorical models, so the resemblance of her style to model letters is no coincidence, even though the most relevant *artes dictandi* postdate the *Epistolae*. But the collection as a whole could not have been meant as a formulary, at least not until Johannes de Vepria pressed it into service as one by excising its minute particulars. It differs from model letter collections in at least three important ways: (1) Its length. Formularies often include paired letters; in the case of love letters, a man's solicitation is usually followed by a woman's refusal. Sometimes the exchange continues until she consents. But no model collection features an exchange of more than a hundred letters, or anything even close, between the same correspondents. (2) Its repetition. In an exchange lasting over a year, the lovers often repeat the same phrases and sentiments, sometimes apologizing for their lack of new inspiration (nos. 13, 56). In a formulary meant for imitation, there would be no point in such redundancy. (3) Its loose ends. As Jaeger has shown, even after de Vepria's editing the exchange is still full of ruptures and discontinuities.[38] For example, the Man accepts the Woman's thanks for an unspecified favor (no. 12); she thanks him again for an unidentified "prologue" (no. 84); angry rebukes are launched (nos. 58, 60) and apologies offered (no. 59) for offenses that are never stated; the lovers ask each other's permission (nos. 67, 71) to do things that remain opaque to the reader.

Von Moos characterizes the EDA not as a formulary, but rather a fictive correspondence—something like an early epistolary novel.[39] This would of course require a later date, which I have already shown to be problematic on stylistic grounds. We begin to see precursors of the epistolary novel only with such works as Machaut's satirical *Voir Dit* (ca. 1362–65), Christine de Pizan's *Cent ballades d'amant et de dame* (ca. 1405–10), and Aeneas Sylvius Piccolomini's *Historia de duobus amantibus* (1444). If we were to take the EDA as an epistolary novel *avant la lettre*, they would surely make a *bad* one. Although many individual letters are stunning set pieces, exemplary both for their style and their convincing representation of various love problems, the work as a whole lacks a cohesive narrative structure. It is vitiated by its many loose ends, impenetrable allusions, and redundancies—which cannot all be explained as a result of scribal abridgment.[40] Von Moos tries to account for this messiness by positing numerous interpolations in de Vepria's exemplar, characterizing the work he finally copied as a cross between some unknown *dictator*'s magisterial fiction and a compilation of loosely related materials.[41] A more economical hypothesis, however, would interpret these features of the *Epistolae* as leftovers from a correspondence that had once been anchored, beyond its rhetorical flourishes, in the minutiae of a couple's everyday life.

In appendix F I have listed some distinctive features of the EDA, which remain without parallels in the most closely related letter collections and *artes dictandi*. These include references to the Woman as a student of philosophy, famed for her "virile" talents (no. 50); the Man's academic prowess in vanquishing a rival teacher (no. 66); his composition of some sort of "prologue" for the Woman (no. 84); an unfulfilled promise related to writing (no. 75); the motif of a competition in love (no. 72); the occurrence of technical philosophical terms, unexpected in love letters (nos. 21, 53); the Woman's theory of love as infinite, unpayable debt (no. 25); her use of an arcane exegetical riddle as a love greeting (no. 27); and the Man's wry acknowledgment of her as a martyr of love (no. 96). All these exceptional features point toward Abelard and Heloise, and one of von Moos's own suggestions strengthens the case. Noting that even a fictional correspondence can have a pragmatic purpose, he remarks that in this extraordinary work, an unparalleled goal of the writer(s) seems to be honoring a long-term, committed erotic relationship that is "marriage-like," yet secret. He suggests the "institution" of clerical concubinage,[42] which was more or less the situation of that famous pair.

Perhaps the most exceptional feature of all is the large number of letters. This is no coincidence, but a plan expressly formulated by the couple early in their relationship. In no. 9 the Woman writes, "I wish, I breathlessly desire that by exchanging letters, as you have bidden, our heartfelt friendship may grow firmer—until that supremely happy day dawns when I shall see your face." However "impossible" we may find the idea of a private correspondence in the early twelfth century, we know at least that Abelard and Heloise engaged in one, because they both say so. Abelard states in the *Historia calamitatum* that he chose to seduce Heloise in the first place because of her love of writing; he anticipated the pleasure of a literary correspondence as one of the joys of an affair with her. "Knowing her knowledge and love of letters I thought she would be all the more ready to consent," he adds.[43] The Woman's "breathless" affirmation in no. 9 could voice that consent. Much later, Heloise charges Abelard with neglecting her in the first decade of their

religious life, recalling that "when in the past you sought me out for sinful pleasures, your letters came to me thick and fast [*crebris me epistolis uisitabas*]."[44]
Doubtless there were not *many* such long, private correspondences at the time; but
there is good evidence for at least one. If we exclude the *Epistolae*—the longest
correspondence between two individuals from the entire Middle Ages—one of
the next longest is the exchange between Abelard and Heloise.[45] The latter survives intact, as we shall see below, because Heloise preserved it. And if she did
something so exceptional once, why should it be impossible that she did it twice?

What Else Does Johannes de Vepria's Manuscript Contain?

Aside from a brief excerpt from Cicero's *De officiis* (fols. 16v–21r) and a few passages from William of Malmesbury's *Gesta regum Anglorum* (fols. 149r–158v),
the anthology consists entirely of model letter collections. Chronologically, the
monk chose writers who span a wide range: Cyprian of Carthage (d. 258),
Sidonius Apollinaris (d. 486), Ennodius (d. 521), Cassiodorus (d. 583), Trans-
mundus of Clairvaux (d. after 1216), Jean de Limoges (d. mid-thirteenth century), and a contemporary rhetorician, Carolus Virulus (d. 1493). The last three
were all *dictatores* or teachers of letter writing. De Vepria selected his texts for
stylistic elegance, rather than theological content or historical importance. In
fact, he abridged most of his authors in the same way as the EDA, excising whatever seemed too particular so as to play up their exemplary content. Further, he
had a humanist taste for rarities, feeling no need to recopy the letters of an Augustine, Anselm, or Bernard. The *Epistolae* are the last item in his anthology,
where they fill nine folios (fols. 159r–167v), written without breaks.[46]

　　Since de Vepria catalogued the library of Clairvaux, we can still trace many
of the manuscripts he used as models. Könsgen's research showed that he was a
careful scribe, and the surviving manuscripts he copied were already at Clairvaux, not borrowed.[47] Unfortunately, however, his catalogue includes no source
for the *Epistolae*. Though Könsgen left no stone unturned in his quest, no such
manuscript has ever been found. Von Moos takes its absence from the catalogue
as evidence that de Vepria found his exemplar elsewhere.[48] Sylvain Piron speculates that the scribe could have lent it to friends as a curiosity or even tried to
have it printed, but to no avail.[49] Anne-Marie Turcan-Verkerk asserts that the
Epistolae, while copied sometime after 1459, were not originally bound with the
rest of de Vepria's manuscript, though she does not deny that they are in the
same hand.[50]

Some have wondered if the two lovers were as anonymous to de Vepria as they are to us. Could he have known, but deliberately suppressed their identity? That seems unlikely, for he did not conceal the name of any other writer. Rather, the letters themselves are so obsessed with secrecy (nos. 38a, 69, 75, 101), envious foes (nos. 28, 54, 85), and the fear of scandal (no. 62) that it would have been imprudent for the lovers to risk using each other's names. If de Vepria had known or even suspected them to be Abelard and Heloise, he would more likely have trumpeted such a discovery. French and Italian humanists admired the famous couple; they either acquired or commissioned several manuscripts of their canonical letters, as well as excerpting them by name in another anthology similar to de Vepria's.[51] So any humanist who thought he had discovered "the lost love letters of Heloise and Abelard" in 1471 could have made his reputation by publishing them.[52] By that date, the enmity of Bernard and Abelard 350 years earlier would no longer have mattered, even at Clairvaux.

How Were the Letters Preserved Before Johannes de Vepria Found Them?

Few endeavors might seem more futile than attempting to trace the provenance of a lost manuscript. If we are sure that Abelard and Heloise did not write the *Epistolae*, it would be pointless even to raise this question. But if we want to explore the possibility that they did, we must try to give a plausible answer.

Generations of research have shown that the pair's canonical letters were disseminated from the Paraclete, where they had remained unknown after Heloise's death until the mid-thirteenth century.[53] At that time they were brought for some reason to the cathedral chapter of Notre-Dame in Paris.[54] Jacques Dalarun, in his attempt to reconstruct the origins of the archetypal manuscript (T), posits a collaboration circa 1237 between Ermengarde, then abbess of the Paraclete, and William of Auvergne, bishop of Paris, to construct an authoritative dossier on religious life for the nuns. It was for that end, he speculates, that Ermengarde sent the bishop her copies of the Paraclete's foundational documents: the *Historia calamitatum* and subsequent letters, Abelard's rule (*Institutio*), and Heloise's customary (*Institutiones nostre*), which William augmented with a selection of canons. The bishop would then have produced two copies of the dossier: one to return to the Paraclete, another to remain in the library of Notre-Dame.[55] It was there that Jean de Meun discovered the letters a few decades later, translated them into French,[56] incorporated the lovers' story into the *Roman de la rose*,[57] and so inaugurated their romantic legend. Although the couple's late medieval fame owes far more to the *Rose* than to direct study of their letters, these nevertheless attracted interest, especially among humanists. Most of the known copies (both extant and lost) date to the fourteenth and fifteenth centuries.[58]

The textual tradition of the *Historia calamitatum* and the seven following letters is remarkably stable. After letter 8, the contents of the manuscripts diverge. Only one (T) includes the complete text of Abelard's rule and Heloise's customary. Two more contain abridged forms of the rule, while another includes material related to the Council of Sens, such as the *Apologia* of Abelard's student Berengar and his late *Confessio fidei ad Heloissam*. All these documents were collected at the Paraclete, the stable institution that preserved them for a century or more until the outside world took an interest. It was Heloise, as abbess for more than thirty years—rather than the harassed and peripatetic Abelard—who had both the motive and the means to conserve these letters that had meant so much to her.

If the "two lovers" of the *Epistolae duorum amantium* were Heloise and Abelard, it would be reasonable to surmise that she was responsible for their preservation too. The letters themselves show that it was the Woman who had the greater stake in them, and she owned the wax tablets on which the pair exchanged messages (no. 14), as usual in a student-teacher relationship. So she most likely copied their letters (or at least some of them) from the wax onto parchment as the exchange proceeded. Further support for this hypothesis derives from a textual crux in no. 23, among the most elaborate of the Woman's letters. Piron has shown that an incoherent sentence in that letter can be emended by removing three words, probably a marginal correction by the author, which the scribe mistakenly incorporated into the text.[59] If he is right, this evidence would not only prove that the Woman preserved the letters, taking such pains that she even revised one of her own after sending it.[60] It further suggests that de Vepria's exemplar was an autograph—thus approximately 350 years old, and most likely in some disarray.

If the Woman was Heloise, she would have had no reason to destroy her old love letters when she professed her vows, for she makes it painfully clear that she took that step for the love of Abelard alone. Knowing Heloise as we do, Jean-Yves Tilliette finds it implausible that she would have saved such letters, as if "inspired by a kind of retrospective *bovarysme* . . . to preserve the traces of a sublime and exemplary passion." In his view, neither Heloise nor anyone else could have known before the time of Jean de Meun (let alone Madame Bovary) that her affair with Abelard was destined to be seen that way.[61] But "a sublime and exemplary passion" was precisely what the Woman of the EDA—whoever she was—claimed for herself. Indeed, that is close to her very phrase (*sublimi et precipua dilectione*, no. 53). In any case, if Heloise had brought the letters with her to the Paraclete, they would have remained there after her death. But here any parallel with the couple's canonical letters ends, for those pertained to the institution as well as the lovers themselves. Abelard and Heloise were its joint founders and, even at her most anguished moments, Heloise appeals to her spiritual daughters as sharers in her own sentiments and pleas.[62] As abbess, she would have had good reason to ensure that the complete exchange, beginning with the *Historia calamitatum* and ending with *Institutiones nostre*, was preserved as the abbey's corporate foundation narrative. The EDA, by contrast, were of purely personal interest. There would have been no need for anyone else to see them but, on the contrary, excellent reasons to keep them secret.

To understand the transmission of the *Epistolae*, we must bear in mind that, before de Vepria, they probably never existed as a bound volume. During the heat of the affair, when Heloise was living in her uncle Fulbert's house, she could certainly not have produced one. So it would have been only a packet of unbound sheets or quires (*libelli*) that she carried with her to Brittany, then to Argenteuil, and eventually to the Paraclete. Moreover, the collection as we have it—a mere nine folios in de Vepria's manuscript—is much too short to fill a volume by itself. So, if it is reasonable to think that Heloise continued to cherish these keepsakes of her past, it is harder to imagine her wasting the resources of her abbey or risking disclosure by producing a bound volume. That would also explain why no such book appears in Clairvaux's library catalogue.

My hypothesis is strengthened by parallel cases. Helmut Plechl, editor of the Tegernsee letter collection, has shown that the massive book was copied from loose originals, not always in logical or chronological order.[63] The Regensburg Songs are scattered here and there in a chaotic miscellany, copied from a scholar's disorganized papers some time after his death.[64] Further, an old inventory from the Cluniac priory of Saint-Marcel, where Abelard died in 1142, indicated that he left behind a "thick bundle" of his own letters, together with those of Heloise. There they remained until the mid-eighteenth century, when they were lent to a person from Dôle and never returned.[65] If Abelard, who had been determined to set the love affair behind him as an aberration, nonetheless preserved unbound copies of their correspondence throughout his life, it is all the more likely that Heloise did the same. Dalarun too suggests that the documents Abbess Ermengarde sent to Paris for copying—the common ancestors of all extant manuscripts—could have been preserved at the Paraclete "in the form of a dossier, *libelli*, or a codex."[66] She might have sent them to be professionally copied in a Parisian scriptorium precisely because they had not yet been bound into an authoritative manuscript. When the first fair copy of any text was produced, the messy, unbound originals were usually discarded, much as authors today destroy their printouts as soon as bound books arrive from the publisher. This could explain why the oldest manuscript of the *Historia calamitatum* dates only to the mid-thirteenth century. In the case of the very unofficial *Epistolae duorum amantium*, it would be all the more likely for any unbound "foul papers" to disappear.

But how could these letters have gotten from the Paraclete to Clairvaux in the first place? By the mid-fifteenth century, as Piron has pointed out, the monks of Clairvaux held *cura monialium* or pastoral responsibility for the Paraclete nuns.[67] The two abbeys were about one hundred kilometers apart, not an easy commute. So at any given time, at least one Cistercian priest would have been in residence at the Paraclete to sing Mass and hear confessions. Latin literacy among religious women, beyond what was necessary to chant the Office, had long since faded almost to the vanishing point. So if some curious priest-monk, rummaging in the Paraclete's library after Mass, had come upon a few interesting old documents and decided to "borrow" them, they would scarcely have been missed. For the ascription to be believed, some such scenario must explain how de Vepria's copy text had arrived at Clairvaux.

How Reliable Is the Sequence of Letters in the Manuscript?

My hypothesis about the copy text has a significant bearing on this question. Whether or not the letters were those of Heloise and Abelard, I believe that de Vepria's exemplar was simply a bundle of loose sheets and gatherings tied together with string, not a bound codex. This would explain an obvious but otherwise inexplicable fact, which is that the last two letters in the manuscript sound very much like the first to be exchanged. After more than a year of intimacy, passion, anger, forgiveness, and countless professions of love, why should the Woman suddenly write, in breathless but formal terms, "to her teacher—the noblest, the most learned," ecstatic because she has only now discovered that their desires are mutual (no. 112)? As von Moos observes, this sounds much more like the beginning than the end of an affair.[68] Immediately after this letter comes a brief fragment (no. 112a) with the marginal note *ex alia*—"from another [letter]." In that note the mood is completely different; the Woman sighs, "I am weary now and cannot reply to you, because you take sweet things as painful and so fill my mind with sorrow. Farewell." Last of all is a poem in elegiacs by the Man (no. 113)—an Ovidian seduction poem to declare himself, as if for the first time, to the object of his affections. No attempt to read these letters in their present order has been persuasive.[69]

Von Moos proposes that the whole final section of the EDA (nos. 89–113) consists of thematically similar material from other sources, tacked on at the end of de Vepria's exemplar.[70] But this seems like a hypothesis of last resort, ignoring the many stylistic as well as thematic echoes connecting the later with the earlier letters. We can solve the mystery more simply by positing that letters 113 and 112 were in fact the first: the Man sent the Woman a poem declaring his love, to which she replied with jubilation. These two letters could once have occupied both sides of a single sheet of parchment. It is possible that the Man transmitted his initial love poem on parchment in the first place as a keepsake, for it is far more carefully crafted than most of his poems and notes. The Woman could have cherished and preserved this token of her teacher's love, copying her own response onto the back.[71] Be that as it may, in the course of centuries or even of de Vepria's own examination, this "cover sheet" could easily have been displaced. The proximity of the apparently late no. 112a, with the scribe's marginal note, suggests that he faced some confusion at this point in his copy text. So, bowing to what I see as compelling narrative logic, I have taken the liberty of beginning my translation with nos. 113 and 112 in that order. I suspect that letters 102–5 and 109–11 also belong to this early phase of the affair, but I have resisted the temptation to do any further rearranging.

Apart from this shift, most of the letters yield sense in the order of their appearance. Indeed, a great many respond directly to those that precede them, picking up some turn of phrase in a salutation or resuming a thread of discussion. If de Vepria had discovered the letters in the form of several small, unbound quires, we would expect those within each quire to follow their correct chronological sequence, while the quires themselves might have been inadvertently shuffled. This would explain some of the more jarring gaps in continuity, as I note in my commentary. Such gaps also suggest that certain letters are missing. Either de Vepria or the Woman herself may have declined to copy them, or they could have been lost or become illegible in the course of time. In one case (no. 75), the Man bitterly regrets "some words [he] composed when provoked by a sudden insult, in the very throes of pain." After realizing how long his beloved has brooded over those offending words, he begs her to "erase them from [her] heart and let them not take root within [her]." The episode may remain obscure because she obediently excised them from her record. Further, at times when the lovers could easily meet, they would have had less need to write (no. 109)—another reason that the record sometimes breaks off and resumes erratically.

Is the Narrative of the EDA Consistent with the Story of Abelard and Heloise?

The probable state of the copy text, exacerbated by de Vepria's omission of all circumstantial details, makes constructing any narrative a perilous project. If we try to read the known story of Abelard and Heloise into these letters, or even to deduce new biographical facts from them, we are on shaky ground. A novelist, of course, could find immense opportunities—as Umberto Eco already has.[72] Deploring my own lack of novelistic imagination, in the previous essay I was able to reconstruct the story of a "typical" affair—a progression from enchantment to disillusionment, marked by many ups and downs along the way—only because I believe that the last two letters are really the first. But what we have in any case is less a satisfying tale with a beginning, middle, and end than a series of extended vignettes—here perhaps six weeks of radiant happiness, there maybe a month of misunderstandings and quarrels, then another love idyll, followed by a long, difficult period of separation and yearning.

Does this seminarrative fit the story of Abelard and Heloise? In some respects it does. The Man's initial poem (no. 113) dovetails with the confident, not to say arrogant, campaign of seduction that Abelard confesses in *Historia calamitatum* (HC) 16. Having considered the available choices for his bed, he selected Heloise especially because of her abundant learning (*per habundantiam litterarum*). He feared no rebuff because he was young, famous, and good-looking, and his campaign quickly succeeded: "We were united, first under one roof, then in heart" (*Primum domo una coniungimur, postmodum animo*, HC 18). Letter 112, construed as the Woman's reply to no. 113, indicates that the teacher indeed met no resistance. Their early letters and at least a few later ones (e.g. no. 109) imply a situation of such proximity that no content needs to be conveyed, only amorous greetings. The delivery of wax tablets by a messenger, perhaps a household servant, could have been justified on the pretext that the student had completed her "homework," which she was now transmitting to her teacher for correction.

Soon after the moment I take to mark the beginning of their sexual relationship (no. 26), we start finding references to absence. The lovers mention their separation in nos. 31, 37, 45, 53, 54, 57, 62, and many times thereafter, suggesting that they had been discovered (perhaps by the "envious") and now had to be more cautious in their meetings. In no. 108, the Woman has returned from a long absence during which her lover yearned to join her, "but shame and fear obstructed the way."[73] If the couple were Abelard and Heloise, their first long period of separation must have followed Fulbert's discovery, which drove

Abelard out of his house: "Separation drew our hearts still closer while frustration inflamed our passion even more; then we became more abandoned as we lost all sense of shame and, indeed, shame diminished as we found more opportunities for lovemaking" (*tantoque uerecundie minor extiterat passio quanto conuenientior uidebatur actio*, HC 21). Their "shameless" phase resulted in Fulbert's second discovery, this time *in flagrante*; Abelard says they were caught in the act like Mars and Venus. Soon afterward Heloise discovered her pregnancy and Abelard secretly "sent" (*transmisi*) her to his sister's farm in Brittany; he did not accompany her. Legally this was the crime of *raptus* or abduction, an offense worse than his initial seduction.[74] Heloise must have arrived in an unfamiliar land to face a welcome, perhaps less than cordial, from total strangers—among whom she would remain for at least six months, until Astralabe was born.

If these were the lovers of the *Epistolae*, the letters written during their separation could date from one or both of these periods. If a pregnant Heloise was languishing in Brittany, feeling alone and neglected by her absent lover, that could account for the dismal tone of the Woman's late letters. On the other hand, the distance from Paris to Le Pallet is almost four hundred kilometers, a journey of at least three weeks by horseback. Messengers from Le Pallet were probably scarce, and the lovers could hardly have been exchanging notes on wax tablets across such a distance. We do know that Heloise sent Abelard at least one substantial letter at this time—her notorious *Dehortatio a nuptiis* (Exhortation against marriage). He quotes that text at considerable length, under its own title, in *Historia calamitatum* 24–26, and Piron discerns a similar rejection of marriage in an enigmatic text from the Woman's no. 79.[75] But in the last clause that Abelard cites from the *Dehortatio*, Heloise asserts that their future meetings will be all the sweeter inasmuch as they are rarer: *nos ipsos ad tempus separatos gratiora de conuentu nostro percipere gaudia, quanto rariora* (HC 26). This does not sound much like the brief, angry notes in which the Woman seems to envision a final parting of the ways. So, if she *was* Heloise, those letters would more likely have been exchanged when both were still living in Paris, but no longer under the same roof. They would belong to a period when the lovers had already weathered one scandal, with a greater one looming before them.

It is thus possible, if not especially easy, to match the couple's known story with the fragmentary indications of the EDA. Needless to say, the latter refer to nothing so concrete as pregnancy and mention no specific locations. Nor is there an obvious way to reconcile the Woman's apparent desire for a breakup late in the EDA with the marriage and ongoing commitment of Heloise to Abelard. But the probable duration of the correspondence, about a year and a half (as measured by the Man's anniversary poem, no. 87) does match that of the famous couple's affair.

Whether the character sketches that emerge from the EDA match those of Heloise and Abelard is something readers must decide for themselves. Let it be said, however, that readers of the couple's monastic letters have tended by a wide margin to side with Heloise in their emotional conflict. Admittedly, her letters are more rhetorically potent; they have all the pathos of Ovid's *Heroïdes*, their ultimate model. But it is also much easier to empathize with her poignant emotional plight than to resonate with Abelard's austere language of sin, penance, and devotion. I would no longer write today, as I once did, that he obtains a "victory for the poetics of castration over the discourse of desire."[76] Yet such issues still need to be evoked, if only because scholars are still human. Like the letters of Abelard and Heloise, the *Epistolae* solicit a strong emotional response—which accounts for much of the intensity in the debate over their authorship. But unlike the monastic letters, much of the story told by these remains unknown and unknowable.

Do the Man's and the Woman's Letters Differ in Style?

Yes, markedly. Their differences, apparent to any close reader, confirm that we are dealing with two individual authors and not a single *dictator*. Many of them were pointed out by Könsgen, others by Mews, and still more have been confirmed by Francesco Stella's lexical research.

As I have already noted, the Woman uses rhymed prose self-consciously and consistently, while the Man avoids it. Her style is ambitious, mannered, and often recherché, with a particular taste for rare words and neologisms. She even uses words found seldom or nowhere else in the corpus of medieval Latin, including the nouns *superciliositas* (arrogance, no. 49), *dehortamen* (dissuasion, no. 23), and *vinculamen* (chain, no. 55); the adjective *dulcifer* (dulcet, no. 98); and three terms of negation: *innexibilis* (inextricable, no. 94), *immarcidus* (unwithered, no. 18), and *inepotabilis* (inexhaustible, no. 86).[77] Her letters also "present a rarer and richer vocabulary of terms for feelings and a tendency toward the sublime," as Stella observes, while the Man appears "more inclined to the abstract, but more banal and less affective."[78] In writing about love, only the Woman mentions *affectus* (feeling, affection) or *caritas* (charity), and she uses *dilectio* almost five times as often as the Man (see appendices A and D). Only she uses the religiously inflected *beatitudo* (happiness); the Man prefers the more secular *felicitas.* Both lovers perceive their relationship as exceptional. But she describes it four times as *specialis* (special), a term he avoids, while he prefers to call it *singularis* (singular) or *unicus* (unique), terms she rarely uses.[79] She is particularly fond of the Ovidian *tot . . . quot* formula (six usages; the Man has none),[80] as well as the rhetorical questions *Quid plura?* and *Quid ultra?* (Why say more?). The Woman composes five greetings such as *par pari* (an equal to an equal, no. 18) or *amans amanti* (a lover to a lover, nos. 48, 84), where the same term designates both sender and recipient. The Man does this only once (no. 68). Other traits of her style include a preference for the intensifying prefix *per-* and for diminutives such as *guttula* (little drop, no. 53) and *scienciole* (modest learning, no. 62).

Although it was the Man who initiated the correspondence, as the Woman tells us (no. 9), she has a greater stake in it. Like a student too eager to impress her teacher, she often despairs of having sufficient skill (nos. 112, 13, 23, 25, 49, 53, etc.). The most extreme instance is no. 23, where she converts her anxiety about writing into a debate between the personified *Affectus* (her warm feeling of gratitude) and *Defectus* (the deficiency of her talent). It must be said that, while she often rises to sublime heights, her prose sometimes ties itself in grammatical knots. This happens at the beginning of no. 25 and more conspicuously in no. 53, where she contrives the tortuous conceit that "if one little drop of knowability were to trickle down to me from the honeycomb of wisdom, I would strive with a supreme effort of my mind to depict a few things in fragrant nectar for you . . . in the markings of a letter." While both lovers take refuge in the ineffability topos, the Man does so *faute de mieux*, scarcely bothering to strive with the exigencies of language. "I love you so much I cannot say how much," he writes, using a familiar proverb (no. 38c), or again, "I love you so much that I cannot rightly express it" (no. 56).

If the Woman is a mannerist, the Man is a determined plain stylist.[81] This is not for lack of ability. He can achieve flights of eloquence when he chooses, most often when he is pleading urgently for sexual favors—as in no. 113 (his seduction poem), no. 22, and the glittering no. 26. In two letters (nos. 24 and 50), he rises to the Woman's challenge and discourses learnedly on the nature of love. Another powerfully rhetorical statement is no. 75, an abject apology written when he was afraid of losing her. More typical, though, is a letter like no. 68, which reads in its entirety: "A sweetheart wishes his sweetheart whatever sweeter thing can be imagined. Farewell—you are sweeter than all things known to be sweet. I beg you earnestly, let me know how you are, for your good fortune is my chief pleasure. Let me know when I can come. Farewell."

In addition to using five "sweet" words (forms of *dulcis*) in two sentences, the Man writes a colloquial Latin that almost qualifies as a vernacular. We see this especially in his use of personal pronouns (see appendix D). Because Latin syntax relies on inflected verbs, there is no need to supply a personal pronoun as the subject of a sentence. Normally this is done only for emphasis. Yet the Man uses *ego* forty-nine times (seven times more often than the Woman) and *tu* forty-one times (more than three times as often). This is an extraordinarily high ratio for *ego* especially. Is the Man betraying his unconscious egotism? Or does he write an informal, almost oral Latin so colloquial that it rarely survives in the written record? An example is no. 74 where he says, *Si tu vales, ego valeo* (if you are well, I am well). This is probably an allusion to Baudri of Bourgueil, who writes in one of his verse letters, *si ualeas, ualeo*.[82] The meaning is exactly the same, but Baudri is elegant where the Man is defiantly plainspoken. Unlike the Woman, who staked enough on these letters to copy and preserve them throughout her life, the Man was making no attempt to produce a literary masterpiece. The everyday Latin of the schools where he taught approached the status of a true vernacular. In many of his missives, he writes a Latin much like what he could have spoken.

Finally, we can note differences in their salutations. Teachers of the *ars dictaminis* devoted more attention to greetings than to the other four parts of a letter combined, for it was here that writers could most easily flatter their recipients, flaunt their authority, profess their humility, and signal the subtle or not-so-subtle gradations of rank on which medieval society relied.[83] For readers new to Latin epistolography, the lovers' salutations may seem bewilderingly complex. But stripped of their curlicues, the formulas are of two basic types:

To X [from] Y: greetings and best wishes. *Or:*
To X [from] Y: to live happily ever after.

Each salutation consists of three parts. First comes a phrase in the dative to identify the recipient, then a phrase in the nominative to denote the sender.[84] The third phrase delivers a wish, using one or more nouns in the accusative ("greetings and best wishes") or else a verb in the infinitive ("to live happily ever after"). For a typical formula, we need look no further than the Woman's first letter in the manuscript (no. 1):

Amori suo precordiali omnibus aromatibus dulcius redolenti, corde et corpora sua: arescentibus floribus tue juventutis, viriditatem eterne felicitatis.

To her heart's beloved, fragrant above all perfumes, (*recipient*)
from her who is his in heart and body: (*sender*)

when the bloom of your youth has faded, [may yours be] the freshness of eternal bliss. (*wish*)

This example places the wish clause in the accusative (*viriditatem eterne felicitatis*), though it is modified by an ablative absolute (*arescentibus floribus tue juventutis*).

An example of the infinitive construction occurs in the Man's letter 6:

Clarissime stelle sue, cuius nuper radiis delectatus sum: ita indeficienti splendore nitere, ut nulla eam nebula possit offuscare.

To his most shining star, in whose radiance I have lately delighted: (*recipient*)
May she shine with such unfailing splendor that no cloud could dim her. (*wish*)

Here the clause for the sender is omitted—an option when the recipient obviously knows who is writing. The wish clause (*ita indeficienti splendore nitere*) is built around an infinitive (*nitere*), modified by the subsequent *ut* clause. Although English cannot use the infinitive this way, the Latin construction is clear enough.

As Carol Lanham has shown, the accusative formula was the older and more common of the two, while the infinitive marked an innovation.[85] Formularies and individual writers show significant differences in their preference for one or the other. Appendix C shows that the Woman is slightly more traditional in this regard; only 20 percent of her letters use the infinitive formula, as opposed to 25 percent for the Man. The Man also shows a penchant for accusative wish clauses with *quid* or *quidquid*, as in no. 2: *quid amplius quam seipsum, quantum corpore et anima valet?* (what more [should he give] than himself, for all he is worth in body and soul?). He uses this convention in fourteen of his letters (27 percent), as compared to only two (5.7 percent) for the Woman. What is more striking, however, is that seven of the Man's letters have salutations with finite verbs. This form of greeting was thought inelegant, and *dictatores* writing soon afterward banned it.[86] So the Man either did not know that rule or chose to disregard it. The Woman employs this novelty only twice, having obviously picked it up from her lover. Finally, in one letter (no. 95) she deliberately omits a wish clause, a violation of the rules that *dictatores* permitted if the writer wanted to express contempt or anger.[87] The Man never does this. Both lovers sometimes violate the custom of writing salutations in the third person by slipping into the first or second person in the course of a complex greeting. (See the example from no. 6 above.) *Dictatores* would later codify this breach of an otherwise firm rule as one of the special liberties permitted in love letters.[88]

On the basis of style alone, we can conclude definitively that we are dealing with two different writers—and thus with a genuine correspondence.[89]

Do the Man's Letters Resemble the Known Works of Abelard?

Very little. Herein lies the greatest stumbling block for the ascription.

In his 2004 article "Lost and Not Yet Found," Jan Ziolkowski undertook a comparative study of Abelard's known works with the Man's letters. He concentrated especially on the poetry, given that we have four short poems by the Man (nos. 20, 38a, 38c, 111) and three longer ones (nos. 113, 87, 108). Abelard himself is acknowledged as one of the greatest poets of his age, the author of an extensive body of hymns (*Hymnarius Paraclitensis*), six devotional poems on Old Testament themes (*Planctus*), and a didactic poem for his son (*Carmen ad Astralabium*). In addition, as both he and Heloise recall in their canonical letters, he had become famous for the love songs that he composed "in amatory meter and rhythmic verse" (*amatorio metro uel rithmo*) during their affair.[90] *Metrum amatorium* denotes elegiac couplets,[91] Ovid's preferred verse form, which is also the meter chosen by the Man for his three longest poems. None of the poems in the EDA are *rithmi*—rhymed, strophic poems meant for singing, like the *Carmina burana*.

Ziolkowski chose to compare the Man's verse letters in elegiacs with Abelard's *Carmen ad Astralabium* in the same meter. He found that the Man's poetry "relies heavily, even monotonously, on [internal] rhyme," whereas the *Carmen* avoids it. Conversely, the Man never uses elision, while Abelard often does. On another technical point, the Man sometimes ends the first half-line of a pentameter with a short syllable, while Abelard always uses a long one in that position. Such discrepancies, Ziolkowski asserts, "speak to a difference in prosodic training and practices," strongly suggesting that the Man could not have been Abelard.[92] Ziolkowski is not the only Latinist to be unimpressed by the Man's poems. Jaeger, a strong proponent of the ascription, calls them mere "yeomanly products of verse making," sometimes compelling and moving in their substance, but undistinguished in their language and metaphors.[93]

Stella's lexical studies again fail to reveal any stylistic connection between the Man and Abelard. He admits that his statistical method for comparing shared locutions (two- or three-word phrases) is experimental, and in fact "practically without precedent in the field of medieval Latin," so that it still lacks any accepted model for interpreting the results.[94] Nevertheless, he cautiously posits that if we compare almost any two Latin textual corpora, even if they are quite distant in genre or chronology, the normal percentage of overlapping locutions will be around 4 percent. Set against this standard, the two lovers of the EDA have a significantly higher ratio of 7.31 percent overlap, while Heloise and the Woman have a ratio of 5.37 percent (roughly the same as that between letters 3 and 5 in Abelard's own corpus). On the other hand, Abelard's monastic letters share only 3.26 percent of their locutions with the Man—a ratio lower than they share even with book 1 of Quintilian's *Institutio oratoria*, written a thousand years earlier in an unrelated genre.[95]

Do these results suffice to sink the attribution? Stella believes they seriously weaken it, although some of his other lexical findings confirm that the *Epistolae* show affinities with "Abelard and his school."[96] Ziolkowski, for his part, finds the Man's letters to be just "barely competent." As for his verse, he asks, "Could Abelard have revealed his hidden pedestrian side, an inner poetaster that he kept hidden from the world at large, only on the wax tablets he dispatched to his paramour?"[97] But Ziolkowski concedes that the ascription could be saved if it were shown that other contemporary poets displayed significant changes in style over the same period—as in fact, they did.[98]

Hildebert of Lavardin, one of the most highly regarded poets of the age, sometimes used end rhyme, sometimes leonine rhyme (especially in shorter poems), and often neither. In a classicizing move toward the end of his life, he rejected rhyme.[99] Marbod of Rennes composed leonine verse over most of his poetic career, but in his penitent *Liber decem capitulorum*, a work of his old age (circa 1102), he abandoned it. That poem begins with the lines:

> Quae iuvenis scripsi, senior dum plura retracto,
> Paenitet et quaedam vel scripta vel edita nollem,
> Tum quia materies inhonesta levisque videtur,
> Tum quia dicendi potuit modus aptior esse.[100]

> Much that I wrote in youth I retract in age
> And repent. Would that I had never written
> On such indecent, frivolous themes—
> And besides, the style could have been more apt.

Marbod goes on to list his specific reasons for rejecting rhymed verse (*dulcisonos numeros concinnaque verba*). In his riper age, he thinks it more fitting to write on useful subjects than to charm the ear with musical language; the constant search for rhymes is onerous and time-consuming; and besides, the incessant use of a single rhetorical device (*color unus*) is monotonous, for variety gives greater pleasure.[101] Several other poets followed this example. Gilo of Paris, for instance, composed the first five books of a Crusade epic in leonine hexameters, but abandoned that form in the sixth, explaining:

> Quod tamen incepi, sed non quo tramite coepi
> Aggrediar, sensumque sequar, non verba sonora
> Nec patiar fines sibi respondere vicissim.[102]

> I will take up the task I began, but not on the path
> I began. Now I will follow sense, not consonance,
> Nor will I let the endings correspond in rhymes.

Not all poets rejected leonine rhymes in the early twelfth century. But many did, so it would not be remarkable if Abelard, a plain stylist in any case, had done likewise.

Aside from poetic flexibility and stylistic change over time, several other factors could account for the discrepancies between Abelard and the Man's verse in the EDA. Most obviously, Abelard was not the same man either physically or spiritually when he wrote the *Historia calamitatum* (1132), some sixteen years later. In that text he represents his love affair as an aberration in an otherwise chaste life, a sinful episode for which (in retrospect) he felt nothing but shame—unlike the erotic nostalgia of Heloise. Few of Abelard's early works survive, and those that do are logical texts like the *Dialectica*, which cannot be compared with fragmentary love letters. His monastic letters, on the other hand, are not only different in genre, but almost opposite. The EDA were written to express an intense erotic passion. Conversely, the monastic letters strive to support Heloise in a chaste life that she still bitterly resented. So one would hardly expect them to quote lavishly from Ovid. In fact, to wean her from her amorous yearnings, Abelard might deliberately have avoided any echo of their previous letters.

Even more to the point, the *Historia calamitatum* and monastic letters are the most rhetorically polished works Abelard ever wrote, along with his hymns for the Paraclete.[103] Much hinged on them, after all. As Mary Martin McLaughlin argued more than forty years ago, Abelard wrote the *Historia* to pave the way for a return to his teaching career in Paris after a disastrous stint as abbot of Saint-Gildas in Brittany.[104] So it was necessary to put the most rhetorically persuasive spin that he could manage on the "calamities" of his past, including a conviction for heresy at Soissons and the notorious love affair. As for his subsequent letters to Heloise, their stakes were no less than the salvation of her soul.[105] Further, we have already seen that those letters were meant not only to meet her personal needs but to edify her nuns. The wide gulf between public and private writing should not be underestimated, for similar differences can be found in other cases. For example, some routine business letters of Einhard, Charlemagne's biographer, happen by chance to survive. In absolute contrast to his eloquent *Vita Karoli Magni* and theological letters, those brief, simple notes are composed in an "extremely bald and unadorned style."[106] The same is true of Fulbert of Chartres and others.[107]

Even in the *Epistolae*, if they are his, Abelard showed that he could write superbly well when he put his mind to it—but in that context, he seldom did. Dashing off a few lines on wax tablets, sometimes with a messenger waiting at his door (nos. 14, 37), the Man of the EDA assured his beloved of his abiding passion. But, unlike her, he did not perceive each love note as a daunting rhetorical challenge to be mastered only with the greatest effort (nos. 23, 53, 79). Other Abelardian works also fall short of high style. His philosophical writings concentrate on thought, not eloquence. Even the *Carmen ad Astralabium*, though its prosody is more careful than that of the love poems, hardly rises to the standard of Abelard's hymns, composed for the loftier end of divine praise.

Moreover, he expressly preferred a plain style. In the introduction to a collection of sermons for the Paraclete, he asserted that their lack of elegance was intentional: "More devoted to lecturing than preaching, I insist on a plain exposition, not eloquent composition—on literal meaning, not rhetorical ornament. It may be that if the language is pure rather than ornate, then the plainer it is, the more suited it will be to the understanding of the simple. And in accord with the quality of the hearers, the very rusticity of uncultivated speech will be a kind of urbanity, a seasoning easy for the intelligence of young girls to savor."[108] Lest we think he was merely condescending to the nuns, he gave exactly the same advice to his son. Ruys is convincing on this point, for she cites numerous passages from the *Carmen ad Astralabium* to that end:[109] "There is an abundance of words where there is no abundance of sense"; "a person's argument takes precedence over his style"; "wisdom declares itself in deeds, not words"; "a person is glorified by his actions, not his sayings."[110] The last two maxims express a core Abelardian belief that is also ubiquitous in the Man's letters in the EDA (nos. 12, 22, 54, 74, 75, 85, 105).

Finally, I mentioned above that the Man uses *ego* uncommonly often—seven times more often than the Woman, although we have roughly the same number of words from each. For what it's worth, a quick search of the *Historia calamitatum* shows that *ego* occurs twenty-four times (excluding two quotations), as opposed to five times in all three letters of Heloise (again excluding quotations). One could object that the *Historia* is intensely personal prose, but then, so are the first two letters of Heloise. So it does appear that, even when he was writing more formally, Abelard had a penchant for the first-person pronoun, which he used considerably more than strict grammar would require. This is a quirk he shares with the Man of the *Epistolae*.

Do the Woman's Letters Resemble Those of Heloise?

Far more than the Man's resemble Abelard's. I have described the Woman's style as mannerist—a term that properly refers to a taste, not a period. The mannerist, writes E. R. Curtius, "prefers the artificial and affected to the natural" because she "wants to surprise, to astonish, to dazzle."[111] Elements of a Latin mannerist style at this time would include an arcane vocabulary, long and grammatically complex periods, *annominatio* or wordplay, exotic metaphors, and an intensive concern with rhyme and prose rhythm, all of which are characteristic of the Woman's letters. I have already given some examples of her taste for rare words and neologisms. Interestingly, the same trait is mentioned in a letter addressed to Heloise by the canon Hugh Metel around 1132.[112] Hugh, a student of Anselm of Laon, had revered his master and had little use for Abelard, Anselm's rival. But he praised Heloise, whom he had never met, for her literary style. In writing, he said, she had risen to positively virile heights: "Fame ... has informed us that you have transcended the female sex. How? In composing letters [*dictando*], writing poetry [*uersificando*], renewing known words with new combinations [*noua junctura nota uerba nouando*]."[113] It is impossible to know which poems or letters of Heloise he had read,[114] since most of her writing is lost—and she had not yet written the only letters securely ascribed to her. But the quality he praises—lexical innovation—is abundantly evident in the *Epistolae*. It is also interesting that he knew of her as a poet because, if we exclude the EDA, no poems by Heloise are known to survive.[115]

As with Abelard and the Man, critics of the attribution can point to differences between the Woman's letters and the known writings of Heloise. For instance, the Woman structured her prose more consistently with rhyme. Here are the first two sentences of one of her finest letters (no. 84). Slashes denote the rhymed endings of *clausulae*, while accents (á, é) mark the speech stresses (as opposed to quantity). The sign | signals internal rhyme within a clause, and è denotes a secondary stress.

Ámans amánti: / gaúdium cum salúte optánti / íllud díco salutáre, quod nón finiátur, | et gaúdium / quod a té non tollátur | per évum. // Post mútuam nóstre visiónis | allocùcionís|que notíciam, / tu sólus michi placébas súpra ómnem Déi creatúram, / téque sólum diléxi, / diligéndo quesívi, / queréndo invéni, / inveniéndo amávi, / amándo optávi, / optándo ómnibus in córde méo prepósui, / téque sólum elégi ex mílibus, / ut fácerem tècum pígnus, / quo pígnore perácto, / dulcèdinísque tue mélle gustáto / sperábam me cúris / fínem posuísse futúris. // [116]

This is very highly wrought prose. All of its *clausulae* are paired by rhymed endings, usually one-syllable rhymes (*gaudium/evum, dilexi/quesivi, milibus/ pignus*). But the passage begins and ends with more noticeable two-syllable rhymes (*amanti/optanti, peracto/gustato, curis/futuris*). In addition, the Woman twice uses internal or chiastic rhyme within *clausulae* (*finiatur/tollatur, visionis/ allocucionis*). The same passage is distinguished by *cursus*, that is, every *clausula* that is set off by a rhymed ending also employs one of four rhythmic cadences.[117] These patterns are as follows, in order of frequency:

cursus planus: eleven cases (*ámans amánti, tollátur per évum, sperábam me cúris*)
cursus tardus: four cases (*finiátur et gaúdium, méo prepósui, elégi ex mílibus*)
cursus trispondaicus: two cases (*Déi creatúram, pígnore perácto*)
cursus velox: one case (*fácerem tècum pígnus*)

Rhymed prose and *cursus* are two essentially independent forms of stylistic ornament. Rhyme was an old technique originating in northern Europe. Used extensively by Hrotsvit as early as the tenth century, it reached its apogee in the eleventh and twelfth centuries.[118] The Woman's predominantly one-syllable rhymes are typical of the early twelfth; her practice is similar to what we see in the Tegernsee love letters. By midcentury, some prose stylists (like many poets) had rejected rhyme altogether, while others refined and perfected it, employing two- and even three-syllable rhymes. The technique of *cursus*, on the other hand, emanated outward from Italy, where it was maintained in certain lay schools and also used in the papal chancery.[119] In the eleventh and early twelfth century it could even authenticate papal documents because it was difficult to learn, not widely taught, and hard to counterfeit.[120] But as it fanned out from Italy, *cursus* gradually made its way into the *ars dictaminis*, becoming more widespread in the course of the twelfth century.[121] It was first theorized in French manuals of the art in the 1180s,[122] though it appears in actual use much earlier.

Because it was hard to combine rhymed prose with *cursus*, many writers selected one or the other, depending on personal taste and early training. For example, Fulbert of Chartres, Bernard Silvestris, and John of Salisbury use *cursus* but not rhyme, while Peter of Celle and Richard of Saint-Victor are masters of rhymed prose but indifferent to *cursus*. Yet in the early twelfth century, a few stylistically adventurous writers combined the two techniques. For instance, the monk Thiofrid of Echternach (in present-day Luxembourg) wrote a stylized work on relics, *Flores epytaphii sanctorum* (ca. 1105), that deploys both rhyme and *cursus*, and Guibert of Nogent did the same in his well-known *Memoirs* or *Monodiae* (1115).[123] Another writer of this type, analyzed in detail by Karl Polheim, is the French monk known as Gallus Anonymus, who moved to Poland ca. 1110 and produced the earliest works of Polish history.[124] His *Chronica et gesta principum Polonorum* (1113–16) are also contemporary with the EDA. These works, spanning a single decade, demonstrate that it was possible to acquire such a doubly ornamented style in northern Europe at the precise time of the *Epistolae*.

Though the Woman employed rhyme more extensively than *cursus*, she was clearly aware of the latter. Heloise, by comparison, used *cursus* more consistently and rhyme more selectively, mainly to set off passages of high emotional intensity. Appendix E compares the opening of no. 84, which I have just analyzed, with a purple passage from Heloise's letter 4. I chose both samples for the same reason: each presents the writer at her most artful, using every technique at her disposal to produce a strong emotional impact. A stylistic comparison shows that both passages use *cursus* extensively, favoring the slower rhythms (*planus* and *tardus*) over the swifter ones (*trispondaicus* and *velox*), while a small number of *clausulae* lack any favored endings. In the passage from Heloise, even the paired *clausulae* without standard *cursus* endings nonetheless display parallel rhythms: *ruínam íntulit, pártem éxtitit*. Both passages also make thoroughgoing use of rhyme, with the difference that Heloise prefers the two- and three-syllable rhymes that were then coming into vogue, and she plays even more deftly with multiple and internal rhyme (e.g., *altior / gradus / grauior / casus*; *potuit / contulit / intulit*; *amissorum / dolor / possessorum / amor*). Both passages heighten their effect with alliteration and assonance: compare the Woman's *amans amanti, pignore peracto, mecum mansisti, certamen certasti* with Heloise's *miserarum miserrimam, maior possessorum precesserat amor, terminaret tristicia*. Other rhetorical figures abound. Both employ *annominatio*, for example, the Woman's *salute/salutare, certamen certasti*, and Heloise's *faceret/effecerat*. The Woman's letter includes a splendid example of *gradatio* or climax: *teque solum*

dilexi, diligendo quesivi, querendo inveni, inveniendo amavi, amando optavi.
Heloise uses apostrophe and anaphora: five sentences in a row begin with *Quam,*
while the *quanto/tanto* construction occurs four times. In short, these two passages could nicely illustrate the maturation of a single, highly self-conscious
writer, as well as a gradual change in stylistic trends over time.

The first half of the twelfth century was a time of rapid transition in Latin
style, as in so many other respects. While leonine verse, a dominant eleventh-century form, continued to be written,[125] it was going out of fashion in
favor of classical meters on the one hand and strophic song on the other—a medium that reached its secular apogee in the *Carmina burana* and its sacred in
the Victorine sequence. Rhymed prose in its most common eleventh-century
mode, the fairly consistent use of monosyllabic paired endings, was abandoned
by some writers, while others came to reserve it for special effects and made it
flashier with the use of perfect two- and three-syllable rhymes. (This development in prose parallels the bravura combination of leonine with end rhyme by a
virtuosic poet like Bernard of Cluny.)

At the same time, the subtler ornament of *cursus* made its way steadily north-
ward from its Italian birthplace. It was not adopted by all writers or used in all
genres, but won its greatest favor in the more belletristic prose forms—epistles,
hagiography, and history—while technical writers and scholastic philosophers
tended to ignore it.[126] Among the writers who did use *cursus,* several patterns can
be found in northern France in the early twelfth century, where for a short time
the *cursus tardus* and the rarer *trispondaicus* were favored. By the century's end,
however, rhythms had become more standardized; the *trispondaicus* (used by both
the Woman and Heloise) dropped out, while the *cursus velox* came to be strongly
favored.[127] If the Woman of the *Epistolae* was Heloise, she would have been following a broader shift in literary fashion—learning to use rhyme less frequently but
more perfectly, while at the same time developing greater proficiency with *cursus.*
Abelard likewise would have changed in tune with the times if he had given up his
early penchant for leonine verse in favor of strophic song (the Paraclete hymns)
and unrhymed elegiacs (the *Carmen ad Astralabium*), while coming to deploy *cursus* in his more polished writing (the *Historia calamitatum* and letters), though
paying it no heed in his philosophical works.[128]

Returning to the Woman of the EDA, we can see in her a talented, ambitious, but youthful writer who still regards herself as a student. Although rhetoric is not the subject she is studying, she yearns for both erotic and intellectual
reasons to impress her teacher. That desire leads her at times to overreach herself, falling into the vices of obscurity and preciosity.[129] What she still needs to

learn is the restraint of a "middle style," like the quieter prose that Heloise uses to ground the emotional and rhetorical pyrotechnics of her mature letters. That middle style, with the even humbler style of her long, truly monastic letter 6, could account for some of the difference that a statistical study of both corpora would doubtless reveal. The Woman of the EDA very rarely attempts a plain style (but see nos. 71, 90). If Heloise is in fact that Woman, her *Epistolae* reveal the apprenticeship of a writer, already famous in her time, who would in later centuries dazzle the world.[130]

For those who make no claim to be connoisseurs of Latin prose style (if any are still with me?), there is another, more obvious way in which the Woman sounds like Heloise. That is her emotional gestalt. As we have seen, the Woman's love is an amalgam more complex than anything in the formulaic letters of the *artes dictandi*. One reason she uses so many alternatives for "love" (*amor, dilectio, amicitia, affectus*) is that she seeks to express the nuances of what she evidently feels: a love compounded of idealistic friendship, flaming passion, sacrificial devotion, and a kind of adoration verging on idolatry. She stakes her whole identity on that love, with an intensity that is more than rhetorical. "With God as my witness," she writes in no. 53, "I love you with a sublime and exceptional love. Hence there neither is nor shall be anything or any fate that can separate me from your love, save death alone." Love letters are by nature hyperbolic, especially in the twelfth century—but this goes beyond topoi. The Woman displays a theatricality, a tragic sensibility, even before anything tragic has happened: "Your honor might seem to have doubled mine—if only we were allowed to live together as equals until the fatal end. But for now, I choose rather to be undone by the danger of death than to live without the sweet delight of seeing you" (no. 79). The histrionic quality of such letters sounds a true Heloisan note, fraught with the same ambivalence that has led some readers to see Abelard's mistress as self-indulgent while, to others, she is the epitome of selfless love. Already the Woman conceives herself as an Ovidian heroine, comparing herself to three of them in a single sentence: "I can no more deny myself to you than Byblis could to Caunus, Oenone to Paris, or Briseis to Achilles" (no. 45). It has long been established that Ovid's *Heroïdes* supplied the chief models for Heloise's first two letters to Abelard.[131]

In the *Epistolae* as a whole, as von Moos observes, "love and love poetry flow together seamlessly in a single art of aesthetic sublimation, 'a secular religion of love,' of which it is hard to say when it is meant seriously, when ironically or even parodically."[132] The Man's allusions to this "secular religion," it seems to me, often have a mischievous or lightly blasphemous tone, as when he represents

sexual relations with his beloved as his *summum bonum* (nos. 26, 46) or inter-
prets Christ's command to "love one another" as a justification of their affair
(no. 52). The Woman, on the other hand, writes with utter seriousness in this
vein (cf. nos. 81, 84, 88). My own studies have corroborated von Moos's assertion
that such a crossover sensibility, a pervasive ambiguity created by the fusion of
sacred and secular, is a phenomenon that becomes widespread only in the thirteenth century.[133] But I know of one early, striking exception—none other than
Heloise. In 1992, long before I had read the *Epistolae duorum amantium*, I represented her as "a kind of mystic manquée":

The female mystics of subsequent generations would delight in imitating every
aspect of [the Virgin's] endlessly rich, varied, and all-absorbing union with [God].
Heloise is, in this respect, a precursor of Mechthild of Magdeburg and even
Margery Kempe, finding a rich and full selfhood in the adoption of multiple
imaginative roles. But the opposite number in *her* totalizing relationship was an
earthly man, and for her, classical models would do just as well as Christian. . . . Heloise prefigures such adepts of abnegation [as Hadewijch and
Marguerite Porete] in her boast that she would follow Abelard without hesitation
to the depths of hell, finding strength at his bidding to destroy her very self.[134]

This "secular religion of love" is already in full force in the Woman's letters—in
her avowal that she would willingly imperil her soul out of charity for her beloved (no. 9), in her appropriation of the virgin martyrs' profession of faith to
describe her devotion to him (no. 84), in her claim that he alone among mortals
possesses "perfect virtue" that "stands out in and through everything" (no. 88). I
agree with von Moos that such an attitude is hardly typical of the early twelfth
century—or perhaps any century. It is, however, typical of the one woman who
has been proposed as an author of the *Epistolae*.

     As I argued in the last section, the Woman's definition of love as a state of
never-ending debt (no. 25) is virtually without precedent or parallel—except in
the letters of Heloise, where it recurs very often. (See comment on no. 25 below.)
Once she had become Abelard's wife, she could present that theme as an extension of the Pauline marriage debt (1 Cor. 7:3–4). Surprisingly, though, its an-
tecedent is already here in the EDA. Somewhat less surprisingly, an ethical
motif so oddly transposed from theology to erotic love breeds a simmering resentment, a sense of being insufficiently appreciated, because no mortal can ever
repay such boundless self-giving. The Woman of the *Epistolae* may or may not
have been ill used; we do not have enough information to know. Yet much like

Heloise, she often flares up in harsh reproach against the one she so fervently claims to love.

This intimate bond of adoration and anger is a characteristic note in the letters of Heloise, and likewise in the EDA. Take no. 94, for example, which de Vepria transmits unabridged: "To her spice of perfect beauty and finest fragrance, bearing a hundredfold yield in the wilderness with tender seed, from his full moon: the delights of inextricable love. You throw your words to the winds. If you stone me for such trifles, what would you do to someone who really injured you? He who forgets a friend until he needs to use him [*qui non est memor amici nisi in tempore usus necessarii*] is not to be praised, nor is he an altogether perfect friend. Farewell." After such an affectionate greeting, the cry of anger comes as a shock, and the last sentence—an ethical maxim, cast in the distancing third person— fairly rings with contempt. Since we have no idea what had actually happened, the effect is mystifying. But compare this passage from Heloise (letter 2.14): "It was desire, not affection, which bound you to me, the flame of lust rather than love [*libidinis ardor potius quam amor*]. So when the end came to what you desired, any show of feeling you used to make went with it. This, most dearly beloved [*dilectissime*], is not so much my opinion as everyone's.... If only I could think of some pretexts which would excuse you and somehow cover up the way you hold me cheap!" (*Vtinam occasiones fingere possem, quibus te excusando mei quoquomodo tegerem uilitatem!*) Here again we have an endearment (*dilectissime*) sandwiched between two accusations—and a desire to make excuses for her beloved, set against the furious suspicion that she has merely been used, possessed, and held cheap (cf. nos. 69, 100). Her last sentence, by the way, alludes to Ovid's *Heroïdes* 3.41, where Briseis (to whom the Woman compared herself in no. 45) asks Achilles, *Qua merui culpa fieri tibi vilis?* (For what fault did I deserve to become cheap to you?) Fortunately, Heloise's story does not end at that point. But her "old, continual complaint," as Abelard would call it (letter 5.1), may have been on the table between them long before the tragic denouement.

How Unusual Were the Lovers of the *Epistolae duorum amantium*?

This question weighs heavily in any debate about the ascription, because Könsgen was surely right: the two lovers were at the very least a couple "like" Abelard and Heloise. Skeptics note that, even if we accept his proposed time and place for the correspondence, we cannot possibly know of every couple that had a love affair in early twelfth-century Paris. Abelard could not have been the only controversial teacher of philosophy, or the only one to lapse from strict chastity (that much at least seems a safe bet). But Heloise's social situation was exceptional, if not unique. It is true that not all girls educated in convents became nuns; some left the cloister to marry in the higher echelons of society. In their new position as ladies of rank, many doubtless continued to use the skills they had acquired in the *ars dictaminis*. Countess Adela of Blois received adulation from the greatest Latin poets of her age, including Baudri of Bourgueil and Hildebert of Lavardin.[135] She may well have written Latin letters in return, even if none survive.

The closest parallels we have to the EDA are the love letters from Tegernsee and the Regensburg Songs, instructive in both their resemblance and their radical difference. Like the *Epistolae*, Tegernsee letters 3–4 and 8–10, as well as the Songs, show how easily the teacher-student relationship could be eroticized. Both corpora derive from the exchange of Latin letters and verses as a pedagogical technique, and given Ovid's central place in the curriculum, it should come as no surprise that such exchanges often focused on love. In the Regensburg Songs, we see a remarkable range of postures and attitudes. The teacher poses one day as seducer, the next as moralist. He lavishes praise on his students' compositions (nos. 12, 37) as well as their beauty (no. 44), just as the Man does in the EDA. Yet these girls were a few years younger than the Woman, probably in their early teens (before the age of monastic profession). One of the most striking features of their verse is its playfulness, the protean array of poses it strikes, ranging from childish petulance to courtly *hauteur* to affectionate concern. The girls often put on airs or tease their master, but they also covet his praise and envy their schoolmates. Sometimes their letters practice the rhetorical art of *ethopoeia* or impersonation. One girl addresses a catty little verse to a rival, impersonating a priest (no. 17), while another pretends to be the teacher's mother (no. 35) and complains that he skimps on his letters home. This playful quality is utterly foreign to the *Epistolae*, where the Woman's letters especially stand out for their high seriousness.

As it happens, we may have some mature writing from one or two of these convent schoolgirls, though there is no way to be certain. Among the many correspondents of Hildegard of Bingen, we find two abbesses from Regensburg (Niedermünster and Obermünster), both writing eloquent letters of friendship in the mid-twelfth century.[136] They could well have received their Latin formation in the same school that bequeathed us the Regensburg Songs. Almost completely unstudied, the letters sent by female superiors to Hildegard offer valuable evidence of the *ars dictaminis* as it was practiced by twelfth-century nuns. More samples come from the Tegernsee corpus. In letters 5–7, we discover that nuns (or novices) could use an emotional, hyperbolic language of affection with one another. Many of its motifs and figures of speech mirror those of the Woman in the EDA: love (*dilectio*) "fixed in the depth of my heart," friendship transcending distance, pledges of everlasting loyalty, endearments centered on *dulcedo* ("sweeter than honey and the honeycomb"), crushing grief over the beloved's absence, urgent pleas for visits and letters, extravagant rhetorical questions, frequent citations from the Psalter and the Song of Songs. Letters 1 and 2 express similar feelings toward male friends, while letter 8 offers a lengthy, florid meditation on Ciceronian friendship. Such exchanges show that nuns were full participants in a monastic *ars dictandi* that had little in common with the treatises of Italian or later French *dictatores*. The Woman had clearly been trained in that art, which must have been taught and practiced far more widely than our meager evidence reveals.

At the time of the *Epistolae*, however, the Woman was not a nun, and she shows no interest in becoming one. Like Adela of Blois, she had completed her monastic education and returned to the world—but, unlike Adela, she had no county to rule, no marriage proposal in sight. Instead, her only apparent goals were to continue her studies and pursue a relationship with her lover. That was precisely Heloise's situation, as described by Abelard in *Historia calamitatum* 16–17 and 29. Despite energetic searching, scholars have yet to identify another such woman.[137] Peter the Venerable, a contemporary of Heloise, recalled hearing a report of her when they were both quite young. She was said to be "a woman not yet free of secular ties, who nonetheless devoted all her effort to literary studies and the pursuit of secular wisdom—a thing that is exceptionally rare [*perrarum*]."[138] What form of life might such a woman have hoped to pursue? In the heyday of the Gregorian reform movement, "educated clerical concubine" would have been a perilous career choice. Nor do we find evidence that, among the rowdy, competitive students who jostled each other in the streets of Paris, nubile women mingled freely in the throng, exchanging witty repartee in Latin with their male peers. Abelard in fact took Heloise as a private pupil, moving into Fulbert's house for ease (as he claimed) in instructing her. He has to explain the logistics in some detail because they were unusual, if not unheard-of. Heloise may well have achieved her early fame because her chosen way of life was so extraordinary. Other women, such as Muriel at Wilton and Emma at Le Ronceray, were likewise renowned for literary skill; but they were nuns.[139] The cloister was the obvious place—indeed, the *only* place—for a woman who wished to pursue a career in letters.

Nowhere in the *Epistolae*, as they come down to us, is it expressly stated that the Woman stood in the position of Heloise. Nevertheless, this is strongly implied. If she had still been a convent pupil, much less a vowed nun, the whole correspondence would have been impossible. Her teacher is hers alone; he is not the *magister* responsible for a whole female community, as in the Regensburg Songs. There is nothing to suggest that these letters were in any way shared or public; we have often noted their obsession with secrecy. No convent girl could have met so repeatedly with a lover, unhindered at least some of the time (no. 109), nor could she have traveled on her own for a lengthy period (no. 108), nor could a messenger have trotted back and forth so frequently with wax tablets (nos. 14, 37) without attracting suspicion. If anyone wanted to separate the lovers, it would not have been the "envious" (no. 28, 69, 85), but the abbess or prioress, who would have acted swiftly. The later twelfth-century story of the Nun of Watton shows just how serious the consequences could be for a religious woman caught with a lover. That unfortunate girl, recruited into monastic life against her will, was found pregnant, compelled to castrate her lover with her own hands, then chained in a prison cell to give birth.[140]

If the Woman of the EDA was neither married nor betrothed, nor under religious vows, we are back to the situation of Heloise—a single, highly educated young woman, living a secular urban life, devoted to some kind of scholarly work in collaboration with her teacher and lover (nos. 71, 84). This would indeed make them a couple "like Abelard and Heloise." To return to Könsgen's question, *was* there another such couple at the time—not simply a student in love with her teacher, but in this precise situation? The fact that we know of none does not mean there was none. Yet the world of the early Paris schools is fairly well documented, and still—we know of none. In the absence of a smoking gun, the case for Abelard and Heloise remains unprovable. But in light of all that we know thus far, it is highly probable.

TRANSLATIONS AND COMMENTARY

Letters of Two Lovers

TRANSLATED FROM EWALD KÖNSGEN, ed., *Epistolae duorum amantium: Briefe Abaelards und Heloises?* (Leiden: Brill, 1974). The mark [. . .] indicates an omission by the scribe, Johannes de Vepria, who signaled his abridgments with double slashes. In elegiac poems, the mark <. . .> indicates a break in the meter, which Könsgen took to imply one or more missing lines. All passages from the letters of Abelard and Heloise are cited from David Luscombe, ed., *The Letter Collection of Peter Abelard and Heloise*, with translation by Betty Radice, revised by Luscombe (Oxford: Clarendon, 2013). On the Tegernsee love letters, see the headnote to my translation below, and see the bibliography for editions of other sources and parallel texts. To avoid encumbering the apparatus, I here give only section and line numbers for classical and medieval works, except when referring to works in Migne's *Patrologia Latina* (PL). In citations from the Psalms, chapter and verse numbers refer to the Vulgate, but 1–2 Samuel and 1–2 Kings are identified as in English Bibles.

ᕽ☚

113 (**Man**)

Love prompts me to join his camp, revere his laws,
  And what I never learned, Love makes me learn.
He is no man but stone whom your beauty cannot move.
  I think that I am moved—no stone am I!
Poets used to paint the limbs of Venus,
<. . .>
But did they ever paint your equal? I think not,
  For goddesses themselves cannot compare.
Should I speak or be silent? By your grace, I will speak.
  I will speak, for betrayers flee from words.
What is hidden beneath your clothes? —My restless mind!
  How I long to caress what I imagine!
But fortune and modesty impede my will,
  And public rumor, sweetest—which I dread.
If I could see you, dear, as often as I wish,
  (Would it could be three times in every day!)
<. . .>
  That night would be more radiant than noon.
Forgive me: Love dictates what I'm forced to write.
  Forgive me, I confess: I love not patiently.
You have vanquished me, whom none could vanquish,
  And so I burn the brighter, for this is my first love:
Never before has the flame pierced to my marrow.
  If ever I loved before, I was but lukewarm.
You alone make me eloquent; none but you
  Has won this glory—to deserve my song.
You have no peer; Nature has set in you
  Whatever excellence this world can hold.
Beauty, birth, character (the source of honor)—
  Make you exceptional in this our city.

What wonder, then, if such elegance allures me,
  If I succumb to you, vanquished by your love?

COMMENT

This Ovidian pastiche is the last item in Johannes de Vepria's anthology, *Ex epistolis duorum amantium*. Yet even a moderately careful reading shows it to be a seduction poem, addressed to a lady who is known to the poet, but not yet his mistress. The Woman replies by addressing the Man formally, if jubilantly, as her teacher and accepting his love (no. 112). Her response indicates that he has only now begun to solicit her favor and extol her in verse. He is clearly not a lover of long standing, much less one with whom she is already disillusioned, as she will be by the end of the exchange. (See pp. 57–58 above for my decision to place these two letters first.) In his opening move, the Man flatters his lady's beauty and proclaims that now, for the first time, he has been "vanquished" by the god of love and the Woman's charms. He seems already to know her well, for he calls her *dulcissima* (sweetest) and *cara* (my dear) and salaciously imagines the body hidden beneath her clothes; but he has not previously declared himself as a lover. If ever he loved before, he says, it was a mere crush ("I was but luke-warm")—but now, Cupid's flame has pierced him to the marrow.

These statements are consistent with Abelard's remarks in *Historia calami-tatum* 14–15, where he boasts that, before meeting Heloise, he had lived in perfect chastity (*vixeram continentissime*); he abhorred prostitutes, had no time for noble ladies, and knew little about "the way of life led by lay women." At the end of his poem, the Man says his lady's beauty, birth, and character mark her as "exceptional [*conspicuam*] in our city [*urbi nostre*]." Later references to France (nos. 49, 89) and a highly competitive academic milieu (no. 66) identify the city almost certainly as Paris. In *Historia calamitatum* 16, Abelard similarly describes Heloise, when he first cast amorous eyes on her, as "very famous throughout the realm" (*in toto regno nominatissimam*). As for her birth or family (*genus*), Heloise's father remains unknown, but Werner Robl has plausibly identified her mother, Hersende, as the first prioress of Fontevraud, a descendant of the Montmorency. Robert of Arbrissel, the abbey's founder, was closely allied with that family.[1] If "fortune" (*fortuna*) impedes the lover's will, it may be because he is of lower rank, or perhaps because of his clerical status.

Written in correct elegiacs, the poem contains more than a dozen Ovidian reminiscences. Both lovers, especially the Man, will draw frequently on this beloved poet. The lovers knew the full Ovidian corpus and perhaps even read his poetry together. Although the *Heroïdes* were not yet widely known in the early twelfth century, they were coming into vogue, due in part to the efforts of Baudri of Bourgueil.[2] Heloise would draw extensively on Ovid's verse epistles in her letters to Abelard, appropriating the urgent, emotionally complex, rhetorically powerful voices of his seduced and abandoned heroines.[3] Further allusions to Virgil and Boethius in this poem introduce other favorite *auctores*. The Man also shows himself well versed in the contemporary poets of northern France. In addition to Baudri, he alludes to Fulcoius of Beauvais, Hildebert of Lavardin, and Marbod of Rennes.

A lightly ominous note is sounded by his fear of "public rumor" (*populi murmura*), which will increasingly dog the couple as their affair progresses. Troubadour poems from this period, sung in the south of France, strongly emphasize love's need for secrecy.

Love prompts me to join his camp (*Urget Amor sua castra sequi*): Ovid, *Amores* 1.2.17–18 (*urget . . . Amor*), 1.9.1 (*habet sua castra Cupido*), 3.8.26 (*castra sequi*); *Ars amatoria* 3.559 (*castris . . . Amoris*)

Love makes me (*cogit Amor*): Ovid, *Metamorphoses* 9.515 (*coget amor*)

He is no man but stone (*Non homo sed lapis est*): Fulcoius of Beauvais, *De nuptiis Christi et ecclesiae* 1.418 (*Non homo sed lapis est*); cf. Terence, *Hecyra* (*The Mother-in-Law*) 214 (*me . . . lapidem, non hominem putas*)

Your beauty cannot move (*non tua forma movebit*): cf. Statius, *Silvae* 2.1.139 (*non te forma movet*)

Goddesses themselves cannot compare (*Exuperat veras nam tua forma deas*): Ovid, *Heroïdes* 18.70 (*forma nisi in veras non cadit illa deas*)

Should I speak or be silent? (*Eloquar an sileam?*): Virgil, *Aeneid* 3.39 (*eloquar an sileam?*)

Fortune and modesty impede my will (*fortuna pudorque meis . . . votis / Obstant*): Ovid, *Metamorphoses* 7.145 (*obstitit incepto pudor*), 8.327–28 (*nec plura sinit tempusque pudorque / dicere*)

That night would be more radiant than noon (*Candidior medio nox foret illa die*): Ovid, *Heroïdes* 16.320 (*candidior medio nox erit illa die*)

Love dictates (*dictat Amor*): Ovid, *Amores* 2.1.38 (*dictat Amor*)

Forgive me, I confess: I love not patiently (*Da veniam fasso, non patienter amo*): Ovid, *Ex Ponto* 1.7.22 and 4.2.23 (*Da veniam fasso*); *Heroïdes* 19.4 (*da veniam fassae; non patienter amo*)

You have vanquished me, whom none could vanquish (*Tu me vicisti, potuit quem*
　　vincere nulla): Hildebert of Lavardin, *Carmina minora* 46.18 (*vincis quod virgo*
　　vincere nulla potest)
First love (*primus amor*): Ovid, *Metamorphoses* 1.452 (*primus amor*); *Amores* 3.9.32
　　(*primus amor*)
Flame pierced to my marrow (*penetravit flamma medullas*): Ovid, *Metamorphoses*
　　14.351 (*flammaque per totas visa est errare medullas*)
If ever I loved before (*Si quis amor fuerat*): cf. Marbod of Rennes, "Ad amicam
　　repatriare parantem"[4]
Make me eloquent (*Facundum me . . . facis*): Ovid, *Metamorphoses* 6.469 (*facundum*
　　faciebat amor)
None but you . . . deserve my song (*hec gloria nulli / Contigit, ut fuerit carmine digna*
　　meo): cf. Baudri of Bourgueil, *Carmina* 137.37 (*Nulla recepit adhuc nisi tu mea*
　　carmina uirgo)
Whatever excellence (*Quicquid precipuum*): Boethius, *Consolation* 3, metr.12.57
　　(*Quidquid praecipuum*)
Beauty, birth, character (*Forma, genus, mores*): proverbial;[5] cf. Hildebert of Lavardin,
　　Carmina minora 35.4 (*genus, et mores, et bona forma*)
What wonder, then (*Ergo quid est mirum*): Fulcoius of Beauvais, *De nuptiis Christi et*
　　ecclesiae 3.125 (*Ergo quid est mirum*)
Vanquished by . . . love (*victus amore*): Ovid, *Metamorphoses* 1.619 (*victus . . . Amore*);
　　Heroïdes 15.176 (*victus amore*)

ॐ

112 (**Woman**)

To her teacher—the noblest, the most learned: greetings in him who is
salvation and blessing.

If you are well and running your course among worldly cares without
stumbling, I am swept up in supreme exultation. It has pleased your
nobility to send my lowly self a letter, and by appealing to me and
promising the solace of your love, you have ravished me up to the third
heaven with a kind of mental lightness stemming, it seemed to me,
from too great a joy. I shall tell the truth more plainly: the boundless

delight of your letter unexpectedly ravished me and assuaged my
desire, as if by some inner revelation.
[. . .]
Already nurtured at the hearth of philosophy, you have drunk from
the fountain of poetry.
[. . .]
To thirst for God and cling to him alone is necessary for every living
creature.
[. . .]
Although it may lie in the future, already I behold the mountaintops
bowing down to you, and I have no doubt that what I desire will, by
God's counsel, be fulfilled in you. Yet no language, no facility with
words, is sufficient to express the joy I feel on reaching the haven of
your love—confident, yet not ungrateful. Though I am utterly incapable of repaying so great a favor, I long with great longing to devote
myself unfailingly to you. [. . .]

COMMENT

The Woman replies to the Man as her teacher, not yet her lover, but she is already
confident enough to use the intimate *tu*, rather than the formal *vos*. Thrilled by his
declaration of love, she leaves no doubt that she feels the same way: his letter "assuaged my desire." With the hyperbole and intensity that will characterize her
throughout the exchange, she compares the joy his poem gave her to a "revelation,"
specifically to St. Paul's experience of being ravished to the third heaven. Already,
too, we see her extravagant protestations of humility. She exults that it has pleased
her teacher's "nobility" to appeal to her "lowly self" (*mee parvitati*) and frets that
she cannot repay his favors in kind. This will be a recurrent theme.

Throughout the correspondence, the Woman uses biblical diction far more
than the Man. Sometimes she adopts a scriptural turn of phrase, such as *omni viventi* (every living creature, Job 30:23) or *cacumina montium* (mountaintops, Genesis 8:5), with no special weight. At other times, as in her allusion to Christ's
longing before the Last Supper (*desiderio desideravi*, Luke 22:15), the echo is more
significant. Her deep knowledge of the Bible and the liturgy indicates that she was
trained in a monastery, for nowhere else could she have acquired such fluency. Yet

she is clearly not a nun. Never does she refer to chastity or virginity, nor does she chastise the Man for his frank sexual interest. She represents her feelings as a combination of *amor* (love in the broadest sense), *amicitia* (friendship), *dilectio* (love based on moral appreciation and choice), *affectus* (tender feeling), and *desiderium* (passionate desire). This complex emotional blend distinguishes her letters from other teacher-student exchanges of the period. Writing from convents, other girls tempered their flirtatious rhetoric with allusions to vowed chastity. For instance, in one of the Tegernsee letters, a young woman consents to her teacher's solicitation of love on one condition: "If I knew that you would love me with a chaste love and preserve the pledge of my chastity inviolate, I do not refuse [the labor or] the love."[6] This Woman's exultation is different; she perceives no contradiction between divine love and her passion for her teacher. Rather, she believes her feelings are grounded in God and wishes her lover eternal blessings. Heloise, more than a decade after her forced entry into monastic life, would still argue for the purity of her love for Abelard, despite its impassioned eroticism. The exceptionality of that stance would be hard to exaggerate, yet we also find it in the Woman of these letters.

Her response begins with a play on words that cannot be reproduced in English. She sends her lover greetings (*salutem*) in Christ who is their salvation (*salus*), using the same Latin noun. This double meaning is ubiquitous; a translator must regrettably make choices.

Because of the scribe's omissions, we do not have the full substance of this letter. But its second paragraph shows that the Woman already knows the Man as a philosopher. Now for the first time, she is delighted to encounter him as a poet. She will praise his poetic gifts again in no. 21. Heloise tells Abelard in her letter 2.13, "You had . . . two special gifts with which you could at once win the heart of any woman—the gifts of composing verse and song [*dictandi . . . et cantandi*]. We knew that other philosophers have rarely been successful in these, whereas for you they were no more than a diversion, a relief from the toil of doing philosophy." The Woman's esteem for her teacher prompts her to predict that, some time soon, the mountaintops will bow down to him—a prophecy of future academic triumph, fulfilled in the acclamation of no. 66.

Johannes de Vepria has preserved only one sentence of a third paragraph: "to thirst for God and cling to him alone is necessary for every living creature." Did the Woman draw an explicit parallel between divine and human love? It would be splendid to have some context, but it is lost forever.

Ravished . . . to the third heaven (*ad tercium celum rapuisti*): 2 Corinthians 12:2
    (*raptum . . . ad tertium caelum*)

Nurtured at the hearth of philosophy (*philosophie laribus nutritus*): cf. Boethius,
　　Consolation 1, pr. 2 (*nostro . . . lacte nutritus*); 1, pr. 3 (*nutricem meam*
　　cuius . . . laribus obversatus fueram, Philosophiam)
Thirst for God (*Sitire deum*): Psalm 41:3 (*Sitivit anima mea ad Deum*)
And cling to him (*et illi adherere*): Psalm 72:28 (*adhaerere Deo*)
For every living creature (*omni viventi*): Job 30:23 (*omni viventi*)
Mountaintops (*moncium cacumina*): Genesis 8:5 (*cacumina montium*)
The joy I feel on reaching the haven of your love (*quantum gaudeo, quod portum tue*
　　dilectionis . . . optineo): cf. Regensburg Songs, no. 9 (*Mens mea letatur corpusque*
　　dolore levatur / Idcirco quia me, doctor, dignaris amare)
I long with great longing (*desiderio desidero*): Luke 22:15 (*desiderio desideravi*)

1 (**Woman**)

To her heart's beloved, fragrant above all perfumes, from her who is
his in heart and body: when the bloom of your youth has faded, may
yours be the freshness of eternal bliss.
[. . .]
Farewell, my life's welfare.

COMMENT

At the beginning of his anthology, Johannes de Vepria copied only the lovers'
elaborate greetings and closings. As noted in "Frequently Asked Questions,"
these salutations follow a standard pattern: a dative clause addressing the recipient, a nominative clause identifying the sender (sometimes omitted), and finally a wish—either a noun clause in the accusative (some variant on *salutem* or
"greetings") or else a verbal clause in the infinitive.[7] Both lovers ring endless
variations on this formula, frequently responding to the previous letter. The
Latin idioms of greeting (*salve*) and parting (*vale*) have wide-ranging connotations that enable elegant wordplay. *Salve* is related to the noun *salus* (greetings,
good health, well-being, salvation), and *vale* (the noun for "farewell") as a verb

means "fare well, thrive, flourish, be strong."[8] The Woman's closing (*vale salus*) is perfectly circular, recalling a line from Baudri of Bourgueil.

For the first time the Woman alludes to the Song of Songs, which was just coming into exegetical fashion. By the end of the twelfth century it would accrue more commentaries than any other book of the Bible.[9] Bernard of Clairvaux would begin his famous sermon cycle in about twenty years.[10] The Woman's "freshness" (*viriditas*) is literally the color green; it connotes the fresh foliage of spring and burgeoning new life, both natural and spiritual. In the 1140s and 1150s, Hildegard of Bingen made this concept a centerpiece of her theological vision.[11]

The scribe's omissions need not have been long. If the lovers lived near each other (see no. 109), they would not have had to include a *narratio* (narrative) or *petitio* (request) in each letter, as the formal *ars dictaminis* required.[12] At this early stage, their letters were mainly a way to exchange florid compliments.

To her heart's beloved (*amori suo precordiali*): Berno of Reichenau, *Epistolae* 6 (*mi praecordialis amor*, PL 142: 1164d)
Fragrant above all perfumes (*omnibus aromatibus dulcius redolenti*): Song 4:10 (*super omnia aromata*); Tegernsee letter 4 (*redolentes aromata summe caritatis*)
Farewell . . . welfare (*Vale salus*): cf. Baudri of Bourgueil, *Carmina* 200.173 (*Dum tibi dico "uale," "uale" hoc intellige: "salue"*)

❧

2 (**Man**)

To his singular joy, the sole consolation of his weary mind, from him whose life without you is death: what more should he give than himself, for all he is worth in body and soul?
[. . .]
Farewell my light, farewell, for whom I would gladly die.

❧

COMMENT

To match the Woman's greeting, "from her who is his in heart and body," the Man offers "all he is worth in body and soul." The proximity of love and death—here expressed twice in two sentences—belongs to the deep core of erotic mythology, medieval or otherwise.

My light (*lux mea*): Ovid, *Amores* 1.4.25 (*mea lux*)
For whom I would gladly die (*pro qua mori velim*): Seneca, *Epistulae morales* 1.9.10
    (*amicum . . . pro quo mori possim*)

3 (Woman)

To her purest love, worthy of intimate faithfulness: I wish you the secret of tender trust through the state of loyal love.
[. . .]
May the ruler of heaven be our go-between; may he be the friend of our faithfulness. Farewell—and may Christ the King of kings make you, sweetheart, fare well forever. Farewell in him who governs all the world.

COMMENT

In rhyming prose, the Woman first broaches her cherished theme of fidelity or trust (*fides, fidelitas*). Habitually expressing herself in religious terms, she audaciously prays that God will be their go-between (*mediator*) in lieu of the cynical confidant(e)s who play that role in Ovidian love affairs. The Woman will repeat this prayer in no. 38b, when she is starting to doubt her lover's loyalty.

Ruler of heaven (*Celi regnator*): Walahfrid Strabo, *Carmina* 49.1 (*caeli regnator*); no. 38b
May [God] be our go-between (*sit inter nos mediator*): *Liber pontificalis* (*Deus omnipotens sit inter nos mediator*, PL 106: 686b)
Christ the King of kings (*Christus, rex regum*): cf. Daniel 2:37 (*rex regum . . . Deus*); the phrase occurs in several liturgical chants.
Who governs all the world (*qui cuncta gubernat in mundo*): cf. Boethius, *Consolation* 3, metr. 9.1 (*qui perpetua mundum ratione gubernas*)

4 (Man)

To her who grows sweeter day by day, beloved even now beyond all
bounds, whom I shall love forever above all things: her only one sends
the same unchangeable constancy of unfeigned trust.
[. . .]
Farewell, my most shining star, my noblest delight, and my sole
consolation. [. . .] Farewell, my health.

COMMENT

The Man's greeting *dilecte et semper . . . diligende* (literally "beloved and to be
loved forever") recurs with variations throughout the exchange (nos. 12, 42, 54,
59, 61), as the lovers seek to outdo each other in their professions of constancy.

Day by day (*de die in diem*): Psalm 60:9, 95:2 (*de die in diem*)

5 (Woman)

To you, my hope and joy, I pledge my trust and myself as long as I live,
with all devotion.

May the giver of every skill and the most generous donor of human
talent fill the depths of my heart with skill in the philosophical art,
that I may greet you in writing, beloved, as I would wish. Farewell,
farewell, hope of my youth.

COMMENT

This conspicuously rhyming note voices a persistent concern. Conceiving the task of letter writing as a rhetorical and even philosophical challenge, the Woman feels stretched to the limit, doubting that she can meet her own exalted standards. This motif recurs often enough to be more than a humility topos (cf. nos. 13, 23, 25). On one level, it expresses the natural timidity of a student writing to her teacher, not wanting to disappoint him. The author of the third Tegernsee letter sounds the same note. But this Woman, like Heloise, reveals a rare degree of literary self-awareness. The *ars dictaminis* has been her particular study, it seems, and now she has a chance to prove her mastery. She might have been pleasantly surprised to learn that she had produced a text for the ages.

Hope of my youth (*spes juventutis mee*): Psalm 70:5 (*spes mea a iuventute mea*)

❧

6 (**Man**)

To his most shining star, in whose radiance I have lately delighted: May she shine with such unfailing splendor that no cloud could dim her.

Because you asked, my sweetest lady—or, to speak more truly, because the fiery flame of love compels me—your beloved could not contain himself, but greets you by means of a letter as best he can, in place of his presence. Be well, then, because I need your well-being. Farewell, for my welfare consists in yours. In you is my hope, in you my rest. Never do I wake so suddenly that my mind does not find you already in it.

❧

COMMENT

The Man addresses his beloved in a courtly vein as "my lady" (*domina mea*), a formality he will soon drop. She has specifically asked him to greet her, an index of how strongly these letters furthered the couple's love. It was an ancient commonplace that a letter could substitute for a friend's physical presence.

By means of a letter (*litterarum officio*): Cicero, *Epistulae ad familiares* 6.6.1 (*litterarum . . . officium*); Augustine, *Epistolae* 23.1 (*officio litterarum*, PL 33: 94); Jerome, *Epistulae* 48.1 (*officio litterarum*)

7 (**Woman**)

To her beloved now and forever, from her who is wholly his in reality and affection: I wish you health, joy, and increase in all that is useful and honorable.

[. . .]

Farewell, farewell, and fare well—for as long as the kingdom of God endures.

COMMENT

The Woman picks up the Man's greeting from no. 4. "From her who is his" translates a single word, *sua*, as in no. 1. Heloise would write to Abelard as *unica sua* (his only one) in letter 4 and *sua singulariter* (she who is singularly his) in letter 6.

8 (**Man**)

To his most beloved lady, whose remembrance no forgetting can obstruct, from her most faithful one: may I forget your name only when I no longer recall my own.

[. . .]

Farewell: rest and sleep in peace. Sleep sweetly, lie gently, may you sleep so soundly that you never stir. Farewell, O my rest, farewell, and ever fare well.

⁂

COMMENT

Abelard and Heloise both had unusual names. So it is interesting that the Man, perhaps alluding to a conversation, promises not to forget the name of his beloved so long as he can recall his own. Long before these *Epistolae* were discovered, several scholars ascribed the poem "Hebet sidus" (*Carmina burana* 169) to Abelard because of a seeming play on *Heloise* as an anagram for *Helios*, the sun. (See comment on no. 20 below.) Abelard offers a different etymology in his letter 5.23, deriving *Heloysa* from *Heloym* (Elohim), a Hebrew name for God.

Whose remembrance no forgetting can obstruct (*cuius memoriam nulla intercipere potest oblivio*): cf. Tegernsee letter 8 (*te de mei memoria nulla poterit delere oblivio*)

Forget your name (*tui nominis oblivionem*): cf. Ovid, *Ex Ponto* 2.11.5 (*Nominis ante mei . . . oblivia*)

Rest and sleep in peace (*in pace in idipsum dormi et requiesce*): Psalm 4:9 (*In pace in idipsum dormiam et requiescam*); I have not translated *in idipsum*.

✦

9 (**Woman**)

To a burning lamp and a city set on a hill: may he fight to conquer, may he run to win.

[. . .]

I wish, I breathlessly desire that by exchanging letters, as you have bidden, our heartfelt friendship may grow firmer—until that supremely happy day dawns when I shall see your face, longed for in all my prayers. As a weary man longs for shade and a thirsty man for water, so do I long to see you.

[. . .]
Nothing will ever be so burdensome for my body, nothing so perilous
for my soul, that I would not do it out of charity for you.
[. . .]
Be strong in God, than whom none is stronger.

COMMENT

With a cascade of biblical metaphors, the Woman wishes her teacher success in
what may have been a *disputatio* or academic competition. Her rhetoric of love
grows ever stronger: in all her prayers (or wishes, *votis*) she longs to see her lover,
employing terms used in Scripture to express longing for God. Biblical diction
lends sublimity to her style. But her willingness to imperil her soul for her beloved sounds an alarming note. Such a theatrical consent to self-immolation was
characteristic of Heloise, who declared apropos of her entrance into religious
life that she would have willingly descended even into hell (*ad Vulcania loca*) at
Abelard's bidding (letter 2.15).

A burning lamp (*ardenti lucerne*): John 5:35 (*lucerna ardens*, John the Baptist)
A city set on a hill (*civitati supra montem posite*): Matthew 5:14 (*civitas . . . supra
      montem posita*)
Run to win (*sic currere, ut comprehendat*): 1 Corinthians 9:24 (*Sic currite ut
      comprehendatis*)
Exchanging letters, as you have bidden (*litteris iuxta preceptum tuum intercurrenti-
      bus*): Abelard, *Historia calamitatum* 16: "Knowing her knowledge and love of
      letters I thought she would be all the more ready to consent, and that even when
      separated we could enjoy each other's presence by exchange of written messages
      in which we could write many things more boldly than we could say them, and
      so need never lack the pleasures of conversation." Heloise, letter 2.16: "When in
      the past you sought me out for sinful pleasures your letters came to me thick and
      fast."
Until that . . . day dawns (*donec . . . dies illucescat*): Song 2:17, 4:6 (*donec aspiret dies, et
      inclinentur umbrae*); Proverbs 7:18 (*donec illucescat dies*); 2 Peter 1:19 (*donec dies
      elucescat*)

I shall see your face, longed for in all my prayers (*votis omnibus desideratam tuam faciem videam*): cf. Tegernsee letter 5 (*tua optata . . . fruor visione*)

A weary man longs for shade (*lassus umbram . . . desiderat*): Job 7:2 (*Sicut servus desiderat umbram*)

And a thirsty man for water (*et siciens desiderat undam*): cf. Psalm 41:2 (*Quemadmodum desiderat cervus ad fontes aquarum*); nuns of Admont[13]

Nothing so perilous for my soul (*nichil tam periculosum anime mee*): cf. Heloise, letter 2.9: "I have carried out all your orders to such an extent that when I was powerless to oppose you in anything, I found strength at your command to destroy myself." Letter 2.15: "At your command, God knows, I would equally have had no hesitation in going ahead of you or following you to Vulcan's pit."

10 (**Man**)

To his most precious gem, ever radiant with her natural splendor, from her purest gold: may he encompass and fittingly frame that gem in joyful embraces.

[. . .]

Farewell, you who make me fare well.

COMMENT

A witty sexual invitation. Just as a jewel is set in a golden ring, the Man wants to "frame" his beloved in his arms.

Purest gold (*aurum . . . purissimum*): 1 Chronicles 28:18 (*aurum purissimum*)

11 (**Woman**)

To him who shines bright with all virtues and holds more delight than the honeycomb: his most faithful one of all gives herself, the other half of his soul, in all faithfulness.

[. . .]

I take God to witness, from whom no secret machinations are hidden or ever can be, how purely I love you, how sincerely, how loyally.

[. . .]

Now then, because I have no leisure for writing, I cry out a hundred times and repeat a thousand times: may you fare well, may your welfare be without peer.

COMMENT

An extravagant profession of love in rhymed prose. The lovers invoke God's all-seeing eye as witness again in nos. 45 and 56, alluding to the liturgical Collect for Purity.

The Horatian expression "half [your] soul" was common in greetings, but it took on new urgency and playfulness in a poem of Baudri of Bourgueil, well known to the Woman:

> Cor pectusque meum dimidiabo tibi;
> Dimidiabo tibi quod erit michi dimidiandum;
> Dimidiabo, si iubeas, animam.[14]

> I will divide my heart and breast with you;
> I will share with you anything of mine that can be divided;
> If you command it, I will share my very soul.

More delight than the honeycomb (*super favum mellis iocundo*): Psalm 18:11 (*dulciora super mel et favum*), Ecclesiasticus 24:27 (*super mel dulcis . . . super mel et favum*)

The other half of his soul (*dimidium anime*): Horace, *Carmina* 1.3.8 (*animae dimidium meae*)

I take God to witness (*Deum testem habeo*): Romans 1:9 (*Testis . . . mihi est Deus*)

God . . . from whom no secret[s] . . . are hidden (*Deum . . . quem neque latet nec latere potest ulla secreti machinacio*): Alcuin, Collect for Purity[15]

꘍

12 (**Man**)

To her who is ardently loved and shall be loved yet more ardently, from him who is faithful above all—and to speak more truly, who alone is faithful: I send whatever the rule of sincerest love requires.

I think there is no need, sweetheart, for you to commend to your beloved in words the fidelity you so plainly show in deeds. If I were to strive with all my strength in your service, I would think I had done nothing; I would judge my labor vain compared with what you deserve. If all this world's goods could be brought together and gathered into one heap and I had to choose between them and your friendship, by the faith I owe you, I would reckon them of no value.
[. . .]
I am certainly glad to have done so. Farewell, my glory, incomparably sweeter than all that is sweet. May you live all your days as gladly as I wish for you, for nothing better is needed.

꘍

COMMENT

Echoing the Woman's hyperbole, the Man declares that no act of his can possibly equal her merits. The comparison of words to deeds is one of his favorite motifs (nos. 22, 54, 74, 75, 85, 105). This is a commonplace; one of the Regensburg Songs (no. 65) remarks that "love does not consist in words, but in gracious deeds."[16] Abelard, however, made the theme particularly his own. In his didactic poem, the *Carmen ad Astralabium*, he warned his son especially against relying on eloquence, noting that "wisdom declares itself in deeds, not words" and advising him, "be sure that you prefer deeds to words."[17] In that context, the maxim justifies his choice of a plain style, contrasting with the Woman's studied elegance.

We see one of the scribe's rare glitches in the sentence, "I am certainly glad to have done so" (i.e., "you're welcome"), which would have closed the previous paragraph. This letter must have been prompted by the Woman's thanking the Man for some favor. Such concrete details did not interest de Vepria, who excised them.

All . . . gathered into one (*totum congeratur in unum*): Cicero, *Tusculan Disputations* 5.117 (*congerantur in unum omnia*)
I would reckon them of no value (*nullius ea precii reputabo*): cf. Song 8:7, 1 Corinthians 13:3; no. 85
My glory (*decus meum*): Horace, *Carmina* 1.1.2 (*decus meum*)

13 (**Woman**)

[. . .] The grateful goodwill of my mind, which is always in your debt for its own sake and in the course of duty, could not send you all the greetings it would like—so it has held back until now, lest it spoil them all by heaping up too many. I think it neither burdensome for you nor difficult for me to write to you often, repeating the same things again and again, for I cannot fail to love you with all the striving of my heart—you, whom I love as myself.
[. . .]
Farewell, you are dearer than life. Know that my death and life are in you.

COMMENT

The Woman belabored her greetings as a finicky shopper agonizes over a choice of gifts. Even when repetition sets in, as it inevitably must in a long correspondence, the act of writing is itself a gift. Here the Woman cites the Great Commandment ("you shall love your neighbor as yourself") and applies it to her love affair, which at this point was probably still chaste.

Could not send you all the greetings it would like (*omnes quas vellet salutes expedire non potuit*): cf. Tegernsee letter 4 (*Affamina salutationis, quibus deberet appellari magnitudo tue dilectionis, haut apparent mee indagini meditationis.*)

Whom I love as myself (*quem sicut memetipsam diligo*): Matthew 22:39 (*Diliges proximum tuum sicut teipsum*)

My death and life are in you (*in te mea mors est et vita*): Marbod of Rennes, "Rescriptum ad amicam" 13 (*In te namque sita mea mors est et mea vita*)

14 (**Man**)

If I could keep your tablets a while longer, sweetheart, I would write much, for much would come to mind. Even if I could always be writing so that I did nothing else, I would doubtless have no lack of matter— that is, your goodness and your acts of kindness toward me, which are so many they could not be numbered. Farewell, my most certain hope.

COMMENT

This is the first reference to wax tablets, the medium of the letters (cf. nos. 62, 66). Such tablets were routinely used for schoolwork, note taking, and rough drafts. They consisted of a double wooden frame into which the user poured hot wax, which cooled to form two writing surfaces that could be inscribed with a stylus. Each pair of tablets could hold up to fifty or sixty lines, providing a natural limit for the length of messages.[18] The Woman might have sent her tablets to her teacher on the pretext that he was to correct her lessons. After reading each letter, the lovers would scrape the wax clean and reuse the same tablets to reply. This method was less expensive than exchanging scraps of parchment, but it still required a trusted (or illiterate) messenger to convey the tablets back and forth. Here the Man seems to write in haste while the messenger waits at the door, as he states explicitly in no. 37.

To preserve their letters, one of the pair must have copied each missive as it was sent or received into a parchment record. This was most likely the Woman, who was more concerned with producing a literary monument to their love. The canonical letters of Abelard and Heloise were disseminated from the Paraclete, where it was Heloise who preserved them. (See pp. 54–57 above.)

✎

15 (**Man**)

To his heart, from her most faithful one: radiant be your night, and would that it were with me! Farewell, my soul, my rest.

✎

COMMENT

A prose version of the sexually suggestive verse in no. 111, probably written around the same time. Is the Man becoming impatient?

Radiant . . . night (*noctem candidam*): Ovid, *Heroïdes* 16.320 (*candidior . . . nox*)
My soul (*anima mea*): cf. 1 Kings 20:17 (David loves Jonathan *sicut . . . animam suam*, "as his own soul")

✎

16 (**Man**)

To his seal, firmly impressed on the inner parts of his mind, from him who is the express likeness of that seal: may our affection be the more enduring in that our common good is achieved, without difference, in the welfare of each of us.

But you, hard-hearted one—how could you have forgotten your soul? For when you have forgotten me, if I am your soul, you have also forgotten your own soul. Farewell, sweetheart. I am wholly with you, and to speak more truly, I am wholly in you.

❧

COMMENT

This is the Man's third letter with no reply from the Woman, but he is not yet unduly troubled. Instead, he begins to develop a philosophical account of their love. The two share a single, common good (*res communis*) which belongs to each of them without difference (*indifferenter*)—a key term in the debate over universals that currently preoccupied Abelard, William of Champeaux, and other Paris philosophers. When the Man offers his definition of love in no. 24, he will call it a *res universalis* that makes two wills into one without difference.

The metaphor of the seal is a rich one, with amorous connotations from the Song of Songs ("set me as a seal upon your heart") and theological ones from the Gospels. When Jesus was asked if it was lawful to pay tribute to Caesar, he asked his opponents whose image appeared on the coin used for the tax. When he was told "Caesar's," he replied, "Render unto Caesar that which is Caesar's, and unto God that which is God's" (Matthew 22:21). In a standard exegetical account, the human soul, "which is God's," is like a coin impressed with the Creator's image or seal.[19] The same metaphor was used in pedagogical theory, likening the student's mind to soft wax ready to be imprinted by the seal of his master's teaching.[20] Here the Man reverses the usual direction of the metaphor and puts himself in the student's place, reshaping "the inner parts of his mind" in the image of his beloved. Abelard would develop a Trinitarian analogy of sealing in his *Theologia "Scholarium,"* where the bronze seal matrix represents the Father, the carved image the Son, and the act of impressing it on wax, the Holy Spirit.[21]

The two lovers have metaphorically exchanged souls. In no. 15 the Man called the Woman "my soul" so now he laments, in a playful syllogism, that she has forgotten her own soul. But that is not really possible because of the lovers' coinherence. The Man is not only "with" his beloved but "in" her, an image he will develop further in no. 22. It would be a mistake to treat such language as mere amorous fluff. It is metaphysics and, on one level, seriously meant.

His seal, firmly impressed (*Signaculo suo . . . artius impresso*): Song 8:6 (*Pone me ut signaculum super cor tuum*)

Express likeness of that seal (*signaculi expressa similitudo*): Ezekiel 28:12 (*Tu signacu-
	lum similitudinis*)
Our common good . . . without difference (*res communis indifferenter*): cf. no. 24
I am wholly with you (*Totus tecum sum*): Regensburg Songs, no. 34.15 (*Totus eram
	tecum, sperabam te quoque mecum*)

17 (**Man**)

To the inexhaustible vessel of all his sweetness, from her most beloved.
Ignoring the light of heaven, may I gaze without ceasing on you alone.

As day was verging upon night, I could contain myself no longer but
seized unasked on the duty of greeting you—a thing you have long
delayed. Farewell. Know that without your welfare, I have neither
health nor life.

COMMENT

She has still not replied and his concern is growing.

18 (**Woman**)

An equal to an equal, to a blushing rose beneath the unwithered
whiteness of lilies: I send what a lover desires for a lover. Even in
wintertime, my breast is ablaze with the fervor of love. What more? I
would write more to you, but a few words will instruct a wise man.
Farewell, my heart and body and all my love.

COMMENT

Responding at last, the Woman's tone is reassuring. She sounds a new note by writing as "an equal to an equal" (*par pari*), offering as her gift "what[ever] a lover desires for a lover." When she addresses the Man as teacher, she feels far from equal. But equality was central to the classical ideal of friendship, which from now on she increasingly adopts as her preferred account of their relationship. Classical friendship, of course, was construed as a relationship between men. In extending it to a heterosexual love affair, the Woman makes a significant contribution to the twelfth century's language of love.[22] Only here and in similar greetings (*amans amanti*, nos. 48 and 84; *dilecta dilecto*, no. 62; *fidelis fideli*, no. 100) does she refer to herself first, as equals were rhetorically entitled to do.[23]

As in many troubadour songs, nature's winter is belied by the lovers' sense of an eternal springtime, bright with flowers.[24] In liturgical symbolism, roses represent martyrdom and lilies, virginity.[25] By extension, they stand for the virtues of charity and chastity. The only prior use of *immarcidus* (unwithered)—a rare and rarified term—refers to saints' crowns in paradise.[26]

A blushing rose . . . whiteness of lilies (*rubenti rose . . . liliorum candore*): Ruricius of
　　Limoges, *Epistulae* 1.11 (*ruborem rosarum, liliorum candorem*)
What a lover desires for a lover (*quidquid amans amanti*): Tegernsee letter 6 (*quidquid amor amori*)
A few words will instruct a wise man (*sapientem pauca monebunt*): proverbial;[27] cf.
　　Plautus, *Persa* 729, and Terence, *Phormio* 541 (*dictum sapienti sat est*)

❧

19 (**Man**)

Few indeed are your words, but I have made them many by rereading them often. I weigh not how much you say, but how fertile is the heart from which you say it. Farewell, sweetheart.

❧

A quick response to say how he cherishes even the Woman's briefest messages.

❧

20 (**Man**)

Starlight patterns the sky, the moon silvers the night,
But the star that ought to guide me is growing dim.
Now if my star should rise and put the dark to flight,
My mind will know no more the darkness of woe.
You are my Lucifer that ought to banish night.
My day is night without you; with you, night is resplendent day.

Farewell, my star, whose splendor never wanes. Farewell, my supreme
hope, in whom alone I take pleasure, whom I need never recall to mind
because I never forget. Farewell.

❧

COMMENT

Another long silence seems to have stretched between the last two letters, and
the Man is worried now. His hexameters address the beloved as his *Lucifer* or
morning star—not the devil but Venus. Alas, that star is growing dim (*sydus
hebet*) because she has not written for so long.

Carmina burana 169, "Hebet sidus," develops the same theme and has long
been ascribed to Abelard, though without certain proof. Its poet calls his lady
someone *cuius nomen a Phebea / luce renitet*: "her name brightly reflects the
light of Phoebus," the sun.[28] Several scholars have endorsed Abelard as its author
because the name *Helois[a]* is a concealed anagram for *Helios*.[29] In these *Epistolae* the Man calls the Woman his sun in nos. 22, 80, 87, 96, and 108, though the
image is hardly rare.

This poem is composed in leonine hexameters, but "Hebet sidus" is a *rith-
mus* in stanzaic form, beginning "Hebet sidus leti visus / cordis nubilo, / tepet
oris mei risus / carens iubilo." (The star of my cheerful gaze grows dim as my

heart clouds over; the smile on my lips is lukewarm, lacking joy.) The singer worships and longs for his beloved, who wastes away in his absence as her youthful bloom withers. Fifty years ago, Peter Dronke argued that "Hebet sidus" could have been written after the lovers' secret marriage when Abelard had placed Heloise at Argenteuil, disguised but not vowed as a nun, to protect her from Fulbert's wrath.[30] If Abelard's authorship of both poems were accepted, the rather ordinary verses in no. 20 might be read as a rough sketch for the later, more sophisticated lyric.

Starlight patterns the sky (*stella polum variat*): cf. Hildebert of Lavardin, *Historia de Mahumete* 16.1304–5 (*variatum / Sicut nocturnum lucida stella polum*, PL 171: 1364d)

The star . . . is growing dim (*sydus hebet*): Lucan, *De bello civili* (*Pharsalia*) 1.662 (*sidus hebet*); *Carmina burana* 169, "Hebet sidus"

Ought to guide (*conducere debet*): Baudri of Bourgueil, *Carmina* 154.669 (*debet conducere*)

Put the dark to flight (*tenebris . . . fugatis*): Ovid, *Metamorphoses* 2.144 (*tenebris . . . fugatis*)

Lucifer: cf. 2 Peter 1:19; Ovid, *Metamorphoses* 2.723

Banish night (*noctem pellere*): Ovid, *Fasti* 6.729–30 (*noctem / pellit*)

In whom . . . I take pleasure (*michi conplaceo*): Matthew 3:17 (*mihi complacui*)

21 (**Woman**)

To her beloved, special from her own experience: the Being that Is / may he be what he is.

When my mind is occupied with many affairs, it fails me, smitten by the sharp hook of love.
[. . .]
Just as fire is unquenchable and nothing can conquer it except water, its naturally powerful antidote, so my love is incurable by any means; it is treatable by you alone. Knowing no gift by which I can enrich you, my mind is troubled. O glory of youth, companion of poets, how lovely you are in form, but nobler still in feeling! Present, you are my joy;

your absence is grief to me. My love for you is equivalent either way. Farewell.

COMMENT

Preoccupied though she is, the Woman writes passionately as ever in her studied prose. It is hard to interpret her enigmatic greeting, *speciali et ex ipsius experimento rei*. She may mean that her beloved is special to her not merely by reputation, as he had once been, but "from experience of the thing itself," the reality of their relationship. The lapidary wish that follows, *esse quod est*, is ambiguous enough to require a double translation. If we construe *esse* as a noun, the Woman is wishing that her beloved might attain to the possession of God, "the Being that Is" (Exodus 3:14). This was a technical term in Trinitarian theology.[31] But if *esse* is a verb, she wishes him to remain in his present state of perfection: "May he be what he is."[32] The double meaning perhaps alludes to a past philosophical discussion. This play on words recalls an even more elaborate one in Tegernsee letter 8, where the woman writes, "I confess that I would call it true being if I could be continually in your presence.... Make it possible, therefore, for me to apprehend true being, which proceeds from nowhere else than your being—your being with me."[33]

Crossing into the Man's Ovidian territory, the Woman evokes the topos of lovesickness. Her closing employs the technical term *equipolenter* (equivalently), which is recondite enough to give us a clue about her education. The term came into use in the late eleventh century, making its way from the advanced study of *grammatica* into exegesis. Introduced in the commentaries of Bruno the Carthusian (d. 1101), who was *magister* at the cathedral school of Reims from ca. 1060 until 1079, the term was used frequently by a few other late eleventh and early twelfth-century exegetes, such as Lanfranc of Canterbury (d. 1089) and pseudo-Bede (a German monk of the late eleventh century).[34] It is not used by Abelard in any extant work and occurs only once in the apologia of his student Berengar. The Woman could have picked it up during her monastic studies, whether of classical poets or the Psalter. It is typical of her to toss such an erudite term into a love letter.

To her beloved, special (*Dilecto suo speciali*): cf. Heloise, letter 6.1: *Suo specialiter sua singulariter* (To him who is specially hers, from her who is singularly his)
Hook of love (*dilectionis hamo*): cf. Isidore, *Etymologiae* 10.4 (*amicus ab hamo ... caritatis*, PL 82: 367c)

Fire . . . unquenchable (*ignis inextinguibilis*): Matthew 3:12 (*igni inextinguibili*); Mark
    9:42 (*ignem inextinguibilem*)
Treatable by you alone (*tibi . . . soli est medicabilis*): cf. Ovid, *Heroïdes* 5.149 (*amor non
    est medicabilis herbis*); Regensburg Songs, no. 3.13 (*non est medicabilis herbis*);
    Heloise, letter 2.9: "you who alone are the cause of my sorrow, be alone in
    granting me the grace of consolation. You alone indeed have the power to make
    me sad, to bring me joy or comfort."
My mind is troubled (*mens mea anxiatur*): cf. Psalm 60:3 (*anxiaretur cor meum*)

❧

22 (Man)

To his gem, more gracious and luminous than the present light, from
him who without you is wrapped in thick darkness. What else should I
wish than for you to exult without end in your natural brilliance?

Scientists often say the moon cannot shine without the sun. So when it
is deprived of that light, losing all benefit of the sun's warmth and
splendor, it shows mortals a dim and pallid sphere. This is plainly a
metaphor for you and me. For you are my sun, always inflaming and
illumining me with the joyous splendor of your countenance. I have no
light except yours; without you I am dull, obscure, weakened, and
dead. And to speak truly, what you do for me is greater than what the
sun does for the lunar orb, for the moon grows darker as it approaches
the sun. As for me, the closer I come to you and the nearer I am, the
more I burn. I am so inflamed that (as you have often noticed), when I
am with you I become altogether fire. I burn down to the marrow of
my bones.

What then shall I repay to match your countless acts of kindness?
Nothing, to be sure, for you transcend your sweetest words in the
abundance of your deeds. You surpass them in the very performance
of love, so that you seem to me poorer in words than in deeds. Among
the other countless gifts you possess beyond others, you have this
outstanding quality too: you do more for your friend than you say,

being poor in words but rich in deeds. This is all the more to your glory because it is harder to act than to speak.

[. . .]

You are immortally buried in my heart; from this tomb you shall never emerge while I live. There you lie down, there you rest. Until sleep comes you are with me; in sleep you do not forsake me; after sleep I see you as soon as I open my eyes, before the light of heaven itself. To others I direct my words, to you my intention. Often I stumble in speech because my thoughts are elsewhere. Who then could deny that you are truly buried within me?

[. . .]

Envious time threatens our love, yet you delay as if we had leisure. Farewell.

COMMENT

In one of his most eloquent letters, the Man develops an astronomical conceit: as the moon can shine only with the reflected light of the sun, so he takes light and warmth only from his beloved. The metaphor of sun and moon was often used for Christ and the church.[35] As with his seal metaphor in no. 16, the Man claims for himself the lesser or passive role. But the conceit soon takes on sexual overtones: he is aflame with love right down to the marrow, echoing Ovid and his initial seduction poem (no. 113). Without his beloved, he says he is "weakened" (*enervis*), a word that can also mean "limp, unmanned." The sexual invitation becomes clearer in the last sentence, where the Man protests that the Woman "delay[s] as if [they] had leisure," despite the threat posed by "envious time." This need not refer to any danger beyond the timeless motif of carpe diem: "Had we but world enough, and time, / This coyness, Lady, were no crime."[36]

The Man expresses gratitude for the Woman's favors, but de Vepria has excised any specific details that would have fleshed out this praise. Alluding to the theme of words and deeds broached in no. 12, he implies that most lovers fall short of their extravagant promises, while his beloved does even more than she promises. The word "friend" (*amicus*) can also mean "boyfriend"; the lovers in the Song of Songs call each other *amicus* and *amica*. This ambiguous term allows the Man and

Woman to discuss the duties of friendship, an ethical topic, with erotic undercurrents.

The third paragraph deploys a remarkable metaphor: the Woman is "immortally buried" in the "tomb" of her lover's heart. This is a memorable twist on the more common idea that the lover finds a home in the heart of the beloved.[37] Behind the gothic imagery lurks the same metaphysical idea we encountered in no. 16: "I am wholly with you, and to speak more truly, I am wholly in you." Human persons are not self-contained, but porous: lovers mingle selves to the point of coinherence.[38] Each abides in the other just as Jesus claims, in the fourth Gospel, that "I am in the Father and the Father in me" (John 14:11). The Man's philosophical definition of love (no. 24) will attempt to explain how this happens. In the meantime, its practical consequence is to impede his teaching: because he directs his words to others but his intention to the beloved alone, he "often stumble[s] in speech." Abelard likewise confesses a drastic decline in the quality of his lectures when he became infatuated with Heloise.

The moon cannot shine without the sun (*luna nisi a sole non luceat*): Bede, *De natura rerum* 20 (*Lunam . . . a sole illustratam*, PL 90: 236a); echoed in Rabanus Maurus, *Liber de computo* 45 (PL 107: 693d)

The moon grows darker as it approaches the sun (*luna, quo soli propior fit, plus obscuratur*): gloss on Bede, *De natura rerum* 20 (*quando [luna soli] appropinquat . . ., obscuratur*, PL 90: 236b)

The nearer I am, the more I burn (*quo tibi vicinior sum, plus ardeo*): cf. Ovid, *Heroïdes* 18.177 (*quo propius nunc es, flamma propiore calesco*)

I become altogether fire (*totus in ignem transeam*): cf. Abelard, *Historia calamitatum* 17 (*in . . . amorem totus inflamatus*)

I burn down to the marrow (*totus medullitus urar*): cf. no. 113

You seem to me poorer in words than in deeds (*pauperior michi in verbis quam in factis videaris*): cf. Heloise, letter 2.15: "It is no use my hoping for generosity in deeds if you are grudging in words."

There you lie down (*ibi cubas*): Song 1:6 (*ubi cubes*)

In sleep you do not forsake me (*in somno me non deseris*): cf. Regensburg Songs, no. 3.6 (*O dum dormito, tua se presentat imago*); Tegernsee letter 5 (*dormiendo quasi vigilando, / non cesso tibi bona optando*)

I stumble in speech (*in verbis cado*): cf. Horace, *Carmina* 4.1.36 (*inter verba cadit lingua*)

My thoughts are elsewhere (*cogitatio mea . . . extranea est*): cf. Abelard, *Historia calamitatum* 19: "As my interest and concentration flagged, my lectures lacked all inspiration . . .; I could do no more than repeat what had been said long ago, and when inspiration did come to me, it was for writing love songs, not the secrets of philosophy."

Envious time (*Invidum . . . tempus*): cf. Horace, *Carmina* 1.11.7–8 (*invida / aetas*)

ॐ

23 (**Woman**)

To the sweetest support of her soul, deeply rooted in her charity, from the one in whose love you are firmly grounded, in whose honeyed passion you are truly founded: I send what is far from anger and hate.

Although I wished to reply to you, the greatness of the task—unequal to my strength—threw me back. I had the will but not the power; I began and faltered, I struggled and fell, my shoulders crushed by the burden. The fervent affection of my mind desired, but the defection of my arid talent refused. I endured the debates and quarrelsome urgings of these two and, having weighed the arguments of each, could not decide to which I should yield. For my mind's affection said:

Affect: "What are you doing, you ingrate? How long will you keep me waiting in this long and surely undeserved silence? Are you not stirred by the generous kindness, the kind generosity of your beloved? Compose a letter full of gratitude, offer the thanks you owe to his abundant goodness! For a favor does not seem welcome or pleasing unless it is repaid with ample thanks."

I thought I should heed these arguments and indeed wished to heed them. But my dry, meager talent resisted, chastising what I had rashly begun with the sharp scourge of reproach, saying:

Defect: "Where are you rushing, you weak, foolish woman? Where is the rash intention of your hasty mind driving you? Will you begin to speak of great things with rude, uncircumcised lips? For you are inadequate to such a magnificent theme. Indeed, whoever takes it upon himself to praise something ought to divide the subject into parts, weigh the qualities of each with the utmost care, and celebrate each according to its worth with suitable praise. Otherwise he insults what he meant to praise, diminishing its beauty with his overwrought account. But where should *you* obtain enough literary skill to speak of the sublime as it deserves? Attend to yourself and to what you wish to do. Manifold and great are the favors for which you intend to give thanks in your letter. Why do you burn with a swarm of tempestuous thoughts? Look at your icy, brutish heart; it lacks the salt of knowledge and swells only with the thick vapor of idleness. Draw in the sails of your boldness, the little boat in which you mean to cross the imperious sea—to be swiftly drowned unless you take heed!"

Oscillating thus between persuasion and dissuasion, I have until now deferred the thanksgiving I owe, obeying the advice of my talent which blushes at its own frailty. Let the excellence of that divine gentleness which abounds in you impute no fault to me, I pray. But since you are the son of true sweetness, let the virtue of your accustomed mildness abound the more toward me. I know indeed, and I confess, that from the riches of your philosophy, the most copious joy has flowed and still flows to me. But—if I may speak without offense—it is still less than enough to make me perfectly blessed in this respect. For I often come with parched throat, desiring to be refreshed with the sweet nectar of your mouth and to drink thirstily of the riches poured out in your heart. What need is there for more words? I swear, with God as my witness, there is no one who lives or breathes in this world whom I would rather love than you. [. . .]
May this farewell, my beloved, sweetly pierce the very marrow of your bones.

COMMENT

Brides who procrastinate with their thank-you notes might take heed to this letter, for no woman ever apologized more fulsomely for delay. The Woman's literary task—thanking her lover for his "manifold and great" favors—overwhelms her with the fear of failure; or so at least she pretends. She converts her struggle into an allegorical debate, with Affect (*affectus*) urging her to express her fervent gratitude, while Defect (*defectus*) protests that her meager talent is unequal to the task. Defect reminds her of the rules of rhetoric by warning that, if she fails, her intended praise will backfire. Having exemplified the rhetorical modes of *persuasio* and *dissuasio*, she next cites appropriate canons for the rhetoric of praise (*laudativum*), a subset of epideictic.[39] Rounded out with the classical metaphor of a literary work as a sea voyage, the letter is an example par excellence of the ironic humility topos. By exaggerating and stylizing her fear of failure, the Woman converts her protestation of weakness into a bravura display of literary skill and learning.

Her salutation plays on St. Paul's letter to the Ephesians, where he asks the community to be "rooted and grounded in love." For good measure she mentions three different types of love: charity (*caritas*), appreciative personal love (*dilectio*), and passionate desire (*amor*), avowing that she possesses all three. These dimensions of love are perhaps meant to correspond to the Apostle's "length and breadth and height and depth." The close of the letter returns to Pauline language: the Woman hopes her lover's mercy will abound the more toward her imagined fault. For those who take him as Abelard, it may come as a surprise that she ascribes to him the virtues of gentleness (*suavitas*) and mildness (*mansuetudo*). The Man describes his own character quite differently as rash and impulsive.[40]

Eroticism also has its place. Craving still more instruction in philosophy, the Woman adds a knowing double entendre: "I often come with parched throat, desiring to be refreshed with the sweet nectar of your mouth and to drink thirstily of the riches poured out in your heart." Abelard speaks of such honeyed teaching in *Historia calamitatum* 18: "with our books open before us, more words of love than of our reading passed between us, and more kissing than ideas."

Deeply rooted . . . firmly grounded (*in eius caritatis radice plantato . . . in cuius dilectione firmiter es constitutus*): Ephesians 3:17 (*in charitate radicati et fundati*)

Unequal to my strength (*impar viribus meis*): Ovid, *Metamorphoses* 5.610 (*viribus inpar*)

Speak of great things (*grandia loqui*): Daniel 7:20 (*loquens grandia*)

Uncircumcised lips (*incircumcisis labiis*): Exodus 6:12, 6:30 (*incircumcisus labiis*)

Otherwise he insults what he meant to praise: The text of this clause is corrupt. The passage reads "Alioquin rei laudande iniuriam facit, qui speciosa eius narracione

eleganciam enormi narracione deterit." Either *speciosa eius narracione* (his
showy account) or *enormi narracione* (too long an account) was probably meant
as a marginal correction to its alternative. When Johannes de Vepria inserted
the extra words into the text, the clause became redundant.[41] My translation
attempts to combine the two senses.

A swarm of tempestuous thoughts (*cogitacionum procellis*): Gregory I, *Regula pastoralis*
  1.9 (*cogitationum procellis*, PL 77: 22c)

Your . . . heart . . . lacks the salt of knowledge (*pectus tuum . . . carens sale sciencie*): cf.
  Gregory of Tours, *Historia Francorum* 5.11 (*salem scientiae vestris pectoribus
  trado*, PL 71: 326a)

Draw in the sails (*Contrahe . . . vela*): Ovid, *Ex Ponto* 1.8.72, and *Tristia* 3.4.32
  (*contrahe vela*); Horace, *Carmina* 2.10.23–24 (*contrahes . . . / vela*)

To cross the imperious sea (*imperiosum pelagus tranare*): Baudri of Bourgueil, *Carmina*
  193.64 (*tranas pelagus*); Horace, *Carmina* 1.14.8–9 (*imperiosius / aequor*)

Abound the more (*magis abundet*): 1 Thessalonians 4:1, 4:10 (*abundetis magis*)

With parched throat (*aridis faucibus*): Virgil, *Aeneid* 2.358 (*faucibus . . . siccis*)

ℐ❧

24 (Man)

To a soul brighter and dearer to me than anything earth has borne,
from the flesh inspired and quickened by that soul: I send what I owe
the one through whom I breathe and move.

The abundant, yet insufficient richness of your letter gives me the
clearest proof of two things, namely your surpassing fidelity and love. As
the saying goes, "From the abundance of the heart, the mouth speaks."
[. . .]
I receive your letters so greedily that they always seem brief to me, for
they both satisfy and rekindle my desire. I am like a man suffering
with fever: the more a drink refreshes him, the hotter he burns. I swear
to God that, when I gaze on them more attentively in a new way, I am
moved in a new way, for my very mind is shaken with glad trembling
and my body is transformed, renewed in bearing and gesture. Such
letters deserve praise because they impel the hearer's understanding to
go wherever they wish.

You often ask me what love is, my sweet soul, and I cannot excuse myself through ignorance, as if I had been consulted about some unknown thing. For love itself has subjected me to its command so completely that it seems not to be external, but something most familiar and intimate, even visceral. Love, then, is a certain power of the soul, neither existing through itself nor self-contained, but always pouring itself into another with a kind of appetite and desire, willing to become identical with the other so that, from two different wills, one single thing may be produced without difference.

[. . .]

Know that, while love may be a universal thing, it has nonetheless confined itself in such narrow space that, as I boldly affirm, it reigns in us alone—it has established its home in me and in you. For the two of us have a complete, sincere, and carefully tended love. Nothing is sweet or restful to one of us unless it profits both alike; we affirm and deny the same things, we have the same views about everything. This can easily be proven, for you often anticipate my thoughts: what I intend to write, you write first, and if I remember well, you have said the same about yourself.

Farewell—and gaze on me as I do on you with unwearied love.

COMMENT

In this important letter, the Man offers a philosophical definition of love at the Woman's request. She will reply with her own reflections on that theme.

He begins with another telling metaphor to express his utter dependence on the Woman. He has already said that if she is the seal, his mind is the soft wax impressed by it (no. 16); if she is the sun, he is the reflecting moon (no. 22). Finally, if she is the soul, he is the flesh it animates. Once again he reverses a familiar gendered image to put his beloved in the superior role. More often, the male was compared to soul or spirit, the female to flesh or body.[42] Here she is not just a figure of Soul, but his own soul, the shaping and quickening form by which he lives. Hence he links her with God, "the one through whom I breathe and move," appropriating a famous passage from St. Paul's sermon on the Areopagus: "in him we live and move and have our being" (Acts 17:28).

Because the Woman had lamented her supposed lack of rhetorical skill (no. 23), the Man takes pains to compliment her, saying that her letters "impel the hearer's understanding to go wherever they wish." That is exactly what effective rhetoric ought to do. But the body of the letter introduces a new theme, the definition of love. This task should be easy, the Man believes, for he is wholly possessed by that passion.

Defining love was a serious philosophical question.[43] The Man's succinct, precise definition can be compared with those of two illustrious contemporaries, both of whom took Augustine as their point of departure. William of Saint-Thierry, in his treatise *On the Nature and Dignity of Love* (early 1120s), defined it as "a power of the soul, leading her by a kind of natural gravity to her place or destination."[44] Just as water naturally tends downward and fire upward, the human soul can be drawn either way by its love. This power is rooted in nature itself, but since nature is corrupt, love now has to be taught. It is indeed "the art of arts." William explicitly contrasts the teaching of God and Nature with that of Ovid, the master of "foul, carnal love," presenting himself as an anti-Ovid.[45] Hugh of Saint-Victor, in his sermon *On the Substance of Love*, defines it as "the delight of somebody's heart toward something on account of something. It is desire in seeking, and delight in thoroughly enjoying."[46] Both definitions draw attention to the choice of object. In contrast, the Man offers a more metaphysical account. Although love is an innate power of the soul, it does not exist through itself (*non per se existens*), nor is it self-contained (*nec seipsa contenta*). The Man affirms the desiring, appetitive nature of love, as acknowledged by Hugh and William, but places more emphasis on its unitive character. Love is "always pouring itself into another" (*semper . . . se in alterum transfundens*), wishing to unite with that other so as to become "the same" or "identical" (*cum altero idem effici volens*). Its effect is to unite two different wills (*duabus diversis voluntatibus*) so as to produce "one single thing . . . without difference" (*unum quid indifferenter*). The *unum quid* is neuter—not a single *will* (which would require the feminine), but a new creation, neither male nor female.

Love is a universal thing (*res universalis*), the Man asserts, which exists within two lovers without difference. This formulation is reminiscent of Abelard's early position on universals, hashed out during a celebrated conflict with William of Champeaux, his former teacher and rival in the Paris schools. Abelard asserts in *Historia calamitatum* 6 that his arguments compelled William to "correct" his previous view, namely that if the same universal is present in several individuals, they must "differ only in the quantity of their accidents," being in essence (*essentialiter*) the same. After Abelard "made him amend, or rather abandon" that opinion, William taught that a shared universal makes two individuals the same "not in essence but in non-difference" (*non essentialiter sed indifferenter*), just as this letter affirms about love. The Man's formulation in no. 16 is similar. According to Constant Mews, Abelard at this early period still spoke of universals as "things" (*res*), a usage he would later forcefully reject—so the question of whether he could have defined love this way circa 1115–17 depends, in part, on the conjectural dating of his early logical works.[47] Incidentally, the Man adds the words *res universalis* to a quotation from Cicero, where the Roman philosopher noted that friendship has the power to concentrate all the love (*caritas*) that theoretically belongs to the whole human race so that it unites just two persons, or a small number.[48] In letter 24 the Man ascribes this power not to *amicitia* or *caritas* but to *amor*, erotic love. Abelard would add the same passage from Cicero to his *Sic et non* when he revised that textbook in the 1120s or 1130s. It is the only passage from the *Laelius* to be included in the whole vast compendium.[49]

Of course the idea that lovers are (or should be) of one mind need not be expressed in philosophical terms. We find a parallel in the Regensburg Songs:

> Sto, stas, sic stamus, mutuo sic nos adamamus
> Unum si velle sit nobis, sit quoque nolle. (no. 34.18–19)

> I stand, you stand, so we stand mutually in love
> If we have but one will, be it yea or nay.

The criterion of a single will (*idem velle atque idem nolle*) derives from Sallust, whose contribution tends to be overlooked because it converges with Cicero's more famous definition of friendship as "agreement in all things human and divine."[50] In a lighter tone, the Man pretends that he and his beloved alone embody true love because they possess such a common will; their thoughts and feelings about everything are just the same. This is of course a wildly optimistic assessment—which, as they and others have learned before and since, could not withstand the test of time.

Twenty years later, in his *Theologia "Scholarium"*—a work of the 1130s, contemporary with his monastic letters to Heloise—Abelard would define love rather differently. "Charity," he there maintains, "is honorable love [*amor honestus*], that is, love directed toward the appropriate end. . . . Love [*amor*] is good will toward another for the other's own sake, by which we desire that [the beloved] should be or live in that state that we believe it is good for him to be in."[51] Here the element of eros, or unitive desire, is absent.

Through whom I breathe and move (*per quem spiro et moveor*): Acts 17:28 (*in ipso . . . vivimus et movemur et sumus*)

From the abundance of the heart . . . (*Ex abundancia cordis os loquitur*): Matthew 12:34, Luke 6:45 (*Ex abundantia . . . cordis os loquitur*). Heloise quotes the same verse at the beginning of letter 6.1.

A man suffering with fever (*in ardore laborantis*): or "toiling in the heat of the day"

Glad trembling (*leto horrore*): Statius, *Thebaid* 1.493–94 (*laetusque . . . / horror*); no. 108

They impel . . . to go wherever they wish (*sensum audientis quocumque volunt impellunt*): Cicero, *De oratore* 1.30 (*voluntates impellere quo velit*)

One single thing may be produced without difference (*unum quid indifferenter efficiatur*): Cicero, *Laelius* 81 (*ut efficiat . . . unum ex duobus*); cf. Abelard, *Historia calamitatum* 6

A universal thing . . . confined . . . in such narrow space (*res universalis . . . tamen in angustum contractus est*): Cicero, *Laelius* 20 (*contracta res est et adducta in angustum*); Abelard, *Sic et non* 138.21

We affirm and deny the same things (*eque annuimus, eque negamus*): cf. Sallust, *De coniuratione Catilinae* 20.4 (*idem velle atque idem nolle*)

You often anticipate my thoughts (*tu sepe meas cogitaciones anticipas*): Baudri of Bourgueil, *Carmina* 90.13–14 (*Dum loquimur, persepe fuit quod cogitat alter / Alterius sermo quatenus anticipet*)

25 (**Woman**)

To her incomparable treasure, more delightful than all the world's delights: I wish bliss without end and health without ceasing.

What love is, what it can do—I too have been intuitively reflecting on this. Having perceived the likeness of our character and concerns—a thing that especially consolidates friendships and reconciles friends—I would repay you in exchange by loving and obeying you in all things.

[. . .]

If our love failed on such trivial provocation, it was never true love. The plain, tender words that we have exchanged thus far were not true, but a mere simulation of love. For once love has affixed its sting in a person, it does not easily depart. You know, my heart's beloved, that the duties of true love are rightly fulfilled only when they are owed without ceasing, so that we do everything in our strength for the beloved, yet do not cease to will beyond our strength.

This debt of true love, therefore, I will strive to discharge—though, alas, I cannot pay it in full. But if my meager talent does not suffice for the task of wishing you well, at least let my unfailing will be worth something to you. For know this, my beloved, and know it well: from the time your love laid claim to the inn (or rather hovel) of my heart, it has remained always welcome, growing more delightful day by day. It has not happened, as it so often does, that constant presence breeds familiarity, familiarity confidence, confidence negligence, and negligence disdain. You began to desire me with great zeal at the time our friendship was born, but you have striven with still greater desire that our love might increase and endure. Hence my mood shifts in accord with your affairs, so that I count your joy as my profit and your adversity as my bitterest defeat.

Fulfilling what you have begun does not seem to me the same as increasing what you have achieved. For in one case, what was lacking is added, and in the other, what was already perfect is crowned with glory. And although we may show pure charity to everyone, yet we do not love all persons equally, so what is general for all becomes special for some. It is one thing to sit at a prince's table, another to be among his counselors; and it means more to be drawn to his love than to be invited to his council. So I owe you fewer thanks if you do not reject me than if you welcome me with open arms. I will speak simply to your clear mind and purest heart. It is no great thing if I love you; rather, it would be the worst possible thing if I should ever forget you. So, my dear, do not make yourself scarce to such a faithful friend! Until now I have somehow been able to bear it, but now—stirred by the singing of birds and the fresh foliage of the woods—as long as I lack your presence, I languish for your love. I would surely rejoice in all these pleasures, if only I could enjoy your company and conversation at will!

As I wish for you, so may God do for me. Farewell.

COMMENT

The Woman begins her meditation by linking love (*amor*) with friendship (*amicicia*), a good classical move. But then she makes two significant, surprising assertions. First, she promises to obey her lover in all things, although he has not (so far as we know) asked this of her.[52] Second, she defines true love as a state of permanent, unpayable debt, for the duties or services of true love (*veri amoris officia*) "are rightly fulfilled only when they are owed [*debentur*] without ceasing." This idea of love as endless debt (*vere dilectionis debitum*) is neither classical nor biblical. On the contrary, believers ask God in the Lord's Prayer to "forgive us our debts as we also have forgiven our debtors" (Matthew 6:12), and Jesus tells several parables about the duty to forgive debt. Rather, the notion seems to be the Woman's own contribution to ethical thought.

Her proximate source may be Anselm's *Cur Deus Homo* (Why God became man, ca. 1094–98), the era's most original treatise on the atonement.[53] Anselm there asserts that man owes God a debt of honor, which is obedience, but through sin he has become an incorrigible debtor. His debt cannot be paid because it is infinite, like God himself, while man is only finite. Any gifts that a sinner might offer God are God's own gifts in the first place, nor can finite man offer anything equal to the infinity of God's offended honor. From this plight the theologian deduces the necessity for redemption by a God-man, who both owes the debt as man and is able to pay it as God. It is characteristic of the Woman to set her lover in the place of God; her sense of unpayable debt may be one consequence of such a displaced theology.

It would be hard to find another writer who insists with such force, in a secular context, on obedience and debt as vital components of love. Yet both emphases recur in the letters of Heloise.[54] She prides herself on her unstinting obedience to Abelard, even against her will or her own better judgment. In letter 2.15–16, she claims that "I carried out everything for your sake and continue up to the present moment in complete obedience to you. . . . I have finally denied myself every pleasure in obedience to your will, kept nothing for myself except to prove that now, even more, I am yours." Similarly, in letter 4.14, she says of her monastic profession that "It was your command [*tua iussio*], not love of God, which hauled me into the religious life." She cites these proofs of obedience as a free expression of her love, not a duty of marriage—an institution she despised. Conversely, however, she insists on Abelard's overwhelming debt to her, responding to his *Historia calamitatum* with the remark that "you have done right by a friend and comrade, paying your debt [*debitum*] to friendship and companionship, but you bound yourself by a greater debt [*maiore debito*] to us who should properly be called . . . not companions but daughters. . . . How great the debt [*debito*] by which you have bound yourself to us needs neither proof nor witness" (letter 2.5). A bit later she adds, "While you spend so much on the stubborn, consider what you owe [*debeas*] to the obedient. . . . Apart from everything else, consider the close tie by which you have bound yourself to me, and repay the debt you owe [*quod debes*] a whole community of devoted women by discharging it the more devotedly to her who is yours alone" (letter 2.7). In closing she pleads once again, "Remember, I implore you, what I have done, and think how much you owe me" (*quanta debeas*, letter 2.16). The present letter seems almost uncannily to anticipate those pleas. Such a forceful emphasis on obedience and debt, most unusual in reflections on love, is one of the strongest pointers to Heloise as the Woman of these letters.

After a lacuna, the writer asks whether love can fail, only to affirm idealistically with St. Jerome that true love (or friendship) never ends. If it does, it was never true in the first place. Abelard would bring the same citation from Jerome into play in *Sic et non* 138, apropos of a theological debate over whether the saving virtue of *caritas*, once acquired, could ever be lost.[55] The Woman in her last paragraph distinguishes between *caritas*, as the universal benevolence owed to all, and personal love for one's friends (*dilectio*). The "special" character she ascribes to *dilectio* recalls the greeting of no. 21. Aelred of Rievaulx would make the same distinction between special friendship and universal charity in his dialogue *On Spiritual Friendship* (1160s).[56]

Since de Vepria finally gives us the (nearly) complete text of a substantial letter, we can observe how faithfully the Woman follows the precepts of the *ars dictaminis*, which asserts that a letter should have five parts. Her *salutatio* includes two of the three standard elements, a dative *inscriptio* designating the recipient ("to her incomparable treasure") and a wish clause in the accusative ("bliss without end and health without ceasing"). There follows a *captatio benevolentiae*, in which the writer seeks to earn the reader's goodwill by pointing out what they have in common ("the likeness of our character and concerns") and stressing her commitment to their relationship ("loving and obeying you in all things"). The substantial *narratio* or narrative must have begun by discussing some "trivial provocation" which had caused a quarrel, but it goes on describe the whole history of their relationship and the nature of love. This leads into a brief *petitio* or request ("do not make yourself scarce") and a still briefer *conclusio* or farewell. In her petition the Woman returns sharply to desire. Like the troubadours, she is stirred by the coming of spring to yearn even more painfully for her absent love.

Treasure . . . without ceasing (*thesauro . . . sine defectione*): Ecclesiasticus 30:23 (*thesaurus sine defectione*)

What love is: The syntax of this paragraph—a single sentence in the original—is not easy to parse. The text may be corrupt or the Woman may be using the figure of *anacoluthon*, in which the syntactic structure shifts in midsentence to make the reader pause and pay closer attention. I have used dashes to suggest the breathless quality of the prose.

Likeness of our character (*morum . . . similitudine*): Cicero, *De officiis* 1.56 (*morum similitudo bonorum*)

Consolidates friendships and reconciles friends (*contrahit amicicias et conciliat*): Cicero, *Laelius* 48 (*contrahat amicitiam*), 100 (*virtus . . . conciliat amicitias*)

Obeying you in all things (*tibi . . . in omnibus obedire*): Heloise, letters 2.15–16, 4.14

It was never true love (*verus amor non fuit*): Jerome, *Epistulae* 3.6 (*amicitia quae desinere potest, vera numquam fuit*)

Love has affixed its sting (*Amor . . . aculeum infigit*): cf. Ambrose, *De Joseph* 10.57 (*amoris aculei . . . corda compungunt*, PL 14: 664b)

The duties of true love . . . owed without ceasing (*veri amoris officia . . . sine intermissione debentur*): cf. 1 Corinthians 7:3 (the marriage debt); Heloise, letter 2.5, 2.7, 2.16

Constant presence breeds familiarity (*assiduitas familiaritatem . . . peperit*): Jerome, *Epistulae* 60.10 (*adsiduitas familiaritatem, familiaritas contemptum . . . fecerat*), 45.2 (*lectio adsiduitatem, adsiduitas familiaritatem, familiaritas fiduciam fecerat*)

What is general for all becomes special for some (*quod omnibus est generale, quibusdam efficitur speciale*): Baudri of Bourgueil, *Carmina* 200.77–78 (*Ergo patet liquido quoniam genus istud amoris / Non commune aliquid, sed spetiale sapit.*)

Welcome . . . with open arms (*obvia manu suscipias*): Jerome, *Epistulae* 49.1 (*obviis . . . manibus excipio*), 53.11 (*obviis te manibus excipiam*)

If I should ever forget you (*si unquam tui oblita fuero*): Psalm 136:5 (*Si oblitus fuero tui*)
I languish for your love (*amore tuo langueo*): Song 2:5, 5:8 (*amore langueo*); Tegernsee
    letter 6 (*de absentia tua / meus semper languet spiritus*)

꒜

26 (**Man**)

To his beloved, whom he does not yet know but longs to know more
intimately, from a young man who burns within himself to seek out the
knowledge of so great a good. May you overflow always with that fount
of goodness, inexhaustible and hidden, and be always refreshed by it.
[. . .]
How fertile with delight is your breast! How brightly you gleam with
inviolate beauty! O body brimful of freshness! O indescribable
fragrance of yours! Display what is secret, reveal what you keep
hidden! Let that whole fountain of your most abundant sweetness
overflow, let all your love release its riches upon me, conceal nothing at
all from your most devoted servant—for I think nothing has been
done as long as I see anything left undone. From hour to hour I am
bound to you more tightly, like a wood-burning fire that grows more
voracious the more fuel it consumes.
[. . .]
You shimmer immortally with perpetual light and inextinguishable
splendor. Farewell.

꒜

COMMENT

A frank sexual invitation. Stimulated by their philosophical exchange, if not by
"the singing of birds and the fresh foliage of the woods" (no. 25), the Man expresses still more passionate yearning. His salutation plays on a theological
motif, desire for knowledge of the *summum bonum*. But in this case, the body of
his beloved is that "great good" that he "longs to know more intimately," in the
sense that Adam knew his wife and she conceived (Genesis 4:1).

Fount of goodness, inexhaustible and hidden (*abstruso et inexhausto boni fonte*): cf.
    Song 4.12 (*fons signatus*); John 4:14 (*fons aquae salientis in vitam aeternam*)
Body brimful of freshness (*corpus succi plenissimum*): Terence, *Eunuchus* 318
    (*corpu'... suci plenum*)
I think nothing has been done ... undone (*nihil actum credo, dum aliquid restare
    video*): Lucan, *Pharsalia* 2.657 (*Nil actum credens cum quid superesset agendum*)
Like a wood-burning fire (*sicut ignis, qui ligna comburit*): Psalm 82:15 (*Sicut ignis qui
    comburit silvam*)
A ... fire that grows more voracious the more fuel it consumes (*ignis ... eo voracior, quo
    in alimentis est copiosior*): Ovid, *Metamorphoses* 8.837–39 (*utque rapax ignis non
    umquam alimenta recusat / ... quo copia maior / est data, ... voracior ipsa est*)

27 (**Woman**)

To her eye: the spirit of Bezalel, the strength of three locks of hair, the
beauty of the father of peace, the depth of Idida.

COMMENT

The Woman responds to this invitation with a brief, enigmatic greeting, which
gives no clue to what transpired between the lovers in person. She calls the Man
"her eye," perhaps because she sees the world through his eyes, or because he longs
to gaze on her without ceasing (no. 17). Her four wishes draw on arcane allusions to
the Old Testament. Bezalel was the chief artisan of the tabernacle, filled "with the
spirit of God, with wisdom and understanding and knowledge in every work"
(Exodus 31:3). The "three locks of hair" (seven in the Bible) denote Samson, the
legendary hero, whose strength depended on his uncut hair. The "father of peace"
must be Absalom, famed for his great beauty. Although Absalom was anything
but a man of peace (he rebelled against his father David and started a civil war), the
etymology of his name (*abba* plus *shalom*) can be interpreted as "father of peace."[57]
Finally, as Isidore of Seville explains, "Idida" was an alternate name for King Solomon, meaning "beloved and lovable to the Lord."[58] In exegetical code, then, the
Woman wishes her lover the blessings of artistic skill, strength, beauty, and

profound wisdom. Though she was being deliberately obscure, it was common to invoke biblical figures in odes and blessings. For instance, a Carolingian poem links three of the same characters : "Sis sapiens ut Salomon, / Fortissimus sicut Samson, / Pulcherrimus ut Absalon" (May you be wise as Solomon, mighty as Samson, peerless in beauty as Absalom).[59]

Sadly, two of these exempla are mentioned by Heloise in letter 4.10, where she sets herself in a long lineage of scriptural Bad Women in order to assume blame for Abelard's downfall. Samson was overcome by Delilah, who extorted his secret and betrayed him (Judges 16:4–21), and Solomon fell through the foreign women in his harem, who lured him into idolatry (1 Kings 11:1–8). Abelard had a special feeling for Samson, the subject of his fourth *Planctus*—a moving poem in which Israel laments its fallen hero.[60]

To her eye (*Oculo suo*): Plautus, *Curculio* 203 (*ocule mi*)
Spirit of Bezalel (*Bezelielis spiritum*): Exodus 31:2–3 (*Beseleel . . . implevi spiritu Dei, sapientia, et intelligentia et scientia*)
Strength of three locks of hair (*trium crinium fortitudinem*): cf. Judges 16:13, 19
Beauty (of Absalom): 2 Samuel 14:25 (*Absalom, vir . . . decorus nimis*)
Idida: Isidore of Seville, *Etymologiae* 7.6.65 (*Idida . . . dilectus et amabilis Domino*, PL 82: 279c)

❧

28 (**Man**)

To his beloved, who will be treasured in memory forever, I wish whatever leads to that being whose fullness knows no lack.

As for those who envy us, may they long have cause for envy and long pine away for our riches, seeing that they wish it so. To separate me from you, even if the sea itself should flow between us, can never be: I shall always love you, always bear you in mind. Do not be surprised if crooked jealousy looks askance on our friendship, so distinguished and so fitting—for if we were wretched, we could surely live with others as we pleased, attracting no envious attention. So let them gnaw, let them slander, let them backbite, let them stew in their own juices, let them turn our goods into their own bitterness. You, however, will still be my life, my spirit, my solace in anguish, and finally, my perfect joy. Farewell, you who make me fare well.

This is the first of several letters dealing with envy and jealous foes (cf. nos. 54, 69, 81, 85, 101)—a theme ubiquitous in the *Historia calamitatum*.[61] Reading between the lines, we might surmise that the consummation so forcefully urged in no. 26 has now taken place—but so has discovery, or at least the threat of it. Yet the Man defiantly faces down the couple's enemies, who vividly recall the *lauzengiers* of troubadour poetry—villains who specialize in slandering lovers and revealing secret affairs. Supremely confident and aglow with sexual triumph, the Man assures his beloved that jealousy will never be able to part them.

As in nos. 21 and 24, the greeting holds an intentional ambiguity. "That being whose fullness knows no lack" (*illud esse . . . cuius plenitudini nichil deficit*) could refer either to God or a state of perfect earthly bliss. The lovers' wordplay on *esse* evokes their philosophical studies.

Pine away for our riches (*nostris opimis rebus . . . marcescant*): Horace, *Epistulae* 1.2.57
    (*Invidus alterius macrescit rebus opimis*)
Let them backbite (*mordeant*): cf. Ovid, *Tristia* 4.10.123–24 (*Livor iniquo /. . . dente momordit*)

29 (**Woman**)

Having given up everything, I take refuge beneath your wings; I submit myself to your authority, resolutely following you in all things. I can scarcely speak these sad words. Farewell.

COMMENT

Has jealousy indeed parted the lovers? Unlike her beloved, the Woman feels not defiant but deeply sad. She speaks as one who has lost everything—beginning, one suspects, with her virginity. Hence her biblical allusion is telling: it evokes the story of Ruth, the Israelite heroine who sleeps (chastely or not) with her kinsman Boaz and ultimately marries him. At the same time she alludes to Ovid's *Tristia*, citing a verse on his wife's sadness when he went into exile.

As in no. 25, but more sorrowfully, the Woman again promises submission, hoping that the one who has led her into suffering will find a way to provide for her.

I take refuge beneath your wings (*sub alas tuas confugio*): Ruth 2:12 (*sub cuius confugisti alas*)

I can scarcely speak . . . Farewell (*Dicere vix possum . . . Vale*): Ovid, *Heroïdes* 5.52 (*vix sustinuit dicere lingua Vale*)

Sad words (*tristia verba*): Ovid, *Tristia* 1.3.80 (*tristia verba*)

❧

30 (**Man**)

May God be gracious to you, sweetheart. I am your servant, most ready for your commands. Farewell.

❧

COMMENT

What did the Woman expect? Far from taking charge of the new situation, the Man now assumes the posture of a courtly lover. It is he who will be the obedient servant, meekly awaiting *her* commands.

I am your servant (*ego servus tuus*): Psalm 115:16 (*ego servus tuus*)

31 (**Man**)

To his sweetheart, his sole remedy in every sickness: may you never experience trouble, never be tried by sickness.
[. . .]
Imagine how much your presence could have achieved if you had such power in your absence! Surely if I could have gazed just once on your delightful face, I would have felt no pain at all.
[. . .]
Let me know where my destiny lies, for it is wholly in your hands. Farewell, and never cease to fare well.

COMMENT

The crisis expressed in the previous letters is still unresolved. Evidently the lovers are now parted and the Man has been ill. Recovering, he assures the Woman of his abiding love and places his destiny (*fortuna*) in her hands, still expecting some command from her.

32 (**Woman**)

As you well know, no one is happier than I at your recovery. Believe me: the noonday sun rises for you, the choir of birds rejoices at your health! While you were sick, the very elements fell into disorder for your sake. Witness the weather, which has been dismal for some time, but now that it senses your recovery, it has changed to share your joy. Look—this little bit of snow has melted as all things return to life. The seasons will smile on them, and for us too, by the grace of God, there awaits our accustomed joy. Only be safe and sound, and all things shall be added to us.

COMMENT

A little late snow has melted, spring warmth has returned, the Man is restored to health—and the Woman's spirits brighten as she anticipates a joyful reunion.

Choir of birds (*concentus avium*): Virgil, *Georgics* 1.422 (*avium concentus*)
The very elements ... changed to share your joy (*elementa ... tibi congratu-lando ... mutata*): cf. Marbod of Rennes, *Carmina* 2.2.2–3 (*Et formam mentis mihi mutuor ex elementis; / Ipsi naturae congratulor*, PL 171: 1717a)
All things shall be added (*omnia adiciuntur*): Matthew 6:33, Luke 12:31 (*omnia adicientur*)

33 (**Man**)

Time to shake off laziness with the warmth of spring, and take up letter writing with new fervor! Unless you want to go first, I shall. Farewell, you who shine more brightly than the moon tonight and please me more than tomorrow's sunrise.

COMMENT

The Man has arrived at a short-term solution to the lovers' impasse. If they can no longer meet freely, they can at least renew their relationship through the ambitious letter writing that we last saw in nos. 22–26. In no. 72 the Man will even propose the idea of a competition in love and, implicitly, in writing. But as we shall see, his plan does not immediately work out.

More brightly than the moon (*luna . . . lucidior*): cf. Song 6:9 (*pulchra ut luna*)

❧

34 (**Woman**)

Farewell—and bear in mind that prudent delay is better than reckless haste. Choose a suitable time for our meeting and let me know. Farewell.

❧

COMMENT

In this hasty note, the Woman again anticipates the long-awaited meeting. But it now brings her as much anxiety as joy, for she fears that her lover's "reckless haste" will cause trouble. A storm is brewing.

❧

35 (**Man**)

To his chosen one from her beloved: may you walk with firm steps on the path of love we have entered.

I would have forgiven you easily, most beloved, even if you had seriously wronged me. He would be too hard a man whom your words, so soft and tender, could not soften! But now you have no need for pardon, for you have not sinned against me at all. Farewell.

❧

COMMENT

The lovers seem to have met and quarreled. This is the only point in the correspondence when the Woman, rather than the Man, seeks forgiveness—though her request does not survive. In any case, he says she has committed no fault. "Sin" is a word the Man rarely uses (nos. 35, 59, 61); the Woman never does.

❧

36 (**Man**)

To his reverend lady: her humble servant offers devoted service.

For this is the way I must address you now, no longer saying *tu* but *vos*, not "sweet" or "dear" but "my lady," for I am not so intimate as before, and you make yourself too much a stranger to me.

❧

COMMENT

Though the Man took no offense during their last quarrel, his partner is seriously upset. We come now to a sequence of eleven straight letters from the Man (nos. 35–44), broken by just one chilly poem from the Woman (no. 38b). She has apparently refused to see him or admit his messenger, prompting this address "to his reverend lady" as, for the first and only time, he uses the formal *vos* rather than the intimate *tu*.

❧

37 (**Man**)

To the only one he waits for, from him who waits with longing: may you be happy, but not wish to be happy without me.

I am your servant, and to you I direct my whole body and mind. When I do not see you, I think that I see no light. Have mercy on your beloved, who is languishing and almost dying, unless you help me soon.
[. . .]

Ask the messenger what I did after I finished writing this letter. At once I hurled myself impatiently onto the bed! Farewell.

༄

At his wits' end, the Man piles on three forms of the term for "expectant longing": *Unice expectacioni sue qui expectans expectat* (cf. no. 70). Again he proffers humble service; again he pleads that he cannot live without his beloved. The letter ends with an impetuous yet self-conscious gesture that is hard to take literally. Stephen Jaeger writes, "The gesture is that of a spoiled child, the attention he calls to it that of a vain and self-aware peacock."[62] For Peter von Moos, the "all too premeditated and artificially staged spontaneity" of this act proves the *Epistolae* to be a literary fiction.[63]

Who waits with longing (*qui expectans expectat*): Psalm 39:2 (*Exspectans exspectavi*)

༄

38a (**Man**)

I'm forced to pour my burning mind into words:
Fire gnaws at my mind and scorches my inmost heart.
As a man branded by the sun seeks hidden waters,
Panting for breath, I yearn to touch your breast—yourself.
Now I will end and close these words with a seal.

༄

Resorting to verse, the Man confides his frustration and remorse. This is the only time either of the pair mentions sealing a letter, presumably for the sake of privacy. Writers of modest rank rarely sealed their letters at this time, and wax tablets were never sealed.[64] But Abelard did own a personal seal. In a vicious letter written circa 1119, soon after his scandalous fall, his enemy Roscelin chided him for it: "It pertains to the crowning disgrace of this incomplete [castrated] man that, in the seal with which you sealed those stinking letters, you yourself designed an image showing two heads, one of a man, the other of a woman."[65]

To pour . . . into words (*pandere verbis*): Otloh of St. Emmeram, *De doctrina spirituali* 3 (*pandere verbo*, PL 146: 266b); Baudri of Bourgueil, *Carmina* 98.93 (*pandere uerba*)

Hidden waters (*latices*): Isidore of Seville defines *latex* as *liquor fontis . . . quod in venis terrae lateat*, *Etymologiae* 20.4 (PL 82: 489b).

38b (**Woman**)

Whether you will or no, I will be faithful to you at heart.
May the ruler of heaven here be our go-between;
May he be the friend of our faith, which consists in dual love.
These verses that I write to you, dearest, I offer
That you may see how I am faithful to you at heart.
For true Fidelity recalls past services,
But if these are subtracted, faith too is thrown to the winds.
So may whatever Fidelity loves always abound for us.
May God's gracious right hand protect you within and without.

COMMENT

In these lofty but distant verses, the Woman wistfully quotes her own greeting from no. 3, a letter written in happier times. Responding in the same metrical form the Man had used, she transforms her rhymed prose into verse. Even as she blesses her lover, calls him "dearest" (*carissime*), and pledges eternal faithfulness, she personifies Fidelity (*fides*) in order to accuse him of not reciprocating her loyalty with the mutual faith that love demands. This will be a recurring charge on her part. Sadly, we do not have enough detail to know what the Man had done—or what the Woman imagined.

The phrase "dual love" (*amore duali*) is unique. *Dualis* is a technical term in grammar that rarely occurs in any other context.

Whether you will or no (*Nolis atque velis*): nos. 61, 84
Ruler of heaven (*Celi regnator*): Walahfrid Strabo, *Carmina* 49.1 (*caeli regnator*); no. 3
These verses . . . I write (*hos versus scribo*): pseudo-Ovid, *De Pyramo* 1.24 (*hos scribo versus*)
Past services (*benefacta priora*): Catullus, *Carmina* 76.1 (*benefacta priora*)[66]
Thrown to the winds (*datur . . . ventis*): Ovid, *Amores* 1.6.42 (*verba dat in ventos*); cf. no. 94

ℐ☙

38c (**Man**)

Source of my life, have mercy on your faithful one,
For all the hope of my life abides in you.
I love you so much I cannot say how much.
This light is night to me, to live without you is death to me.
So may you live and thrive and vanquish all that is hurtful,
Just as I wish and pray and desire with all my strength.

ℐ☙

COMMENT

Protesting that he is indeed faithful, the Man too resorts to self-citation as he continues to plead for mercy. Of the third line (*Diligo te tantum, non possum dicere quantum*), Jaeger remarks that the verse is "carpentered with all the sophistication of two sticks nailed together" and "may thrill a girl by its sentiment, but surely not by its form."[67] In fact, the rhyming maxim was proverbial.[68]

This light is night to me (*Hec michi lux nox est*): no. 20
To live without you is death to me (*sine te michi vivere mors est*): no. 2

❧

39 (**Man**)

To his beloved, sweeter than honey and the honeycomb: if any sweetness can be added to her who already possesses it all. You are my life, you are my desire. Farewell.

❧

COMMENT

The recourse to "sweetness" sounds a poignant note, for bitterness now seems to be the Woman's governing mood.

Sweeter than honey (*super mel et favum dulci*): Psalm 18:11 (*dulciora super mel et favum*); Ecclesiasticus 24:27 (*dulcis . . . super mel et favum*); Tegernsee letter 6 (*super mel et favum dulciori*)

❧

40 (**Man**)

To his noble and most lovable friend: be steadfast with me, I beg, as I wish to be with you. Be with me, be my spirit, be my joy. Farewell, lovelier and sweeter than the cherry tree.

❧

COMMENT

Compliments again fail to produce the desired result.

ↂ

41 (**Man**)

To the only one on whom my mind and eyes gaze without flinching: I send whatever my striving is worth, with the whole intention of my body and spirit.

I have no command for you; do what you will. Write me anything—two words at least—if you can. Farewell.

ↂ

COMMENT

In his instructions on marriage, St. Paul told the Corinthian church that "concerning virgins I have no command from the Lord"—words that the Man strangely echoes here. Perhaps the Woman had asked by messenger what he "commanded" her to do (cf. no. 29). But he refuses that role, alluding instead to the famous axiom of St. Augustine: "love and do what you will." The maxim would gain greater currency in the late twelfth century, but Abelard cited it in *Sic et non* and again in his commentary on Romans.[69] It was also known to Ivo of Chartres, Robert of Arbrissel, and Hildebert of Lavardin.[70]

I have no command (*preceptum in te non habeo*): 1 Corinthians 7:25 (*preceptum Domini non habeo*)

Do what you will (*fac quod vis*): Augustine, *In epistolam Joannis ad Parthos*, tractatus 7.8 (*dilige et quod vis fac*, PL 35: 2033)

ↂ

42 (**Man**)

To his beloved, to be loved forever, from him who grieves alone on the rooftop, burning with cares: I send the well-being I would wish to have with you, but not for you to have without me.
[. . .]

Such hostility is not the way of a lover, but of someone who wants to break up and seeks opportunities for coldness. Once you were not like this toward me; you did not reckon friendship down to the penny. As for me, I cannot compete with you in harshness, for I am too soft-hearted toward you. Accept my letter, though you find it too burdensome to send me yours. Tell me then, sweetheart, how long will I be tortured? How long will I burn up inside—and find no relief for the raging flames in the refreshment of your sweet speech? There is still much to be said. From day to day I burn hotter in love for you—and you grow colder. [. . .]
Conceal nothing, you may speak plainly. Farewell.

✶

COMMENT

Increasingly desperate, the Man begins to suspect from her long silence that the Woman wants to end the relationship. Insisting that he loves her more than ever, despite her coldness, he confesses that he still cannot guess the reason for her anger and begs her to "speak plainly."

Alone on the rooftop (*solitarius in tecto*): Psalm 101:8 (*solitarius in tecto*)
Seeks opportunities for coldness (*occasiones frigidas querentis*): Proverbs 18:1 (*occasiones quaerit qui vult recedere ab amico*)
Reckon friendship down to the penny (*amiciciam ad calculum . . . vocabas*): Cicero, *Laelius* 58 (*ad calculos vocare amicitiam*); no. 50
How long will I be tortured? (*quousque torquebor*): cf. Tegernsee letter 2 (*Que est enim fortitudo mea, ut sustineam pacienter et non defleam nunc et semper?*)

✶

43 (Man)

To his lily—not the lily that fades, but one that knows not how to change its fragrance, from her heart, who sends as much as he is worth, with all the strength of his body and mind.

Nature has without doubt poured into you all the sweetness there is,
for wherever I turn I find nothing sweet anywhere but you alone.
Holding you before my mind, then, I live, I think and feel, I rejoice
and forget all toils, I am stronger in all affairs. Therefore I, who
flourish in you, passionately wish you perpetual flourishing. Farewell,
bear me always in mind.

૭✦

COMMENT

Resuming a softer tone, the Man appeals again to the woman's natural "sweetness" (*suavitas*) and his own dependence on her. The famous canon lawyer Huguccio, or Uguccione da Pisa (d. 1210), wrote an updated version of Isidore's
Etymologiae in which he placed the noun *suavitas* in the same linguistic family
as *sanguis* (blood), *sanitas* (health), *sodalitas* (companionship), and *sacramentum* (sacrament)—all sources of life or health—together with *suasio* (persuasion).[71] It is no wonder that *suavitas* and its synonym *dulcedo* play a key role in
the *Epistolae*.

   In his euphonious opening (*lilio suo, non illi lilio quod marcescit*), he recalls
her amorous words in no. 18, where she had called him a rose "beneath the unwithered whiteness of lilies." The lily symbolizes innocence, chastity, and virginity; it is the flower of the Annunciation. Perhaps the Man hints that,
although his beloved is no longer a virgin, she has neither "faded" nor "changed
her fragrance" for him, but is still "perpetually flourishing."

Nature has . . . poured into you all the sweetness (*quidquid est suavitatis, in te Natura
   transfudit*): cf. Hildebert of Lavardin, *Carmina minora* 46.7–10[72]

૭✦

44 (Man)

To his complete joy, without whom I am truly a luckless exile: live
happily, rejoice supremely—if it is right for you to have joy without me.

Farewell. I swear to God, I have uttered this "farewell" with tear-filled eyes.

COMMENT

Because neither his harsh letter 42 nor his tender 43 produced any response, the Man seems at last to have abandoned hope. Weeping, he pens his last farewell.

Tear-filled eyes (*oculis stillantibus*): cf. Juvenal, *Satires* 6.109 (*stillantis ocelli*)

45 (**Woman**)

To her house of cedar, from the ivory pillar on which the whole house rests: I send the whiteness of snow, the gleam of the moon, the brightness of the sun, the splendor of the stars, the scent of roses, the beauty of lilies, the sweetness of balsam, the fruitfulness of the earth, the cloudless calm of the sky, and whatever charms are encompassed within them.

Let the harp with the tambourine serve you, making sweet music! If my will could achieve its desire, most beloved, all that I say now by letter I would discuss with you in person.
[. . .]
When you departed, I departed with you in spirit and in mind; nothing was left at home but my dull and useless body. How much your long absence since your going has tormented me, he alone knows, whose knowledge probes the secrets of every heart. Just as the thirsty land longs for rain from heaven in the dog days of summer, when Sirius blazes, so my grieving and anxious mind yearns for you. Now glory be to God in heaven and joy to me on earth, because I know that you are alive and well—you whom I love above all. For as often as Fortune has cast me down, the comfort of your sweetness has revived

me. You ride in that chariot whose wheels are virtues, which is why
you are far more precious to me than gold and topaz. I can no more
deny myself to you than Byblis could to Caunus, Oenone to Paris, or
Briseis to Achilles.

[. . .]

What more? I send you as many joys as Antiphila had when she
welcomed her Clinia. Do not delay your coming; the sooner you come,
the sooner you will find cause for joy. May you live and flourish, that
you may behold the time of Elijah.

COMMENT

There seems to be no connection between the Man's sad note of farewell (no.
44) and this jubilant "welcome home" from the Woman. She mentions no quarrel, no reconciliation—only her lover's long absence and imminent return. So
there are probably some missing letters or some disruption in the sequence.[73] In
any case, their estrangement is past. The matters that she would have preferred
to discuss in person are unknown, thanks to the scribe's excisions.

Wishing her lover effusive blessings, the Woman recalls her anxiety in his
absence, not knowing even if he was still alive. Though her style is hyperbolic,
she reminds us that long-distance communication was not easy; many letters no
doubt failed to reach their intended recipients. Exchanging letters, in fact, was
so chancy that lovers who had to part for long periods exchanged hearts instead—a topos formalized in the later twelfth-century romances of Chrétien de
Troyes.[74] Like the Man in nos. 16 and 22, the Woman alludes to their coinherence: when he left, her mind and spirit went with him, leaving nothing behind
"but my dull and useless body."

This letter's rich blend of biblical and classical allusions is typical of the
Woman's (and Heloise's) style. Rejoicing as she anticipates a reunion, she compares herself to three eager but ill-starred Ovidian lovers: Byblis, madly in love
with her brother Caunus; Oenone, the first wife of Paris, abandoned for Helen;
and Briseis, the concubine of Achilles, whose exchange prompted his bitter feud
with Agamemnon. Oenone and Briseis are among the unhappy women of
Ovid's *Heroïdes*, whose letters to their ex-lovers would supply Heloise with
models for her letters to Abelard.[75] Antiphila and Clinia are star-crossed lovers,

eventually reunited, in a comedy by Terence. But even as she evokes these classical love stories, the Woman recalls a passage from St. Jerome. The church father imagined the righteous person riding in Christ's chariot, drawn by a team of horses representing the cardinal virtues. Since the Woman's beloved travels in the same allegorical chariot, he may be blessed to behold the messianic age, heralded (in a recondite allusion) by the return of Elijah.

House of cedar (*cedrine domui*): 2 Samuel 7:2, 1 Chronicles 17:1 (*domo cedrina*); cf.
    Song 1:16 (*tigna domorum nostrarum cedrina*)

Ivory pillar (*eburnea statua*): cf. Song 7:4 (*turris eburnea*)

On which the whole house rests (*supra quam domus innititur tota*): cf. Judges 16:29
    (*columnas, quibus innitebatur domus*)

Fruitfulness of the earth (*terre fertilitatem*): Ovid, *Metamorphoses* 5.481 (*fertilitas*
    terrae)

Whatever . . . encompassed within them (*quidquid in eorum . . . comprehenditur*
    ambitu): cf. Esther 13:10 Vulg. (*quidquid caeli ambitu continetur*)

The harp with the tambourine (*cithara cum timpano*): Psalm 150:3–4
    (*cithara . . . timpano*)

I departed with you in spirit and in mind (*tecum discessi spiritu et mente*): Heloise,
    letter 2.15: "For my mind was not with me but with you, and now, most of all, if
    it is not with you it is nowhere."

Probes the secrets of every heart (*qui cuiusque cordis rimatur secreta*): cf. no. 11; Alcuin,
    De ratione animae: Elegiacum carmen, PL 101: 648a (*qui cernit cordis secreta*);
    Heloise, letter 4.14: "God, who searches our hearts and loins and sees in our
    darkness"

Thirsty land longs for rain (*area siciens imbrem expectat*): Joel 1:20 (*area sitiens imbrem*)

Dog days of summer, when Sirius blazes (*ardentis tempore Syrii*): the star Sirius,
    ascendant during the so-called dog days (24 July–23 August)[76]

Glory be to God . . . and joy to me on earth (*Deo in celis gloria michique gaudium in*
    terra): Luke 2:14 (*gloria in altissimis Deo et in terra pax*); Gloria, Ordinary of
    the Mass

As often as Fortune has cast me down (*quociens Fortuna deposuit*): cf. Heloise, letter
    4.6: "O Fortune who is only misfortune, who has already wasted on me so many
    of the shafts she uses in her wider battle that she has none left with which to vent
    her anger on others."

Chariot whose wheels are virtues (*vadis in rotis virtutum*): Jerome, *Epistulae* 52.13
    (*habeto prudentiam, iustitiam, temperantiam, fortitudinem . . . haec te quadriga*
    velut aurigam Christi . . . ferat)

More precious . . . than gold and topaz (*super aurum et topazium*): Psalm 118:127 (*super aurum et topazion*)
Byblis . . . to Caunus: Ovid, *Metamorphoses* 9:454–665
Oenone to Paris: Ovid, *Heroïdes* 5
Briseis to Achilles: Ovid, *Heroïdes* 3
Antiphila . . . [and] Clinia: Terence, *Heauton Timorumenos* (*The Self-Tormentor*)
The time of Elijah (*Helye tempora*): Malachi 4:5 (*ego mittam . . . Eliam prophetam, antequam veniat dies Domini*)

❧

46 (**Man**)

To his fiercely desired hope, to a good so great that, once it is possessed, nothing more could be desired. Would that I might deserve to be incorporated in that good, which I desire with such impatience that it can scarcely be believed or uttered.

How much I delight in your letter, my spirit, and how exultantly I would rush to meet your love for me, I would rather show in deed than describe in words. I long to see you so much that I pine away with longing. Farewell my soul, my fair one, my every joy. No woman is lovelier, no woman better.

❧

COMMENT

The Man just as ardently awaits their reunion. His longing to be "incorporated in that good" that is her body recalls the erotic-metaphysical conceit of no. 26. The Woman is his *summum bonum*, the end of his desire—and, now more than ever, he prefers deeds to words.

My spirit (*anime mi*): Terence, *Heauton Timorumenos* 406 (*anime mi*)
My fair one (*formosa mea*): Song 2:10 (*formosa mea*)

47 (**Man**)

To his soul, to one more radiant than anything earth has brought
forth beneath the sky, from the most wretchedly unhappy of men: I
wish you all the happiness that one who lacks all happiness can wish.

O luckless night! O hateful slumber! O cursed idleness of mine!
Farewell, my sole refreshment, my only food, my only rest. Wherever I
am, there truly are you.

COMMENT

Did the longed-for tryst fail to occur because he overslept, after all that? Or did
he stay too long, like the lover in a lyric *alba*, and risk discovery?

My only food (*solus cibus meus*): cf. Marbod of Rennes, "Rescriptum rescripto eiusdem"
(*tu meus ipsa cibus*)

48 (**Woman**)

A lover to a lover: I send the freshness of love.

No one should live or increase in good if he does not know how to love
and control his passions. What need is there for more words? Ablaze
with a fire of passion for you, I want to love you forever. Farewell, my
one salvation, the only one in the world that I could love.

COMMENT

This time she is forgiving and, despite the risk or the missed assignation, echoes her amorous greeting of no. 18. But she cannot resist a rebuke, while casting it in the form of a neutral *sententia*: no one deserves to live who cannot love properly (*diligere*) and control his own passions (*amores regere*). The Man's lack of self-control is becoming a chronic reproach.

Abelard, looking back in repentance on his love affair, would chastise himself for the "intemperate lust" (*mee libidinis . . . intemperantia*) that compelled him to have sex with Heloise even in the nuns' refectory at Argenteuil (letter 5.17) and during the forbidden days of Holy Week (letter 5.20).

49 (**Woman**)

To her rose that cannot wither, blooming with the flower of beatitude, from her who loves you above all men: may you grow as you flourish, flourish as you grow.

You know, O greatest part of my soul, that many people love each other for many reasons. But no friendship of theirs will be so firm as one that stems from integrity, virtue, and intimate love. In my judgment, the friendship of those who seem to love each other for the sake of riches or pleasures will by no means endure, since the very things on whose account they love seem not at all enduring. Thus it happens that, when riches or pleasures fail them, their love also fails, because they did not love those goods for each other's sake, but each other for the sake of the goods.

My love, however, is joined to you by a very different pact. For it was not the idle weight of riches that compelled me to love you; nothing teaches the way to wickedness more readily than those, once the thirst for possession starts to blaze. No, it was virtue alone, the sole excellence, the source of all that is honorable, all that is prosperous. Virtue is sufficient to itself, needing nothing; it restrains all greedy desires, checks amorous passions, tempers joys, casts out sorrows. It furnishes all that is fitting, all that is pleasing, all that is cheerful; it can find nothing better than itself. I have indeed found in you this supreme good, the most outstanding of all, and that is why I love you. Because this good is agreed to be eternal, beyond doubt I shall love you eternally. Believe me then, O you whom I long for: neither wealth, nor honors, nor all that the partisans of this world desire, could separate me from the love of you. Truly, that day will never come, so long as I can remember myself, that could pass without remembrance of you. And know this: I have not the least doubt that I may hope for the same from you.

It is a sign of great rashness that I send you artful writings. For not even someone learned right down to his fingertips, one who had made the artful arrangement of words into a habit through long practice and training of the affections, could paint the face of language elegantly enough to deserve the scrutiny of so great a teacher—let alone I, who seem hardly skilled enough to produce trifles "that neither taste of bitten fingernails nor bang the desk." Before so great a teacher, I say—a teacher by his virtues, a teacher by his character, to whom French stubbornness rightly yields, whom the arrogance of the whole world rises as one to honor—before such a teacher, anyone who thinks himself even slightly learned would become in his own judgment utterly mute and speechless.

And so let your goodness trust me, for if I did not know you to be endowed with the unfailing friendship of true love, I would not presume to send you unpolished letters in so crude a style. But since the spur of your unfailing charity and sweetness has driven me into a passion for your love, even if it should (God forbid!) displease you, the fervent affection of my love has found that perfect devotion can never be cast out by any intervening trouble. If I could have what I wish in this regard, this letter and many more would surely be sent your way. I would write to you as often as if my affairs required it, nor would I let my stylus take a single day's holiday—even if you found it tiresome to write to me.

You certainly aroused my hunger with the beginning of your letter, but you have not yet fully satisfied it. For when I was pining away as usual with intimate desire for my friends, you would have greatly relieved my pain if you had written something longer. Nevertheless, I welcome this tiny compendium of charitable greetings like an angel, reading and rereading it every hour. Sometimes I even kiss it in your place, trying to satisfy my impassioned longing. For nothing in this life is more delightful to me, you might think, than to speak with you, write to you, or hear you speaking. Indeed, the honeyed sweetness of your writing clings to my heart. Whenever I recall it, it leads me from sorrow to joy, from mourning to cheerfulness. God knows, nothing can be believed more truly! But if you scarcely believe it, I feel sure that the day will come, please God, when you must confess that you have heard nothing truer. Now let my declaration cease, for I have rendered an account of the way our love must be preserved.

As the vault of the sky holds nothing to equal the sun,
So the ends of the earth enclose nothing equal to you.
While you live, thrive, and may joy be yours after death.

Lest my unkempt speech weary you longer, I commend you to the heavenly Savior. Farewell, you whose remembrance blots out all my troubles. Fare well without end.

COMMENT

With letter 49, the longest in the correspondence, the Woman resumes the lofty tone of nos. 22–25, as if in response to the Man's challenge in no. 33. Her theme is pure friendship as defined in Cicero's dialogue *De amicitia* (*Laelius*). Unlike worldly friendship grounded in pleasure, riches, or ambition, true friendship is based on virtue alone and demands the highest integrity. Cicero's dialogue was popular throughout the twelfth century. In the 1160s the Cistercian abbot Aelred of Rievaulx produced a Christianized version, *Spiritual Friendship*.

Both lovers, especially the Woman, represent their love as such a friendship. In exuberant praise of Virtue per se and her lover's own virtue, the Woman claims that this excellence alone is the ground of her love. Because Virtue is eternal, so will her love be. To corroborate that claim, she reaches for St. Paul's epistle to the Romans: just as "neither death, nor life, nor angels, nor principalities, nor things present, nor things to come" can separate believers from the love of God (Romans 8:38–39), so "neither wealth, nor honors, nor all that the partisans of this world desire" can separate her from her beloved. Heloise likewise claimed in letter 2.10–11 that her love for Abelard was pure and disinterested: she loved him for himself alone because of merit, not the gifts of fortune. Her famous rejection of marriage was based on the same ideal; since a wife receives material gains from her marriage, her love cannot make the same claim to be disinterested.

Writing in the highest possible style, the Woman performs another elaborate humility topos, reminiscent of her allegorical apologia in no. 23. Playing the self-conscious student, she apologizes for writing "unpolished letters in so crude a style"—a broad joke in this context—as she blushes to think how her attempt at "artful writings" (*litteratorie . . . verba*) will pass muster with "so great a teacher."[77] So great is he, not only in eloquence but in virtue and character, that "French stubbornness [*francigena cervicositas*] rightly yields" to him, and "the arrogance of the whole world" (*tocius mundi superciliositas*) rises to honor him. The Woman's rare nouns paint a vivid picture: stiff necks are compelled to bow, lifted eyebrows must be taken down a notch. But her adjective *francigena* has captured more notice. If the lovers are based in Paris, it would make little sense to mention that the teacher's vanquished rivals were French unless he himself was not. Abelard of course came from Brittany, which was not part of medieval Francia. Although other "foreigners" may have taught in Paris, the university's role as a great international mecca lay still in the future. So this reference, in the context of praise for a celebrity teacher, plays a key role in the ascription to Abelard and Heloise.[78]

In calling her lover "a teacher by his virtues, a teacher by his character," the Woman offers what would have been highest praise in the old cathedral schools, with their ideal of the eloquent, charismatic master on whom pupils strive to model themselves. But in the new schools of dialectic, such as Abelard's, the standard of excellence had become ruthless brilliance in argument. Hence to an initiate of those schools, as Jaeger notes, the Woman's praise might already have had a hollow ring, hard to distinguish from mockery—as if a historian today were to call his teacher "a truly great positivist."[79]

After promising once again to write frequently, the Woman concludes with a *petitio* pleading for more and longer letters from her beloved. Lovesick, she has been avidly reading, rereading, and even kissing his last note, which she calls a "tiny compendium of charitable greetings." Love letters were cherished not only for their content, but as much or more because they had been in physical contact with the beloved, representing his longed-for presence.[80] Yet the Woman's description cannot possibly refer to the Man's most recent letter in our manuscript; the deeply embarrassed no. 47 is hardly a vehicle of "honeyed sweetness." So we must reckon yet again with either missing letters or disarray in the sequence. The letter ends as it began in high style, with leonine distichs and a rhyming prose conclusion.

Greatest part of my soul (*maxima pars anime mee*): Ovid, *Ex Ponto* 1.6.16 (*magnaque pars animi . . . mei*); Baudri of Bourgueil, *Carmina* 6.16 (*meae maxima pars animae*); Regensburg Songs, no. 35.5 (*mihi pars o maxima fame*)

Riches or pleasures . . . not at all enduring (*divicias vel voluptates . . . nullam videantur diuturnitatem habere*): Cicero, *Laelius* 20 (*[bona terrena] caduca et incerta*); *De officiis* 3.43 (*honores, divitiae, voluptates . . . amicitiae numquam anteponenda sunt*)

They did not love . . . but each other for the sake of the goods (*non propter se res, sed se propter res dilexerunt*): cf. Augustine, *Contra Faustum* 22.78 (*homo iniquus . . . propter se ipsas diligit res*, PL 42: 451)

Once the thirst for possession starts to blaze (*cum habendi sitis incanduit*): Boethius, *De institutione arithmetica*, Praef. 3.8 (*cum habendi sitis incanduit*)

Virtue alone, the sole excellence, . . . [compelled me to love you] (*te diligere [compulit] . . . sola excellentissa virtus*): Cicero, *Laelius* 20 (*summum bonum . . . ipsa virtus amicitiam et gignit et continet*); cf. Heloise, letter 2.10: "God knows I never sought anything in you except yourself; I wanted simply you, nothing of yours" (*te pure non tua*), letter 2.11: "For a person's worth does not rest on wealth or power; these depend on fortune, but worth on his merits."

Tempers joys, casts out sorrows (*gaudia temperat, dolores extirpat*): cf. Boethius, *Consolation* 1, metr. 7.25–28 (*Gaudia pelle . . . Nec dolor adsit*)

Neither wealth, nor honors . . . could separate me from the love of you (*non opes, non dignitates, non omnia . . . poterunt me a tui dilectione secernere*): cf. Romans 8:38–39 (*neque mors, neque vita, . . . neque creatura alia poterit nos separare a charitate Dei*)

Partisans of this world (*sectatores huius seculi*): cf. Cassian, *Collationes* 13.4 (*mundanae sapientiae sectatores*, PL 49: 903b)

So long as I can remember myself (*qua mei meminisse valeam*): cf. no. 8

Neither taste of bitten fingernails nor bang the desk (*demorsos ungues non sapiunt nec pluteum cedunt*): Persius, *Satires* 1.106 (*nec pluteum caedit nec demorsos sapit unguis*), quoted in Quintilian, *Institutio oratoria* 10.3.21. "Banging the desk" would be a crude way of marking rhythm.[81]

French stubbornness (*francigena cervicositas*): Cf. Abelard, *Historia calamitatam* 46 (*invidiam Francorum*) and 60 (*Francorum invidia*)

Arrogance (*superciliositas*): this very rare word occurs only once in the *Patrologia Latina*: Guibert of Nogent, *Tropologiae in Amos* 4.1 (PL 156: 418b).[82]

Who thinks himself even slightly learned (*qui sibi videtur sciolus*): Jerome, *Commentaria in Ezechielem* 1.2 (*qui sciolus sibi videtur*, PL 25: 61bc); *Epistulae* 48.3 and 125.16 (*videntur sibi scioli*)

Mute and speechless (*elinguis et mutus*): Boethius, *Consolation* 1, pr. 2 (*elinguem . . . mutumque*)

Unpolished letters in so crude a style (*impolitas tam rudis stili litteras*): cf. Tegernsee letter 3 (*doctoris aures pudor sit inculto sermone interpellare*)

Nothing in this life is more delightful to me . . . than to . . . write to you (*Nichil . . . hac in vita michi delectabilius esse existimes quam te . . . scribere*): cf. Cicero, *Epistulae familiares* 12.30.1 (*quid mihi iucundius quam . . . aut scribere ad te aut tuas legere litteras?*)

The ends of the earth enclose (*clauditur orbis*): Virgil, *Aeneid* 1.233 (*clauditur orbis*)

༄

50 (Man)

To the only disciple of philosophy among all the girls of our age, the only one in whom Fortune has fully enclosed all the gifts of the manifold virtues, the only beautiful, the only gracious one, from him who by your gift feeds on ethereal breezes, who lives only when he is certain of your grace: may you advance ever higher—if she who has attained the summit can advance.

[. . .]

I marvel at your genius! You argue so subtly about the laws of friendship that you seem not to have read Cicero, but to have given Cicero himself those precepts.

[. . .]

To come to my response—if it can rightly be called a response when nothing equal is offered—let me reply in my own way. You say truly, O sweetest of all women, that we are not bound by the same kind of love as those who seek only their own good—the ones who turn friendship into a business venture, whose loyalty stands and falls with Fortune, who do not prize virtue as its own reward, who reckon friendship down to the penny, who count their returns with anxious fingers, and in short, for whom nothing is sweet without profit.

Not Fortune, I say, but God has joined us by a very different pact. I chose you among many thousands for your countless virtues, truly seeking no other benefit save that I might rest in you, that you might lighten all my woes, and that among all earthly goods, your charm alone might refresh me and make me forget all sorrows. You are my feast in hunger, my refreshment in thirst, my rest in weariness, my warmth in the cold, my shade in the heat. In every tempest, in short, you are my true, health-giving temperance.

Perhaps because of some good opinion you had of me, you too saw fit to make my acquaintance. I am your inferior in many ways, or to speak more truly, in all ways, for you surpass me even in the respect where I seemed to excel. Your talent, your eloquence, far beyond your age and sex, now begin to extend into virile strength. What humility, what courtesy you display toward all! With such great worth, how marvelous is your temperance! Do these virtues not magnify you above all people, do they not set you on the heights where you can shine like a candelabra to be admired by all? As for me, I believe and confidently affirm that there is no mortal, no kinsman, no friend, whom you would prefer to me or, to speak more boldly, compare with me. For I'm not made of lead, I'm no blockhead, I'm not so hard-nosed that I can't keenly smell out where true love exists and who loves me from the heart.

Farewell, you who make me fare well. Let me know how I can stand in your grace, for your grace alone is my festival.

❧

COMMENT

In his response, abridged by de Vepria, the Man hails his beloved as "the only disciple of philosophy among all the girls [*puellas*] of our age." This may be more than a lover's compliment; many young women studied rhetoric in the cloister, but we know of no others (except Heloise) who studied philosophy with secular masters. The statement suits well with Heloise's reputation for learning and Abelard's sober praise of her virtues (*Historia calamitatum* 64; letter 3.1). Among these virtues, the one that stands out here is temperance. In ascribing this cardinal virtue to his beloved, the impulsive Man displays some self-knowledge: "In every tempest [*intemperie*], . . . you are my true, health-giving temperance [*temperies*]." He seems almost daunted by the Woman's talents, which surpass what can be expected of her sex and even "begin to extend into virile strength." This was a standard way to compliment a woman in a misogynist age, but the Man also expresses true humility: "I am your inferior in many ways, or to speak more truly, in all ways, for you surpass me even in the respect where I seemed to excel." He may be referring to eloquence.

Accepting the Woman's account of their love as Ciceronian friendship, the Man agrees that they have been united by God, not Fortune. Strikingly, for the first time he names their love *dilectio*, a word the Woman has often used. Hitherto he has always called it *amor*.[83] Derived from *diligere*—to love, prize, or esteem—*dilectio* is a Christian Latin coinage, an alloy of friendship and charity.[84] But, unlike the Woman, her lover does not claim to be disinterested. Rather, he asks "that I might rest in you, that you might lighten all my woes . . . and make me forget all sorrows." Extolling his beloved as "my feast in hunger, my refreshment in thirst, my rest in weariness, my warmth in the cold, my shade in the heat," the Man's praise recalls the Golden Sequence for Pentecost, "Veni sancte Spiritus." The authorship and date of that sequence are uncertain, but if it was a Parisian composition, it could conceivably have been known to the Man by this point.[85] Like the Holy Spirit, the Woman offers perfect *temperies* and counters every harmful extreme. Abelard would dedicate his oratory to the Spirit under the name of the Paraclete, defending his choice against those who protested its novelty (*Historia calamitatum* 54–57). The Woman, however, would eventually grow frustrated with being cast as her lover's personal paraclete.

Feeds on ethereal breezes (*etheriis auris vescitur*): Virgil, *Aeneid* 1.546–47 (*si vescitur aura / aetheria*)
Who seek only their own good (*qui sua tantum querunt*): 1 Corinthians 13:5 (*Charitas . . . non quaerit quae sua sunt*)

Turn friendship into a business venture (*amiciciam questum faciunt*): Ovid, *Ex Ponto*
2.3.19–20 (*Illud amicitiae... uenerabile nomen / prostat et in quaestu... sedet*);
Ambrose, *De officiis ministrorum* 3.22.133 (*virtus est enim amicitia, non quaestus*,
PL 16: 182b)

Loyalty stands and falls with Fortune (*fides cum fortuna stat et cadit*): Ovid, *Ex Ponto*
2.3.10 (*cum fortuna statque caditque fides*)

Prize virtue as its own reward (*virtutem sui ipsius precium... putant*): Ovid, *Ex Ponto*
2.3.12 (*virtutem pretium qui putet esse sui*)

Reckon friendship down to the penny (*amicicam ad calculum vocant*): Cicero, *Laelius*
58 (*ad calculos vocare amicitiam*); no. 42

Count their returns with anxious fingers (*quod ad se rediturum sit, sollicitis articulis*
supputant): Ovid, *Ex Ponto* 2.3.17–18 (*reditus iam quisque suos amat et... /*
sollicitis subputat articulis)

Nothing is sweet without profit (*sine lucro nichil dulce est*): Terence, *Heauton Timoru-*
menos 234 (*nil iam praeter pretium dulcest*)

God has joined us (*Nos... Deus coniunxit*): Matthew 19:6, Mark 10:9 (*Quod... Deus*
coniunxit)

I chose you among many thousands (*ego te inter multa milia... elegi*): Song 5:10
(*electus ex millibus*); Tegernsee letters 6 (*electa es ex milibus, / te diligo pre*
omnibus) and 8 (*tu solus es ex milibus electus*)

My refreshment in thirst, my rest in weariness, my... temperance (*tu in siti refectio,*
tu in lassitudine quies, tu... vera temperies): cf. "Veni sancte Spiritus," sequence
for Pentecost (*Consolator optime, dulcis hospes animae, dulce refrigerium; / In*
labore requies, in aestu temperies, in fletu solatium; *Analecta hymnica* 54: 153)

You surpass me (*me excedis*): cf. Regensburg Songs, no. 37.11 (*Longe precellis, longe me*
carmine vincis)

Your talent, your eloquence, ... extend into virile strength (*Ingenium tuum, facundia*
tua... iam virile in robur se incipit extendere): Hugh Metel, *Epistola* 16, to
Heloise: "Fame... has informed us that you have transcended the female sex.
How? In composing letters [*dictando*], writing poetry [*uersificando*], renewing
familiar words with new combinations [*noua iunctura nota uerba nouando*]—
and what is more excellent than all these things, you have surpassed feminine
softness and hardened into virile strength."[86] Peter the Venerable, *Epistola* 115, to
Heloise: "At a time when... wisdom can scarcely find a foothold not only, I may
say, among women who have banished her completely, but even in the minds of
men, you have surpassed all women in carrying out your purpose, and have gone
further than almost every man."[87]

A candelabra to be admired by all (*de candelabro luceas et omnibus spectabilis fias*):
   Matthew 5:15 (*accendunt lucernam, et ponunt eam . . . super candelabrum, ut luceat omnibus*)
I'm not made of lead, I'm no blockhead (*Non . . . plumbeus sum, non stipes*): Terence,
   Heauton Timorumenos 877 (*stipes asinu' plumbeus*)
I'm not so hard-nosed (*non corneum rostrum habeo*): cf. Persius, *Satires* 1.47 (*neque enim mihi cornea fibra est*)

❧

51 (**Man**)

To the complete and undivided joy of his soul: may this day and every season be happy. Let me know how you are, sweetheart, for I cannot be well unless your good health gives me cause. Fare well and happily for as long as the wild boar loves the mountaintops.

❧

COMMENT

A quick, casual note seasoned with a tag from Virgil.

The wild boar loves the mountaintops (*iuga montis amabit aper*): Virgil, *Eclogues* 5.76
   (*iuga montis aper . . . amabit*)

❧

52 (**Man**)

To the lily from the privet: may you flourish forever. Because we do not fulfill the Lord's commandment unless we love one another, we should obey divine Scripture. Farewell, until your welfare becomes tiresome to me.

❧

COMMENT

The Man mischievously applies Christ's new commandment to the couple's affair. His conclusion employs the figure of *adynaton*, a form of hyperbole invoking an impossible condition (cf. the greeting in no. 72).

To the lily from the privet (*Lilio ligustrum*): Martial, *Epigrams* 1.115.2–3 (*candidior puella . . . lilio, ligustro*)
The Lord's commandment . . . love one another (*mandatum Domini . . . dilectionem ad invicem habeamus*): John 13:34 (*Mandatum novum do vobis: Ut diligatis invicem*); Romans 13:8 (*invicem diligatis*)

53 (**Woman**)

To him who shines wonderfully with the light of wisdom in his distinguished nobility, flourishing like a resplendent lily and a vernal rose in the youthful bloom of his whole body, from her who lacks all skill: I wish all that tends to the advancement of true love.

If one little drop of knowability were to trickle down to me from the honeycomb of wisdom, I would strive with a supreme effort of my mind to depict a few things in fragrant nectar for you, my gracious love, in the markings of a letter. But in all Latinity, I have found no word that can plainly say how intent is my mind upon you, for with God as my witness, I love you with a sublime and exceptional love. Hence there neither is nor shall be anything or any fate that can separate me from your love, save death alone. Therefore it is my daily desire and longing to be revived by the refreshment of your presence. One day will seem like a month to me, one week like a year, until the sweetest countenance of your love shall appear.

[. . .]

Such great sorrow arises and springs up in my heart that a whole year would not suffice in the least to describe it. My body is saddened, my spirit altered from its usual good cheer. Farewell.

COMMENT

In the vein of exaggerated humility that she often adopts, the Woman writes as one "who lacks all skill" to her lover "shin[ing] wonderfully with the light of wisdom." But that humility is offset by her claim to exalted preeminence in the art of love, requiring a radical ineffability topos: "in all Latinity, I have found no word that can plainly say how intent is my mind upon you, for with God as my witness, I love you with a sublime and exceptional love." Again, as in no. 49, she deploys the rhetoric of Romans 8 to avow that nothing can ever part her from her beloved. Heloise was given to similar hyperboles about the unique, exceptional quality of her love. In letter 2.12 she boasts, "What married woman, what virgin did not long for you in your absence and burn with love in your presence? What queen or powerful lady did not envy my joys and my bed?" Similarly, in letter 4.7 she laments that Fortune, "to make me the saddest of all women, first made me blessed above all." Not to be outdone, the Man too hopes that their love will "become immortal" (no. 72).

In her rather precious metaphor of the "honeycomb of wisdom" whose nectar should furnish her with ink, the Woman employs the rare word *scibilitas* (knowability), which has been much discussed. The context hardly requires a technical term in dialectic; her meaning would have been clearer if she had just written *scientia* (knowledge). But the abstraction *scibilitas* is an Abelardian coinage. Apart from two of Abelard's logical works and this letter, it does not appear again in medieval Latin until Albertus Magnus and Ramon Llull.[88] So it looks very much as if the Woman drops it into this sentence as an affectionate *hommage*, much as a graduate student would footnote her mentor's new article.[89] The adjective *scibilis* also occurs in one of Abelard's epitaphs: "Petrus hic iacet Abaelardus / cui soli patuit scibile quidquid erat" (Here lies Peter Abelard, to whom alone / all that was knowable was clearly known). Since it was Heloise who arranged for Abelard's burial at the Paraclete, it may have been she who composed those lines.[90]

The letter ends on a sad note as the lovers' long separation continues.

Light of wisdom (*sapiencie lumine*): Wisdom 6:23 (*lumen sapientiae*)

A resplendent lily and a vernal rose (*candentis lilii et vernantis rose*): Baudri of
  Bourgueil, *Carmina* 34.1 (*uernans rosa*); cf. no. 18

Knowability (*scibilitas*): Abelard, *Dialectica* 1.2.3 and *Logica "Ingredientibus"*[91]

Anything or any fate that can separate me from your love (*nec erit res vel sors que tuo
  amore me separet*): Romans 8:38–39 (*neque creatura alia poterit nos separare a
  charitate Dei*); no. 49

❧

54 (Man)

To his beloved, to be loved forever, from her most faithful one: may
our love never end and grow ever stronger.

If you, O sweetest of all things, were to doubt the loyalty of your
singular friend, or if I myself were not absolutely sure of your love,
then we would have to write longer letters to commend our mutual
love and call on more arguments to defend it. But now, because our
love has grown so strong that it shines by itself without assistance,
there is little need for words; we have abundance in deeds. Nevertheless, it makes sense for us sometimes to visit each other this way and
let a letter take the place of our physical presence, because the devouring envy of the wicked does not allow us to be united at our pleasure.
What more? Just that, with many sighs, I often pray that God almighty
will long preserve you unharmed for me.
[. . .]
We must allow those to depart whom we cannot retain. Good counsel
will come of that.

❧

COMMENT

Although the Man expresses complete trust in the Woman's love, their meetings are still rare because of "the devouring envy of the wicked." His letter again

casts their enemies in the mold of the *lauzengiers*, the envious spies of troubadour lyric. After a lacuna, he adds enigmatically, "We must allow those to depart whom we cannot retain." Is he still referring to "the wicked"—perhaps false friends or unreliable servants?

Sweetest of all things (*omnium rerum dulcissima*): Horace, *Satires* 1.9.4 (*dulcissime rerum*)

Mutual love (*mutui amoris*): Cicero, *Epistulae familiares* 13.50 (*amor . . . mutuus*); Horace, *Epodes* 15.10 (*amorem mutuum*)

Devouring envy (*edax . . . invidia*): cf. Ovid, *Amores* 1.15.1 (*Livor edax*)

55 (**Woman**)

To him who is dearest of all that live, to be loved above life itself, from his intimately devoted friend: I wish whatever is best, with all my heart and soul.

I think you are not unaware, my sweet light, that ashes sprinkled on a dormant fire never quench it. Even if they keep it from shining, they cannot stop its continual burning. In the same way, no random events can by any means efface the memory of you, which I have bound to my heart with a golden chain. What more? I take God as my witness that I love with you true and unfeigned love. Farewell, my supreme sweetness.

COMMENT

This letter marks the first appearance of a favorite metaphor: the smoldering fire banked in ashes, which burns hotter than ever though it gives little light (cf. nos. 75, 88). Such is the couple's secret love. The Woman uses not the ordinary word for chain (*vinculum*), but an abstract coinage (*vinculamen*), otherwise unknown in medieval Latin. This exemplifies the *nova junctura*, or art of neologism, for which Hugh Metel says Heloise was known; see comment on no. 50.

Ashes sprinkled on a dormant fire never quench it (*nunquam superpositi cineres*
suffocant sopitum ignem): cf. Virgil, *Aeneid* 8.410 (*cinerem et sopitos suscitat ignis*)
I take God as my witness (*Deum . . . testem habeo*): Romans 1:9 (*Testis . . . mihi est*
Deus); no. 11
My supreme sweetness (*maxima dulcedo mea*): cf. Tegernsee letter 5 (*O dulcedo mea*)

℈

56 (**Man**)

To his desirable one above all that can be desired, from her friend who
shares one soul with her: I wish whatever good is reserved uniquely for
lovers.

Your speech, sweeter than honey, gives the clearest proof of your
absolute fidelity.
[. . .]
I cannot decide what to say to you, for I love you so much that I cannot
rightly express it. It has come to this, O supreme repose of my life—it has
come to this, I say: I can find no name for your perfection. As long as you
are well, nothing can sadden me. When you are ill, nothing can delight
me. So, if you wish to take perfect care of your beloved, be well; then I
too will be well. God, from whom nothing can be hidden, knows you lie
so deep within my heart that my every thought is directed to you.

Farewell, sweetest—not only of women, but of all things in the universe.

℈

COMMENT

The Man uses an ineffability topos to express a love beyond the reach of language—a more colloquial version of the Woman's declaration in no. 53. As in
no. 22, he insists that his every thought and intention is directed to her.

Sweeter than honey (*super mel dulcis*): Psalm 18:11 (*dulciora super mel et favum*);
 Ecclesiasticus 24:27 (*super mel dulcis . . . super mel et favum*); no. 39
God, from whom nothing can be hidden (*deus, quem nichil latere potest*): Alcuin,
 Collect for Purity (*Deus . . . quem nullum latet secretum*); no. 11

57 (**Woman**)

To her loveliest adornment from his friend, not for beauty but for
virtue's sake: I wish the fullness of supreme delight.

Much time has now passed—as you know, alas!—since we were last
joined in intimate conversation. But know that, although I cannot
enjoy your presence at my pleasure, nothing can make me stop gazing
at you with my inner eyes and loving your good health and prosperity.

Farewell, most beloved, and love me with my own love for you.

COMMENT

A last wistful love note as the couple's separation drags on, before another quarrel intervenes.

58 (**Woman**)

To a friend, as I suppose, from her who was once loved above all others
in words, but is now unjustly deprived of the privilege of love. May you
have what no eye has ever seen, what has never pierced the depth of
any heart. Farewell, sir. Relieve my burden more willingly.

COMMENT

We do not know what happened, but the Woman is suddenly furious. This is her only use of the formal, frigid plural *Valete*, which I have translated "Farewell, sir" to convey its distant flavor. The Man had resorted to a similar strategy in no. 36. Despite the couple's endless assurances of fidelity, separation has placed an immense strain on their relationship. "What no eye has ever seen" alludes to St. Paul's evocation of heaven, but here it is transposed, invoking the longed-for presence of the earthly beloved.

Privilege of love (*amoris privilegio*): Abelard, letter 7.39 (*privilegium amoris*). Like
    many exegetes, Abelard uses this phrase for the intimate friendship between
    Jesus and John the Evangelist.
What no eye has ever seen . . . depth of any heart (*quod nec oculus visu percepit, nec in*
    interiora cordis pertransiit): 1 Corinthians 2:9 (*Quod oculus non vidit . . . nec in*
    cor hominis ascendit)

59 (**Man**)

To his most beloved, to be loved above all that is or can be, I wish
perpetual health and the most abundant growth in all goods.
[. . .]
Unavoidable business stood in the way, setting its left foot against my
desire. I am the guilty one—I who compelled you to sin.

COMMENT

This apology tells us nothing of what we want to know, except that there has been a serious incident. The "unavoidable business" (*causa necessaria*) suggests a planned meeting that had to be cancelled. But the last sentence is darker: *Ego nocens sum qui te peccare coegi*, "I am the guilty one—I who compelled you to sin." Whatever happened, it made the Woman so angry that, despite her professions of eternal love, in the next letter she tried to end the relationship.

It is hard to imagine how such a strong-willed person could have been "compelled" to sin. Sexual violence? The Woman was willing enough in general, but she might not have been willing on all occasions. In *Historia calamitatum* 18, Abelard acknowledges that he sometimes struck Heloise "to avert suspicion," but claims that "these blows were prompted by love and tender feeling rather than anger and irritation." He even claims that she enjoyed them. But in letter 5.20 he confesses, "Even when you were unwilling, resisted to the utmost of your power, and tried to dissuade me, as yours was the weaker nature I often forced you to consent with threats and blows." Such a scenario could have provoked the Woman's fury and the Man's abject apology. But nothing else in the correspondence confirms this suspicion.

Setting its left foot against my desire (*meo desiderio pedem sinistrum opposuit*): cf.
    Ovid, *Ex Ponto* 4.6.7–8 (*Fortuna . . . votisque malignum / opponit nostris insidiosa pedem*)

ॐ

60 (**Woman**)

To him who until now has been faithfully loved, but must be loved no longer with the bond of an ailing passion: I send a firm guarantee, all the same, of my love and fidelity.

With a great pledge of charity, I had made myself intimate with you for as long as your true love remained firmly rooted. What is more, I had set all my hope upon you as an unconquerable tower. You also know, if you will concede so much, that I was never double-minded toward you, nor do I wish to be. Now think and think again about these things—and others like them. As for me, in truth I have always borne a great deal for your sake, fully and perfectly enough. No writing can express how strongly, how intensely I began to love you. [. . .]
If the covenant we had established had to be broken, although this is very bitter to say, at least it will not be broken a second time. Keep away from me with your bluster! I will no longer listen to your words.

From the quarter whence I expected to receive much good, there have sprung tearful and heartfelt sighs.

May almighty God, who wishes no one to perish and loves sinners with more than fatherly love, illumine your heart with the splendor of his grace and lead you back to the way of salvation, that you may know what is his well-pleasing and perfect will.

Farewell. Your wisdom and knowledge have deceived me, so from now on, let all our writing perish.

COMMENT

In this resolute letter, the Woman suddenly and shockingly wishes to end the relationship to which she had been so profoundly committed. While promising her continued affection (*dilectio*), she renounces the grand passion (*amor*) that she believes is now "ailing" and unable to sustain the affair. Verbs in the pluperfect relegate their relationship firmly to the past.

But what has the Man done? This is far from clear. The letter suggests that he has broken their "covenant" (*fedus*) by being "double-minded" (*duplici animo*), implicitly comparing him to the "double-minded man" in the epistle of James, who "is inconstant in all his ways." Yet she never charges him with taking a new lover. She also has a sense of being put upon, of having "always borne a great deal" for her lover without being sufficiently appreciated. So, with a prayer for the sinner's conversion, she advises him to put himself right with God because she will have nothing further to do with him. As for their letters (*omnis nostra scriptura*), they are to "perish." Fortunately, the lovers were reconciled before she could implement her decision and destroy them.

My hope . . . as an unconquerable tower (*spem meam quasi turrim invictam*): cf. Psalm
   60:4 (*spes mea, turris fortitudinis*)
Double-minded (*duplici animo*): James 1:8 (*vir duplex animo*)
Think and think again (*cogita et recogita*): Abelard, letter 5.19: "Think and think again
   of the great perils in which we were" (*cogita et recogita*)
Fully and perfectly (*plene et perfecte*): Colossians 4:12 (*perfecti et pleni*)

The covenant we had established (*fedus quod pepigeramus*): Deuteronomy 5:2, 1
    Samuel 20:16 (*pepigit . . . foedus*)
I will no longer listen (*ultra non audiam*): Deuteronomy 18:16 (*ultra non audiam*)
God, who wishes no one to perish (*Deus, qui neminem vult perire*): Roman Missal,
    prayer for Good Friday (*Deus, qui . . . neminem vis perire*)
Illumine your heart with the splendor of his grace (*illuminet cor tuum gracie sue*
    splendore): Roman Missal, prayer for Good Friday (*illumina . . . corda nostra*
    gratiae tuae splendore)
His well-pleasing and perfect will (*voluntas eius beneplacens et perfecta*): Romans 12:2
    (*voluntas Dei . . . beneplacens et perfecta*)
Your wisdom and knowledge have deceived (*sapiencia et sciencia tua me decepit*): Isaiah
    47:10 (*sapientia tua et scientia tua . . . decepit te*)

꾀

61 (**Man**)

To his lady, beloved now and forever, from her most wretched friend,
for whom there is little difference between life and death. Whether
you will or no, may the friendship we have begun take a course that
will never end.

I do not know what sin of mine could have been so great that you want
so suddenly to cast aside every last feeling of mercy and intimacy
toward me. For it must have been one of these two things: either I have
sinned against you terribly, or else you had little love before to have
cast it aside so easily, so carelessly. For my part, unless you advise me
more fully, I cannot recognize any fault I have committed against
you—unless you want to call it a fault to lament one's miseries and
troubles before someone from whom a remedy is hoped for, consolation expected.
[. . .]
These are not the words of a friend; they are not the words of one who
was ever kindhearted, but of someone who seeks occasions—of someone, I say, who has long been waiting for some excuse to break up. By
what word or action, I beg you, did I provoke such outrageous words?

You have thrown me half-dead into the waves, you have inflicted new wounds on my old ones, you have added sorrow to sorrow.
[. . .]
If you loved me, you would have said less. Whoever you may appoint as judge between us, I will clearly prove that you have sinned against me more than I against you. Surely anyone who carefully studies your words will find that they are not those of a lover, but of one who seeks separation. Nowhere in them do I see a tender heart; rather I find a cruel breast, impregnable to love.
[. . .]
Nevertheless, my soul, dry your tears, although I cannot dry my own.
[. . .] Farewell. I received your tear-stained letter; I send you my own with tears.

ᴈᴄ▸

COMMENT

For the first time in this exchange, the Man is angry and feels more sinned against than sinning. His guess about his alleged fault is intriguing. It seems that when the lovers last met, he devoted much time to "lament[ing his] miseries and troubles" in order to be consoled. In fact, this is precisely what he sought from his beloved. In no. 50 he had expressed a confident wish that she would "lighten all [his] woes" and "make [him] forget all sorrows."

If these lovers are Abelard and Heloise, we will see the same scenario repeated in their canonical letters. Hard pressed by his enemies and fearing for his life, Abelard would write to Heloise in letter 3, begging her to pray for his safety and, if he died, to arrange his burial at the Paraclete and offer suffrages for his soul. These requests outraged Heloise, who felt that he should offer *her* consolation instead of asking it for himself: "Instead of bringing us the healing balm of comfort as you should have done, you increased our desolation and made the tears to flow which you should have dried" (letter 4.2). He in turn replied sharply: "When I am suffering in despair of my life, would it be fitting for you to be joyous? Would you want to be partners only in joy, not grief...?... Say no more, I beseech you, and cease from complaints like these, which are so far removed from the true depths of love!" (letter 5.11–12). Both lovers had mastered the rhetorical genre of the *planctus*—and both, it seems, were readier to ask for comfort than to give it. If they are the authors of the *Epistolae*, it is poignant to see this pattern emerging so early.

Whether you will or no (*velis, nolis*): nos. 38b, 84

A fault to lament one's miseries (*culpam . . . miserias suas . . . deplorare*): cf. Heloise, letter 4.2–3; Abelard, letter 5.11–12

Who seeks occasions . . . to break up (*qui occasiones querit . . . ad amoris scissionem*): Proverbs 18:1 (*occasiones quaerit qui vult recedere ab amico*); no. 42

Thrown me . . . into the waves (*in mediis fluctibus involvisti*): Exodus 14:27 (*involvit eos . . . in mediis fluctibus*)

You have inflicted new wounds on my old ones, . . . added sorrow to sorrow (*vulneribus meis nova vulnera inflixisti et dolorem doloribus addidisti*): cf. Psalm 68:27 (*super dolorem vulnerum meorum addiderunt*)

A cruel breast, impregnable to love (*pectus durum et amori inexpugnabile*): Ovid, *Metamorphoses* 11.767–68 (*inexpugnabile amori / pectus*)

62 (**Woman**)

From his beloved to her beloved: I send whatever can be most blessed in the sight of God, most honorable and joyful among mortals.

If I had such a clever way with words that I could reply prudently to your message, I would answer you as suitably as I could with a willing spirit. Nonetheless, although I cannot give satisfaction, I will reply as best I can to the measure of my modest learning.
[. . .]
Let the matter between us be handled in such a way that you incur no danger, nor I scandal.

O the cruelty of men! How true is that oft-cited proverb: "a man's devotion is bound to a throw of the dice."
[. . .]
If you had had to suffer chains, irons, prison, fetters, or even the sword, I had still hoped that you could not have resisted coming to me

by any means possible, to discuss with me face to face the things you
told me in your letter.

I do not want any more tears to burst from your eyes, for it is improper
for a man to weep when he should maintain the severity of strict honor.
Dearest, it is time that we cast aside these bitter, tearful subjects; let us
apply our hands to the wax for more cheerful and fortunate things. So,
my beloved, write something cheerful, sing something cheerful, live
happily and prosperously! When shall I see you, sweetheart—you who
have almost forgotten me? Grant me at least one cheerful hour.

COMMENT

After receiving her lover's tear-stained letter, the Woman relents. Unfortunately,
the scribe's omissions have deprived us of the more concrete portions of no. 61,
in which the Man imparted some news that she would rather have discussed in
person. She is still upset that he avoids visiting her, held back by fear, but her
words could apply to any illicit affair: "let the matter . . . be handled in such a
way that you incur no danger, nor I scandal."

Heloise was deeply influenced by Stoic ethics.[92] So is the Woman of these
letters, who thinks "it is improper for a man to weep." This belief was common
but not universal, for weeping did not always render a man effeminate. After all,
Jesus wept (John 11:35). So did Roland, so did Tristan; and monks were encouraged to weep in contrition. The Woman nonetheless finds tears unacceptable for
a man, who should maintain "the severity of strict honor." So she declares a mor-
atorium on bitterness.

Oft-cited proverb: *pietatem viri talo ligari.* I have been unable to locate any such
    proverb, but a model letter in Bernard de Meung's *Flores dictaminum* (late
    twelfth century) uses a similar expression.[93]

Chains, irons, prison, . . . sword (*Si vincula, si ferrum, si carceres, . . . si gladium*):
    Hebrews 11:36 (*et vincula, et carceres, . . . in occisione gladii*)

I had still hoped that you could not have resisted coming (*sperabam te abstinere non
    potuisse, quin . . . ad me venires*): cf. Regensburg Songs, no. 61.4 (*Si tibi plana
    fides esset, secret[e] venires*)

It is improper for a man to weep (*indecens est virum flere*): cf. Hugh Primas 3.11 (*Non est flere viri*)

Severity of strict honor (*honesti rigoris . . . severitatem*): cf. Peter Damian, *Epistolae* 7.254 (*severitatis honestae rigorem*, PL 144: 449b)

You who have almost forgotten me (*fere mei oblite*): cf. Tegernsee letter 2 (*a memoria tua funditus videor deleta*)

ℨ⟶

63 (**Man**)

To his most beloved: I send whatever sincere devotion requires of those who love each other uniquely.
[. . .]
The letter you sent was marked by mature judgment and a rational, orderly composition. I have certainly never seen one more aptly arranged. As for me—God willing, sweetheart, I shall grant you many of the most sweet and cheerful hours. Farewell, my spirit.

ℨ⟶

COMMENT

Much relieved, the Man pedantically thanks the Woman for her "rational, orderly composition" and promises a visit. The couple's bitterest quarrel to date has ended.

ℨ⟶

64 (**Man**)

To his most beloved: I send the greeting I long to bring you in person. Farewell, and see that I never see your tears, but be cheerful—sure of the fidelity of your faithful one.

ℨ⟶

Again he promises joys to come, assuring her of his fidelity.

⊰⊱

65 (**Man**)

To his soul from her soul: may we long be one in one soul.

⊰⊱

This simple greeting repeats the word "soul" in three cases, a triple token of harmony: *Anime sue, anima eius: in una anima diu unum esse.*

⊰⊱

66 (**Woman**)

With an auspicious omen, Clio, assist my task!
Adorn my tablets with song, declaim sweet verses.
Awake, my mind, with such a patron's riches!
All instruments, resound, favored by the breath of Jove.
Lo, how the light advances, night is fading away,
Lo, now the light has come, night withdraws in dismay.
See how the band of clerics shines with the master's light
As their teacher's splendor banishes the old one's night.
Muses, therefore, sing praise with sonorous voices!
Clio, sing first: "Hail forever, flower of clerics!"
Speak next, Euterpe: "Flourish and gather favor!"
Let Thalia say: "Increase like the crescent moon!"
Melpomene, assent: "For as long as winter freezes!"
And add, Terpsichore: "Hail, happy throughout all ages!"
I ask Calliope too, proclaim sweet hymns.

Let Urania speak as well: "May he live enriched with virtues!"
Polymnia, adorn him with manners, crown him with honors.
And now let Erato say: "May he be glad in this world,
Glad in this world, but then rejoice in the next,
Where the blessed in mutual love rejoice without end."
"Hail, live, and thrive," resound all Muses together.
"Gather as many joys as there are drops in the ocean's waves,
As many as the blades of grass or all the fish in the sea."
What more need I say? May he flourish in peace. Amen.

Farewell, breath of my life.

COMMENT

This ode in leonine hexameters celebrates an academic victory of the beloved.[94]
For his partisans, the new teacher is the "light" that has banished his disgraced
predecessor's "night." As he assumes his position of honor, presumably a teaching chair, the Woman invokes the Muses to acclaim him in a solemn *adventus*.
The nine Muses are not linked here with particular arts or poetic modes. They
merely shower the teacher with blessings here and hereafter. As Jaeger notes, the
formal genre of the poem harks back to Carolingian panegyric. Such acclamations were used at solemn public occasions such as a royal birth, coronation, or
inauguration of a bishop; they commonly invoked the Muses or other classical
deities and ended with a triadic "hail," like the *salve, vive, vige* (hail, live, and
thrive) at the end of this lyric. The Woman's mastery of the form shows her deep
familiarity with "the neo-classical idiom of the humanist poetic traditions,"
which flourished in both French and German cathedral schools.[95]

    If the master was Abelard, the best-known "victory" of his early career was
a triumph over his old teacher, William of Champeaux. Having bested William
in a debate over universals, Abelard boasted in *Historia calamitatum* 7, "My
own teaching gained so much strength and authority from this [victory] that
the most vigorous supporters of my master who had hitherto been the most hos-
tile among my critics now flocked to join my school. Even [William's] successor
as head of the Paris school offered me his chair so that he could join the others as
my pupil, in the place where his master and mine had won fame." The debate

took place at the new abbey of canons of Saint-Victor, which William had founded around Easter 1111. But in 1113 he left Paris to become bishop of Châlons. There is some uncertainty about William's immediate successor, who may have been Joscelin de Vierzy, later bishop of Soissons (1126–52). In the turmoil of cathedral politics, this master in turn was soon replaced by another, probably Goswin, who became a monk of Anchin around 1113. If Abelard succeeded Goswin, the timing would fit the presumed dates of the love affair in 1116–17. Yet the poem casts aspersions on the previous master, who departs in disgrace (*confusa*)—not, it would seem, voluntarily. Two separate occasions may have been conflated with some poetic license.[96]

One allusion in the poem also has implications for its date. When the Woman calls her teacher "flower of clerics" (*flos cleri*), she quotes the first line of Marbod of Rennes' epitaph for Anselm of Laon: "Princeps doctorum, flos cleri, gloria vatum" (prince of teachers, flower of clerics, glory of poets). *Flos cleri* was not a common phrase; in the entire *Patrologia Latina* it appears only in this epitaph.[97] Anselm had been a famous biblical exegete who, with his students, was largely responsible for the *Glossa ordinaria*. The young Abelard came to Laon to attend his lectures but, dissatisfied with them, humiliated the master in his old age by setting himself up as a rival. In retaliation, Anselm "persecuted" the cocky young philosopher (as Abelard puts it) by forbidding him to continue lecturing at his school (*Historia calamitatum* 10–12). It was this banishment from Laon that prompted Abelard's return to Paris, where he soon afterward met Heloise. Anselm died on 15 July 1117. So, if Heloise was the author of this poem, she must have seen Marbod's epitaph almost as soon as it was written. This would not have been surprising in Paris, given Anselm's celebrity and his prior connection with Abelard. She could even have pilfered Marbod's phrase with deliberate irony to praise her own master, who had vanquished the deceased one.

If Abelard was not the master acclaimed in this lyric, we would have to posit another famous, competitive teacher of philosophy who also happened to have a highly literate, poetically gifted girlfriend. The floor is open for nominations.

Assist my task (*ceptis assis*): Virgil, *Aeneid* 10.461 (*coeptis . . . adsis*)
Their teacher's splendor banishes the old one's night (*Splendor doctoris noctem*
      fugatque prioris): cf. *Historia calamitatum* 7
Hail forever (*semper aveto*): Alcuin, *Carmina* 7.16 (*semper aveto*)
Flower of clerics (*flos cleri*): Marbod of Rennes, *Carmina* 2.24.1 (*flos cleri*, PL 171: 1722b)
As long as winter freezes (*spirant dum frigora brume*): Ovid, *Tristia* 4.7.1 (*frigora brumae*)

Enriched with virtues (*virtutibus auctus*): Walahfrid Strabo, *Carmina* 2, *Vita B.*
    Blaithmaic 26.17 (*virtutibus auctus*)

Blades of grass (*virent herbe*): Fulcoius of Beauvais, *De nuptiis Christi et ecclesiae* 1.200
    (*uirent herbae*)

As many as . . . the fish in the sea (*quot pisces sunt maris amne*): Ovid, *Ex Ponto* 2.7.28
    (*quotque natent pisces aequore*)

Flourish in peace, amen (*pace fruatur, amen*): Baudri of Bourgueil, *Carmina* 26.10
    (*pace fruaris. Amen.*)

67 (**Man**)

Farewell, my sweetest, and grant your beloved your permission.
Farewell, and may you think of me as you do of yourself. You are the
goal toward which I always aim; you are the end and repose of my
journey. Farewell, more lovable than anything speech can name.

COMMENT

The Man asks his lover's permission (*licenciam*) to do something, unknowable
for lack of context. She would already have known the details.

End and repose (*terminus et requies*): cf. Boethius, *Consolation* 3, metr. 9.27–28 (*tu*
    requies . . . / . . . terminus idem)

68 (**Man**)

A sweetheart wishes his sweetheart whatever sweeter thing can be
imagined. Farewell—you are sweeter than all things known to be

sweet. I beg you earnestly, let me know how you are, for your good fortune is my chief pleasure. Let me know when I can come. Farewell.

COMMENT

Forms of sweetness (*dulcissime, dulcior,* and the like) occur five times in two sentences, setting a new record. In fact, versions of *dulcis* and *dulcedo* occur no less than eighty-seven times in the whole correspondence. A meeting seems imminent—but, as we learn from no. 69, it never takes place.

Whatever sweeter thing can be imagined (*quicquid dulcius excogitari potest*): cf. the hymn "Jesu dulcis memoria" (*nil cogitatur dulcius*)[98]

69 (**Woman**)

Go, letter of mine, and bear my complaints
  To my friend, greeting him on my behalf.
Convert my friend, I beg, though unwilling:
  Tell him I lack my just reward.
<...>
  Gullibly, I believed his deceptive speech.
Let him remember those tears he shed for me
  When he told me he would surely die
If he could not possess one so beautiful—
  And then he praised what he now holds cheap.
Ask where is his weeping, where now his pleas,
  And the pledge of faith that he freely gave me?
Why does he never come? why does he break my heart?
  Ah! I never deserved to be so deceived.
Let no envious eye, I pray, read these verses:
  I want no hearts full of guile to know them.

Any eloquence that might appeal to you, beloved, exceeds the capacity of my mind. For, just as the human heart chose the chief seat of its exaltation in the midst of blood, my mind has exalted you as its supreme desire in every kind of love. My soul thirsts with incomparable love for the fountain that is the sight of you; it can never lead a blessed life without you.

[. . .]

With every surge of blood, my heart is stung by as many stabs of pain as there are letters in these words. O prize of my heart, what have you done? No matter what force drives you from me, I marvel how you could be so suddenly changed, you whom I sealed in my heart with a firm anchor of love. For this reason I have taken to sackcloth and ashes, and day and night tears spill from my eyes. What more? Above all, the sharpest arrow of pain is piercing me, and harder than diamond will be the man who remains unmoved by my sighs of misery.

Fare well in eternity and after, if that can be.

COMMENT

Despite the Man's latest assurance of love, the Woman is angry again, recalling no. 60. In verse and prose alike she complains of neglect, echoing an age-old female lament. Once her lover wept and pleaded, praising her beauty to the skies, making endless promises, swearing he would die if he could not possess her. But now that he does possess her, he holds her cheap (*vile*) and never visits. She, on the other hand, has bound her welfare so completely to his that she can have no joy without him. Her rather confused analogy of the heart seems to make loving equivalent to bleeding. Having set her lover in the place of God, the Woman assumes the posture of a penitent, weeping in sackcloth and ashes, mourning that she has been deceived.

The letter is an unabashed plea for pity and reassurance. Heloise in her monastic letters would voice the same complaints.

Go, letter (*Littera, vade*): Ovid, *Tristia* 3.7.1–2 (*Vade . . . / littera*)

Though unwilling (*licet invitum*): Marbod of Rennes, *Carmina* 2.44.99 (*licet invitus*, PL 171: 1733d)

Tell him (*Dic quia*): Hildebert of Lavardin, *Carmen in libros Regum* 4.228 (*Dic quia*, PL 171: 1256b)

What he now holds cheap (*quod modo vile facit*): Heloise, letter 2.14: "If only I could think of some pretexts which would excuse you and somehow cover up the way you hold me cheap!"

Pledge of faith (*pignus fidei*): Regensburg Songs, no. 34.8 (*fidei pignus*)

Let no envious eye . . . read these verses (*Hos, rogo, ne versus oculus legat invidiosus*): cf. Tegernsee letter 2 (*Cave diligentius, / ne tercius interveniat oculus*)

Hearts full of guile (*pectora plena dolo*): cf. Ecclesiasticus 19:23 (*interiora eius plena . . . dolo*); Nigellus Wireker, *Speculum stultorum* 2822 (*pectora plena dolo*)

My soul thirsts . . . for the fountain (*Anima mea . . . ad fontem . . . sitit*): Psalm 41:2–3 (*Quemadmodum desiderat cervus ad fontes . . . / Sitivit anima mea ad Deum*)

Never lead a blessed life without you (*neque unquam beatam vitam sine te ducere valet*): cf. Heloise, letter 4.4: "If we lose our life in you, we shall not be able to go on living when you leave us."

Stabs of pain (*doloris aculei*): Jerome, *Epistulae* 108.1 (*doloris aculeos*); Augustine, *De civitate Dei* 5.20 (*doloris aculeos*)

Prize of my heart (*pars pectoris mei*): Symmachus, *Epistolae* 4.22 (*pars pectoris mei*, PL 18: 229b); cf. Psalm 72:26 (*Deus cordis mei et pars mea*)

Sackcloth and ashes (*cineris . . . et cilicii*): Matthew 11:21 (*cilicio et cinere*)

Day and night tears spill from my eyes (*per diem ac noctem lacrimas deducunt oculi mei*): Jeremiah 14:17 (*Deducant oculi mei lacrymam per noctem et diem*)

The sharpest arrow (*acutissima . . . sagitta*): Psalm 44:6, Isaiah 5:28 (*sagittae . . . acutae*)

❧

70 (**Man**)

To his long-awaited desire, whom he will always long for: I wish all the good that can be desired or longed for. Farewell.

❧

COMMENT

The keyword *expectare* is repeated in three forms. In the liturgy it has connotations of patient waiting and fervent hope, as the prophets awaited the Messiah. What is "expected" in this sense is beyond one's control; one can only hope and wait.

Long-awaited . . . always long for (*expectato . . . et semper expectando*): Psalm 39:2
 (*Exspectans exspectavi*); no. 37

71 (**Woman**)

Terrified by the Lord's saying that "it is hard to kick against the goad," I send you this unadorned letter to prove how devotedly I submit myself to your commands in all things. The East is far from the West, yet loyalty is repaid with loyalty for those who are divided over long periods of time. They will not be divided for an instant if the chain of true love has bound them together, for wherever they dwell, they will still be joined in soul and in mind. I had many things to say, but I am hampered by too great a bitterness of spirit. Would that I could sit at your side this very hour and talk with you! For a little sadness might be allowed, but my many heartfelt sighs increase when I think of the times I have spent diligently working for you, utterly neglected though I am. Out of many things I will do just one: I greet you with a kiss of true peace.

Farewell, and grant me leave to go.

COMMENT

Unwilling to adopt the Man's passive attitude, the Woman will not resign herself to patient longing, but avows her "bitterness of spirit." One senses her unspoken, though almost audible protest: no matter how great the challenges, her lover could visit if he really wanted! Or at least he could write more often. Grief at his absence feeds resentment of his indifference.

The letter contains a complaint that has been overlooked, I suspect, because of a difficulty in the Latin text. Deleting a superfluous comma, the passage reads, *dum studiosa mei laboris tempora in te funditus perpendam neglecta*. Chiavaroli and Mews translate, "when I consider that times set aside for my work are completely abandoned because of you."[99] But how could the Woman have sacrificed her working hours for a lover she never saw? Rather, I would read *funditus neglecta* as modifying not *tempora*, but the implied subject *ego*. Feeling "utterly neglected" by her absent lover, the Woman resents "the times I have spent diligently working for you" (*in te*).[100] It sounds as if her teacher had employed her as a kind of unpaid research assistant. Indeed, this might be the earliest complaint of its kind in the long history of exploitative labor relations between eminent men and the women who loved them. The Woman's request for "leave to go" (*licenciam eundi*) echoes the Man's language in no. 67, though its context is equally obscure. Is she asking for a dispensation from her tasks, and if so, what might they have been?

The First Authenticity Debate disclosed some evidence that Abelard and Heloise worked with a shared dossier of quotations. For instance, Heloise's letter 6 on monastic observance contains a long quotation from Augustine's *De bono coniugali*, which also occurs in Abelard's *Sic et non*. There is similar overlap between letter 6 and Abelard's *Rule* for the Paraclete, which he composed in direct response to that letter. Shared quotations are also found in Heloise's *Problemata* (a set of biblical queries posed by the Paraclete nuns) and various Abelardian texts. Peter Dronke addressed this problem by suggesting that the couple "read certain texts together at one stage of their lives, and that, when they were separated, they still read texts in the same manuscripts, exchanging these (or sometimes perhaps making copies for each other) when necessary." Or they could have had "a commonplace-book, in which quotations were stored by topic. . . . [I]t could have been kept jointly, added to jointly, or even copied out by one of the two for the other."[101] Heloise could certainly have maintained such a dossier, searched out quotations for Abelard, or copied manuscripts for him. Through Fulbert she would have had access to the well-stocked library of Notre-Dame, and she had no lack of learning, dedication, or leisure for such tasks. If such a scenario underlies this letter, the Woman may be complaining less about the labor itself than about a sense that she and her diligent toil have been *funditus neglecta*—utterly neglected.

Surprisingly in the light of what follows, the Woman begins her letter by avowing yet again her total submission—as promised in no. 25, where she pledged to obey her teacher in all things. Although this letter is brief, it presents a complex emotional spectrum of submissiveness, idealism, bitterness, resentment, and desperate yearning. Attentive readers of Heloise's letters 2 and 4 will recognize that jumble of feelings, whose ultimate model can be found in Ovid's *Heroïdes*. Antiquity's greatest female impersonator crafted his women's voices from a potent amalgam of passion and anger, gendered obedience and fierce independence. Heloise—and the Woman of the *Epistolae*—absorbed the model well.

Hard to kick against the goad (*difficile est contra stimulum calcitrare*): Acts 9:5, 26:14 (*durum est . . . contra stimulum calcitrare*)

The East is far from the West (*distat ortus ab occidente*): Psalm 102:12 (*distat ortus ab occidente*)

Those who are divided over long periods of time . . . will still be joined in soul and in mind (*per multa temporum spacia disiunctis . . . anima tamen juncti erunt et mente*): Tegernsee letter 5 (*Quamvis nos disiungant maxima intervalla locorum, tamen coniungit nos equanimitas animorum*); Regensburg Songs no. 42.1–2 (*non queat adtenuari / Tempore vel spacio*)

Chain of true love (*vinculum vere dilectionis*): Jerome, *Epistulae* 82.11 (*dilectionis vinculo*); pseudo-Jerome, *Regula monachorum* 1 (*vinculo dilectionis*, PL 30: 393d); nos. 55, 76, 84

I had many things to say (*multa habui loqui*): John 8:26 (*multa habeo . . . loqui*)

Bitterness of spirit (*mentis amaritudine*): cf. Job 3:20, 7:11 (*amaritudine animae*)

⨀

72 (**Man**)

To one who in her wrath does not forsake mercy, from him who is restored to grace: may you live happily until I should wish to forgo your grace.

This is how our love will become immortal: if each of us strives to surpass the other in a friendly, joyful competition; and let neither of us consent to be outdone by the other. It may happen that a friend will grow weary of loving if he sees himself less loved by his friend than he deserves. So I would never want to have said that I love you more than I feel loved; such a remark is silly and breeds discord. Rather, I think it is much better to say that in our mutual love, I do not want to be the lesser, and I have no idea which of us surpasses the other.

[. . .]

Someone once said, on seeing a thornbush that produced the most beautiful flowers, "My lady is like that! No thorn is sharper than when she is angry, and no flower more pleasing and bright than when she is pleased."

[. . .]

Farewell, and take good care that you compare no mortal to me, for I will firmly persist in the same intention toward you. Be well, beloved, and remember that I am yours forever.

COMMENT

To celebrate the end of another quarrel, the Man resorts to theological language. Like God, his beloved is "wrathful" (*irata*) yet "does not forsake mercy," while he, like a penitent sinner, has been "restored to grace." These biblical dynamics recur throughout the relationship. The Woman reserves the rights to pass judgment, to reproach, to maintain silence, and to withdraw her favor if her covenant partner falls short of her demands, as he often does. He in turn repents, apologizes, and promises to amend. Rarely is this pattern reversed.[102] Only once does the Woman seek forgiveness, though in a letter that is no longer extant (see no. 35); and only once does the Man express anger (no. 61)—though, even in that case, he ultimately confesses a fault (no. 74). The couple's dynamics recall troubadour lyrics and the later development of courtly love, in which the Woman holds a dominant, morally superior position. But two competing patterns complicate the lovers' relationship. In one, the Woman compensates for her lofty tone by adopting a markedly inferior stance: she humbles herself before her teacher, laments her defects, exalts his virtues, and pledges complete submission. In yet a third pattern, the lovers adopt the language of friendship—a classical, purely masculine heritage—to posit equality on both ethical and affective planes. The interplay of these patterns renders the couple's exchange extraordinarily complex and—like all deep human relationships—contradictory.

In this letter, the Man hits on an inspired way to resolve these tensions. From now on, the lovers' subliminal jockeying for power is to become an overt, formal contest. They will engage in a *concertatio amoris*, a "friendly, joyful competition" to see which can outdo the other in showing affection, in the hope that—as the Man says in no. 85—"both of us will win." As an acknowledged topos of male friendship, *concertatio* encouraged two friends to compete in self-improvement and the cultivation of virtue.[103] A striking twelfth-century instance is afforded by the friendship of Bernard of Clairvaux and William of Saint-Thierry. William had accused Bernard of loving him less because Bernard's letters were neither so long nor so frequent as William's. The Cistercian replied with a rhetorical tour de force, asking how his friend could presume to have knowledge of his heart:

If man sees only the face because God alone beholds the heart—then I wonder, and indeed I cannot wonder enough, how or by what means you were able to weigh and distinguish between your love and mine. . . . Perhaps what you say is true, that I love you less than you love me; but I say with certainty that you cannot be certain of this. . . . Inasmuch as there is greater charity in you—I speak to you as my father—then you have all the more reason not to despise my potential. For even if you love more because you are more able, yet you do not love more than you are able. As for me, even if I love less than I should, nonetheless I love as much as I can.[104]

To head off this kind of jealousy at the pass, the Man specifies that neither he nor his partner should ever presume to declare victory. Significantly, this motif had no previous place in heterosexual relations; it is part of the lovers' bold attempt to fuse *amor* with *amicitia*. In effect, their competition in love will be a competition in rhetoric. Because their meetings have become dangerous and rare, the lovers must now display their passions primarily through writing. One premise of their competition must be a settled conviction on either side that the beloved is supreme among mortals; no invidious comparisons may be entertained. In her Letter 2.11, Heloise cites an *auctoritas* from Cicero's *De inventione*: "Unless you come to believe that there is no better man nor worthier woman on earth you will always still be looking for what you judge the best thing of all." Spouses, like lovers, must give up such futile searches by persuading themselves that the perfect partner is the one they already have. Heloise adds that for other married couples, this is a happy illusion, but for herself and Abelard, it was actually true.

"Immortal love" was not yet the romantic cliché it later became. In fact, the phrase itself was rare. We find it in a famous poem from the *Carmina burana*, the *Altercatio Phyllidis et Florae*, in which two girls debate the merits of knights versus clerics as lovers. The cleric's girlfriend praises *Amor indeficiens, Amor immortalis* (unfailing Love, immortal Love); but she is describing the God of Love, not their relationship.[105] The Man of the *Epistolae*, however, uses *immortaliter* for his beloved and their relationship twice in nos. 22 and 26. Given the Woman's claim to a "sublime and exceptional love" in no. 53 and the Man's boast of their extraordinary friendship in no. 28, it seems that this couple consciously aspired to an exemplary love, if not the legendary status that Abelard and Heloise were ultimately to attain.

Our love will become immortal (*amor noster immortalis erit*): cf. *Carmina burana* 92, *Altercatio Phyllidis et Florae*, stanza 24 (*Amor immortalis*)

Friendly . . . competition (*amabili concertacione*): Cicero, *Laelius* 32 (*sintque pares in amore et . . . inter eos sit honesta certatio*); Cassiodorus, *Variae* 9.4 (*amabili concertatione*, PL 69: 769d)

Compare no mortal to me (*neminem mortalium michi compares*): cf. Heloise, letter 2.11, citing Cicero, *De inventione* 1.31.51–52

73 (**Woman**)

May you too be well, beloved, worthy of all delights.

Hail, flower of youth, light and imperial glory!
  Imperial glory, hail, flower of youth!
When Nature fashioned you, she blessed you
  With strength within and acclaim without,
And gave to your form such splendid beauty
  That I am dumbstruck and cannot describe it.
I could say much more of you, if any would believe
  What my mind perceives of your value.
Now I shall make an end, though I could say more:
  May you live in joy, may you seldom grieve.

As many as the stars in heaven, girls on the earth,
  Or crashing waves on the sea—so many times I say: farewell.

COMMENT

The Woman opens the competition with a poem in her lover's praise, professing to
be dumbstruck (*stupeo*) at his beauty and hailing him—oddly for a French
woman—as if he were an imperial prince. Formally, the repetition of the first half-
line at the end of the second was characteristic of late antique poets, and popular
again in the late eleventh and early twelfth centuries. It was a technique especially
favored by Baudri of Bourgueil.[106] *Flos juvenilis* (flower of youth) in the sense the
Woman uses here, "illustrious young man" (rather than youth as a stage of life), is a
rare, nonclassical usage. That sense is attested earlier, albeit ironically, only in a
long, polemical poem that might have interested Abelard and Heloise for quite
particular reasons. The poem defends a master of the Würzburg schools in a dispute between the students of Würzburg and Worms, which became such a cause
célèbre circa 1030 that the Würzburg students disseminated their defense of the
calumniated teacher far and wide. The bishops of both cities, local potentates, and
possibly the king himself adjudicated the dispute.[107]

  The Woman's closing lines exemplify a kind of flourish to which she was
especially partial, using the *quot-tot* construction (cf. nos. 45, 66, 69, 79, 107).
Ovid favored this topos, which abounds in medieval letters. Notker of St. Gall
produced a comprehensive example:

> As many as the sky has stars and the earth pebbles,
> As many as the wood has leaves or the ocean sands,
> As many as the raindrops that fall from the cloudy sky,
> As many as the river's fish or all the birds of the world,
> As many as the flowers in the field and grass in the meadow,
> So many blessings may the Triune God grant you.[108]

Flower of youth (*flos juvenilis*): *Nomen ut herbarum*, apologia for the school of
    Würzburg (*flos iuvenilis*);[109] cf. *Carmina burana* 169, "Hebet sidus"[110]
Nature ... blessed you (*te Natura beavit*): Marbod of Rennes, *Carmina* 1.24.21 (*te
    Natura beavit*, PL 171: 1660c)

Such splendid beauty (*Forme splendorem tantum . . . atque decorem*): In *Historia*
    calamitatum 16, Abelard says that when he set out to seduce Heloise, he feared
    no rebuff because of his youth and "exceptional good looks" (*iuuentutis et forme*
    gratia preminebam).
Of your value (*de probitate tua*): Baudri of Bourgueil, *Carmina* 32.4 (*ex probitate tua*)
As many as the stars in heaven, girls on the earth (*Quot celo stelle, quot sunt et in orbe*
    puelle): Ovid, *Ars amatoria* 1.59 (*Quot caelum stellas, tot habet tua Roma*
    puellas); Tegernsee letter 4 (*Quot celum stellas retinet, quot pontus harenas*)
I say: farewell (*tibi dico vale*): Baudri of Bourgueil, *Carmina* 200.173 (*tibi dico "uale"*)

74 (**Man**)

Now at last I understand, sweetheart, that you belong to me with all your
heart and all your soul, since you are willing to forget every wrong that
I—foolish and thoughtless, with a mind far too reckless, too soft to resist
my sorrows—have carelessly inflicted on you, my beloved. That remark
was empty; it meant nothing and had no weight. And if you are willing
to compare words with deeds, my spirit, you will realize that those were
only words, not supported by any action. You ask about my health? If
you are well, I am well; if you are happy, I am happy. I want in fact to
adapt myself to you in every turn of fortune. Farewell, my spirit.

COMMENT

After a conversation, it seems, the Man finally understands why the Woman
had been so angry. We will glean more information in no. 75, but for now, he
confesses to a careless remark and a mind "too reckless, too soft to resist my sorrows" (cf. nos. 61–62). He still hopes that he has offended only in words.

With all your heart and all your soul (*ex toto corde et ex tota anima*): Deuteronomy 6:5
    (*ex toto corde tuo et ex tota anima tua*); Matthew 22:37 (*ex toto corde tuo et in tota*
    anima tua)

If you are well, I am well (*Si tu vales, ego valeo*): Baudri of Bourgueil, *Carmina* 103.23
(*Si ualeas ualeo*)

I want . . . to adapt myself . . . fortune (*ad omnes . . . fortunas tuas me coaptare volo*): cf.
the Woman in no. 25: "my mood shifts in accord with your affairs, so that I
count your joy as my profit and your adversity as my bitterest defeat."

❧

75 (**Man**)

To his only delight: whatever can be found most delightful in this life.
[. . .]
What an idiotic promise! What a rash, all too thoughtless remark!
What a saying from a man who was plainly either out of his mind or
drunk! For who is so filled with knowledge, so circumcised in his lips,
that he might dare to promise so great a thing of himself? Never mind
the learned scholars of this age. If Cicero himself had made such a
boast, even his copious eloquence would have failed to fulfill it, for he
could have brought forth nothing worthy of so great a promise. If
Ovid had applied his fullest powers to his verse, he could by no means
have made good on such a start. Who am I, then, or what talent do I
have, that I could compose a letter to prove myself worthy of your
golden bosom, your ivory arms, your milk-white neck?

But never mind words, which are like the wind. What deed, what labor
could be great enough to purchase such marvelous delight? If I were to
cross the ocean in the hope of winning such a good, my labor would be
slight. If I were to climb the Alps in the most bitter cold, or seek you in
the midst of flames at the risk of my life, in all these things I would
seem to have done nothing. So I must humbly beg for your grace. Do
not measure this letter against my promises, lest I incur the reproach
of that proverb: "The mountains will labor and a ridiculous mouse be
born." For I can say nothing worthy of so arrogant a promise.
[. . .]
For some time now, my fair one, you have doubted the fidelity of your
beloved because of some words I composed when provoked by a

sudden insult, in the very throes of pain. Would I had never composed them! You have stamped them too deeply on your memory, and I beg you to erase them from your heart and let them not take root within you—as I never did myself, I swear to God! Rather, as soon as they left my hands, at once I wanted to call them back, if only a word once spoken knew how to return.

I am the same toward you as I was before; look not to words, but to deeds! You have not become stale to me; every day you are renewed in my heart, just as the pleasant weather is renewed every year with the coming of spring. The season itself caresses us with kindness; let us take full advantage of its opportunities. We shall be able to love wisely—which is a rare thing indeed, for someone once said, "Who has ever loved wisely?" We, however, shall truly be able to love wisely, for we shall take prudent care for our reputation yet at the same time mingle our joys with supreme delight. A covered fire burns hotter than one that is allowed to breathe freely.

Farewell, my lovely delight.

COMMENT

Now at last we learn what caused the last bitter quarrel. Some time ago the Man had been stung by a "sudden insult" (*subita impulsus contumelia*). Perhaps one of the "envious"—his enemies—had challenged his right to possess the Woman or his worthiness of her. In a reckless moment, he responded by promising to write some kind of letter or poem in her praise, firmly establishing that he deserved her; and he had been foolish enough to inform her in writing of that promise. Immediately he thought better of it, for few courses of action could have been more dangerous. But rather than saying this, he appeals to an ineffability topos. Neither Cicero nor Ovid—the standards of eloquence in prose and verse, respectively—could remotely do justice to the Woman's worth. Indeed, not even the most heroic feats could merit anything so sublime as her beauty.

Meanwhile, the Woman has continued to wait for the promised text, long after her beloved forgot that he had ever made such an "idiotic promise." When the expected letter is not forthcoming, after some weeks or even months, she doubts her lover's "fidelity" (*fides*)—not to her sexually, but to his promised word. She even begins to wonder if she has grown old and stale (*vetus*) in his eyes.[111] But only now, it seems, has she confessed the cause of her simmering resentment. While praying to be released from his promise, the Man does his best to fulfill it, although he begs her not to read his present letter as the one he had boasted he would write, lest it seem an absurd little mouse born to laboring mountains. We do not have his earlier boasting letter, perhaps because the Woman obeyed his request and destroyed it.

If it seems surprising that so trivial a cause could have provoked such anger, we might think of this broken promise as symptomatic. From nos. 69 and 71, we know that the Woman feels neglected and bitter at the Man's prolonged absence. The suitor who had once begged with tears for her love and sexual favors now takes her for granted or, as she puts it, holds her cheap. All the same, it is significant that a promise about *writing* has led to this crisis. The Woman has poured her whole self into these letters—and the longer the couple's enforced separation, the more they come to matter. But in order to meet his enemy's challenge, the Man would have had to produce a semi*public* letter, an act precluded by the secrecy of their affair. Hence he reminds his beloved of the need to "love wisely" and protect their reputations, recalling the metaphor of hidden fire that she had introduced in no. 55. Yet even as the Man apologizes for one boastful promise, he cannot help making another: he and his partner *will* be able to love wisely. The allusion to Ovid is inexact, but telling; what the poet actually said is "whoever loves wisely will conquer" (*Quisquis sapienter amabit / Vincet*).

Was such behavior typical of Abelard? In *Historia calamitatum* 11, he reports making another rash promise that got him into considerable trouble. As noted earlier, the young philosopher had embarked on a course of biblical studies under Anselm at Laon, but soon grew disillusioned with the aging teacher (see comment, no. 66). When his fellow students rebuked him for claiming expertise in a field he had just taken up, Abelard met their challenge by promising to lecture on the most obscure biblical passage they could propose. After they had settled on a prophecy of Ezekiel, he arrogantly rejected their advice to spend more than a single night preparing. Though he claims that his lectures succeeded brilliantly, his defiance resulted in Anselm's banishing him from the school. Here we see the Man of the *Epistolae* meeting a verbal challenge with a similar rash promise.

Circumcised in his lips (*labiis circumcisus*): Exodus 6:12, 6:30 (*incircumcisus labiis*); no. 23

If Cicero . . . If Ovid: cf. Tegernsee letter 8 (*Si exsuperat mihi ingenium Maronis, / si afflueret eloquentia Ciceronis*)

Ivory arms (*eburneis brachiis*): Ovid, *Amores* 3.7.7–8 (*eburnea . . ./ bracchia*)

Milk-white neck (*lactea cervice*): Virgil, *Aeneid* 10.137 (*cervix . . . lactea*)

If I were to cross the ocean, . . . if I were to climb the Alps . . . or seek you in the midst of flames . . . in all these things I would seem to have done nothing: cf. 1 Corinthians 13:1–3 (*Si linguis hominum loquar et angelorum . . . si habuero omnem fidem ita ut montes transferam . . . si tradidero corpus meum ita ut ardeam, charitatem autem non habuero, nihil mihi prodest*)

To climb the Alps in the most bitter cold (*si Alpes in asperrimo frigore transcendam*): cf. Ovid, *Amores* 2.16.19 (*si premerem ventosas horridus Alpes*)

The mountains will labor . . . mouse be born (*Parturient montes, nascetur ridiculus mus*): Horace, *Ars poetica* 139 (*Parturient montes, nascetur ridiculus mus*)

My fair one (*formosa mea*): Song 2:10 (*formosa mea*); no. 46

If only a word . . . return (*si vox emissa reverti nosset*): Horace, *Ars poetica* 390 (*nescit vox missa reverti*); cf. Tegernsee letter 10 (*Sermonem ceptum quis enim retinere valebit?*)

Who has ever loved wisely? (*quis unquam sapienter amavit?*): cf. Ovid, *Ars amatoria* 2.511–12 (*Quisquis sapienter amabit / Vincet*)

A covered fire burns hotter (*ignis fortius estuat, qui tegitur*): Ovid, *Metamorphoses* 4.64 (*tectus magis aestuat ignis*); no. 55

76 (**Woman**)

To the dearest of all that bind with the bond of love, from a friend whose companionship is certain: I wish you the summit of the most inviolate love.

My writing hand can by no means express how intimately I cherish you, for a sweet feeling within me urges that you should be my special beloved above all. In no way can I make you see how ardently I burn with affection for you.

[. . .]

I confess truly, beloved, that I would often have come to a standstill in the road, like a listless sheep, if the magisterial skill of your teaching had not constantly recalled me when I strayed from the sloping path. "But now let us block the streams; the meadows have drunk enough." This is what I mean to decree: from now on our quarreling must cease. Harsh anger has swollen enough already through our mutual recriminations.

[. . .]

Why do I delay with prolix ramblings? Please grant me one request, which is this: never presume to trouble me, your soul, with such uncertainty.

Farewell, my bright star, my golden constellation, my gem of virtues, sweet medicine for my body.

COMMENT

Mollified, the Woman declares an end to quarreling, reassures the Man of her affection, and expresses renewed gratitude for his teaching.

She probably picked up the adjective *specialis* (special) from the letter-poems of Baudri of Bourgeuil.[112] In his letter to the nun Constance, Baudri characterizes his attachment to her as *spetialis amor, quem nec caro subcomitatur / Nec desiderium sauciat illicitum* (a special love which is not secretly in league with the flesh, nor tainted by illicit desire).[113] It is not clear to me that the Woman uses *specialis* with the same implications of purity, but she is quite partial to the term, using it four times to describe *dilectio* (nos. 21, 25, 76, 79). Conversely, the Man avoids *specialis* but calls their relationship *singularis* (singular) four times (nos. 2, 4, 54, 56) and *unicus* (unique) no fewer than nine times. (See appendix D.) Whether the distinction is semantically significant or not, it is consistent and thus, as Constant Mews has observed, helps to explain the famously enigmatic salutation of Heloise's letter 6: *Suo specialiter sua singulariter* (To him who is specially hers, from her who is singularly his).[114] In that greeting Heloise allows herself one last, brilliantly succinct evocation of their earlier letters, and their love, before changing the subject to monastic observance—in obedience, as always, to Abelard's command.

To the dearest of all that bind with the bond of love (*cunctorum vinculo amoris alligantium carissimo*): The grammar yields the best sense if *vinculo* is taken as an ablative. Cf. Boethius, *Consolation* 2, metr. 8.13–15 (*Hanc rerum seriem ligat / Terras ac pelagus regens / Et caelo imperitans amor*)

Special beloved (*specialis dilectus*): cf. Baudri of Bourgueil, *Carmina* 99.131 (*specialis amicus*), 200.79 (*spetialis amor*)

Listless sheep (*pecus ignavum*): Virgil, *Georgics* 4.168 (*ignavum . . . pecus*)

Let us block the streams . . . drunk enough (*claudamus rivus, sat prata biberunt*): Virgil, *Eclogues* 3.111 (*Claudite iam rivos . . . sat prata biberunt*)

Harsh anger has swollen enough . . . (*satis iam dire iactis mutuo sermonibus intumuere ire*): Statius, *Thebaid* 1.411–12 (*mox ut iactis sermonibus irae / Intumuere satis*)

Gem of virtues (*gemma virtutum*): Jerome, *Epistulae* 64.22 (*gemmis . . . virtutum*)

Medicine for my body (*corpori meo . . . medicamentum*): cf. Ecclesiasticus 6:16 (*Amicus fidelis medicamentum vitae*)

꩜

77 (**Man**)

To his joy: joy and gladness. What shall I say to you, sweetheart, but what I have often said before? I hold you in my whole heart, I embrace you with my inner arms, and the more I drink of your sweetness, the more I thirst. All my riches have been gathered in you alone; all that I can do is yours. That we may do our best to care for each other, you are I and I am you. To have said this should be enough. Farewell; may the strong hand of almighty God protect you.

꩜

COMMENT

The Man reiterates that he belongs entirely to his beloved as he carries the theme of coinherence (nos. 16, 22) to its furthest point: "you are I and I am you." The phrase echoes a comedy of Plautus, where its context is farcical: two rivals claim to be *unianimi* (of one mind), even declaring that *ego tu sum, tu es ego*, because they both love the same prostitute. But, as von Moos notes, verbal proximity does not always indicate the source of inspiration.[115] In this case the Man's intentions are entirely serious. They belong rather to the world evoked by Karl Morrison in *"I Am You,"* his profound study of the hermeneutics of empathy.[116] One is reminded of the Man's earlier definition of love, which unites two wills so as to produce "one single thing... without difference" (no. 24). He and his beloved now constitute that *unum*.

You are I and I am you (*tu es ego et ego sum tu*): Plautus, *Stichus* 731 (*egu tu sum, tu es ego*)

ℑ•

78 (**Man**)

If a man has not, let him write earnestly to obtain what he has not. As for me, I am secure; I have come sailing into the harbor. Let him who is shipwrecked offer vows; since I am safe in the harbor, I have no need of vows. Farewell.

ℑ•

COMMENT

In an exultant mood, the Man boasts of his success in love. No longer among the "have-nots," he has reached his goal and need make no further vows—or votive offerings or prayers (*vota*). Metaphors of ships and sailing could often be sexual innuendos.[117]

A man [who] has not (*qui non habet*): Matthew 25:29, Mark 4:25, Luke 19:26 (*qui non habet*)

Obtain what he has not (*ut quod non habet, reperiat*): James 4:2 (*non habetis, propter quod non postulatis*)

I have come sailing into the harbor (*ego navigando ad portum veni*): Terence, *Andria* 480 (*Ego in portu navigo*)

I am safe in the harbor (*ego in portu sedeo*): Terence, *Andria* 480; Virgil, *Aeneid* 7.201 (*portuque sedetis*)

৶

79 (**Woman**)

To him who deserves to be embraced with the passion of a special love, the blazing fire of your love sends you as many greetings as there are fragrant flowers in springtime.

If a person's inner self conceives of some great plan in meditation, it rarely comes to fruition without a kind of violence from the outer self. For despair of fulfilling the plan may cripple it, or else exhausting toil gravely harms it before it can be carried out. So it happens that the effort or labor of the whole self fails, more often than not, to arrive at the desired goal.

As for me, I have long struggled with an impassioned effort of heart and body over the question of how to address you, my noble gem. But the difficulty of my expected failure has kept me until now from completing what my affection intends. For I know—and I confess— that I am wholly inadequate in body and mind alike to render thanks for each and every one of your favors. Yet for one particular gift which I hold more precious than gold and topaz, for as long as this spirit thrives in its body, it will never weary me to write to you, my love. For no written account, no willing declaration, can ever express how much joy and exultation your honeyed love confers on me.
[. . .]
Your honor might seem to have doubled mine—if only we were allowed to live together as equals until the fatal end. But for now, I choose rather to be undone by the danger of death than to live without the sweet delight of seeing you.
[. . .]
Since you have become all things to me, save the grace of God alone, I have no need to desire anything more throughout all time, except that

he who can grant a thousand days as easily as one may increase the days of your life.

COMMENT

Much of this letter is devoted to one of the Woman's pet themes, her sense of inadequacy in greeting and thanking her beloved (cf. no. 23). She begins with a labored account of why so many human endeavors, including her literary project, come to grief. But the letter takes an ominous, melodramatic turn at the end: "Your honor might seem to have doubled mine—if only we were allowed to live together as equals until the fatal end" (*usque ad finem fatalem*).

What is this "fatal end" that entails even "the danger of death"? It sounds very much as if the lovers are at risk because they have been discovered and will soon be parted. In *Historia calamitatum* 21, Abelard says of this phase in his affair with Heloise: "How I blushed with shame and contrition for the girl's plight, and what sorrow she suffered at the thought of my disgrace! All our laments were for one another's troubles, and our distress was for each other, not for ourselves. Separation drew our hearts still closer while frustration inflamed our passion even more; then we became more abandoned as we lost all sense of shame and, indeed, shame diminished as we found more opportunities for lovemaking." He further recalls that, when he proposed marriage, Heloise did her best to dissuade him, even writing a letter-tract that he quotes at length in the *Historia calamitatum*.[118] Jaeger, following Piron, takes the Woman's puzzling statement that "your honor might *seem* to have doubled mine" (*tuus honor meum geminasse videretur*) to express her rejection of marriage.[119] As a legally wedded pair, the lovers might "seem" to gain the respect of society, but its price would be the loss of that pure, disinterested quality that Heloise so prized in her love. When she failed in her *dissuasio* she remarked, prophetically and theatrically, "We shall both be destroyed. All that is left us is suffering as great as our love has been" (*Historia calamitatum* 27).

Inner self . . . outer self (*hominis interioris . . . exterioris*): cf. Romans 7:22 (*secundum interiorem hominem*); 2 Corinthians 4:16 (*is, qui foris est . . . is, qui intus est*); Ephesians 3:16 (*in interiorem hominem*)
More precious than gold and topaz (*auro et topazio preciosius*): Psalm 118:127 (*super aurum et topazion*); no. 45

Joy and exultation (*leticie et exultacionis*): Psalm 44:16 (*laetitia et exsultatione*)
Honor . . . doubled (*honor . . . geminasse*): Ovid, *Ex Ponto* 3.4.99 (*geminabit honorem*)
You have become all things to me (*omnia factus sis michi*): 1 Corinthians 9:22 (*omnibus omnia factus sum*)

❧

80 (**Man**)

To her who is more welcome than winter sun and sweeter than summer shade, from him who is intimately on fire with your warmth and gently refreshed by your soothing breath. May you live gently and experience nothing except what is sweet.

If I hunger, you alone satisfy me; if I thirst, you alone refresh me. But what have I said? You do indeed refresh me. But you do not satisfy me, for I have never had enough of you, and I think I never will. Live in gladness; may it never fail you. Farewell.

❧

COMMENT

Ignoring the Woman's baleful hints, the Man returns to the theme of her tempering influence (no. 50). But he himself is not temperate, for the more he drinks of love, the more he thirsts (no. 77), and the more he tastes, the more he hungers. Like Lady Wisdom, the beloved feeds a truly insatiable desire.

More welcome than winter sun and . . . summer shade (*Hiberno sole gratiori et estiva umbra dulciori*): Ovid, *Metamorphoses* 13.793 (*solibus hibernis, aestiva gratior umbra*)
You do not satisfy me (*reficis et non saturas*): Ecclesiasticus 24:29 (*Qui edunt me adhuc esurient, / Et qui bibunt me adhuc sitient*)

81 (**Woman**)

To my most beloved and, to tell the truth, most expert in love, whom I can never thank enough, yet I endorse the praise offered by all things that together serve you—and all beauty. Farewell. May they perish who are trying to part us!

COMMENT

Like a worshipper overwhelmed by gratitude to God, the Woman feels that she owes her lover thanksgiving far beyond her means, so she calls on the creation to help her—even as she confirms the threat of a final parting.

82 (**Woman**)

I send you the greeting I would want sent to me:
  I know of nothing more wholesome than this.
If all that Caesar ever possessed were mine,
  Riches so great would profit me nothing.
<...>
  I will never have joys unless you give them—
And grief and woe pursue us in every season.
  Nothing is wholesome for me unless you give it.
Of all things that the universe contains,
  You alone will be my everlasting glory.
Just as stones on the ground dissolve in fire
  When a pyre that is built above them burns,
So our body wholly dissolves in love.
  And so farewell: live as long as the Sibyl,
May you vanquish Nestor in a ripe old age.

Have mercy on me, for I am truly constrained by the love of you.
Farewell.

COMMENT

Obeying the Golden Rule, the Woman greets her beloved as she herself would
wish to be greeted. That "wholesome" salutation turns out to be none other than
the famous claim, amplified in Heloise's letter 2.10, that all the wealth of Caesar
Augustus could not compare with the joy of love in freedom. In each case, the
point turns on the disinterested character of the woman's love. Heloise reaches
for this hyperbole to reinforce her claim that she never sought anything from
her beloved save himself alone, *te pure non tua concupiscens*. The Woman's point
here is similar: even fabulous wealth, apart from her beloved, would be mean-
ingless.[120] Psalmlike, her poem formulates the terms of an erotic mysticism:
nothing will ever be joyful, nothing healthful, unless it comes from the hands of
her lover—who alone will be her everlasting glory (*semper eris gloria sola michi*).

Her final image may invoke the phoenix, or perhaps the suicide of Dido.
Just as a funeral pyre burns so forcefully that even the stones beneath the wood
"dissolve in fire," so her body dissolves in love. But what she actually says is "our
body" (*nostrum corpus*) in the singular. Does she mean "my body," using the au-
thorial *we*, or does she mean (as her lover has so often said) that the two have
become one? Probably both. The lyric, Jaeger writes, "suggests a physical union
so complete and ecstatic that the single body into which two are transformed
vanishes and is scattered abroad (*late vanescit*) like ashes in the wind."[121]

In keeping with its classical themes, this is the Woman's only poem in unrhymed distichs.[122]

I send you the greeting I would want sent to me (*Quam michimet vellem mitti, tibi*
       mitto salutem): cf. Matthew 7:12 (the Golden Rule); Ovid, *Tristia* 5.13.1–2 (*Hanc*
       tuus . . . mittit tibi Naso salutem, / mittere si quisquam, quo caret ipse, potest);
       Baudri of Bourgueil, *Carmina* 98.1 (*Quam michi non habeo, mitto*
       tibi . . . salutem)
If all that Caesar ever possessed (*Si quicquid Cesar unquam possedit, haberem*): cf.
       Marbod of Rennes, "Rescriptum ad amicam" 5–6;[123] Heloise, letter 2.10: "God
       is my witness that if Augustus, emperor of the whole world, thought fit to
       honour me with marriage and conferred all the earth on me to possess forever, it

would seem to me dearer and more honourable to be called not his empress [*imperatrix*] but your whore [*meretrix*]."

All things that the universe contains (*quas totus continet orbis*): Ovid, *Metamorphoses* 7.59 (*quas totus possidet orbis*)

Live as long as the Sibyl (*vive per tempora longa Sibille*): Ovid, *Metamorphoses* 14.132–53

83 (**Woman**)

May this day dawn for you happily, pass happily, end happily. What more? You know that I love you on equal terms. Farewell. You are clearer than glass and stronger than steel.

COMMENT

In this hasty note, the Woman states with odd formality that she loves her partner "on equal terms" (*condicione pari*), recalling her use of *equipolenter* (equivalently) in no. 21 and *par pari* (an equal to an equal) in no. 18. She may be alluding to the terms the Man had set for their competition: each should strive to surpass the other in love, and neither should consent to be outdone (no. 72). Alternatively, she recalls a celebrated formula St. Jerome had used to assert that adultery committed by a married man is just as serious as if the woman were married.[124]

Equal terms (*condicione pari*): Jerome, *Epistulae* 77.3 (*pari condicione*)
Clearer than glass (*vitro . . . lucidior*): Horace, *Carmina* 1.18.16 (*perlucidior vitro*)

84 (**Woman**)

A lover to a lover: joy with salvation, I say, for one who desires that salvation that can never end and the joy that for all eternity cannot be taken from you.

Ever since we first knew each other by sight and speech, you alone have pleased me above every creature of God, and you alone have I loved. In loving I sought you, in seeking I found you, in finding I desired you, in desiring I chose you, and in choosing I set you in my heart before all others. You alone have I chosen from thousands that I might make a pledge with you. When that pledge was fulfilled and I had tasted the honey of your sweetness, I hoped that I had put an end to future cares.
[. . .]
Birds love the shade of the forests; fish lurk in streams of water; stags climb up the mountains; and as for me, I love with you a stable and undivided mind. Until now you have remained with me; you have manfully fought the good fight with me; but you have not yet received the prize.
[. . .]
If the one in whom I have placed (and still place) all my hope and confidence should falter in loyalty, if the bond of his love should not hold firm, I have absolutely no idea whom I could ever trust again.

Whether you will or no, you are mine forever and always will be. Never will my desire for you be altered, nor will I withdraw my whole spirit from you. In you I have what I sought, I hold what I desired, I embrace what I loved. Your ways alone suit me. No one but Death will ever take you from me, for I would not hesitate to die for you. Farewell, and remember our love in every hour.

I will repay you for your prologue, which you composed for me, with thanksgiving and the service of love. May your heart be glad; depart, whatever is sad.

COMMENT

Attaining the summit of erotic adoration, the Woman sets her lover rhetorically, figuratively, and affectively in the place of God. Echoing the salutation of no. 48, *amans amanti*, she wishes him *gaudium cum salute* (joy with salvation or health), but the greeting becomes akin to a prayer when she specifies not temporal well-being, but never-ending joy and eternal salvation. Like the bride in the Song of Songs, she says she has chosen her beloved from thousands, making her covenant or pledge (*pignus*) with him alone. The impassioned rhetoric of her declaration "in loving I sought you, in seeking I found you" (*teque solum dilexi, diligendo quesivi, querendo inveni, inveniendo amavi*, and so forth) is a splendid example of the figure of *gradatio* or climax.[125] While not a quotation, it may deliberately recall the famous close of *De civitate Dei*, where Augustine speaks of the joys of the blessed: *ibi vacabimus et videbimus, videbimus et amabimus, amabimus et laudabimus* (there we shall be still and we shall see; we shall see and we shall love; we shall love and we shall praise).[126]

In adopting this sacred register, the Woman assumes agency and initiative in her love affair. Far from being merely a girl who responded favorably to a seduction poem (nos. 113, 112), she portrays herself as the active wooer in a love quest pursued with all her heart and mind and soul and strength. A little further she declares, "In you I have what I sought, I hold what I desired, I embrace what I loved." These lines allude unmistakably to the passion of St. Agnes, the prototypical virgin martyr: "Behold, now I see what I desired, now I hold what I hoped for; I am united in heaven to the one I loved on earth with my whole devotion."[127] As Sarah McNamer notes, "St. Agnes is the exemplary *sponsa Christi* in the eleventh century: she is the virgin martyr who proved her worthiness to be Christ's spouse by suffering torments and violent death.... [Her] exemplarity was enshrined liturgically . . . via the rich quotation from her *vita* in the liturgy for consecration of virgins."[128] The same lines are echoed in the *Epithalamica*, an Easter sequence sung at the Paraclete and ascribed by Chrysogonus Waddell to Abelard:

Iam video quod optaveram,	Now I see what I had longed for,
iam teneo quod amaveram;	now I clasp what I had loved;
iam rideo quae sic fleveram,	now I laugh, who had wept so much:
plus gaudeo quam dolueram:	I rejoice even more than I had grieved.
Risi mane, flevi nocte,	At morn I laughed, I wept at night;
mane risi, nocte flevi.[129]	I laughed by morn, by night I wept.

In light of the relationship between this liturgical piece and letter 84, David Wulstan (following a hint by Mews) reascribes the sequence to Heloise.[130] As Dronke has shown, however, there are good reasons to be skeptical.[131]

Just as newly professed nuns exulted to possess Christ, the convent-educated Woman exults to possess her earthly lover, and like a virgin martyr, she proclaims her willingness to die for him. Such a love can only be eternal. So the Woman boldly claims—as she has done before—that her love will never change. Love is her element, so to speak. As the forest is to birds, rivers to fish, and mountains to stags, so is the beloved to her constant mind. But the exalted register of this language enables her, perhaps unconsciously, to slip into the tone of moral superiority that comes so easily to her. Her desire will not change, yet his might ("whether you will or no"), and she even hints darkly that he could "falter in loyalty," leaving her bereft. Although she has chosen to make him her god, he is in fact not God—and on some level, she knows this.

Thirty years ago Dronke took the Woman's Pauline phrase "you have not yet received the prize" to imply that this love affair (unlike that of Abelard and Heloise) was never consummated.[132] But that seems unlikely in view of the many erotic hints in the exchange, including a passage in this very letter: "when that pledge was fulfilled and I had tasted the honey of your sweetness." Here I agree with von Moos: the "prize" probably refers to victory in the *concertatio amoris* (no. 72).[133] Indeed, it would be uncharacteristically coarse for a lover as idealistic as this Woman to call her own body "the prize."

The "prologue" for which the Woman thanks her partner cannot be identified. It could have been a prologue to one of his own works or, conceivably, one of hers.[134] But the suggestion of a joint literary project reinforces the hint in no. 71. Abelard, of course, would compose a great many works for Heloise in her monastic life.

For a stylistic comparison of this highly wrought letter with a passage from Heloise, see appendix E and p. 70 above. The letter also displays many parallels with the Tegernsee love letters, especially nos. 8 and 10 (both from the same woman). Although one was trained in a northern French and the other in a Bavarian convent, these two accomplished writers had a similar grammatical and rhetorical education.

Since we first knew each other by sight and speech (*Post mutuam nostre visionis allocucionisque noticiam*): cf. Tegernsee letters 6 (*iocundissime allocutionis / ac visionis tue / dulcedinem*) and 8 (*a die, qua te primum vidi, cepi diligere te*)

You alone have pleased me (*tu solus michi placebas*): Ovid, *Ars amatoria* 1.42 (*tu mihi sola places*); Tegernsee letter 8 (*mihi [nisi] tu nemo placebit*)

Chosen from thousands (*elegi ex milibus*): Song 5:10 (*electus ex millibus*); no. 50; Tegernsee letters 6 (*electa es ex milibus*) and 8 (*Tu solus es ex milibus electus*)

I hoped that I had put an end to future cares (*sperabam me curis finem posuisse futuris*): *Ovidius puellarum* 2 (*Sperabam curis finem fecisse futuris*); Tegernsee letter 10

(*Dicit quidam sub nomine Ovidii de amore: Sperabam curis finem fecisse futuris*)[135]

Stags climb up the mountains (*cervi ascendunt montana*): cf. Psalm 103:18 (*montes excelsi cervis*)

Fought the good fight (*bonum certamen certasti*): 1 Timothy 6:12 (*certa bonum certamen*); 2 Timothy 4:7 (*bonum certamen certavi*)

Not yet received the prize (*nondum bravium accepisti*): 1 Corinthians 9:24 (*unus accipit bravium*)

The one in whom I have placed . . . all my hope and confidence (*in quem omnem spem meam fiduciamque positam . . . habeo*): troped introit for St. Stephen's Day (*in quo omnem spem meam fiduciamque positam habeo*);[136] Tegernsee letter 8 (*in te omnem spem meam fidutiamque positam habeo*)

I have . . . no idea whom I could ever trust again (*cui postea credere possim, prorsus ignoro*): cf. Tegernsee letter 2 (*mortales cuncti discedant, fidem et dilectionem a me ulterius non querant*)

Whether you will or no (*Velis, nolis*): nos. 38b, 61

I have what I sought, I hold what I desired (*quod quesivi, habeo, quod optavi, teneo*): Vita S. Agnetis 2.11 (*quod credidi, video; quod speravi, iam teneo; quod concupivi, complector*); cf. *Epithalamica*, Easter sequence from the Paraclete (*Iam video quod optaveram, iam teneo quod amaveram*)[137]

✣

85 (Man)

If there can be any alterity or division within the same body, then to the best part of his own body, which is divided from him, he wishes undivided, incorrupt, and integral affection, with unending sweetness of the liveliest love.

If you want to note the words of your beloved closely, sweetheart, you can plainly note that I would like to say more than I can. In searching for words I fall short, because my affection surpasses the ordinary measure so far that it can by no means be fully expressed in ordinary words. So, if you observe any sluggishness in me or judge any failure, the fault certainly does not lie in my love growing colder. Rather, it stems from the excessive distraction of someone who cannot decide what is best to say—someone who wills much, but accomplishes less. Nor is it fitting to repay in words alone the favors you provide in deeds.

If all that the world holds precious were gathered into one heap, compared with your favors it would seem utterly vile; it would be judged of no worth. So great is your sweetness, so amazing your constancy, so indescribable your way of speaking, so complete the beauty and grace of everything about you, that it would seem to be great insolence if anyone presumed to find its equivalent in words. May our flame always increase with new nourishment. The more hidden it is, the more let it blaze, deceiving the envious and treacherous. And let it never be certain which of us loves the other more, for thus the competition between us will always be most beautiful, and both of us will win. Farewell.

✉

COMMENT

The only new element in this letter is the conceit of its salutation—a play on the motifs of integrity and division. The lovers are one body, like Christ and the Church, yet that body is divided in space and the Woman represents its "best part," that is, the heart. So, to the one who is physically "divided from him" (*divise a se*), the Man wishes the most "undivided" love (*indivisam dilectionem . . . et integram*).

His other themes are familiar. Like the Woman, but more straightforwardly, he laments his inability to express his love; he notes that words often fall short of deeds (cf. nos. 12, 22, 54, 74) and proclaims that all the world's treasures cannot compare with his beloved (no. 12). Once again he hopes that their love, like a blazing but hidden flame (nos. 55, 75), will deceive its envious foes, and their amorous competition (no. 72) make both of them victors.

Gathered into one heap (*in unum congeratur*): Cicero, *Tusculan Disputations* 5.117
    (*congerantur in unum omnia*); no. 12

86 (**Woman**)

To her inexhaustible fount of sweetness, from an indivisible part of his soul: after the cares of Martha and the fertility of Leah, may you possess the best part, which is Mary's.

The measureless force of my love for you, which incessantly, indefectibly, indubitably, and indescribably holds its steadfast course, compels me to write you a few words, beloved, to the best of my ability and power. But I have absolutely no idea what is most important to say. As often as you anticipate me with your sweetest words, so often you show me the affection of your sincere and intimate love. So, with no doubt whatsoever, love and desire for you burn in me always and never grow cold.

If by the will of God I could take the form of a bird, how quickly I would fly off to visit you!
[. . .]
If by the grace of God, what I have just now desired could come to pass, there is nothing in all the world that I would desire more—with God as my witness, before whom it is difficult to utter deceiving words. Your affection is a rich feast for me, yet I can never be sated with your love. In your life is my health; you are my whole desire and all my good.

Farewell, half of my heart, the fire of all my love and gladness.

COMMENT

The Woman closely echoes the themes of the Man's previous letter, wishing her lover some contemplative peace ("the best part, which is Mary's"), perhaps after the labors of teaching.

The cares of Martha (*sollicitudinem Marthe*): Luke 10:41 (*Martha, Martha, sollicita es*)
The fertility of Leah (*fecunditatem Lie*): Genesis 29:31–35

The best part, which is Mary's (*optimam partem Marie*): Luke 10:42 (*Maria optimam partem elegit*)

Love . . . compels me to write you a few words (*vis tui amoris . . . me cogit pauca . . . scribere*): Ovid, *Heroïdes* 4.10 (*scribere iussit amor*); Baudri of Bourgueil, *Carmina* 99.137 (*amor me scribere pauca coegit*)

If . . . I could take the form of a bird (*O si . . . acciperem volucris speciem*): Psalm 54:7 (*Quis dabit mihi pennas sicut columbae*); Tegernsee letter 5 (*Quis dabit mihi genus volatile, / ut volitem more aquile, / ut ad te veniam?*)

Half of my heart (*cordis dimidium*): Horace, *Carmina* 1.3.8 (*animae dimidium*); no. 11

ℑ❧

87 (**Man**)

Quickly yet slowly this year has passed for me
  Since your love, my dear, first bound me to itself.
When I think of your inexhaustible beauty
  And the goodness that is innately yours,
It seems scarce one brief hour since we met;
  You are ever new to my desires and cares.
Yet if I think how rarely you can meet your love—
  It seems to me that countless years have passed.
Each day that I am forced to spend without you
  Feels to me, sweet love, like thrice ten years.
Dismal is that day, deprived of light,
  When the sun of your face does not dawn on me.
Your countenance is my sun, my certain light,
  Whenever I may chance to see your face.
My stars are two, if you should ask, no more:
  I mean to say, those starry eyes of yours.
When I enjoy them, I think nothing lacking;
  Lacking them, I think that I lack all.
So I can be called happier than all men—
  Yet I can be said to have nothing good,
So what I said before is proven true.
  In this way the space of a year has passed.

Now a new year comes and love must begin anew:
  Our fidelity wishes to hold a different course.
Love must be harmed no more with bitterness:
  Only the sweet henceforth, my life, I'll give you.
Nothing I'll say or do unless it pleases you.
  I shall hold myself wholly at my lady's will;
Let us have discord in nothing at all.
  Command what you will, I'll obey at once!
No longer shall bitterness wound your tender body,
  Nor shall I give cause for more harsh poems.
Forgive me, fair one, if ever I have written
  Any word that justly merited your wrath.
I did it without forethought, without reason—
  Impulse itself was my poor adviser.
If anyone could recall a word once uttered,
  That remark, I swear, I would recall!
When I bring back to mind your tears, beloved,
  I myself cannot restrain my own tears.
Receive one, then, who confesses his faults;
  Receive him and remember his guilt no more.
Receive him, dearest, I beg with ample tears;
  Even on bended knees I pray you!
May their last day's light have risen on my eyes
  If there lives a woman I would prefer to you.

COMMENT

This poem in elegiacs, at forty-six lines the longest in the correspondence, is the Man's anniversary gift. Much like lovers today, the couple must have recognized some specific date as the beginning of their love. The position of this letter suggests that their affair lasted for a year and some months—probably a year and a half at most.

The Man praises his lover's beauty, as she might expect on such an occasion. He assures her that she is "ever new" to him, not stale as she sometimes fears (nos.

75, 98). Her face is still his sun, her eyes his guiding stars. But separation continues
to take a toll. Gallantly he promises to turn over a new leaf, from now on playing
the obedient courtly lover: "I shall hold myself wholly at my lady's will." No more
will he wound her with "bitterness," no more provoke "harsh poems" like no. 69.
Again he apologizes for the rash promise that had so deeply offended her (no. 75).
In fact, fully half the poem is devoted to this penitential theme, culminating with
the Man "on bended knees" and no fewer than three mentions of tears. We are left
with an impression of the Man's profound commitment to the relationship, along
with his concomitant fear that, despite the Woman's assurances of love, he is unworthy and may indeed lose her.

Each day . . . without you . . . years (*una dies ter denos continet annos . . . sine te*): cf.
    Baudri of Bourgueil, *Carmina* 90.31 (*Sola dies sine te mecum decernitur annus*)
Lacking them, I think that I lack all (*His ego dum careo, defore cuncta puto*): no. 111
What I said before (*quod diximus ante*): Marbod of Rennes, *Vita B. Maurilii* 2.129
    (*quod diximus ante*, PL 171: 1645a)
A new year comes (*novus est annus*): Ovid, *Fasti* 1.149 (*novus incipit annus*)
Love must begin anew (*novus est amor incipiendus*): Ovid, *Remedia amoris* 452 (*novus
    est inveniendus amor*)
Command what you will (*Tu, quod vis, jubeas*): Augustine, *Confessions* 10.29 (*jube
    quod vis*)
Your tender body (*Corpus sic tenerum*): pseudo-Ovid, *De Pyramo* 3.266 (*Corpus sic
    tenerum*)
Impulse . . . my poor adviser (*Qui male consuluit, impetus ipse fuit*): Statius, *Thebaid*
    10.704–5 (*male cuncta ministrat / impetus*)
If anyone could recall (*si quis revocare valeret*): Fulcoius of Beauvais, *De nuptiis Christi
    et ecclesiae* 5.72 (*Si tum reuocare ualeret*)
Cannot restrain my own tears (*Non possum lacrimas ipse tenere meas*): cf. Ovid,
    Metamorphoses 2.796 (*vixque tenet lacrimas*)
Their last day's light . . . on my eyes (*Lux oculis hodierna meis extrema sit orta*): Ovid,
    Heroïdes 9.167 (*Et tu lux oculis hodierna novissima nostris*)

88 (**Woman**)

To the foundation of her firmest love, from the house that is well built upon it and perfectly finished: may we be bound by a stable, neighborly covenant.

Mountains and forests and all the shady groves of the woods reply, so how should the glory of replying to you be difficult for me? For hard work disappoints the worker, while a willing mind hastens to its task. Or rather, nothing is difficult that is willingly done.

Rarely do we find anyone on this high sea who can claim such settled happiness, such perfect virtue, that he need not often regret the faults of his uncultivated body—except you alone, whose virtue stands out in and through everything. That is why, firmly attached, you cleave to my heart and always will. Not for a single hour, sleeping or waking, will you ever leave it.

There is no firm love that is so quickly deflected by deceit, nor will there ever be. Any injury you have ever inflicted on me has not yet faded from my heart's remembrance. Yet I will forgive you now for everything, so fully, purely, and sincerely that I will never again be moved by such an injury from you. I will remain with you—faithful, stable, immutable, unbending—and even if I should come to know all men individually, I would never leave you unless driven off by force and utterly cast out. I am no reed shaken by the wind, nor will either harshness or softness in anything remove me from you.

The fire of love for you will be constantly renewed and increase within me. Its flames blaze higher and never cool; the more it is hidden and guarded within, the more it increases and multiplies. Although I may not see you with my bodily eyes as often as I would wish, as I would choose, as I would desire, you do not slip away from my mind's intention. For a fire is more easily preserved if it is carefully buried in ashes and produces no smoke. In this way let us also love one another.

Farewell; rejoice with a never-ending joy.

COMMENT

The Woman makes firmness and stability her keywords. She will be like the wise man in the parable, building her house upon a rock—but her firm "foundation" is her lover. Though she has often questioned his fidelity before, she now claims that he alone possesses "perfect virtue," come what may. So, while she cannot forget past injuries, she freely forgives them, offering pardon as proof of her love. The four adjectives she applies to her own constancy (*fida, stabilis, immutabilis, et non flexibilis*) balance the four adverbs she used in no. 86 (*indesinenter, incessanter, indubitanter, inennarabiliter*). Another way she evokes the eternal is by frequently yoking verbs in the present to the future tense, cementing them with an "always" or a "never": *semper adheres et adherebis*; *neque . . . recedis neque recedes*; *non est nec unquam erit.*

Since the lovers can so rarely meet, this virtue of total loyalty to an absent, increasingly idealized beloved looms larger every day. In the first two canonical letters of Heloise we see how, even after fifteen years in religious life, she still measures her conscience against the standard set here, which is that of absolute fidelity and obedience to her old lover.

The house that is well built upon it (*fundamento domus bene superedificata*): Matthew
    7:24–25 (*aedificavit domum suam . . . fundata . . . super petram*); 1 Corinthians
    3:10 (*ut sapiens architectus fundamentum posui; alius autem superaedificat*);
    Ephesians 2:20 (*superaedificati super fundamentum*)
The house . . . perfectly finished (*domus . . . optime consummata*): 1 Kings 6:9 (*aedificavit domum et consummavit eam*)
Forests and . . . woods reply (*nemora silvarumque omnia respondent*): Virgil, *Eclogues*
    10.8–9 (*respondent omnia silvae. / Quae nemora*)
Hard work disappoints the worker (*Fallit . . . labor laborantem*): cf. Horace, *Satires*
    2.2.12 (*studio fallente laborem*); Ovid, *Metamorphoses* 6.60 (*studio fallente
    laborem*)

Firmly attached, you cleave to my heart (*cordi meo firmiter infixus semper adheres*): cf.
     Tegernsee letter 5 (*ante omnes, qui sunt in mundo, cordis mei fixa es profundo*)
Reed shaken by the wind (*harundo vento agitata*): Matthew 11:7, Luke 7:24 (*arundi-
     nem vento agitatam*)
Love one another (*invicem diligamus*): 1 John 4:7 (*diligamus nos invicem*); no. 52

ॐ

89 (**Man**)

To his only joy: I wish well-being, if I can give you what I do not have
except from you. If the words I send seem to be somewhat fewer than
you desire, consider not the words but the will of the sender. Abundance makes me poor. Indeed, many words wish to burst out all at
once, and so obstruct one another. While I delay in hesitation, time
flies. Farewell, gem of all France.

ॐ

COMMENT

Apologizing for his brevity, the Man frets: "while I delay in hesitation, time
flies." Some decision has to be made, but what is the issue? Could the Woman be
pregnant?

Abundance makes me poor (*Inopem me copia facit*): Ovid, *Metamorphoses* 3.466
     (*inopem me copia fecit*)

ॐ

90 (**Woman**)

To her leafy grove, fragrant with every kind of virtue, from his lily
flower: I wish you growth in trust and increase in love.

I would write much to you, my beloved, with a willing spirit and a devoted mind—except so many cares impede me, pulling my mind in different ways. So, because of my heart's excessive pain, I can scarcely utter any words of greeting. But now I appeal to you by your loyalty and your concern for my love: just as you welcomed me from the beginning into your love, protect the one you welcomed, and do not cast our love out of your mind.

Live and fare well, and in faring well, rejoice forever.

COMMENT

Strain is showing again. Weighed down by "many cares" and suffering "excessive pain," the Woman anxiously begs her beloved for protection. What threat could she be facing?

Fragrant with every kind of virtue (*omnigenarum virtutum odore redolenti*): cf. Berno
     of Reichenau, *Epistolae* 9 (*omnigenarumque virtutum decori*, PL 142: 1166c)
Lily flower (*flos et lilium*): Song 2:1 (*flos campi et lilium*)

91 (Man)

To his resplendent moon that banishes all darkness—a moon, I say, whose splendor does not wane, from him for whom day never comes without you: may you shine forever, and rejoice forever in the increase of that delectable light.

The cares you endure for your beloved, sweetheart, are all the sweeter to me because they provide yet greater proof of your loyalty. So if I were present, I would wash away all your cares, I myself would wipe those sweetest tears from your starry eyes. I would enfold your anxious breast in embraces and renew your happiness completely. Farewell.

COMMENT

A tender but frustrating note. Grateful for his partner's loyalty as proven by her suffering, the Man muses on how kindly he would treat her if he were present. But in fact, he is absent. The anxiety remains.

Wipe those . . . tears from your . . . eyes (*lacrimas . . . oculis tuis abstergerem*): Revelation 7:17, 21:4 (*absterget Deus omnem lacrymam ab oculis eorum*)

92 (**Woman**)

To her most radiant light, her solstice that never slips into shadow, but always brings shining color, from her for whom no sun burns by day nor any moon by night except you: may you blaze more keenly, shine more splendidly, and never wane in the fervor of our love. Be seasoned with salt and do not lose your savor. Farewell.

COMMENT

Once again the Woman borrows her lover's imagery: each is the light of the other's eyes. But she also warns him, alluding to the Sermon on the Mount, not to be like that "spendsavour salt" that is good for nothing except to be trodden underfoot.[138]

No sun burns by day nor any moon by night (*nisi . . . sol uret in die nec luna per noctem*): Psalm 120:6 (*per diem sol non uret te, neque luna per noctem*)

Be seasoned with salt (*salis condimentum habere*): Matthew 5:13 (*Vos estis sal terrae. Quod si sal evanuerit, in quo salietur?*); Mark 9:49 (*si sal insulsum fuerit, in quod illud condietis?*); Colossians 4:6 (*Sermo vester semper in gratia sale sit conditus*)

❧

93 (**Man**)

To his resplendent light that shines in the midst of darkness: may you know no waning of your sweetest light. No one is unhappier than we, who are pulled by love and shame in two directions at once.

❧

COMMENT

Although the "resplendent light" of their love still shines, the darkness of shame—or public exposure—casts a spreading gloom. Divine light shines in the darkness, and the darkness cannot overcome it. But can this brave yet fragile love match that triumph? The Man's despondent note proposes no solution.

Light that shines in the midst of darkness (*luci . . . que in mediis tenebris lucere solet*): John 1:5 (*lux in tenebris lucet*)
Pulled by love and shame (*amor simul et pudor in diversa rapiunt*): Ovid, *Metamorphoses* 1.618–19 (*Pudor est qui suadeat . . . / dissuadet Amor*), *Heroïdes* 15.121 (*Non veniunt in idem pudor atque amor*), *Amores* 3.10.28 (*hinc pudor, ex illa parte trahebat amor*)

❧

94 (**Woman**)

To her spice of perfect beauty and finest fragrance, bearing a hundred-fold yield in the wilderness with tender seed, from his full moon: the delights of inextricable love.

You throw your words to the winds. If you stone me for such trifles, what would you do to someone who really injured you? He who forgets a friend until he needs to use him is not to be praised, nor is he an altogether perfect friend. Farewell.

COMMENT

The Woman is angry again. Despite her exuberant greeting, which invokes the fruitful seed of the Gospel, she protests that her lover "stones" her for mere trifles (*pro talibus*), which remain unspecified. Perhaps the couple had met face to face and quarreled, or there may have been another angry letter that she chose not to preserve. Resorting to the cold, third-person language of a *sententia* or moral maxim, she avers that her partner has fallen short in the duties of friendship. Rather than loving in the pure, disinterested way she had claimed for herself (no. 49), he conveniently forgets her until he has need of her services. In short, she feels used.

A hundredfold yield (*centuplicato*): Matthew 13:8 (*dabant fructum . . . centesimum*); Regensburg Songs, no. 42.2 (*tempore vel spacio . . . centuplicato*)
Throw your words to the winds (*Verba das ventis*): Ovid, *Amores* 1.6.42 (*Verba dat in ventos*); no. 38b
Nor . . . altogether perfect (*nec ex omni parte perfectus*): Cicero, *Laelius* 21.79 (*nec quicquam difficilius quam reperire [amicum] quod sit omni ex parte in suo genere perfectum*)

95 (**Woman**)

To her storm-tossed ship that has no anchor of fidelity, from her who remains unmoved by the shifting winds of your faithlessness.

You have no sympathy with me but have changed your ways; so nowhere is fidelity secure. I have no small regret that I so firmly set you alone in my heart beyond all others. For a worker labors in vain if there is no one to reward his labor. Waiting in suspended hope, I scarcely kept hoping. But what did that fruitless hope profit me? Farewell.

COMMENT

Having received no reply, she states her accusation more forcefully. Her lover has abandoned her, leaving her to hope in vain—like a worker cheated of his pay. The Woman has made such charges before (nos. 60, 69, 71); now she goes so far as to regret that she ever loved him. Even amid the passionate effusions of no. 84, she had remarked ominously that "If the one in whom I have placed . . . all my hope and confidence should falter in loyalty, if the bond of his love should not hold firm, I have absolutely no idea whom I could ever trust again." Now she believes this has happened—"so nowhere is fidelity secure."

This is the only letter whose salutation includes no wish clause. Such an omission, according to the *artes dictandi*, signifies anger or contempt.[139]

Storm-tossed ship (*Navi periclitanti*): Jonah 1:4 (*navis periclitabatur*)
A worker labors in vain . . . reward his labor (*frustra laborat, cui laboris mercedem nemo recompensat*): proverbial, e.g. *Nil valet ille labor, quem premia nulla sequuntur.*[140]

96 (**Man**)

To his lovely one, for whose praise neither mind nor tongue suffices: what else should I wish but this, that everything the burning love of your most beloved perpetually desires for you may come to pass?

My love for you truly increases day by day and does not diminish with the passing of time. Rather, just as the sun is renewed every day, your delectable sweetness flourishes anew, puts forth shoots, and vigorously grows.

Farewell, my martyr. Remember me just as I remember you.

COMMENT

Disregarding the Woman's reproaches, the Man claims that he loves her more every day. But in his absence, how can she believe it? "Farewell, my martyr," he writes, striking a rare humorous note. We smile, for the Woman does seem to have a martyr complex. But has she truly been ill used, or does she suffer from neediness or, as we would now say, a sense of entitlement? It is impossible to know. In a worst-case scenario, if the Woman was Heloise, we can imagine her pregnant and alone, watching her body swell as she nervously waits for Fulbert to notice, with no more than moral support from her lover.

To his lovely one (*Speciose sue*): Song 2:13 (*speciosa mea*)

97 (**Man**)

To half my heart and part of my soul, I send what I am: I am yours while I live. Farewell, although you have sent me no greeting.

COMMENT

She has retreated into silence, and he is worried.

Half my heart and part of my soul (*Cordi dimidio, parti anime*): Horace, *Carmina* 1.3.8 (*animae dimidium*); cf. nos. 11, 49, 86

98 (**Woman**)

To a beginner, the sweetest of lovers, from a foundation of stable friendship: may you never know the shadows of infidelity. May you become neither cold nor lukewarm in the dulcet fire of our love, but burn more ardently than before and always hold me without wearying, as I deserve, with a spark of friendship in your breast.
[. . .]
My prayers profit me nothing because I and what is mine have become worthless to you. You have merely endured the pleasure of a long-desired joy as if you were angry.

COMMENT

This letter is puzzling. The Woman calls her lover a *tyro*, a new recruit in the army—in this case, Cupid's (no. 113)—although their affair has lasted for more than a year. As she has often done before, she prays that he will be faithful both in friendship and the fire of their passion (*nostri amoris ardore*). Her sense of her own worth is strong; would that he cherished her as she deserves (*me promeren-tem*)! Yet from this hopeful beginning she slides to a disconsolate close. Convinced that her beloved has grown weary of her, she ends on a baffling note, crushed that he has "merely endured" (*sustulisti*) what should have been a great joy, as if it made him angry (*iratus*).

In *Historia calamitatum* 21, Abelard recalls that Heloise sent him a "supremely jubilant" letter (*cum summa exultatione*) in which she announced her pregnancy and asked for counsel. That letter is lost, though it is clear that Abelard did not take this as good news. The present correspondence mentions nothing so concrete as pregnancy, nor do we have any hint of the couple's debate over marriage.[141] If such matters had in fact been discussed, de Vepria would have excised them. But whoever she was, the Woman by now felt seduced and abandoned.

Neither cold nor lukewarm (*frigidum nec tepidum*): cf. Revelation 3:16 (*tepidus es, et nec frigidus, nec calidus*)

99 (**Man**)

To her who well knows and perfectly fulfills the laws of love, from her friend who is the same as ever: I send the same constancy of a unique love.

COMMENT

As he has done before (no. 75), the Man protests that his feelings have not changed in the least, hoping that a compliment will sweeten his plea. Since she has called him a "beginner" (*tyro*) in love (no. 98), he responds by deferring to her own expertise.

100 (**Woman**)

Faithful to faithful one: I send a knot of integral love, which is never untied. It is fitting and right that a possession, possessed by its possessor, should be attentively cultivated. It should not become worthless in his heart, but grow more and more valuable by the hour.

COMMENT

Although she still oscillates between calling her lover "faithful" and bewailing his faithlessness, the Woman increasingly feels that he has used her and thrown her away. This contemptuous note rings three changes on the word "possession," reversing the Ciceronian idealism of nos. 49 and 50. A true friend is utterly indifferent to possessions. But the Woman here complains that she herself has become a possession, and a devalued one at that—last year's shiny toy, thrown on the scrap heap as new interests beckon.

Knot of . . . love (*nodum . . . amoris*): This phrase became common in the later twelfth
century; it occurs in Alan of Lille, Walter of Châtillon, and Baldwin of Ford. A
medieval proverb states that *Firmissimus inter pares est nodus amoris* (The
firmest knot of love exists between equals).[142]

A possession, possessed by its possessor (*possessio, que possidetur a possessore*): cf. Heloise,
letter 2.9: "at your command I changed my clothing at once along with my
mind, in order to prove you the unique possessor [*possessorem*] of my body and
my mind alike."

101 (**Man**)

To his starry eye: may it always see what is pleasing, never perceive
what could displease it.

I am who I was. As for my passion for you, nothing in me has
changed—except the flame of love for you springs higher every day.
This change alone I must confess, this alone I rightly concede: my love
for you constantly increases. But I now address you more cautiously, if
you will take note; I approach more cautiously. Shame tempers love
and modesty restrains it, lest it burst out to infinity. In this way we can
both satisfy our sweet desires and gradually stifle the rumor that has
arisen about us. Farewell.

COMMENT

Protesting that his love is unaltered, the Man confesses the reason for his apparent coldness. Shame (*pudor*) and modesty (*verecundia*) have made him more
cautious, but above all, he dreads discovery. Expanding on a reference to shame
in no. 93, he admits that dangerous rumors are abroad, still hoping it will be
possible to quell them.

I am who I was (*ego sum qui fui*): Exodus 3:14 (*ego sum qui sum*)

102 (**Woman**)

To one flowing with milk and honey, from the whiteness of milk and the sweetness of honey: I wish you the flowing liquid of all delight, the increase of wholesome joy.

With the supreme intention of my heart I wish that you—most beloved, dearest to my heart, utterly suited to my love, most perfectly matched to my desire—may flourish always and live always in sweetness. What I hold most precious I give you, and that is myself—firm in fidelity and love, stable in my longing for you, never changing.

Farewell, be happy—and let nothing offend you nor injure me through you.

COMMENT

Letters 102–5, as well as 108–11, echo a much earlier phase in the correspondence, before the bitterness and fears of discovery that haunt the most recent letters. They may represent a dislocation in de Vepria's exemplar, perhaps a quire or individual leaves that had fallen out of chronological order. But the intervening letters 106–7 were plainly written just before the end of the affair.

In this letter, untouched by reproach, the Woman joyfully offers the gift of self to a lover represented as perfect in every way. Saluting him as the biblical promised land "flowing with milk and honey," she describes herself as the *quidditas*, the essential property of everything he is—the whiteness of milk, the sweetness of honey.

Flowing with milk and honey (*Lacte et melle mananti*): Deuteronomy 26:15 (*lacte et melle mananti*)

103 (**Man**)

To her who is brighter than silver, more resplendent than any precious stone, surpassing all spices in taste and fragrance, from him who is refreshed by your ever-new gifts and joys: may you always delight in charming newness.

Love cannot be idle, for it always rouses itself for a friend, always strives to perform new services, never sleeps, never lapses into laziness. This maxim is clearly proven in you, my spirit. Persevering firmly in the course of a love once begun, you always show your friend by new signs how you feel about him. How much I value your gifts, how much weight they have with me, I will reveal to you in person.

COMMENT

Celebrating the newness of love and his beloved's charms, the Man uses his favorite pet name, "my spirit" (*anime mi*), as he thanks the Woman for her energetic performance of love's service. The idea that love "always rouses itself for a friend" recalls Luke's parable of the friend at midnight, who rises from bed to assist a friend in need.

More resplendent than any precious stone (*omni precioso lapide splendidiori*): Proverbs 8:19 (*melior . . . lapide pretioso*)
Love cannot be idle (*Amor ociosus esse non potest*): Gregory I, *Homiliae in Evangelia* 2.30.2 (*Nunquam est Dei amor otiosus*, PL 76: 1221b)
Rouses itself for a friend (*Se . . . semper in amicum erigit*): Luke 11:5–8. Cf. Abelard, letter 3.9, where this parable is cited.

104 (**Woman**)

To her insatiable sweetness of love, deliciously surpassing all delights, from her to whom nothing in all the world is more precious: may your worth be renewed with ineffable glory.

The fire of my love for you, which is always increasing in me, compels me to write. But I have no idea what is best to say, unless I reveal to you the evidence of a love planted deep in my heart. Rightly do I grieve for the one I love so tenderly, so intimately, whose sweet kindness excels mere human goodness. And he whom it is not given me to see with my bodily eyes never slips from the intention of my mind. So the increase of this pain can be healed in no other way unless, like a turtledove, I keep the pledge of love for you inviolable, wishing in word and prayer that the years of your life may be multiplied, and that at last you may attain to the eternal crown of immortality. Farewell.

COMMENT

As in no. 86, the Woman has "no idea what ... to say" except that she is insatiable in love. Though she grieves over their separation, she does not blame her beloved for it, but wishes him only well. This separation may be the same one lamented by the Man in no. 108, occurring at an early stage in the affair.

I have no idea what is best to say (*quid potissimum dicam, ignoro*): no. 86; cf. Tegernsee
    letter 3 (*Quid dignum digno / valeam scribere ignoro*)
Like a turtledove (*in modo turturis*): Song 2:12 (*vox turturis*); Tegernsee letter 6 (*quasi*
    turtur)
Years of your life may be multiplied (*tibi multiplicentur anni vite*): Proverbs 4:10
    (*multiplicentur tibi anni vitae*)
Attain to the ... crown of immortality (*adipiscaris ... coronam immortalitatis*): James
    1:12 (*accipiet coronam vitae*)

❧

105 (**Man**)

To the supreme consolation of his weary spirits, to his utter joy and
unshakable hope, to the dwelling place of all that is joyful, from him
for whom your breath is a honeyed draught and your gaze the most
radiant light: what else should I wish but the longest life, sufficient for
your great sweetness?

I gladly accept, sweetheart, that you make your love for me a necessary
cause of your writing, as I hold you tightly clasped in the most binding
chain of true love. Your actions, which abound in such frequent favors,
prove how readily I should believe your words, for it is plain that your
love is not cold. Even when your tongue is silent, you speak sufficiently
in deeds to the one you swear that you love.

❧

COMMENT

The Man writes in the full flush of intoxicated love. Whether in words or in actions, his beloved brings him nothing but joy. His greeting formula, *quid aliud
nisi ut . . . ?*, recalls nos. 22 and 96. The "chain of love," a metaphor often used by
the Woman (nos. 55, 71, 76, 84), would soon take visual form in the motif of a
woman leading a man by a tether wound tightly about his neck.

Even when your tongue is silent . . . in deeds (*lingua etiam tacente, factis sufficienter
       loqueris*): cf. 1 John 3:18 (*non diligamus verbo neque lingua, sed opere et veritate*)

❧

106 (**Man**)

[. . .] Nothing is worse than a fortunate fool. Now for the first time I
recognize the good fortune I had before, now I have leisure to look
back on happy times—for hope is fading, and I do not know if it will

ever be restored. I am paying the price of my own folly, for I am losing that good thing that I did not know how to keep as I should have, that good of which I have been utterly unworthy. It is flying elsewhere, it is forsaking me, for it knows I am unworthy to possess it. Farewell.

COMMENT

In the original sequence, no. 106 could not possibly have followed the exuberant no. 105. Rather, it belongs to the final phase preceding the apparent breakup, along with nos. 93–101. Now the Man is losing his beloved and knows it. After a scribal lacuna, he calls himself a fool who did not recognize his good fortune until it was too late. Strikingly, he accepts full blame for the Woman's defection, saying he did not know how to keep "that good thing" (*bonum illud*) that is now "flying elsewhere." In his earlier erotic letters (nos. 26, 46), he had likewise described her as "so great a good"—one he had desired to "know" (in the intimate biblical sense) by being "incorporated" into it. Resuming the impersonal neuter, he now adopts the Woman's scornful language of "possession" (no. 100), only to admit that he has indeed failed to value the good that he once enjoyed.

Nothing is worse than a fortunate fool (*Nichil insipiente fortunato gravius*): Cicero, *Laelius* 54 (*nec quicquam insipiente fortunato intolerabilius fieri potest*)

107 (**Woman**)

[. . .] One whose mind is divided among many things accomplishes less in each one of them.
[. . .]
I saw a woman standing before me, advanced in age, comely of aspect, her whole body elegant beyond human measure. Gazing at me with fierce eyes, she spoke in just reproach, uttering these words: "Why do you behave so negligently? Do you not see that neither noble birth, nor an attractive figure, nor a beautiful face helps anyone unless the grace

of the Holy Spirit comes first, and he inwardly receives the riches of wisdom and knowledge so that, fortified by these, he can safely resist worldly cunning?"

[. . .]

My mind restored to full strength, I answered her with this reply.

[. . .]

Farewell. I send you as many good wishes as there are leaves on the trees.

COMMENT

This letter, sadly mangled by the scribe, is hard to interpret. Von Moos, justifiably annoyed with de Vepria's cutting, observes that he had little patience with allegory or metaphorical extravagance, "but delighted only in manneristic *colores rhetorici*, sententious formulas, and semi-philosophical discussions about ideas of love."[143] In any case, the Woman represents herself as a Boethian seer confronted by Lady Philosophy or a similar figure. As in *The Consolation of Philosophy*, this celestial visitor gazes at the seer with "fierce" (*torvis*) eyes and utters a reproach, apparently rebuking the Woman for yielding to carnal love. Despite her beauty and noble birth, she had lacked the spiritual wisdom to recognize her seducer's "cunning" (*secularibus calliditatibus*) for what it was. When she had earlier tried to end the relationship in no. 60, she told the Man that his "wisdom and knowledge [had] deceived" her. Now, with the help of Lady Philosophy, she reaches the same conclusion more firmly.

But the Lady's words could have an alternative meaning, not inconsistent with the first. Both lovers alike possessed the gifts of beauty and fortune, so the heavenly figure could be indirectly reproaching the Man as well. Despite his immense gifts, he has squandered them through spiritual folly. Lacking the integrity and courage to remain with his beloved in her time of need, he perhaps yielded to the "worldly cunning" of friends who urged self-protection, or the advancement of his career, above the pleas of a pregnant or otherwise desperate girlfriend. The Lady's further speech and the Woman's reply, if we had them, would have clarified the message.

It is hard to know if the Woman's *vale,* with her wistful good wishes for the future, was meant to be a final farewell or an invitation to renew the dialogue. I would suggest the former.

I saw a woman . . . beyond human measure (*Vidi michi assistere mulierem etate senem . . .*): Boethius, *Consolation* 1, pr. 1 (*Astitisse mihi . . . visa est mulier reverendi admodum vultus . . . ultra communem hominum valentiam . . . aevi plena foret*); cf. Tegernsee letter 5 (*in somnis astas / quasi Philosophia*)
With fierce eyes (*torvis oculis*): Boethius, *Consolation* 1, pr. 1 (*torvis . . . luminibus*)
The riches of wisdom and knowledge (*diviciasque sapiencie et sciencie*): Romans 11:33 (*O altitudo divitiarum sapientiae et scientiae Dei*)

✨

108 (**Man**)

Hail, my sun, my cloudless day, my light!
  You are my sweetness; without you nothing is sweet.
If you should ask who sends you such sweet words,
  It is he who is yours—you are his life.
Tears have been his drink since you went away,
  Grief mingled with sighs has been his food.
Life was a burden, for gentle death I prayed;
  Day brought no gladness, rest no pleasure.
Often I wished to leave, to follow my lady—
  But shame and fear obstructed the way.
As soon as I heard news of your return, sweet friend,
  Your dear one's spirit was restored.
I was all on fire, glad trembling shook my bones,
  I am risen and can scarcely seize my joys!
No wonder, beloved, if I favor your return,
  For the season itself favors glad caresses.
The stars shine fairer, the sun shows a brighter face,
  The kindly earth caresses with its blossoms.
All Nature preens itself to sing your praise:
  All things—O you my life!—now chant your praise.

✨

COMMENT

This poem in elegiacs probably laments the same period of separation that the Woman grieves in no. 104. While it could belong to a late phase in the relationship, with its reference to "shame and fear" (the fear of rumors), its exuberant tenderness suggests to me an early date. Here it is the Woman who has travelled out of town, while later on it is the Man who makes himself scarce and dares not visit. Just as she expresses no bitterness in no. 104, her lover shows no hint as yet of the defensive tone he adopts in many of his late letters.[144]

The Man's symbolic repertoire often relies on the heavens: he calls the beloved his sun and moon, light and splendor, brilliance and radiance. The poem also stresses the leitmotif of sweetness (*dulcedo*). As in troubadour song and the *Carmina burana*, springtime is the season of love *par excellence*; all nature sings the praise of the beloved.

Hail . . . my light (*lux mea, salve*): Paulinus of Nola, *Poemata* 27.148 (*lux mea, salve*, PL 61: 651c)

Without you nothing is sweet (*te sine dulce nichil*): Prudentius, *Cathemerinon* 3.11 (*te sine dulce nihil*)

Tears have been his drink (*Cui potus lacrime . . . fuere*): Psalm 41:4 (*Fuerunt mihi lacrimae meae panes*), 79:6 (*pane lacrimarum*), 101:10 (*potum meum cum fletu miscebam*); cf. Ovid, *Metamorphoses* 10.75 (*dolorque animi lacrimaeque alimenta*)

Grief [and] sighs (*dolor et gemitus*): Isaiah 35:10 (*dolor et gemitus*); Baudri of Bourgueil, *Carmina* 172.4 (*dolor et gemitus*); Marbod of Rennes, *Carmina* 1.57.5 (*dolor et gemitus*, PL 171: 1685a)

Glad trembling (*horror . . . letus*): Statius, *Thebaid* 1.493–94 (*laetusque . . . / horror*); no. 24

The stars shine fairer (*Gratius astra nitent*): Boethius, *Consolation* 3, metr. 1.7 (*Gratius astra nitent*)

Shows [its] face (*exerit orbem*): Lucan, *Pharsalia* 8.160 (*exerit orbem*)

The kindly earth (*tellus . . . alma*): Ovid, *Metamorphoses* 2.272 (*Alma . . . Tellus*)

109 (**Woman**)

Since both of us can now see each other in a moment, our letters need no greetings. Yet I desire you to be well, clothed with the beauty of virtues, adorned with the gems of wisdom, endowed with honorable character, and arrayed with the ornaments of perfect harmony.

Farewell, fount of refreshment. Farewell, flower of delicious fragrance. Farewell, remembrance of gladness, oblivion of sadness.

COMMENT

In this early letter, the Woman has returned from her journey and the lovers now live very near each other. Yet she cannot resist the pleasure of a fulsome greeting, which draws on a literary topos found in both monastic allegory and episcopal courts. Wisdom and virtue afford clothing for the saintly soul, the skillful teacher, or in this case, the lover. She wishes him to be adorned with the *ornatus* of all *composicio*—a difficult term that I have translated as "harmony." It refers less to prose style than to that elegant, harmonious personal bearing that counted for so much in the charismatic culture of the age. This quality is a precursor of the later twelfth-century *courtoisie*, or courtliness.[145] The Woman uses a Greek word for wisdom (*sophia*), a conspicuous mark of learning, and rhymes "gladness" and "sadness" (*leticie / tristicie*).

If the writers were Abelard and Heloise, their new proximity could indicate the moment when Abelard moved into Fulbert's house, supposedly to save money on lodgings and more easily instruct his pupil, but in fact, to pursue his plan of seduction (*Historia calamitatum* 17).

Gems of wisdom (*sophie gemmis*): Marbod of Rennes, *Carmina* 2.44 (*gemma sophiae*, PL 171: 1735c)

Ornaments of perfect harmony (*omnisque composicionis ornatu*): cf. Adso of Montier-en-Der, *Vita S. Frodoberti* 31 (*compositio ornatusque*, PL 137: 616a); Hugh of Saint-Victor, *De arrha animae* (*compositio ornatus tui*, PL 176: 966c) ᴥ

110 (**Man**)

To his only one: a joy no sickness can mar.

God is my witness, beloved, that whenever I start to read your letters, I am flooded with so great a sweetness within that I am often forced to reread the letter I have just read, for the magnitude of my joy distracts my attention. You can easily imagine, then, how much pleasure I take in the actual presence of your charming self and how much weight your living words carry, when even a word sent from afar makes me so happy. Farewell.

ᴥ

COMMENT

Overwhelmed by the joy of reciprocated love, the Man in this early letter can barely concentrate on the text that gives him such pleasure. This may have been the first greeting in which he addressed the Woman as *unice sue*—"to his only one." (See comment on no. 76.) The gesture of appealing to God as their witness (*Deo teste*) is shared by both lovers.

To his only one (*Unice sue*): Heloise, letters 2.16 (*Vale, unice*), 4.1 (*Unico suo post Christum, unica sua in Christo*); Tegernsee letter 7 (*unice sue rose*)

ᴥ

111 (**Man**)

May your night be lucid, lacking nothing but me,
  And lacking me, my lovely, think that you lack all.
See me in your dreams, dream of me when you wake,
  And just as I am yours, be mine, my spirit.

ᴥ

COMMENT

This sprightly quatrain echoes (or more likely, anticipates) a line in no. 87. The lovers have now declared their mutual affection ("just as I am yours, be mine"), and the Man confidently expects his beloved to share his wish for a night together.

Think that you lack all (*defore cuncta putes*): no. 87
Just as I am yours, be mine, my spirit (*velut ipse tuus sum, michi sis animus*): cf.
    Terence, *Eunuchus* 196 (*meus fac sis postremo animus quando ego sum tuus*)

112a (**Woman**)

Where desire and love abide, there effort always burns bright. I am weary now and cannot reply to you, because you take sweet things as painful and so fill my mind with sorrow. Farewell.

COMMENT

Beside this fragment is a marginal note reading *Ex alia <epistola>*, testifying to the disarray we have noted at several points—presumably due to the jumbling of loose leaves or quires in de Vepria's exemplar. This is the last letter, or snippet of a letter, to appear before the Man's seduction poem (no. 113). But that does not mean it was the last to be written. It might originally have been part of no. 98, where the Woman similarly complains that her beloved has responded with anger to what should have been a joy.

    Almost shockingly, she parodies the famous antiphon for Maundy Thursday: *Ubi caritas et amor, Deus ibi est* (where charity and love abide, God is there). Instead she writes that *Ubi est amor et dilectio* (where desire and love abide), there "effort always burns bright" (*semper fervet exercicium*). This is an odd choice of words, hard to translate. Again, it is possible that the Woman refers to a desired pregnancy—initially "sweet" for her until she learned, to her dismay, that her lover found it "painful" (*gravis*, which can also mean "pregnant"). But we cannot know for certain. The fragment shows us a brilliant, passionate Woman in a tired and anxious mood—and that, sadly, is the last we will see of her.

Where desire and love abide (*Ubi est amor et dilectio*): Antiphon for Maundy
    Thursday, "Ubi caritas et amor." Cf. Tegernsee letter 3 (*Si consistat absque dolore,
    / non potest dici amor, / unde constat maximus labor*);[146] Hugh of Saint-Victor,
    Adnotatiunculae in Threnos Jeremiae (*Ubi est amor tuus, ibi est animus tuus.
    Qualis est affectio tua, talis etiam est cogitatio tua.* PL 175: 290d)

Love Letters from Tegernsee

THESE MAINLY FEMALE-AUTHORED letters are preserved in a manuscript from the Bavarian abbey of Tegernsee: Munich, Bayerische Staatsbibliothek, MS Clm 19411, fols. 69r–70r (nos. 1–7), 100v (no. 10), and 113v–114v (nos. 8–9).[1] The only evidence for dating is the *terminus ante quem* provided by the manuscript itself, written by twelve scribes between 1160 and 1186. This substantial codex includes 307 letters on ecclesiastical affairs, in addition to the ten letters of love and friendship, and *artes dictandi* by Alberic of Monte Cassino, Henricus Francigena, and Adalbertus Samaritanus, all dated between 1110 and 1120. Other contents include excerpts on the seven deadly sins, etymologies, and logic; a Greek alphabet; lyric and devotional poetry; collections of proverbs; the *Ludus de Antichristo*; and a large section of Otto of Freising's *Gesta Friderici*. In short, the context and provenance of the codex tell us little about the love letters except that they originated in Germany, presumably in an abbey of nuns or canonesses.[2] I have translated from the edition of Helmut Plechl and Werner Bergmann, *Die Tegernseer Briefsammlung des 12. Jahrhunderts*, MGH Briefe der deutschen Kaiserzeit 8 (Hanover: Hahnsche Buchhandlung, 2002), 343–66.[3] My numbering follows that of Étienne Wolff's French translation.[4]

1 *Amico amica*: H. to Her Friend and Kinsman S.

To her beloved S., sweetest to her of all her kinsmen, from H.: fidelity and love.

Would that you could know, my beloved, how many troubles I have endured since I parted from you! For day and night your delightful face is before my mind, and rightly so, for none of my kin have welcomed me with such friendly conversation and gifts. Therefore, sweetest of all lovable men, repay favors with worthy favors. Love the one who loves you from her heart and let there be no reproach, for the love I bear is not at all feigned or pretended. Why say more? Gold could more easily be changed into tin than my mind be torn away from your love. So do not delay your coming to me! Farewell, farewell.

COMMENT

This letter is typical in its use of extravagant language, which may strike modern ears as erotic, to strengthen the bond between friends or relatives. An *amicus* can be a friend, a kinsman (as here), or a lover. But the letter uses forms of *dilectio* and *diligo* seven times, while the more passionate *amor* occurs only once. In her *narratio* the writer gives an account of her loneliness and sorrow, justifying her *petitio* or request—that her kinsman should visit soon. Such pleas for a loved one's visit do not appear in model love letters.[5] But for a young cloistered nun, unable to leave her convent, the visits of close friends would be of vital importance.

Repay favors with worthy favors (*dignis digna repende*): Regensburg Songs, no. 31.2
    (*dignis digna rependam*)
Let there be no reproach (*nec ulla de me tibi sit reprobatio*): ambiguous, depending on
    how *de me* is construed. Dronke translates, "You shall never have a reproach
    from me," and Wolff, "Ne me blâme en aucune façon."
Love . . . not at all feigned (*non est prorsus simulata . . . dilectio*): Romans 12:9 (*dilectio*
    sine simulatione)

2 *Amico amica derelicta*: An Abandoned Friend N. to Her Friend H.

To H., formerly dearest but now most perfidious, from N.: the reward that his deeds deserve.

My soul will be consumed with grief and filled with sorrow because I seem to have been utterly blotted out of your remembrance—I, who always hoped to receive trust and love from you until the end of my life. What is my strength that I should bear this patiently and not weep now and forever? Is my flesh bronze or my mind a rock, are my eyes made of stone, that I should not grieve my bitter misfortune? What have I done? What have I done? Was I the first to reject you? How have I been found guilty? Truly, I have been cast off through no fault of my own. If you seek a fault it is you, *you* who are to blame! For time and again I have sent you messages, yet never received the comfort of your words in the greatest affair or the least. So let all mortals depart and seek trust and love from me no longer!

Take great care that no third person's eye sees this. Farewell, farewell—and mend your ways.

COMMENT

Is the writer a woman who has been seduced and abandoned, furiously berating the lover who has forgotten her and spurned her messages? Or is she more like the nun in no. 1—as she might feel if six months had passed with no word from her kinsman? The warning against unauthorized readers suggests the first possibility, while the context (a monastic letter collection) points to the latter. Given the high emotional temperature of medieval letters, it is impossible to be sure. But it seems more likely that the writer is grieving hyperbolically over her friend's epistolary silence.

The reward that his deeds deserve (*dignam mercedem secundum opera sua*): Matthew
      16:27, Romans 2:6 (*reddet unicuique secundum opera eius*)
I seem to have been utterly blotted out of your remembrance (*a memoria tua
      funditus videor deleta*): cf. EDA no. 62 (*fere mei oblite*)
What is my strength that I should bear this? (*Que est enim fortitudo mea, ut
      sustineam?*): Job 6:11 (*Quae est enim fortitudo mea, ut sustineam?*)
Is my flesh bronze? (*Numquid caro mea est enea?*): Job 6:12 (*Nec caro mea aenea est*)
What have I done?. . . Was I the first to reject you? (*Quid feci, quid feci, numquid
      prior te abieci?*): Regensburg Songs, no. 35.7 (*Quid tibi, quid feci, quid me, dic
      deseruisti?*)
Let all mortals depart and seek . . . no longer (*mortales cuncti discedant, fidem et
      dilectionem a me ulterius non querant*): cf. EDA no. 84 (*cui postea credere possim
      prosus ignoro*)
Take great care that no third person's eye sees this (*Cave diligentius, ne tercius
      interveniat oculus*): cf. EDA no. 69 (*ne versus oculus legat invidiosus*)

⁂

3 A Convent Student to Her Teacher

My faithful one, accept this reply to your letter. I don't know what I
can write that is worthy of you, especially since it would be a shame to
assault a teacher's ears with unrefined speech. Yet it would be wrong to
let it pass in silence, so I will answer you as best I can. What you are
trying to gain from me seems a hard, difficult thing for me to grant—
namely, my absolute trust, which I have never promised to any mortal.
Yet, if I knew that you would love me with a chaste love and preserve
the pledge of my chastity inviolate, I do not refuse [the labor or] the
love. If it exists without pain it cannot be called love, which is the
source of the greatest toil.

Beware lest anyone see these lines, for they were written without
permission.

⁂

COMMENT

This young student is in the same position as the Woman of the EDA after receiving the Man's seduction poem (no. 113). Both feel anxiety about writing: no rhetoric they can command will be worthy of their teachers' ears. But the Woman of the EDA, living in the world, eagerly reciprocated her teacher's feelings (no. 112), while this convent pupil is more cautious. What the teacher has requested so far (in a letter not transmitted) is not yet her love, but a likely precursor to it—her "absolute trust" (*integritatem mee fidei*). Being no fool, she admits that this would be hard for her to grant and insists twice on her pledged chastity (*casto amore*; *pignus pudicicie mee*). This situation is paralleled in the Regensburg Songs (nos. 27–28) and the more sophisticated exchange between Baudri of Bourgueil and Constance.

The final lines play ambiguously on the rhyming nouns *amor, dolor,* and *labor*. In the manuscript, they read "non recuso *laborem · vel* amorem · si consistat absque dolore ; non potest dici amor · unde constat maximus labor."[6] The emphasized words are underlined in the manuscript and probably meant for deletion. Depending on how one punctuates the quatrain, two opposite readings are possible. If we omit *laborem vel* and put a semicolon after the second line, as the manuscript does, we would have a healthy-minded view of love:

Non recuso amorem	I do not refuse [your] love
si consistat absque dolore;	if it exists without pain;
non potest dici amor	that cannot be called love
unde constat maximus labor.	which entails the greatest hardship.

This reading is followed by Kühnel's German translation and Wolff's French version.[7] But if we put a period after the first line, we get something totally different:

non recuso [laborem vel] amorem.	I do not refuse [the labor or] the love.
Si consistat absque dolore,	If it exists without pain
non potest dici amor,	it cannot be called love,
unde constat maximus labor.	which is the source of the greatest toil.

Plechl's edition follows this second interpretation (without *laborem*), as does Peter Dronke in his translation (with *laborem*).[8] I have hesitantly chosen this version because of its Ovidian resonance, by which love is understood as involving both pain and labor (or hardship or struggle). In the EDA (no. 112a), the

Woman similarly notes that "where desire and love abide, there effort always burns bright" (*ibi semper fervet exercicium*).

I don't know what I can write that is worthy of you (*Quid dignum digno valeam scribere, ignoro*): cf. EDA no. 104 (*quid potissimum dicam, ignoro*)

A shame to assault a teacher's ears with unrefined speech (*doctoris aures pudor sit inculto sermone interpellare*): cf. EDA no. 49 (*Magne temeritatis est litteratorie tibi verba dirigere . . . impolitas tam rudis stili litteras non tibi mittere presumerem*)

Beware lest anyone see these lines (*Cave, nequis videat ista dicta*): no. 2 above; EDA no. 69 (*Hos rogo ne versus oculus legat invidiosus*)

4 The Teacher to His Female Friend

The eloquent greetings which should hail the greatness of your love are hardly clear to my searching thoughts. For my joys are more than the sands in the sea if all your good fortune holds fast. I have received a most pleasing letter from your honeyed sweetness, fragrant with the perfumes of supreme charity. But as I perused it with desire, I was a little disappointed, for I found there that it is a hard, difficult thing for you to grant what I ask of you. What more? Whatever you should reply or say to me, you will hold me as a captive, bound by your love and under your power.

Farewell, farewell. As many as the stars in heaven or sands in the sea—so many praises may your life deserve.

COMMENT

Refusing to take "no" (or even a mitigated "yes") for an answer, the teacher makes a move typical of lyric lovers. The words of his beloved do not really matter because, whatever she says, he will remain "a captive, bound by [her] love [*amore*] and under [her] power." But he is plainly disappointed by her insistence on chastity.

In sharp contrast to the EDA, the teacher's letter in this collection is more florid than any of the women's messages. Versions of his closing *quot-tot* formula occur several times in the EDA and in *artes dictandi*.

The eloquent greetings . . . searching thoughts (*Affamina salutationis . . . haut apparent mee indagini meditationis*): **cf. EDA no.** 13 (*omnes quas vellet salutes expedire non potuit permultas, ne plures enumerando, offendere sibi videretur universas*)
Fragrant with the perfumes of supreme charity (*redolentes aromata summe caritatis*): cf. EDA no. 1 (*omnibus aromatibus dulcius redolenti*), no. 94 (*optimi odoris aromati*)
As many as the stars in heaven (*Quot celum stellas*): Ovid, *Ars amatoria* 1.59 (*Quot caelum stellas*); EDA no. 73 (*Quot celo stelle*)

⁊ꙮ

5 A Religious Woman to Another Young Woman

[To?] G., a dear one to her dearest, a sweetheart to her sweetest: I wish you everything that excels all that is and that shall be.

Although great distances divide us in space, yet the goodwill of our spirits unites us—along with true friendship, which is not feigned but firmly fixed in my heart. For you stand before me in dreams like Lady Philosophy, uttering gracious and comforting words. If only it were permitted to wish for death, so that no one would ever see me again by the light of day—because I must live without the longed-for sight of you, full of loyalty and love. Who will give me wings like a bird, so that I might fly like an eagle and come to you and snatch some joy for my heart? For I have received you into a place set apart in my spirit, above all our sex, if you will never depart from it at anyone's urging. I wish to establish this firmly if you will meet me with the same loyalty. What more? I want to love you until the moon falls from the sky, for before all others in the world, you are fixed in the depth of my heart.

Farewell—sleeping or waking, I never cease to wish you good. May you fare well and be as blessed as Io! O my sweetness, may the fullness of joy come upon you. I send a gift that is not worthy, just a token of loyalty to you. The convent of young girls also greets you, precious pearl.

COMMENT

This passionate letter of friendship sounds so "lesbian-like" that its last sentence comes as a surprise.[9] Not only the writer but her whole convent, or at least its younger inhabitants (*conventus iuvencularum*), send greetings to her "precious pearl." The recipient may have been a fellow novice or convent pupil who had professed her final vows elsewhere, or finished her studies and returned to the world.

The familiar topoi of *amicitia* are all present. True friends remain united in spirit, despite physical distance; their friendship, rooted deep in the heart, is unfeigned and eternal. It is also unique and exclusive, setting the cherished friend apart from all others—even though the same writer might address multiple correspondents in the same terms. The many stylistic parallels with the EDA, especially the Woman's letters, testify to nuns' shared epistolary culture.

A dear one to her dearest, a sweetheart to her sweetest (*cara karissime dulcissime dulcis*): *Karissime* and *dulcissime* are datives of address, not adverbs.[10] The salutation is unusual because its terms for sender and recipient are chiastically intertwined, a token of their intimacy. It is not clear which is denoted by the initial G.

All that is and that shall be (*totum quod est et quod erit*): cf. EDA no. 59 (*omne quod est vel esse potest*)

Although great distances divide us (*Quamvis nos disiungant maxima intervalla locorum*): cf. EDA no. 71 (*Multum distat ortus ab occidente, sed fides rependitur fide per multa temporum spacia disiunctis*); Regensburg Songs, no. 42.1–2 (*Salve . . . quod non queat adtenuari / Tempore vel spacio terrarum*)

Firmly fixed in my heart (*cordi meo infixa*): EDA no. 88 (*cordi meo firmiter infixus*)

You stand before me . . . like Lady Philosophy (*astas quasi philosophia*): Boethius, *Consolation of Philosophy* I, pr. 1 (*adstitisse mihi supra verticem visa est mulier . . .*); EDA no. 107 (*Vidi michi assistere mulierem, etate senem . . .*)

Comforting words (*verba consolatoria*): Zechariah 1:13 (*verba consolatoria*)

I must live without the longed-for sight of you (*tua optata non fruor visione*): cf. EDA no. 9 (*donec . . . votis omnibus desideratam tuam faciem videam*)

Who will give me wings like a bird (*Quis dabit mihi genus volatile?*): Psalm 54:7 (*Quis dabit mihi pennas sicut columbae?*); EDA no. 86 (*O si nutu Dei acciperem volucris speciem*)

Before all others . . . you are fixed in the depth of my heart (*ante omnes, qui sunt in mundo, cordis mei fixa es profundo*): cf. EDA no. 84 (*teque . . . omnibus in corde meo preposui*)

Sleeping or waking (*dormiendo quasi vigilando*): EDA no. 88 (*dormiendo neque vigilando*)

Be as blessed as Io (*prosis velut Io*): Io was one of the more fortunate maidens raped by Jove in that she eventually regained human form (Ovid, *Metamorphoses* 1.568–667, 722–46). The name is chosen more to rhyme with *cupio* than for any thematic significance.

My sweetness (*O dulcedo mea*): EDA no. 55 (*maxima dulcedo mea*), no. 108 (*Tu mea dulcedo*)

The convent of young girls also greets you, precious pearl (*Salutat te dulcis margarita et conventus iuvencularum*): Kühnel and Wolff both take *dulcis margarita* as nominative, but it makes better sense as a vocative. The passionate writer would not use such an endearment for a third party, nor would she denote herself in the third person.[11]

🙊

6 A Religious Woman B. to Her Friend G.

To G., sweeter than honey and the honeycomb, B. sends whatever love desires for love.

O my unique, my special one, why do you linger afar for so long? Why do you want your only one to perish—she who loves you with soul and body, as you yourself know, and sighs for you every hour, every moment, like a hungry little bird? Ever since I have had to do without your sweetest presence, I have not wanted to hear or see any other human being. But just as a turtledove, having lost her mate, always perches on a dry little branch, so I lament without end until I can enjoy your faithful love once more. I look around and do not find my lover, nor anyone to comfort me with a single word. When I consider within myself the sweetness of your most delightful words and looks, I am crushed with a grief too great, for I find nothing to compare to your love—which is sweeter than honey and the honeycomb. Set beside it, the gleam of gold and silver is worthless.

What more? In you are all gentleness and virtue; therefore my spirit always languishes in your absence. You have no gall of treachery; you are sweeter than milk and honey; you are chosen from thousands. I love you before all others; you alone are my love and desire; you are the sweet refreshment of my spirit; nothing in the whole wide world is pleasing to me without you. Everything that was sweet to me with you is burdensome and tedious without you. Hence I want to say truly: if it were possible, I would buy you at the price of my life without delay, for you alone are the one I have chosen according to my heart. Therefore I always pray to God: may bitter death not seize me before I have enjoyed the dear and longed-for sight of you.

Farewell—take from me all that belongs to fidelity and love. Accept the stylus I am sending, and with it, my constant spirit.

COMMENT

This ardent letter may be a response to no. 5, if the G. in the salutation of no. 5 denotes its sender. At the end of that letter the writer mentions a token gift, while this writer encloses a stylus—a charming plea to continue their correspondence. If G. in no. 5 denotes the recipient, however, we might have here a collection of three letters (nos. 5–7) all addressed to the same religious woman (G.) by two or three of her intimates.

Like the lovers of the EDA, the writer calls her beloved *unica* and *specialis*, using rhetoric similar to theirs. But her exuberance and ardor exceed her rhetorical invention, for she calls her friend "sweeter than honey" three times, while forms of *dulcis* and *suavis* occur eight times. Comparing this letter with no. 1, addressed to a kinsman, we can see that the language here is "hotter." *Amicitia* is not mentioned; the beloved is called *amantem* (lover) rather than *amica*, and love is not only *dilectio* but also *amor et desiderium*. The gender of the beloved seems immaterial to the theme—the unbearable pain of absence, which is also a frequent theme of the EDA.

Sweeter than honey and the honeycomb (*super mel et favum dulciori*): Psalm 18:11
(*dulciora super mel et favum*); Ecclesiasticus 24:27 (*super mel dulcis*); EDA nos. 11
(*super favum mellis*), 39 (*super mel et favum dulci*)

Whatever love desires for love (*quidquid amor amori*): cf. EDA no. 18 (*quidquid
amans amanti*)

A turtledove, having lost her mate (*turtur perdito masculo*): cf. EDA no. 104 (*in modo
turturis*)

I look around and do not find my lover (*Circumspicio et non invenio amantem*): cf.
Song 3:1 (*Quaesivi quem diligit anima mea . . . et non inveni*)

I find nothing to compare to your love (*nil invenio tale, quod velim tue dilectioni
comparare*): cf. EDA no. 72 (*neminem mortalium michi compares*)

The gleam of gold and silver (*auri et argenti nitor*): Ovid, *Ex Ponto* 3.4.23 (*nitor
argenti . . . et auri*)

In you are all gentleness and virtue (*In te omnis suavitas et virtus*): cf. EDA no. 43
(*quidquid est suavitatis, in te natura transfudit*)

My spirit always languishes (*meus semper languet spiritus*): cf. Song 2:5, 5:8 (*amore
langueo*); EDA no. 25 (*amore tuo langueo*)

Milk and honey (*lacte et melle*): Deuteronomy 26:15 (*lacte et melle*); EDA no. 102 (*lacte
et melle*)

Chosen from thousands (*electa es ex milibus*): Song 5:10 (*electus ex milibus*); EDA nos.
50 (*te inter multa milia . . . elegi*), 84 (*elegi ex milibus*)

Nothing . . . is pleasing to me without you (*nil mihi absque te iocundi*): EDA no. 108
(*te sine dulce nichil*)

Buy you at the price of my life without delay (*vite precio te emerem non segniter*):
Boethius, *Consolation of Philosophy* 2, pr. 4 (*vitae pretio non segnis emeres*)

You alone . . . I have chosen according to my heart (*sola es, quam elegi secundum cor
meum*): cf. EDA no. 84 (*in corde meo . . . teque solum elegi*)

⁊ℰ

7 A Religious Woman A. to Her Friend G.

To G., her only rose, A. sends a chain of precious love.

What is my strength that I should endure, that I should have patience
while you are away? Is my strength the strength of stones that I should
await your return—I, who do not cease mourning night and day, like

someone who has lost hands and feet? Everything that is joyous and delightful seems, without you, like mud to be trampled underfoot. Instead of rejoicing I weep; never does my spirit seem happy. When I remember the kisses you gave me and the merry words with which you caressed my little breasts, I want to die because I am not allowed to see you. What shall I do—most wretched me? Where shall I turn—poor little woman?

O if only my body had been consigned to the earth until your longed-for return, or if the translation of Habakkuk were granted to me so that I could come just once and gaze on my lover's face—then I would not care if I died that very hour! For no woman born in the world is so lovable and charming and loves me with such intimate love, without feigning. So I shall not cease my endless mourning until I can deserve to see you.

Truly, as some wise man said, great is the misery of a person who cannot be with the one he cannot be without! As long as the world endures, you will never be erased from the center of my heart. Why should I say more? Return, sweet love! Do not delay your journey any longer; you should know that I cannot bear your absence any longer.

Farewell, and remember me.

COMMENT

The three letters of love between women are arranged in order of increasing intensity. This remarkable message is one of very few surviving testimonies to a medieval lesbian relationship. While the theme of the absent beloved is common to other letters in this collection, one sentence goes beyond the topoi of friendship: "When I remember the kisses you gave me and the merry words with which you caressed my little breasts [*refrigerasti pectuscula*], I want to die because I am not allowed to see you." Were the two discovered and separated? As Dronke remarks, this recollection of a *past* erotic encounter differs from a robust metaphor or the anticipation of a future meeting.[12]

Ernstpeter Ruhe is so distressed by the writer's apparent lesbianism, which he says would indicate "an otherwise wholly unknown species in the history of the genre," that he thinks the text must need emendation.[13] But the writer clearly uses feminine grammatical forms for both herself (*miserrima, pauperrima, mortua*) and her beloved (*nata, grata, que*). There is no ambiguity. As Dieter Schaller points out, heterosexual love is just one of many sentiments conveyed in what we have chosen to call "love letters." The medieval *epistola familiaris* can also encompass friendship, love of family, religious enthusiasm (*Schwärmerei*), devotion, flattery, pleas for help or counsel—and in this case, same-sex passion.[14]

The writer is not without learning. She mischievously cites a passage from Augustine's *De Trinitate*, where the theologian laments the misery of humankind without God, and adapts the saying of "some wise man" to express the personal misery of living without her beloved. Her letter also alludes to a famous Old Testament episode (dramatized in *The Play of Daniel*) in which an angel seizes the prophet Habakkuk by the hair and flies him off to feed Daniel in the lions' den. The writer's wish that she too could magically travel by such means recalls a letter from Alcuin to Archbishop Arno of Salzburg, which interestingly is known only from Salzburg manuscripts. Hence Schaller suggests that the women responsible for these letters might have lived in that city.[15] The freedom of mobility assumed in this letter suggests that they might in fact have been canonesses rather than cloistered nuns. Tegernsee had frequent communications with Salzburg, so it would not have been surprising if the monks had ties with a women's community there. It seems more surprising that they preserved such a letter—and unthinkable that any monk would have written it in the persona of a woman.

I cannot take seriously Plechl's suggestion that even this should be regarded as a "model letter" (*Musterbrief*) because it demonstrates stylistic parallels with others in the collection.[16] If no letter can be considered genuine unless it is totally free of formulas and topoi, what would be the point of writing model letters in the first place?

To ... her only rose (*unice sue rose*): cf. EDA nos. 49 (*rose immarcessibili*) and 110 (*unice sue*)

Chain of precious love (*vinculum dilectionis preciose*): cf. Jerome, *Epistulae* 82.11 (*dilectionis vinculo*); EDA nos. 71 (*vinculum vere dilectionis*), 105 (*vere dilectionis cathena*)

What is my strength that I should endure? (*Que est fortitudo mea, ut sustineam?*): Job 6:11 (*Quae est ... fortitudo mea, ut sustineam?*); no. 2 above

Is my strength the strength of stones? (*Numquid fortitudo mea fortitudo est lapi-*
    dum?): Job 6:12 (*Nec fortitudo lapidum fortitudo mea*)

Love, without feigning (*sine simulatione . . . dilectione*): Romans 12:9 (*dilectio sine*
    simulatione); cf. no. 1 above; EDA no. 55 (*sincera dilectione*)

If the translation of Habakkuk were granted to me (*si translatio mihi concederetur*
    Abacuc): Daniel 14:32–38; Jerome, *Epistulae* 3.1 (*O si mihi nunc Domi-*
    nus . . . Ambacum ad Danihelum translationem repente concederet); Alcuin,
    Epistolae 10 (*O si mihi translatio Abacuc esset subito concessa*)

Great is the misery of a person who cannot be with the one he cannot be without
    (*magna miseria est hominis cum illo non esse, sine quo non potest esse*): Augustine,
    De Trinitate 14.12.16 (*Magna . . . hominis miseria est cum illo non esse, sine quo*
    non potest esse, PL 42: 1049)

⁊ṧ

8 A Religious Woman to Her Teacher

To H., flower of flowers, crowned with a wreath of morals,
a model of virtues, indeed the very norm of virtues,
N.—who is like honey, guileless as a dove—
wishes whatever is joyful and favorable
in the present life or sweet in eternal life,
what Thisbe wished for Piramus, and finally, herself—
once again herself, or whatever she prizes above herself.

More beloved than all who are beloved, if the talent of Virgil
abounded in me, if I overflowed with the eloquence of Cicero—or of
any other outstanding orator or excellent poet, so to speak—I would
confess myself unequal, all the same, to respond to the page of your
exquisitely polished speech. So I want you not to laugh at me if I bring
forth something less elegant than I wish, because, in spite of that, you
may tenderly come to feel with me what I have in mind. Therefore,
because it is a property of good minds to desire intimacy with others
like them, and because it should be my heartfelt wish to comply with
your teachings in every way, it has pleased me to reply to your sweet
letter in the present one, though it is unequal to yours.

Our first, last, and central theme has always been friendship—true friendship, than which there is nothing better, nothing more joyful, nothing more lovely. Thus the very order of things grants me license to speak of it. True friendship, as Tullius Cicero attests, is agreement in all things divine and human, together with charity and good will. It is also, as I have learned from you, more excellent than all human goods, more eminent than all other virtues, gathering what is scattered, preserving what is gathered, and more and more enhancing what is preserved. There is nothing truer than this description or definition. If anyone relies upon it, he can find no firmer foundation.

Let us rely on it, for we are strengthened by it.
Friendship is a fine thing, the kind hope of the desperate.
She restores the fallen, revives the sick and heavy-laden,
lets no one go astray; and she commands that we freely love.
To speak briefly, she orders all things fittingly.
We say boldly, she reigns and powerfully commands.

Leaving this subject, then (not that it should be dismissed), I turn my stylus to you—to you, I say, whom I have enclosed in the marrow of my heart, deserving all the praise that human reason can give. For, from the day I first saw you, I began to love you. You mightily penetrated the inner depths of my heart and there (this is marvelous to say!) you prepared yourself a seat by addressing me with your most delightful conversation. Lest it be tossed out on some impulse, you established it most firmly with your epistolary speech like a three-legged stool, or rather a four-legged throne.

Hence it is that no forgetfulness could wipe you out of my memory, no darkness overshadow you. No tempest of winds and clouds, even the most violent, could ever shake you. For where there is variety, one thing after another, how can that be called stability? I confess that I would call it true being if I could be continually in your presence. Since that true being is denied me, I hold all being, whatever it is, to be false. Make it possible, therefore, for me to apprehend true being, which proceeds from nowhere else than your being—your being with me.

Faithfulness too is called the queen of all virtues, as not only Scripture bears witness, but also the doctrine of secular teachers, which is not to be rejected. You desire this, I desire this. You seek this from me, I seek this from you. I attach this firmly to your heart in both words and deeds. If you were to depart from this, you would be plunged into the abyss. If you were to separate from this, what would you do but stray from the destiny of the good? If you adhere to this, you will come to shine like a ray of the sun. By cultivating it you will capture the citadel of virtues. By clinging to it you will attain a blessed life. By holding it fast, you will be able to seize the anchor of your hope. Why? Because faithfulness promotes hope, it cements love. We are bound by its bonds, we rejoice together in its affections. What more? Whoever God fires up with faith gives birth to every good.

You alone have been chosen from thousands, you alone have been received into the inmost sanctuary of my mind, you alone are sufficient for me in all things—but only if, as I hope, you do not fall away from my love. As you have done, I have done; I have cast aside all pleasures for the sake of your love. I depend upon you alone; in you I have set all my hope and my confidence.

Now because you have warned me to beware of knights as if they were monsters, you do well. Indeed, I myself know why I should beware, lest I fall into a pit. But, saving my fidelity to you, I do not altogether reject them, though I will not succumb to that vice with which you charge them. For they are the ones, so to speak, by whom the laws of courtesy are upheld. They are the fount and origin of all honor. Now enough about them, so long as they do not stand in the way of our love.

Not unmindful of my promise, I will remember you always and everywhere, for in this way "my bow will be restored in my hand, and my glory renewed." I preserve a stable mind and fidelity for you alone because by this means I heap up for myself gold and silver—that is, a joyful spirit, which is more to be prized than gold and silver. Whatever is especially valuable to you,

This I too embrace, this I follow at all times.
My mind has truly decided to cleave to you always.
Be assured, you neither have nor will ever have
any successor; no one will please me but you.
I would have written more but I said, there is no need.

Du bist min, ih bin din:	You are mine, I am yours:
des solt du gewis sin.	of this you may be certain.
du bist beslossen	You are locked
in minem herzen:	in my heart:
verlorn ist daz sluzzellin:	the little key is lost:
du muost och immer dar inne sin.	you must remain there forever.

COMMENT

This expansive letter belongs to a genre peculiar to the eleventh and early twelfth centuries: the Latin letter of friendship from a young religious woman to her teacher. It is a *prosimetrum*, a prose letter spangled with passages in leonine hexameter at beginning, middle, and end. Its florid vocabulary and exhaustive review of the topoi suggest that, like some of the Woman's letters in the EDA (especially nos. 25 and 49), it was composed as much to display the writer's learning and rhetorical skill as her feelings.

   Like the Woman, this writer loves her teacher in a high-minded, Ciceronian way and is eager to rehearse the glories of friendship. Her praise shades into personification as she allies Friendship with Wisdom, the virtue that "orders all things fittingly." While the writer describes her affection for her teacher as love at first sight, it has more to do with his words than his sex appeal. It was his "delightful conversation" (*iocundissime confabulationis*) that first attracted her, while his "epistolary speech" (*epistolari sermone*) cemented the bond. As we learn from letters 9 and 10, she is determined to preserve her chastity, yet one could never guess that from her extravagant praise of their unique love ("chosen from thousands") and her urgent admonitions to be faithful. In fact, her rhetoric closely resembles the Woman's in EDA no. 84, one of her most passionate letters. This writer's didactic tone suggests that, even if her beloved is officially the teacher, she too assumes a pedagogic role, like the *domna* in *fin'amor* whose lessons are supposed to make her lover more virtuous.

In a strange metaphysical passage, the writer says that for her, the only "true being" (*verum esse*) is to live constantly in the presence of her beloved. Every other mode of existence seems to her "false"; for her, true being proceeds only from her lover's being with her (*de tuo esse, mecum esse*). This bit of extravagance recalls the way the Woman of the EDA plays with a metaphysical concept (*esse quod est*) in the salutation of no. 21. The Man of the EDA similarly speaks of the lovers' coinherence: "I am wholly with you, and to speak more truly, I am wholly in you" (no. 16); "you are immortally buried in my heart" (no. 22); "you are I and I am you" (no. 77). Friends and lovers were intertwined in their very being—a key part of the medieval ontology of love.

The teacher's warning to "beware of knights" (in a letter that is not extant) suggests jealousy on his part, recalling the many twelfth-century debates between a *miles* and a *clericus* as to which makes the better lover.[17] Interestingly, the woman (who was doubtless the sister and daughter of knights) promises to resist any attempts at seduction, but she will not reject knights outright because it is they who uphold the laws of courtesy (*iura curialitatis*); they are the wellspring of all honor in the world. In fact, she might well have returned to the world to marry one after completing her convent education.[18]

In this recension, the letter ends with some celebrated love verses in Middle High German. These lines, which played a major role in arguments about the origin of Minnesang,[19] could have originated either at Tegernsee or wherever this letter was written. What has not been noticed, however, is that they could not have been its original ending, for the man's response (letter 9, which follows directly in the manuscript) attacks a very different conclusion, in which the woman had refused his sexual advances. So the letter could have circulated in other recensions; perhaps the monks at Tegernsee were not the only ones to include it in a model collection. Given its many points of resemblance with the EDA, an alternative version might even have been known in France.

What Thisbe wished for Piramus (*quod Piramo Tispe*): a formulaic greeting in love
        letters[20]
The talent of Virgil . . . the eloquence of Cicero (*si exsuperaret mihi ingenium
        Maronis, si afflueret eloquentia Ciceronis*): cf. EDA no. 75 (*Si ipse Tullius . . . Si
        ad metrum totas Ovidius vires suas intenderet*)

I would confess myself unequal . . . to respond (*imparem tamen me faterer esse ad respondendum*): cf. EDA nos. 23 (*impar viribus meis rei magnitudo*), 50 (*si responsio jure vocari potest, ubi nichil par redditur*)

If I bring forth something less elegant than I wish (*si minus lepide, quam volo, aliquid profero*): cf. EDA no. 49 (*impolitas tam rudis stili litteras . . . mittere presumerem*)

To comply with your teachings in every way (*tuis preceptionibus in omnibus velle obsecundare*): cf. EDA no. 25 (*tibi rependere et in omnibus obedire*)

True friendship, as Tullius Cicero attests (*Amicicia vera attestante Tullio Cicerone*): cf. EDA no. 50 (*tam subtiliter de amicicie legibus argumentaris ut non Tullium legisse, sed ipsi Tullio precepta dedisse videaris*)

Agreement in all things . . . and good will (*divinarum humanarumque omnium rerum cum karitate et benivolentia consensio*): Cicero, *Laelius* 20 (*omnium divinarum humanarumque rerum cum benevolentia et caritate consensio*)

More excellent . . . , gathering what is scattered, preserving what is gathered, . . . enhancing what is preserved (*excellentior est omnibus rebus humanis . . . , dissociata congregans, congregata conservans, conservata magis magisque exaggerans*): Though not found in any extant work of Cicero, this praise of friendship was sometimes ascribed to him.[21]

Orders all things fittingly (*disponit cuncta decenter*): cf. Wisdom 8:1 (*disponit omnia suaviter*)

Reigns and powerfully commands (*regit imperat atque potenter*): cf. the Royal Acclamations (*Christus vincit, Christus regnat, Christus imperat*)

Whom I have enclosed in the marrow of my heart (*quem teneo medullis cordis inclusum*): Cicero, *Epistulae ad familares* 15.16 (*qui mihi haeres in medullis*)

From the day I first saw you, I began to love you (*a die, qua te primum vidi, cepi diligere te*): cf. EDA no. 84 (*Post mutuam nostre visionis . . . noticiam, . . . teque solum dilexi*)

No forgetfulness could wipe you out of my memory (*te de mei memoria nulla poterit delere oblivio*): cf. EDA no. 8 (*cuius memoriam nulla intercipere potest oblivio*)

True being . . . proceeds from nowhere else than your being (*verum esse . . . non alias procedit nisi de tuo esse*): cf. EDA no. 21 (*esse quod est*)

Faithfulness . . . queen of all virtues (*Fides . . . omnium virtutum regina*): Prudentius, *Psychomachia* 716 (*Virtutum regina Fides*)

Chosen from thousands (*ex milibus electus*): Song 5:10 (*electus ex milibus*); EDA nos. 50 (*te inter multa milia . . . elegi*), 84 (*elegi ex milibus*); letter 6 above

Received into the inmost sanctuary of my mind (*in mentis mee penetrabilibus quoddam penetrale receptus*): cf. Ovid, *Tristia* 1.1.105 (*in nostrum . . . penetrale receptus*)

If . . . you do not fall away from my love (*si tamen ab amore meo . . . non deficis*): cf.
　　EDA no. 84 (*Si fides illius titubat, vinculumque eius dilectionis non firmiter se*
　　continet)

In you I have set all my hope and my confidence (*in te omnem spem meam fidutiam-*
　　que positam habeo): troped introit for St. Stephen's Day (*in quo omnem spem*
　　meam fiduciamque positam habeo);[22] EDA no. 84 (*in quem omnem spem meam*
　　fiduciamque positam . . . habeo)

I should beware, lest I fall into a pit (*caveam, ne incidam in caveam*): or "lest I be
　　trapped in a cage"

My bow will be restored in my hand, and my glory renewed (*arcus meus instaurabi-*
　　tur et innovabitur gloria mea): Job 29:20 (*Gloria mea . . . innovabitur, / Et arcus*
　　meus in manu mea instaurabitur)

I heap up for myself . . . more to be prized than gold and silver (*super aurum et*
　　argentum amplectendam mihi coacervo): cf. Proverbs 3:14 (*Melior est . . . negotia-*
　　tione argenti, / Et auri); Ecclesiastes 2:8 (*Coacervavi mihi argentum et aurum*)

You neither have nor will ever have / any successor (*successor nemo futurus / est tibi,*
　　sed nec erit): Regensburg Songs, no. 34.8–9 (*fidei pignus semper servabo . . . / Ne*
　　qua succedat)

No one will please me but you (*mihi ni tu nemo placebit*): cf. EDA no. 84 (*tu solus*
　　michi placebas)

I would have written more but I said, there is no need (*Scripsissem plura, dixi non*
　　esse necesse): a closing formula. The German lines replace an earlier epilogue
　　deleted by the Tegernsee scribe (see comment on no. 9 below).

9 The Teacher to the Woman

Having read your intimate letter most diligently, I was delighted by
your extravagant praise of fidelity and friendship. I felt renewed like a
field at the end of winter, when it is strewn once more with merry
flowers. Even if all the parts of my body were turned into tongues, I
could not reply sufficiently to such great praise. If I had as many
absorbent holes as a sponge, I could not drink in such exalted words.

Yet, in accord with that maxim of Horace, you should not have joined
a horse's neck to a human head, nor should a beautiful woman's body

have ended in a hideous fish. To my amazement, you set a chimera
before me when, from a single fountain, you poured sweet and bitter
waters alike. When the field of my heart, watered by you, had begun to
blossom and bear fruits of fidelity and friendship—suddenly a stream
of bitter liquid fell on it and withered all of its delicious charms.
Indeed, you allured my heart when you extended your branches
toward me, beautifully adorned with the leaves of words. But then you
drove me off, lest I should pluck any fruit from your tree to taste it.
This is like that fig tree in the Gospel that bore no fruit; it is like poetic
talent without training. Why should such a tree take up space?

If faith without works is dead and the fulfillment of love is shown in
deeds, you caught yourself in a contradiction when you did not fulfill
your good beginning with a suitable ending, nor bring your sweet
eloquence to a fitting close. Rather, contrary to the law of friendship,
you opposed your *nolle* (I won't) to my *velle* (I will). So the first part of
your letter should utterly reject its harsh epilogue, contrary to friendship—and what you have magnificently expressed in words, you ought
to fulfill in friendly deeds.

If you cannot be moved or converted by prose, my friend,
then be governed by a discourse in verse.
The last words you wrote, you surely cannot defend,
for your rulings contradict the precepts, so very true,
of the learned Ovid—they are quite unsound.
One who defies his decrees comes to a bad end.

Whom do you wish to hurt? You pronounced harsh, evil words after
gentle ones!

It's right that you should prove what you write: "I'm in love!" So please—
why shouldn't I seek the goal that love desires?
The hymen is natural: let me penetrate that threshold!
What you say against this, I take as a mere cliché
fitting for ugly women—you should never be that way!
I reckon you will send another messenger with your reply,

for parchment won't do; there are things it would rather not say.
If any daylight is left me, let your door be open!
Then I will come for certain, I will snatch you in my arms.
I would have written more to you, S., if it had been allowed;
There is no need, I said, to reveal my name.

COMMENT

In this letter the teacher pounces. Having duly praised his student's essay on friendship, he couches a seduction bid in highly rhetorical terms. In the *Ars poetica*, Horace warned against hybrids: centaur and siren have no place in his aesthetic. But the woman's letter—with its lost original ending, now replaced by German verses—was just such a chimera, her teacher asserts. For it defiled "a beautiful woman's body" (her praise of friendship) by ending with the "hideous fish" tail of her chastity. Going further, this rhetorical devil cites Scripture for his purpose: an affectionate but chaste woman is like a barren fig tree, like faith without works, like love without deeds. The "law of friendship" he cites is a maxim of Sallust, also known to the Man of the EDA: *idem velle atque idem nolle*. True friends have a single will, whether to wish or to refuse. But the woman, by opposing her "I won't" to her teacher's "I will," violated that law. So, to mend both faulty rhetoric and defective friendship, she needs—obviously!—to sleep with him.

The letter concludes with a poem in leonine hexameters, but it is heavily abbreviated. For the entire second half of each line, and many words in the first half, the manuscript supplies only the initial letters of each word. A Polish philologist in the 1920s, Ryszard Ganszyniec, ventured to reconstruct these lines with the aid of their internal rhymes.[23] It is his conjectural verse—edited by Plechl and Bergmann, with many textual queries—that I translate here. So, needless to say, these verses should be taken with a barrel of salt. But despite uncertainties in detail, the gist is clear enough and explains why the lines were abridged in the first place. Whether the Tegernsee scribe found the abbreviations in his exemplar or supplied them himself, the obscenity of the poem probably offended him. Obscene verse was not exactly rare,[24] but this example seems all the more shocking by contrast with the woman's lofty moralism. It may be that the same scribe who abbreviated the cleric's verse (whether at Tegernsee or elsewhere) also changed the ending of the woman's letter 8, replacing her sexual *nolle* with the Middle High German lines that have so fascinated scholars of *Germanistik*.

The sequence of letters 8 and 9 is not unlike EDA nos. 25 and 26. There too, the Woman's earnest meditation on friendship inspires the Man's sexual pleading. By contrast with this Tegernsee letter, the Man's invitation seems far more tender. In that case, the wished-for consummation did take place, whereas the woman in the Tegernsee exchange continued to resist—as we shall see in letter 10 below.

If all the parts of my body were turned into tongues (*si omnia mei corporis membra verterentur in linguas*): Jerome, *Epistulae* 108.1 (*si cuncta corporis mei membra verterentur in linguas*)

Maxim of Horace (*humano capiti cervicem equinam . . . mulier formosa superne in atrum piscem*): *Ars poetica* 1–4 (*Humano capiti ceruicem pictor equinam / iungere si uelit et . . . atrum / desinat in piscem mulier formosa superne*)

From a single fountain, you poured sweet and bitter waters alike (*ex fonte uno dulcem et amaram simul aquam perfudisti*): James 3:11 (*Numquid fons de eodem foramine emanat dulcem et amaram aquam?*)

Fig tree in the Gospel (*evangelica illa ficus sine fructu*): Matthew 21:19 (*videns fici arborem . . . nihil invenit in ea nisi folia*); Mark 11:13–14 (*Cumque vidisset a longe ficum . . . nihil invenit praeter folia*)

Why should such a tree take up space? (*Quid etiam terram occupat?*): Luke 13:7 (*quid etiam terram occupat?*)

Faith without works is dead (*fides sine operibus mortua est*): James 2:20, 26 (*fides sine operibus mortua est*)

The fulfillment of love is shown in deeds (*plenitudo dilectionis exhibitio est operis*): Romans 13:10 (*plenitudo . . . legis est dilectio*); Gregory I, *Homiliae in evangelia* 2.30.1 (*Probatio . . . dilectionis, exhibitio est operis*, PL 76: 1220c); EDA no. 103 (*Amor ociosus esse non potest*)

Contrary to the law of friendship (*velle meo nolle tu tuum contra legem amicicie posuisti*): Sallust, *De coniuratione Catilinae* 20.4 (*idem velle atque idem nolle*)

I would have written more to you . . . There is no need, I said (*Scripsissem tibi S. plus . . . dixi non esse necesse*): an impudent echo of the woman's closing verse, *Scripsissem plura, dixi non esse necesse*. After the teacher's accurate summary of her letter, with its *multiplici laude fidei et amicitiae*, this echo proves that letter 9 is indeed a response to no. 8.

10 The Woman to Her Teacher

To her own from his own: herself to himself.

Someone under the name of Ovid says of love: "I had hoped to put an end to future cares." In my case, I want to apply this verse differently, for I had hoped to have no need of future writings. Yet "once again I am called to arms" and compelled to embark on modes I did not desire. For who will be able to hold back a speech once begun?

I do not want you to be angry with me when I bring forth what the passion of my mind conceives. To tell the truth, I wrote you a more intimate letter than any man before you could ever wrench from me. But you men are sly, or to put it better, deceitful. It is your habit to ensnare us simple young girls in talk because so often, as we proceed with you in our simplicity of mind onto the battlefield of words, you stab us with the sound reasoning (as you imagine) of your darts. Hence it is that you compared the letter I recently sent you to certain monstrous animals, which do not exist, but nonetheless have meaning. And you did this repeatedly, not fearing in this way to incriminate your friend. For with a wildly irreverent, unbridled spirit exceeding measure, you imprudently loosed the reins of your hasty speech when you equated my words— which I thought to be good and wholesome, proceeding from a good conscience and an unfeigned faith—to a chimera and a siren. This comes from no other place, as I am firmly led to believe, than *"what the billy goat"* and so forth— because you think that, after our tender words, you should proceed to acts. But that is not so, nor will it be.

I would please you less if I gave myself entirely *to everyone with whom I exchange friendly words. When you turned my message inside out,* you became notorious in my eyes. *Never do that again! My friend, follow my teaching, which can do you no harm. If you were not dear to me, I would* just let you race into the abyss of ignorance and blindness, if I may say so. *But you deserve better than that,* for in you there are fruits of honor and decency. *I would have written much more to you, but you are so well trained* that you know how to gather much from few words. *Be ever constant and happy.*

COMMENT

This little gem of a letter—witty, affectionate, yet fierce—could serve as a model to show cloistered women how to refuse their too-importunate "friends." The writer does not want to break off relations with her predatory teacher, for she continues to use the familiar *tu*, not the distancing *vos*. But she calls him out on his duplicity. This teacher and his ilk, she argues, encourage their students to turn girlish crushes into love by writing over-the-top letters about fidelity and friendship, mastering the hyperbolic mode of their day. Then, once the teacher has baited his trap—or, in the writer's metaphor, lured a "simple young girl" onto the battlefield of words—he strikes, perverting his victim's "good and wholesome [words]" in order to proposition her. Undeceived, the writer rebukes her would-be seducer in no uncertain terms. "Follow *my* teaching," she writes; then he will not disgrace himself. To avoid her own disgrace, the student be-comes the teacher. Like several young women in the Regensburg Songs (nos. 6, 22, 28, 31, 53), she has no compunction about taking on the role of moral arbiter.

Her letter begins with a grammatical riddle: *Suo sua sibi se.* This teasing salutation is hard to translate. I have chosen the most obvious interpretation, but another possible reading would be "his own self to himself"—as if the woman were her teacher's better angel, trying to restore him to his true ethical self after he had been led astray by lust.[25] Heloise engages in similar play in the greeting of her third letter: "Suo specialiter, sua singulariter."

Strikingly, the woman quotes the beginning of a late eleventh or early twelfth-century comic dialogue, the *Ovidius puellarum*, which is also cited by the Woman of the EDA (no. 84). She bristles at having her letter compared to a chimera because, as Ganszyniec has shown, misogynist poets of the age (includ-ing Marbod) used the mythical beast as code for "prostitute." A harlot is called a chimera—lion in front, goat in the middle, and snake in her tail—because she is leonine in her pride, stinking in her filth, and serpentine in her cunning.[26]

While it provides evidence for a diffuse epistolary culture, this letter was clearly written in Germany. The elliptical words "what the billy goat..." (*daz der boch*) are in German, alluding to a vernacular proverb. And the final paragraph blends German and Latin; I have italicized the German passages in my translation. Although the letter is obviously a reply to no. 9, it appears by itself in the manuscript (fol. 100v), while nos. 8–9 are found later on fols. 113v–114v. This is an indication that the Tegernsee monks were copying originals on loose leaves.

I had hoped to put an end to future cares (*Sperabam curis finem fecisse futuris*): *Ovidius puellarum* 2, ed. Lieberz (*Sperabam curis finem fecisse futuris*); EDA no. 84 (*sperabam me curis finem posuisse futuris*)

Once again I am called to arms (*rursus ad arma vocor*): *Ovidius puellarum* 3 (*Rursus ad arma vocor*)

Compelled to embark on modes (*cogor inire modos*): Boethius, *Consolation of Philosophy* 1 metr. 1.2 (*cogor inire modos*)

Who will be able to hold back a speech once begun? (*Sermonem ceptum quis enim retinere valebit?*): Job 4:2 (*conceptum sermonem tenere quis poterit?*); Horace, *Ars poetica* 390 (*nescit uox missa reuerti*); EDA no. 75 (*si vox emissa reverti nosset*)

Ensnare ... in talk (*capere ... in sermone*): Matthew 22:15, Luke 20:20 (*ut caperent eum in sermone*)

Certain monstrous animals, which do not exist, but nonetheless have meaning (*monstruosis non existentibus quibusdam animalibus, significatione tamen rerum non carentibus*): cf. Boethius, commentary on Aristotle's *De interpretatione* 1.1 ('*hircocervus*'... *significat aliquid, sed nondum verum vel falsum*), 1.3 (*chimaera ... non est nec omnino subsistit et potest de ea vere dici*)

With a[n] ... irreverent, unbridled spirit (*irreverenti et infronito animo*): Ecclesiasticus 23:6 (*animae irreverenti et infrunitae*)

Wholesome [words]: reading *salutaria* for MS *solitaria*

A good conscience and an unfeigned faith (*conscientia bona et fide non ficta*): 1 Timothy 1:5 (*conscientia bona et fide non ficta*)

A chimera and a siren (*chimere et sirene*): The MS has the corrupt reading *hernini*, which Plechl and Bergmann emend to *sirene*, Kühnel and Dronke to *Charybdi*. Cf. letter 9, "nor should a beautiful woman's body have ended in a hideous fish. To my amazement, you set a chimera before me." Horace mentions both Chimaera and Charybdis in *Carmina* 1.27. For the chimera as an image of illicit love, cf. Regensburg Songs 2 and 4; Marbod of Rennes, *Vita S. Thaisidis* (*Ut domus absque sera fuit omnibus illa chimaera*, PL 171: 1630c), and *Liber decem capitulorum* 3.46–57.

What the billy goat (*daz der boch*): German proverb, *Was der Bock an ihm selber weiss, dasselbig zeihet er die Geyss* (What the billy goat knows as his own faults, he reproaches in the nanny goat)

Fruits of honor and decency (*fructus honoris et honestatis*): Ecclesiasticus 24:23 (*fructus honoris et honestatis*)

From the Regensburg Songs

THE REGENSBURG SONGS are a collection of lyrics scattered randomly through a twelfth-century manuscript (Munich, Bayerische Staatsbibliothek, Clm 17142) preserved by the monks of Schäftlarn. The MS is a barely legible miscellany whose texts are datable to 1106; it includes grammatical notes, scholia, proverbs, political poems, and other teaching materials copied from a schoolmaster's working papers after his death. Among these are love letters and playful verses, all in leonine hexameters or distichs, exchanged between one or more teachers and a class of convent pupils in Regensburg. Thirty-nine of the sixty-eight pieces are unfinished drafts or epigrams of just one to four lines; the rest are short poems of five to thirty-eight lines. I have translated these selections from the edition of Anke Paravicini, *Carmina Ratisponensia* (Heidelberg: Carl Winter, 1979).

No. 2 (Teacher)

A lion in front, a goat in the middle, with a viper's tail—
This monster denotes the terrible face of love.
Fierce as a lion, it rushes into the illicit act
And grows filthy as a goat in carrying out the crime.
The serpent follows, stinging the heart with its sordid guilt.
With the foul poison of its sin, it burns a mind
That repents its evils too late, after rumors erupt.
It is safer to be alone than to bear such grievous ills!

COMMENT

The chimera, a hybrid monster, symbolizes illicit love. Sometimes it was linked specifically with prostitutes (see comment on Tegernsee letter 10). See also no. 4 below.

A lion in front, a goat in the middle, with a viper's tail (*Prima parte leo, medio capra, vipera cauda*): Fulgentius, *Mythologiarum libri* 3.1 (*Cymera . . . id est fluctuatio amoris . . . Dum enim amor nouiter venit, ut leo feraliter inuadit; . . . capra quae in medio pingitur perfectio libidinis est; . . . postremus draco . . . . uulnus det penitentiae uenenumque peccati*)

No. 3 (Teacher)

What a flower asks a flower, sparkling in springtime,
Is what the man who loves you above all demands:
The games of Hymen! Welcome the name of a lover!
Now the ardor of love returns to my unruly veins.
Alas, what is happening? Sweet dreams deceive me:

O even as I sleep, your image appears to me,
Plies me with kisses, and in embracing vanishes!
You're mine, my care, more fleeting than a gentle breeze.
All too inconstant, you make sport of constant loves.
But when love blazes, its heat is fierce, unbearable!
Its fervor—shall I check it?—demands the strongest medicine.
Yet what use is medicine, what can a herbal potion do?
It does nothing for me; love is not treatable with herbs.
But you, my fair one—what a wholesome remedy!
With you is sweet loving; love is the sweetest ardor.
But in this sweet season, you are nursing barren loves—
If you yield no more to me, let yourself at least be kissed.

COMMENT

Resounding with Ovidian echoes, this song gains piquancy from its position,
sandwiched between two poems that warn against sinful love.

What a flower asks a flower (*Quidquid flos flori*): cf. Tegernsee letter 6 (*quidquid
amor amori*)

The name of a lover (*nomen amantis*): Ovid, *Metamorphoses* 1.474 (*nomen amantis*)

Even as I sleep, your image appears to me (*O dum dormito, tua se presentat imago*): cf.
EDA 22 (*in somno me non deseris*); Tegernsee letter 5 (*dormiendo quasi vigilando
non cesso tibi bona optando*)

More fleeting than a gentle breeze (*tenuique fugatior aura*): Ovid, *Metamorphoses*
8.179 (*tenues volat . . . per auras*), 13.807 (*fugacior aura*)

When love blazes (*cum fervet amor*): cf. EDA no. 18 (*estuat . . . pectus meum amoris
fervore*), no. 42 (*in amore tuo ferveo*), no. 92 (*fervore . . . amoris*)

Not treatable with herbs (*non est medicabilis herbis*): Ovid, *Heroïdes* 5.149 (*amor non
est medicabilis herbis*); EDA no. 21 (*amor meus . . . tibi . . . soli est medicabilis*)

Nursing barren loves (*lactas steriles . . . amores*): Ovid, *Metamorphoses* 1.496 (*ster-
ilem . . . nutrit amorem*)

Let yourself at least be kissed (*vel ad oscula danda patebis*): Ovid, *Metamorphoses* 4.75
(*vel ad oscula danda pateres*)

❧

No. 4 (Teacher)

When you stroll in a field where a dismal form is creeping,
Gaze not on the savage beast, but fear the chimera,
For the lion will bite, the she-goat defile, and the viper poison you.

❧

No. 5 (Student)

You could be called a sphinx or a monkey—you look like one,
With your hideous face and your unkempt hair!

❧

No. 6 (Students)

The chorus of vestals sends you men gifts of peace,
Granting your company the right to govern us,
But only so far as Virtue demands an honest price.

❧

COMMENT

These aristocratic convent pupils never forget that, by virtue of their social rank,
it is they who hold the real authority. In no. 5, a student impudently insults the
new master. Here the students welcome him, but only on condition that he behave himself.

Chorus of vestals (*vestalis chorus*): Lucan, *Pharsalia* 1.597 (*Vestalemque chorum*)

No. 7 (Student)

Correct the little verses I present to you, teacher,
For I accept your words as the light of the Word itself.
But it makes me so sad that you prefer Bertha to me!

COMMENT

Perhaps Bertha was the teacher's pet. In these school poems, it is hard to distinguish between academic rivalry and romantic jealousy.

No. 8 (Teacher)

Be glad that Fortune made you my first girlfriend!
But this constant rain is seriously bothering me,
For I'm afraid it's falling to punish our sins.

Be glad that Fortune made you my first girlfriend (*Gaude quod primam te sors mihi
fecit amicam*): cf. no. 17 below (*quam primam sibi sors bona fecit amicam*)

No. 9 (Student)

My mind is joyful, my body is freed from pain
Because you, teacher, have honored me with your love.

෨෫

No. 11 (Student)

You, whom I cherish above all other friends—
Your situation seriously worries me.

෨෫

No. 12 (Teacher)

Be well, you deserve boundless praise for your letter—
Although, dear love, as what you have written suggests,
I beg you not to worry about my affairs. It is enough
For me to take care and watch out for you in every way.

෨෫

No. 14 (Student)

With your lamp, O Christ, cast darkness from the hearts
Of us who trace the holy footsteps of your word.

෨෫

No. 15 (Teacher)

You are dear to me because you have given precious gifts:
A shiny and well-turned bowl, ideal for drinking,
And garlic too, which my medicine requires.
If you were to add more, you will never lack thanks.

Well-turned bowl (*Vas bene tornatum*): *Eupolemius* 3.271 (*bene tornatis . . . vasis*)[1]

No. 16 (Teacher)

Psst! It's me—you know who. Now don't betray your lover!
I beg you, come to the Old Chapel at dawn,
But knock lightly because the sacristan lives there.
What my heart now conceals, the bed will reveal to you.

No. 17 (in the Person of a Priest)

The provost of the Old Chapel wishes you luck,
Emma, whom good fortune has befriended.
But you're not the first—half a dozen have gone before.
You're number seven, the last—and not the favorite.

COMMENT

The teacher's come-on receives a fitting reply in this witty message to the last
(and least) of his supposed paramours.

Whom good fortune has befriended (*quam primam sibi sors bona fecit amicam*): cf. no.
8 above (*Gaude quod primam te sors mihi fecit amicam*)

No. 22 (Students)

Clever Mercury has given me this flower
With which I can resist vices and filthy pleading,
So no foolish man can lay claim to me.

Let men who enjoy lewdness renounce our company—
And the one whose talk is too crude for our companions.
If you number yourself among those, begone!
Even men tested in a thousand ways are scarcely admitted,
Yet we welcome them modestly—in moderation.
As for those whose pledge Virtue wants us to trust,
She takes care to fashion them well, with great refinement,
That they may grow secretly in good and skillful speech
And outstanding manners, being polished in every way.
Before you come to us, therefore, preen your feathers—
If Reason gave you any when she formed you—
Lest you be defiled in any way with inveterate guile.
But the man who is famed for courtesy like ours—
Our vestal chorus wishes him salutary gifts.

COMMENT

Like the court ladies that some of them would become, the convent girls represent themselves as arbiters of courtesy and refinement, warning the new teacher that he must measure up to their high standards. Mercury, the god of eloquence, figures prominently in these poems. In Martianus Capella's beloved late antique textbook *The Marriage of Philology and Mercury*, he weds the goddess of learning, who brings the seven liberal arts as her dowry. The "flower" of line 1 is Mercury's gift of eloquent speech, which is metaphorically represented as a charm against sexual harrassment.

Clever Mercury has given me this flower (*Hunc mihi Mercurius florem dedit ingeniosus*): Ovid, *Metamorphoses* 14.291 (*pacifer huic dederat florem Cyllenius album*); cf. no. 35 below
Fashion . . . with great refinement (*extrema . . . fingere lima*): cf. Ovid, *Tristia* 1.7.30 (*defuit et coeptis ultima lima meis*)
Vestal chorus (*vestalis chorus*); no. 6 above; Lucan, *Pharsalia* 1.597 (*Vestalemque chorum*)

No. 24 (Student)

I believe you are testing my dutiful intentions,
Because you ask me for a cord for your tablets.
From this little thing, see how great my devotion is:
My courtesy promptly grants your request.
So, when you attach what I've made you to your side,
Bear me attentively on the tablet of your heart.

COMMENT

Small gifts cement the affectionate relationship between teacher and students
(cf. no. 15). The teacher would have used the requested gift (*perpendiculum tabularum*) to hang his writing tablets from his belt for easy access. I have not found
perpendiculum attested elsewhere in the same sense, but the meaning seems
clear enough.

No. 26 (Teacher)

I'm safe, as I should be—I've followed perfect models.
And so I will always be, for literature is my mead.
Why should I let myself be hurt by such a nun?
No, I'll drive the men away and more easily conquer a girl!

COMMENT

This little poem is an enigma. Perhaps the teacher, rebuffed by a nun who was already vowed and therefore off limits, is resolving to try his luck with a younger girl.

❦

No. 27 (Teacher)

A ring sent among gifts is a pledge of love.
So let's hasten to make a pact, as the custom is!

Pledge of love (*pignus amoris*): EDA no. 104 (*pignus amoris*)

❦

No. 28 (Student)

My nurse Integrity does not know the pact you name,
And wants me never to learn such a custom.

❦

COMMENT

The "pledge of love" (*pignus amoris*) and its accompanying "pact" (*fedus*) are frequent motifs. In this epigrammatic exchange (cf. nos. 31 and 33), the student shows that she has learned the difference between seduction and honorable friendship (*Honestas*).

❦

No. 29 (Student)

I cannot bear parting from you so often
When every one of our girls is chasing you!

No. 31 (Student)

Men taught by Virtue to make an honorable pact
I will not chase away, but repay with their just rewards,
Though I have not learned to be joined in a private pact.

Repay with their just rewards (*dignis digna rependam*): Tegernsee letter 1 (*dignis
digna repende*)

No. 32 (Teacher)

Newly veiled virgins, sanctify yourselves to the Lord,
Lest the ring seal him to you in vain as Bridegroom.
The master calls the newly veiled to obey new rules:
Let them learn to be wise and lay frivolity aside.

COMMENT

Every year at the bishop's visitation, girls who had reached the canonical age and
were destined for religious life would receive the nun's veil and formally profess
their virginity. After this milestone, there was to be no more flirtation or playful
love notes, but a more mature and serious life: *ut sapiant et opus levitatis omittant.*

No. 33 (Teacher)

A choice love is hidden in a friendly breast.
Love that runs silently conquers all pacts.

No. 34 (Teacher)

I will repay you worthily, considering your letter kindly.
You wrote that you are devoted to me with all your heart;
I too am devoted, though I am far away in the flesh.
Let my spirit itself be with you, ever the same.
We are one spirit, treasuring the gift of fidelity.
If my mind should deceive the intentions of such a friend,
I will refuse her, lest anyone call her a companion in sin.
I will be kind and keep this pledge of loyalty forever,
Lest she have a successor—even if all beauty should fade.
I say "farewell" before the wings of poetry fail.
But now, to advise a friend gently, I have more to say.
These verses reply to yours, written as best you could.
The words indeed reveal the lofty flight of your heart.
But when you descended, tell me where you left me?
I was wholly with you; I hoped you were also with me.
But this coming and going of yours agitates me!
When you ascend to me, I don't know where you part from me.
I stand, you stand, so we stand mutually in love
If we have but one will, be it yea or nay.

COMMENT

In this poem of ennobling love, the teacher pledges fidelity and promises to maintain a friendship with his old student, even after her youthful beauty fades. Line 7
is a tour de force, hard to interpret: *Hanc renuam, ne quam quis nequam dixerit
equam.* The second section critiques the student's previous letter, written *pro potuisti*. She did her best, but perhaps her verses had used an incoherent metaphor.

We are one spirit (*Spiritus est unus*): cf. 1 Corinthians 6:17 (*Qui ... adhaeret Domino,
    unus spiritus est*)

Pledge of loyalty (*fidei pignus*): EDA no. 69 (*pignus fidei*)
Lest she have a successor (*Ne qua succedat*): cf. Tegernsee letter 8 (*successor nemo futurus / est tibi, sed nec erit*)
I was wholly with you (*Totus eram tecum*): EDA no. 16 (*Totus tecum sum*)
If we have but one will, be it yea or nay (*Unum si velle sit nobis, sit quoque nolle*):
    Sallust, *De coniuratione Catilinae* 20.4 (*idem velle atque idem nolle*); EDA no.
    24 (*eque annuimus, eque negamus*); Tegernsee letter 9 (*velle meo nolle tu tuum
    contra legem amicicie posuisti*)

No. 35 (in the Person of the Teacher's Mother)

From G., set down instead of H., a name that stands for Gem,
To the one her kindly care was accustomed to nurse:
A mother desires no other greeting for her son
But what she owes the spirit that governs him in life.
O glory of my desire, O greatest part of my fame,
Tell me, I ask, fine young man, tell me, my sweet son,
What have I done to you, tell me, why have you abandoned me?
There is no need for you to ask for a flower of Mercury,
For you still have the herb that was given you by my care,
Exuding the sweet scent of delicious spice.

COMMENT

Like no. 17, this is a poem in character (*ethopoeia*). The student pretends to be her teacher's mother, complaining that he never writes home. Laments over a loved one's failure to write were a common genre. Tegernsee letter 2 is a fine specimen, and there are several in the EDA (nos. 37, 42, 97). As in no. 22 above, the "flower of Mercury" is eloquence. The speaker perhaps means that her "son" cannot use inability to write as an excuse because she herself, his mother, gave him (or at any rate paid for) his early education.

O greatest part of my fame (*mihi pars o maxima fame*): cf. EDA no. 49 (*o maxima pars anime mee*)

What have I done to you, tell me, why have you abandoned me? (*Quid tibi, quid feci, quid me, dic deseruisti?*): Psalm 21:2 (*quare me dereliquisti?*); Matthew 27:46, Mark 15:34 (*ut quid dereliquisti me?*); Tegernsee letter 2 (*Quid feci, quid feci, numquid prior te abieci?*)

Flower of Mercury (*florem . . . Mercurialem*): no. 22 above; Ovid, *Metamorphoses* 14.291 (*huic dederat florem Cyllenius*)

Sweet scent of delicious spice (*dulcem pigmenti suavis odorem*): cf. EDA nos. 94 (*optimi odoris aromati*), 103 (*omnia pigmenta odore . . . superanti*)

❧

No. 37 (Teacher)

I used to be rich in song when I had need of little,
But I laid song aside once I began to get rich.
It is no longer safe to compete with you in song!
You claim that Mercury's offspring serve you;
Now his children's services are mine.
Indeed, I know the learned Minerva herself taught you;
She gave you a fiery gaze and a skillful heart,
Feasted you richly, bade you blaze so brightly
Lest you conceal the flames that burn in your breast—
Disgraceful flames, with which you scorch even me!
You far surpass, you far excel me in song.
I confess myself vanquished, at last I'm compelled to yield.
Orpheus himself meets his just destruction
When he presumes to challenge your sex in writing.
Marsyas mocked the puffy cheeks of the Tritonian goddess;
Hence he was flayed and flowed away like a river,
And all males have given up competing with females.
Enough! Recalling these examples, I remind myself
That I should avoid this contest, for I am not your equal.

❧

COMMENT

Now that his student has reached a high level of proficiency in Latin, the teacher half boasts, half laments that he can no longer compete with her. In a previous poem (no. 36), a group of students had sent their teacher a poetic "gift" of the three Graces, the daughters of Philology and Mercury.[2] Graciously acknowledging the gift, he flatters this student: she has gained her skill not from him, but from Minerva herself. He then cites mythological examples of women's superiority over men. Orpheus, in one version of his legend, rejected heterosexual love after his failure to redeem Eurydice. In the end he was torn apart by the Maenads, or priestesses of Bacchus. The flute player Marsyas challenged Apollo to a musical contest and lost; hence he was flayed alive. But Ovid tells his story briefly and elliptically, without naming Apollo. Instead he mentions the "Tritonian flute" (*Tritoniaca . . . harundine, Metam.* 6.384), and since "Tritonia" was another name for Athena, it is easy to see an example of female victory in this tale. This poem shows that in the early twelfth century, at least in some quarters, women's advanced Latin learning seemed not exceptional but normal.

It is no longer safe to compete with you (*Iam non est tutum contendere*): cf. Ovid, *Heroïdes* 4.11 (*non est contemnere tutum*)

Flames that burn in your breast (*gestent tua pectora flammas*): cf. Virgil, *Aeneid* 1.44 (*transfixo pectore flammas*)

Vanquished . . . I'm compelled to yield (*Victum . . . manus dare cogor*): Ovid, *Heroïdes* 4.14 (*dabit victas . . . manus*), 17.260 (*dabo . . . victa manus*)

Orpheus (*Treicius vates*): Ovid, *Metamorphoses* 11.2 (*Threicius vates*, i.e., Orpheus)

Marsyas: Ovid, *Metamorphoses* 6.382–400

I am not your equal (*non sum par tibi*): cf. EDA no. 50 (*Tibi . . . impar sum, quia in hoc eciam me excedis, ubi ego videbar excedere*)

No. 42 (Student)

I send you a greeting that cannot be diminished
By time or distance, were it a hundredfold greater.

May the right hand of God, who sees all men of proven virtue,
Be ever present and send you happiness often.

I send you a greeting (*Salve mitto tibi*): cf. EDA no. 82 (*tibi mitto salutem*)
A hundredfold greater (*centuplicato*): cf. EDA no. 94 (*centuplicato*)

⁊❧

No. 44 (Student)

I cannot decide what I should specially write to you,
  Who have said so many things in my praise.
Whether you say them in jest or in earnest
  I cannot tell; my mind is still uncertain.
For, leaving out all that is truly distinguished,
  You praised my beauty, as if it were worthy—
As if, consumed by a horrid fever, it deserved any praise.

I cannot decide what I should specially write to you (*Quid tibi precipue scribam
    nequeo reputare*): Ovid, *Ars amatoria* 2.273 (*Quid tibi praecipiam . . . mittere
    versus*); cf. EDA no. 104 (*quid potissimum dicam ignoro*)

⁊❧

No. 46 (Student)

Your loyalty is hollow, your love not lasting!
He who gave you a heroic name wasted its meaning.
What good is a name if you will not preserve its honor?
Those who seek to be heroic will shine with such names.
From now on, you should instead be called [Weakling].
Now I'll briefly explain why, I'll solve this riddle.
When I sent you my little verses, reasonably polished,
You never bothered to send me a fitting reply.
This failing is of course entirely your fault.

Trouble in the realm kept you from answering?
You alone could have treated this pestilence.
No breastplate protected your foolish breast,
And your sword was covered with so much rust
That even if it struck the foe, he received no wound.
I wonder which hand of yours bore a suitable shield?
Your right, I suppose, as befits a cowardly slave!
But perhaps you'll say, "I had no messenger!"
She who gave you my letter would have brought me yours,
If you wished to send one, if you even knew how to write.

COMMENT

This lyric, like the "mother's" poem (no. 35) but more savagely, abuses the teacher
for not answering the student's last letter—or, as we might say now, grading her
assignment promptly. His name, presumably that of some Germanic hero, has
been wasted on him; the insulting epithet she wants to give him instead (line 5)
has been lost from the manuscript. The speaker compares him to a cowardly
knight, so timid that he carries his shield in his right hand. A proper knight, of
course, would hold a sword in his right hand, a shield in his left.

The writer makes light of "trouble in the realm" (*turbatio regni*), but this
was a serious political crisis. A revolt against the controversial emperor Henry
IV had been led by his own son in 1104, with backing from Pope Paschal II on
the ground that the emperor had been excommunicated. Though imprisoned
and forced to abdicate in December 1105, Henry escaped and defeated his son's
army in March 1106, but died soon afterward. An earlier poem (no. 43) had announced the king's death (*Qui regnum tenuit, nature debita solvit*), lamenting
that he had been succeeded by a "foolish boy" (*puer insipiens*).

Lack of a messenger must have been a common excuse for not writing. But
the last lines preemptively reject that excuse—showing too that women could
serve in the role of messengers.

I wonder which hand of yours bore a suitable shield? / Your right, I suppose (*miror
clipeum tua que ferret manus aptum. / Dextra, reor*): Ovid, *Ars amatoria*
1.693–94 (*clipeo manus apta ferendo est: / Pensa quid in dextra . . . habes?*)

No. 47 (Teacher)

Don't blame it on me if I didn't reply
  To your letter as quickly as I should have.
I don't hold on to what I write to friends until the ninth year.
  And I'm sorry, it was your peers and slaves
Who caused this delay, you know;
  I hadn't expected their sudden return.

COMMENT

The student's teasing has gone too far and the teacher is not amused. Alluding to
Horace's *Ars poetica*, he reminds her that he has other students (*consimilesque
tui*), as well as fellow "slaves" (*sclavi*)—perhaps members of his own religious
house who had unexpectedly returned.

I don't hold on to what I write to friends until the ninth year (*Non servo nonum
  quod amicis scribo per annum*): Horace, *Ars poetica* 386–89 (*Siquid tamen olim /
  scripseris, . . . / . . . nonumque prematur in annum / membranis intus positis*)

No. 49 (Student)

I will pray for your health, though I'm angry with you:
I've learned from experience that the gods are plotting against me.
For, beneath a cloak of empty friendship, you deceive me:
You embrace me in words, but other girlfriends in deed.
Why should I complain? May my prayer be fulfilled on my rivals:

Let all the snakes that the dread Medusa has for hair
Leap on those nymphs that now tempt your constancy!

COMMENT

In this charming piece of invective, the student imagines a fitting punishment
for her rivals in love (*alias amicas*), who may be classmates demanding their own
fair share of the teacher's attention.

No. 50 (Student)

Because you made me glad with a place of honor,
Many have hurt me with bitter darts of envy.
Before they do real harm and dig deeper wounds,
Let your goodness anticipate and chase them off.

COMMENT

Like nos. 7 and 49, these lines comment on student rivalries. The only gendered
pronoun is *illas* in line 4, denoting the envious girls. For this reason I assign the
poem to a student, though Paravicini ascribes it to the teacher.

No. 53 (Student)

We to whom the Lord has given—or will give—good looks
Are not amused by the honor of hyperbolic praise.
It's not that I'm angry if I'm called charming or beautiful,

If that praise is bestowed simply and not wantonly.
The man I hate is the one with a treacherous heart:
All the arrows he shoots are drenched in black poison.

COMMENT

Dominus, the subject of line 1, is omitted by Paravicini but supplied in Dronke's edition.[3]

No. 57 (Student)

Writing and speaking skillfully, the handmaids of Mercury
Remain with me, to keep babbling arrogance at bay.
Look to yourself prudently, then, lest you suffer a worse fate
Than the raven, who lost his snowy form because of his tongue.

COMMENT

The "handmaids of Mercury" (*Mercurii famule*) are probably the Graces, as in no. 37. Like many of these songs, the poem extols eloquence as not merely an ornament but a moral virtue. It is no less important to know when to keep silent. In Ovid's *Metamorphoses* (2.596–632), a raven tells Apollo that his girlfriend Coronis has been unfaithful. Apollo kills her in a rage, then repents and punishes the raven by turning it from white to black.

No. 60 (Student)

These apples, plucked from the proud branches of the Hesperides,
The star of Athena's maidens gives to their king,
Who is nobler than Hercules, because as victor he did not take all.

COMMENT

A somewhat mysterious epigram. Line 2 reads *Doxa puellarum dat regi Palladiarum*. Stealing the golden apples of the Hesperides was the eleventh labor of Hercules.

No. 61 (Teacher)

Is this the reward you give me, faithless one, for my letter—
To flee from me, silly girl, and not want to remember
How many well-meaning favors I have lavished on you?
If your fidelity were perfect, you would come in secret,
And bring me whatever secret you possess.

COMMENT

As in no. 16, the teacher adopts an Ovidian pose and plays at seducing a student.

❧

No. 65 (Teacher)

Love does not consist in words, but in gracious deeds.
Because I see that you are my friend in both words and deeds,
If I live and thrive, I will repay you with an equal favor.

Love does not consist in words, but in gracious deeds (*Non constat verbis dilectio sed benefactis*): cf. EDA no. 12 (*Non opus esse reor . . . ut fidem tuam quam factis evidenter exhibes, verbis . . . commendes*) .

"To a Fugitive Lover"

This letter-poem is found in a late twelfth-century manuscript: Zürich, Zentralbibliothek, MS C 58/275, fol. 11v. Beginning in leonine hexameters, it shifts at line 19 into elegiacs. The poem is no. 116 in Jakob Werner, ed., *Beiträge zur Kunde der lateinischen Literatur des Mittelalters aus Handschriften gesammelt*, 2nd ed. (Aarau: Sauerländer, 1905), 45–46. Werner speculates that the anthology was compiled by a German cleric who had studied in France, perhaps at Orléans and Paris. While this poem could have been written by either a man or a woman, it is an exercise in *ethopoeia* or impersonation; there is no reason to think it autobiographical. Modeled on Ovid's *Heroïdes*, the epistle voices the lament of a seduced, abandoned, and pregnant woman. It is a powerful *dissuasio* for any girl tempted by a clerical seducer.

All things disgust me. My limbs are contorted with pain,
They endure a peasant's fate. Do I need to explain?
My senses fail me, body and voice waste away.
Come back to me, then, or else you deserve to die!

5 Let death be far from you—I beg you, come back.
Only your returning could restore my mind.
May the Lord grant this, lest my mind groan in travail;
May the living God bring you back as my friend.
Think, think how my crazed mind is perishing!

10 There will be no end where the dire Fury reigns—
Truly, the Fury's reign will never end.
Writing fails me, for grief is crushing my heart.
What shall I say to you, absent and—alas!—fleeing me?
What good is it to assault distant ears with verses?

15 You have turned harder than stone as I seek you;
I cannot vanquish you, stony and distant.
Please come and meet me, I will make you less lonely!
I would discuss many things with you if I had time—
        And a place that was fitting for our tears.

20 But these are not granted, so let my letter speak for me;
        Let parchment take the place of my living voice.
Woe is me, what have I done to deserve this,
        That I cannot speak with you in a secret place?
If you refuse to talk privately, then at least

25   Grant that my parchment may say a few things.
I thought the Rhine would pour its golden streams
        Into the Danube, before you'd refuse a private talk!
Why should I now cause you greater shame
        Than I did before? I am quite unable to say.

30 Whatever in me displeases you . . . came from you!
        Did you not test what was mine? Why now do you carp?
Then I was a gem, a flower, a lily of the field—
        Then no woman in the world was my equal!
I am no different now, though I'm no longer virgin,

35   Nor can I ever be again—as I lament without end.
I weep day and night that the Fates did not take

My life along with my tender maidenhood.
To win a conquest by deceit is utterly base.
When you were wooing, you often gave me presents—
40   And for those goods, I have had to bear many evils.
Because of you, I have suffered many a beating
  That my delicate limbs can scarcely bear.
But the shame hurts more than lashes hurt my limbs;
  Words cause more agony than whippings.
45 What gave me pleasure once, now brings only tears.

APPENDICES

affectio / affectus—both terms have a similar range of meanings—feeling, mood, disposition, affection—with strong positive connotations. *Affectus* occurs only in the Woman's letters. I have translated both terms as "feeling" or "affection."

amica / amicus / amicitia—an *amicus* or *amica* is a friend, but the terms are strongly gendered; they can also mean "boyfriend" and "girlfriend." The bride and bridegroom in the Song of Songs are styled *amica* and *amicus*. By using these terms, the lovers evoke both the sacred text and the Ciceronian ideal of pure friendship (*amicitia*), which requires that a friend be loved in a disinterested way for himself alone, not for the sake of pleasures or riches. When the lovers wish to discuss friendship in a gender-neutral sense, they use the generic masculine *amicus*.

amor—the most general Latin term for love, with a semantic range as broad as the English word. Both lovers use it frequently. *Amor* is rare in the Vulgate, appearing only three times in the New Testament, but is central to the Ovidian tradition. I normally translate it as "love," but when it appears in conjunction with *dilectio*, I have used "desire" or "passion" to emphasize its sexual connotations.

anima / animus—The ubiquitous biblical *anima* means "soul"—the immaterial entity that gives life to the body, as well as the moral self that survives death. *Animus*, a classical term, is less common in the Bible and has a broader semantic field: mind, spirit, thought, courage, purpose, and the like. It is also a term of endearment, which I translate as either "mind" or "spirit" according to context. The Man calls the Woman both *anima* and *animus* as pet names, using the terms interchangeably.

caritas—charity; altruistic love or benevolence; the supreme Christian virtue, eulogized by Paul in 1 Corinthians 13. Only the Woman uses this term, defining it as the universal goodwill owed to all people, in contrast to the special love of friendship or erotic desire.

dilecta / dilectus / dilectio—*Dilectio* is not a classical term for love, but a Christian coinage from the verb *diligere*, to love or esteem. It appears frequently in the Vulgate and in ethical and devotional texts, connoting a love based on free will and moral choice, though it can also be a synonym for either *amor* or *caritas*. The Woman uses *dilectio* often, the Man less so, beginning only in letter 50 when he picks it up from her. *Dilecta* and *dilectus*, more often in the superlative, are the couple's favorite epithets for "beloved."

dulcis / dulcedo—These terms for "sweet" and "sweetness" occur in almost every letter—a total of eighty-seven uses, in addition to twenty-five for their synonyms *suavis* and *suavitas*. Alternative translations include "pleasant," "charming," "lovely," and "delightful." I translate the vocatives *dulcissime* and *dulcissima* as "sweetheart."

fides / fidelitas—In the letters, these common terms refer not to the theological virtue of faith, but the relational virtue of trust, loyalty, or fidelity.

gratia—grace, charm, favor. The theological sense of "grace" sometimes overlays a more secular meaning, as when the Man after offending his beloved seeks to regain her *gratia* or favor. Closely related are the adjective *gratus* (pleasing, welcome, thankful) and the expression *gratias agere*, to give thanks.

indifferenter—a philosophical term, "without difference," current in the early twelfth-century debate over universals. The term was a hallmark of Abelard's teaching in that controversy; the Man uses it twice in a similar sense.

ingenium—genius, talent, native ability. The Man praises the Woman for her *ingenium*, while she bewails her lack of that quality.

intentio—intention, moral purpose. In the ethical philosophy shared by Abelard, Heloise, and the Woman of the letters, the morally significant dimension of any act is less the action itself than the agent's *intentio*.

salve / salus—*Salve* is the standard epistolary term of greeting. From the verb *salvere*, it means "hail" or less formally "hello" (and occasionally "good-bye"), as well as "be in good health." The noun *salus* can denote health, welfare, greetings, and good wishes, but also has the specifically Christian sense of "salvation." The lovers play endlessly on the range of meanings inherent in these terms. I have generally favored secular meanings, using "salvation" only when a reference to God or eternity seems to warrant it.

singularis / solus / unicus—one and only; sole, singular, unique, unparalleled. The Man especially uses these terms for the Woman and their relationship, but the lovers share a strong sense of exceptionality.

specialis—special; the Latin word is stronger than its English cognate. The
   Woman prefers this term to *singularis* and *unicus*. In its philosophical
   sense, *specialis* means "pertaining to the species," as opposed to the
   individual (*singularis*) or the genus (*generalis*), but she seems not to use
   that technical sense. For Baudri of Bourgueil, a "special" love or friendship
   was a chaste but intimate relationship between a man and a woman.

vale / valitudo—*Vale,* parallel to *salve,* is the standard closing formula of a
   letter. It derives from *valere* and means simultaneously "farewell" and "fare
   well." The additional senses of *valere* are even broader than those of *salvere*:
   to be strong, well, or healthy; to prevail; to be (of) worth. As a noun, *vale*
   is "a word of parting" but also (like its synonym *valitudo*) means health,
   welfare, well-being.

verba / res / facta—The familiar contrast between words (*verba*) and deeds (*res*
   or *facta*) is central to the Man's ethical thinking. He often insists that
   when *verba* are insufficient or faulty, one must privilege *facta*. This contrast
   is also a favorite theme of Abelard.

virtus—virtue, moral excellence. The term is broader than English "virtue." In
   classical usage it implies strength, courage, and valor; it derives from *vir*
   (man) and originally entailed a gendered ideal of virility. When the
   Woman insists that her love and friendship depend on the Man's *virtus*,
   this meaning may lie beneath the surface.

Appendix B. Citations, Allusions, and Parallels

	Man	Woman	Total
Scripture and Liturgy			
Torah	3	7	10
Psalms	11	18	29
Song of Songs	7	6	13
Wisdom books	4	6	10
Prophets	2	7	9
Other OT	1	10	11
Gospels	9	15	24
Epistles	5	22	27
Other NT	2	2	4
Liturgy	3	8	11
Total	47	101	148
Classical Authors			
Catullus	0	1	1
Cicero	10	6	16
Horace	8	5	13
Juvenal	1	0	1
Lucan	3	0	3
Martial	1	0	1
Ovid	38	22	60
Persius	1	1	2
Plautus	1	1	2
Quintilian	0	1	1

Sallust	1	0	1
Seneca	1	0	1
Statius	4	1	5
Terence	6	1	7
Virgil	5	8	13
Total	**80**	**47**	**127**

Early Christian Authors

Ambrose	1	1	2
Augustine	2	1	3
Bede	2	0	2
Boethius	3	8	11
Cassian	0	1	1
Cassiodorus	1	0	1
Gregory	1	1	2
Isidore	0	1	1
Jerome	0	9	9
Paulinus of Nola	1	0	1
Prudentius	1	0	1
Symmachus	0	1	1
Total	**12**	**23**	**35**

Medieval Authors

Abelard[a]	1	3	4
Adso Dervensis	0	1	1
Alcuin[b]	0	1	1
Baudri of Bourgueil	6	11	17
Berno of Reichenau	0	2	2
Fulcoius of Beauvais	3	1	4
Gregory of Tours	0	1	1
Guibert of Nogent	0	1	1
Hildebert of Lavardin	3	1	4
Hugh Metel	1	0	1

Hugh of Saint-Victor	0	2	2
Hugh Primas	0	1	1
Marbod of Rennes	3	7	10
Nigellus Wireker	0	1	1
Otloh of St. Emmeram	1	0	1
Peter Damian	0	1	1
Peter the Venerable	1	0	1
Ruricius of Limoges	0	1	1
Walahfrid Strabo	0	3	3
Total	**19**	**38**	**57**

Anonymous Medieval Texts

Carmina burana	2	1	3
De Pyramo	1	1	2
Liber pontificalis	0	1	1
Nomen ut herbarum	0	1	1
Ovidius puellarum	0	1	1
Proverbial sayings	2	3	5
Total	**5**	**8**	**13**

Other Letter Collections

Abelard-Heloise	9	16	25
Admont nuns	0	1	1
Regensburg Songs	3	6	9
Tegernsee letters	8	22	30
Total	**20**	**45**	**65**

[a] Excluding the *Historia calamitatum* and correspondence with Heloise.
[b] Excluding liturgical texts.

Appendix C. Salutation Types

Excludes poems and fragments with salutation omitted by the scribe.

Salutation Type	Man	Ratio	Woman	Ratio
Accusative	18	34.6%	23	65.7%
Accusative with *quid* or *quidquid*	14	26.9%	2	5.7%
Infinitive	13	25.0%	7	20.0%
Finite verb	7	13.5%	2	5.7%
No wish (omitted as a mark of anger)	0	0%	1	2.9%
Total letters or fragments	52	100%	35	100%

Appendix D. Word Frequencies

	Man	Woman
Personal Pronouns[a]		
Ego	49	7
Tu	41	13
Nos	10	9
Terms for Love[b]		
Affectio	2	2
Affectus	0	9
Amicitia	8	7
Amor	47	52
Caritas	0	5
Dilectio	9	41
Terms for Exceptionality[c]		
Immortalis, -iter	3	0
Singularis	4	0
Specialis	0	4
Unicus, -a	9	2

[a] The Man uses *ego* seven times more often than the Woman and *tu* more than three times as often. His high frequency of both pronouns may be, in part, an index of his more colloquial style. The plural *nos* shows no such disparity.

[b] The Man uses *amor* more than five times as often as *dilectio*; he does not use *affectus* or *caritas* at all. The Woman's ratio of *dilectio* to *amor* is roughly 4:5. The partners do not differ significantly in their frequencies of *affectio, amicitia,* or *amor.*

[c] In describing the exceptional character of their love, the Man shows a strong preference for *immortalis, singularis*, and *unicus,* the Woman for *specialis.*

Woman, Letter 84

Ámans amánti: / gaudium cum *salúte optánti* / illud dico salutare quod non *finiátur,*| *et gaúdium* / quod a te non *tollátur* | *per évum.* // Post mutuam nostre visionis | *allocucionís*|*que notíciam,* / tu solus michi placebas supra omnem *Déi creatúram,* / teque *sólum diléxi,* / *diligéndo quesívi,* / *queréndo invéni,* / *inveniéndo amávi,* / *amándo optávi,* / optando omnibus in corde *méo prepósui,* / teque solum *elégi ex mílibus,* / ut *fácerem tècum pígnus,* / quo *pígnore perácto,* / dulcedinisque tue *mélle gustáto* / *sperábam me cúris* / fínem *posuísse futúris.* // [. . .] Nemorum umbrosa *díligunt volúcres,* / in aquarum rivulis latent pisces, / cervi *ascéndunt montána,* / ego te diligo mente stabili et integra. // Hactenus *mécum mansísti,* / mecum viriliter bonum *certámen certásti,* / sed nondum *brávium àccepísti.* //

Cursus: Fourteen planus, four tardus, three trispondaicus, two velox: twenty-three *clausulae* with *cursus*, two without

Heloise, Letter 4.7

O me *miserárum misérrimam,* / infelicium *ínfelicíssimam,* / que quanto uniuersis in te feminis *preláta sublimiórem* / obtinui gradum, tanto hinc *prostráta grauiórem* / in te et in me pariter *perpéssa sum cásum!* // Quanto quippe altior | ascendéntis grádus, / tanto grauior | corruéntis cásus. // Quam mihi nobilium potentium feminarum fortuna umquam preponere *pótuit aùt equáre?* // Quam denique adeo deiecit | et dolore *confícere pótuit?* // Quam in te mihi *glóriam cóntulit!* // Quam in te mihi ruínam íntulit! // Quam mihi uehemens in utramque pártem éxtitit, / ut nec in bonis | nec in malis | *módum habúerit!* // Que, ut me miserrimam *ómnium fáceret*, / omnibus ante *beatiórem effécerat*, / ut, cum quanto perdidi pensarem, *tánto me maióra* / *consúmerent laménta* / *quánto me maióra* / *opprésserant dámna*; / et tanto *maíor amissórum* / *succéderet dólor* / quanto *maíor possessórum* / *precésserat ámor*, / et summe uoluptátis gaúdia / summa meroris *termináret tristícia*. //

Cursus: Four planus, eight tardus, six trispondaicus, two velox: twenty *clausulae* with *cursus*, five without

Key

/ denotes the end of a *clausula* set off by rhyme, *cursus*, or both.
// denotes the end of a sentence.
| denotes internal or chiastic rhyme within a *clausula*.
é denotes a strong stress, è a secondary stress (according to speech accent, not quantity).
Italicized words with scansion denote *cursus* patterns.

Types of Rhyme

One-syllable: *gaudium / evum*; *lamenta / damna*
Two-syllable: *amanti / optanti*; *contulit / intulit*
Three-syllable: *sublimiorem / graviorem*

Types of *Cursus*

Planus: *ámans amánti*; *perpéssa sum cásum*
Tardus: *finiátur et gaúdium*; *infelicíssimam*
Trispondaicus: *Déi creatúram*; *prostráta graviórem*
Velox: *brávium àccepísti*; *preláta sublìmiórem*

I have assessed *cursus* patterns by the simpler rules of the early twelfth century, counting only the number of weak syllables between the two final stresses and after the last stress in a *clausula*. In the late twelfth century, theorists also began to take account of the number of words and the number of syllables in each word.

Without parallels in the Tegernsee letters, Regensburg Songs, or twelfth-century *artes dictandi*.

Situation and Specific Events

- Collection of over one hundred letters between the same two correspondents
- Man requests a continuing correspondence and Woman complies (no. 9)
- Correspondence is structured as a competition in love (no. 72)
- Man praises Woman for her "virile" talent and her fame (no. 50)
- Frequent references to the Woman's study of philosophy with the Man
- Woman's poem celebrating the Man's academic triumph over a rival (no. 66)
- Woman represents love as a continual, unpayable debt (no. 25)
- Woman's letter concerning her lover's illness (no. 32)
- Shared literary endeavor: the Man composes a "prologue" for the Woman (no. 84) and she does some kind of work for him (no. 71)
- Specific promise related to writing, unfulfilled by the Man, offends the Woman (no. 75)
- Frequent references to envious foes who try to separate the lovers
- Pattern of repeated quarrels and reconciliations, including an attempted breakup (no. 60)
- Man's poem celebrating the lovers' first anniversary and repenting past sins (no. 87)
- Man laments that he is losing the Woman through his own folly (no. 106)

Language and Rhetoric

- Man's metaphors of himself as the impression of his lady's seal (no. 16), the moon to her sun (no. 22), and flesh to her soul (no. 24)

- Man wishes to be incorporated into the *summum bonum* that is his beloved (nos. 26, 46)
- Woman poses an exegetical riddle as a greeting (no. 27)
- Woman employs rare technical terms such as *scibilitas* (no. 53) and *equipolenter* (no. 21)
- Woman's hyperbole, "if all that Caesar ever possessed were mine" (no. 82)
- Woman stages an allegorical debate between *Affectus* and *Defectus* (no. 23)
- Metaphor of secret love as a fire banked by ashes, burning hotter than ever (nos. 55, 75, 88)
- Man calls Woman a "martyr" of love (no. 96)

Appendix G. Abelard, Heloise, and the Paraclete

A complete dossier of Abelard and Heloise's relationship from beginning to end would include the following items, some of which are lost.

1. An unabridged version of the *Epistolae duorum amantium*, if they are judged to be authentic—or if not, the lost love letters mentioned in *Historia calamitatum* (HC) 16 and Heloise, letter 2.16

2. Abelard's lost love songs, both metrical and strophic (*carmina amatoria* mentioned in HC 19; *amatorio metro uel rithmo composita carmina* in Heloise, letter 2.13)

3. Heloise's exultant letter announcing her pregnancy (lost, mentioned in HC 21)

4. Heloise's lost *Dehortatio a nuptiis* (cited in HC 24–26; cf. Heloise, letter 2.10)

5. *Historia calamitatum*: Abelard's autobiography or "letter of consolation to a friend"

6. Letters of Heloise and Abelard, conventionally numbered 2–8

7. Abelard's rule for the Paraclete (*Institutio*), appended to letter 8

8. Heloise's customary for the Paraclete (*Institutiones nostre*)

9. Abelard's letter 9, exhorting the Paraclete nuns to biblical study

10. *Problemata Heloissae*: exegetical queries, with Heloise's preface and Abelard's replies

11. *Hymnarius Paraclitensis*: Abelard's cycle of liturgical hymns, with preface to Heloise

12. *Planctus*: Abelard's six devotional songs on Old Testament themes

13. *Expositio in Hexaemeron*: Genesis commentary for the nuns, with preface to Heloise

14. *Sermones*: thirty-three sermons for the Paraclete nuns, with preface to Heloise

15. *Carmen ad Astralabium*: Abelard's didactic poem in elegiacs for their son

16. Documents pertaining to Abelard's second condemnation for heresy at the Council of Sens (1141), including his *Confessio fidei ad Heloissam* and Berengar's *Apologia*, preserved by Heloise at the Paraclete

17. Heloise's correspondence with Peter the Venerable, abbot of Cluny, concerning Abelard's death and burial, his absolution from the charge of heresy (procured by Peter to be hung over Abelard's tomb), and her attempt to secure a prebend for Astralabe

18. Epitaphs for Abelard, at least one of which was composed by Heloise

19. Necrology of the Paraclete, with obituaries for Abelard, Heloise, and Astralabe

Notes

Preface

1. Ewald Könsgen, ed., *Epistolae duorum amantium: Briefe Abaelards und Heloises?* (Leiden: Brill, 1974).

2. The chief alternative to Könsgen's position—both the twelfth-century date and the thesis of a genuine exchange by two lovers—is the view of Peter von Moos, who reads the correspondence as a sophisticated literary fiction created by one or more late medieval authors: "Die *Epistolae duorum amantium* und die *säkulare Religion der Liebe*: Methodenkritische Vorüberlegungen zu einem einmaligen Werk mittellateinischer Briefliteratur," *Studi Medievali* 44 (2003): 1–115. I will discuss von Moos's arguments below in the section on "Frequently Asked Questions."

3. Könsgen, *Epistolae*, 103. The subtitle itself has been a topic of controversy. In a later article, Könsgen explains that *Briefe Abaelards und Heloises* was added by the series editor, Karl Langosch, but Könsgen himself insisted on the question mark. "'Der Nordstern scheint auf den Pol': Baudolinos Liebesbriefe an Beatrix, die Kaiserin—oder *Ex epistolis duorum amantium*," in *Nova de veteribus: Mittel- und neulateinische Studien für Paul Gerhard Schmidt*, ed. Andreas Bihrer and Elisabeth Stein (Munich: K. G. Saur, 2004), 1114.

4. For an overview of this debate and its ideological stakes through the early 1970s, see Peter von Moos, *Mittelalterforschung und Ideologiekritik: Der Gelehrtenstreit um Héloise* (Munich: Wilhelm Fink, 1974). For its later stages see John Marenbon, "Authenticity Revisited," in *Listening to Heloise: The Voice of a Twelfth-Century Woman*, ed. Bonnie Wheeler (New York: St. Martin's Press, 2000), 19–33.

5. Charlotte Charrier, *Héloïse dans l'histoire et dans la légende* (Paris: Champion, 1933). For Heloise as the inaugural figure in a genre of romantic fiction, see Peggy Kamuf, *Fictions of Feminine Desire: Disclosures of Heloise* (Lincoln: University of Nebraska Press, 1982), and Linda S. Kaufmann, *Discourses of Desire: Gender, Genre, and Epistolary Fictions* (Ithaca, NY: Cornell University Press, 1986).

6. For example, Bernhard Schmeidler wrote a series of four articles making a case for Abelard's authorship of the whole exchange, including "Der Briefwechsel zwischen Abälard und Heloise als eine literarische Fiktion Abälards," *Zeitschrift für Kirchengeschichte* 54 (1935): 323–38. The same author raised the same kind of doubt about Hildegard of Bingen, the other great female Latinist of the twelfth century: "Bemerkungen zum Corpus der Briefe der hl. Hildegard von Bingen," in *Corona Quernea: Festgabe Karl Strecker* (Leipzig: Hiersemann, 1941), 335–66.

7. The editor J. T. Muckle, a priest, concluded that Heloise's original letters must have been rewritten by a forger because, if Abelard had seen them, he "would have chided her and tried to set her right in regard to such extravagant and sinful dispositions"—even more

forcefully than he did. "The Personal Letters between Abelard and Heloise: Introduction, Authenticity and Text," *Mediaeval Studies* 15 (1953), 59 and 67.

8. John F. Benton, "Fraud, Fiction and Borrowing in the Correspondence of Abelard and Heloise," in *Pierre Abélard—Pierre le Vénérable: Les courants philosophiques, littéraires et artistiques en Occident au milieu du XIIe siècle, Colloques internationaux du Centre national de la recherche scientifique, Abbaye du Cluny, 1972*, ed. René Louis and Jean Jolivet (Paris: Éditions du Centre National de la Recherche Scientifique, 1975), 469–506.

9. D. W. Robertson, Jr., *Abelard and Heloise* (New York: Dial Press, 1972).

10. John F. Benton, "A Reconsideration of the Authenticity of the Correspondence of Abelard and Heloise," in *Petrus Abaelardus (1079–1142): Person, Werk und Wirkung*, ed. Rudolf Thomas, Jean Jolivet, David E. Luscombe, and Lambertus M. de Rijk (Trier: Paulinus-Verlag, 1980), 41–52. In this article Benton adopts the thesis of Abelardian authorship for the entire dossier.

11. Hubert Silvestre, "Réflexions sur la thèse de J. F. Benton relative au dossier 'Abélard-Héloïse,'" *Recherches de théologie ancienne et médiévale* 44 (1977): 211–16, and "Die Liebesgeschichte zwischen Abaelard und Heloise: Der Anteil des Romans," in *Fälschungen im Mittelalter*, part 5: *Fingierte Briefe, Frömmigkeit und Fälschung, Realienfälschungen*, MGH Scriptores 33 (Hanover: Hahn, 1988), 121–65; Deborah Fraioli, "The Importance of Satire in Jerome's *Adversus Jovinianum* as an Argument Against the Authenticity of the *Historia calamitatum*," in *Fälschungen im Mittelalter*, part 5, 167–200. Silvestre ascribed the letters at first to some "vindictive" thirteenth-century forger, but later to Jean de Meun. Fraioli argued that they were written by an enemy of Abelard and Heloise in order to ridicule them.

12. *Abélard et Héloïse: Correspondance*, ed. and trans. Paul Zumthor (Paris: Union Générale d'Éditions, 1979); Georges Duby, *Dames du XIIe siècle*, vol. 1: *Héloïse, Aliénor, Iseut et quelques autres* (Paris: Gallimard, 1995), 73–110; Peter von Moos, "Le silence d'Héloïse et les idéologies modernes," in *Pierre Abélard—Pierre le Vénérable*, ed. Louis and Jolivet, 425–68.

13. Zumthor, *Abélard et Héloïse*, 11–12.

14. Peter Dronke, *Abelard and Heloise in Medieval Testimonies* (Glasgow: University of Glasgow Press, 1976), "Heloise's *Problemata* and *Letters*: Some Questions of Form and Content," in Thomas et al., *Petrus Abaelardus*, 53–73, and *Women Writers of the Middle Ages: A Critical Study of Texts from Perpetua (†203) to Marguerite Porete (†1310)* (Cambridge: Cambridge University Press, 1984), 107–43; David E. Luscombe, "The Letters of Heloise and Abelard Since 'Cluny 1972,'" in *Petrus Abaelardus*, 23–31, and "From Paris to the Paraclete: The Correspondence of Abelard and Heloise," *Proceedings of the British Academy* 74 (1988): 247–83; Barbara Newman, "Authority, Authenticity, and the Repression of Heloise," *Journal of Medieval and Renaissance Studies* 22 (1992): 121–57, repr. in *From Virile Woman to WomanChrist: Studies in Medieval Religion and Literature* (Philadelphia: University of Pennsylvania Press, 1995), 46–75.

15. M. T. Clanchy, *Abelard: A Medieval Life* (Oxford: Blackwell, 1997).

16. Peter von Moos lists these reviews, none of which endorses the ascription to Abelard and Heloise, in "Vom Nutzen der Philologie für den Umgang mit anonymen Liebesbriefen: Ein Nachwort zu den *Epistolae duorum amantium*," in *Schrift und Liebe in der Kultur des Mittelalters*, ed. Mireille Schnyder (Berlin: Walter de Gruyter, 2008), 25 n.4.

17. Constant J. Mews, *The Lost Love Letters of Heloise and Abelard: Perceptions of Dialogue in Twelfth-Century France*, with a translation by Neville Chiavaroli and Constant J. Mews (New York: St. Martin's Press, 1999).

18. Jan M. Ziolkowski, "Lost and Not Yet Found: Heloise, Abelard, and the *Epistolae duorum amantium*," *Journal of Medieval Latin* 14 (2004), 198.

19. Peter von Moos, "Kurzes Nachwort zu einer langen Geschichte mit missbrauchten Liebesbriefen: *Epistolae duorum amantium*," in *Abaelard und Heloise: Gesammelte Studien zum Mittelalter*, vol. 1, ed. Gert Melville (Münster: Lit, 2005), 286–87. Von Moos repeats these arguments in "Vom Nutzen der Philologie."

20. For a useful though now somewhat dated account of the controversy, see Réka Forrai and Sylvain Piron, "The Debate on the *Epistolae duorum amantium*: Current *status quaestionis* and Further Research" (9 March 2007), posted at http://www.tdtc.unisi.it/digimed/files/Piron-status%20quaestionis.pdf.

21. Könsgen, "Der Nordstern scheint auf den Pol," 1114.

22. Constant J. Mews, "Philosophical Themes in the *Epistolae duorum amantium*: The First Letters of Heloise and Abelard," in Wheeler, *Listening to Heloise*, 35–52, "Bernard of Clairvaux, Peter Abelard and Heloise on the Definition of Love," *Revista Portuguesa de Filosofia* 60 (2004): 633–60, "Discussing Love: The *Epistolae duorum amantium* and Abelard's *Sic et Non*," *Journal of Medieval Latin* 19 (2009): 130–47, "Abelard, Heloise, and Discussion of Love in the Twelfth-Century Schools," in *Rethinking Abelard: A Collection of Critical Essays*, ed. Babette S. Hellemans (Leiden: Brill, 2014), 11–36, and "Between Authenticity and Interpretation: On *The Letter Collection of Peter Abelard and Heloise* and the *Epistolae duorum amantium*," *Tijdschrift voor Filosofie* 76 (2014): 823–42.

23. C. Stephen Jaeger, *Ennobling Love: In Search of a Lost Sensibility* (Philadelphia: University of Pennsylvania Press, 1999), 160–70.

24. C. Stephen Jaeger, "*Epistolae duorum amantium* and the Ascription to Heloise and Abelard," in *Voices in Dialogue: Reading Women in the Middle Ages*, ed. Linda Olson and Kathryn Kerby-Fulton (Notre Dame, IN: University of Notre Dame Press, 2005), 125–66, "A Reply to Giles Constable," in Olson and Kerby-Fulton, *Voices in Dialogue*, 179–86, and "The *Epistolae duorum amantium*, Abelard and Heloise: An Annotated Concordance," *Journal of Medieval Latin* 24 (2014): 185–224.

25. Sylvain Piron, trans., *Lettres des deux amants attribuées à Héloïse et Abélard* (Paris: Gallimard, 2005), 175–218, "Heloise's Literary Self-fashioning and the *Epistolae duorum amantium*," in *Strategies of Remembrance: From Pindar to Hölderlin*, ed. Lucie Doležalová (Newcastle upon Tyne: Cambridge Scholars, 2009), 103–62, "Héloïse et Abélard: L'éthique amoureuse des *Epistolae duorum amantium*," in *Histoires de l'amour, fragilités et interdits, du Kâmasûtra à nos jours*, ed. Jocelyne Dakhlia, Arlette Farge, Christiane Klapisch-Zuber, and Alessandro Stella (Paris: Bayard, 2011), 71–94, and "La 'collection' des lettres d'Abélard et Héloïse," review of *The Letter Collection of Peter Abelard and Heloise*, ed. David Luscombe, *Cahiers de civilisation médiévale* 57 (2014): 337–42.

26. Eva Cescutti and Philipp Steger, trans., *Und wärst du doch bei mir, Ex epistolis duorum amantium: Eine mittelalterliche Liebesgeschichte in Briefen* (Zurich: Manesse, 2005); Graziella Ballanti, trans., *Un epistolario d'amore del XII secolo (Abelardo e Eloisa?)* (Rome:

Edizioni Anicia, 1988). The Italian translation has an odd feature . Könsgen used vertical lines in his edition to mark the rhyming clauses characteristic of the Woman's prose. Ballanti converts these into dashes and reproduces them in her unrhymed Italian text, making it look like a pastiche of Emily Dickinson.

27. Dronke, *Abelard and Heloise in Medieval Testimonies*, 24–26, and review of *Listening to Heloise*, ed. Wheeler, *International Journal of the Classical Tradition* 8 (2001): 134–39; Peter Dronke and Giovanni Orlandi, "New Works by Abelard and Heloise?" *Filologia mediolatina: Studies in Medieval Latin Texts and Their Transmission* 12 (2005): 123–77.

28. Ziolkowski, "Lost and Not Yet Found," 190–95; Dronke and Orlandi, "New Works by Abelard and Heloise?" 146–77; Francesco Stella, "Analisi informatiche dei lessico e individuazione degli autori nelle *Epistolae duorum amantium* (XII secolo)," in *Latin vulgaire— latin tardif VIII: Actes du VIIIe colloque international sur le latin vulgaire et tardif,* ed. Roger Wright (Hildesheim: Olms-Weidmann, 2008), 560–69.

29. Giles Constable, "The Authorship of the *Epistolae duorum amantium:* A Reconsideration," in *Voices in Dialogue,* ed. Olson and Kerby-Fulton, 167–78.

30. Peter von Moos, "Abaelard, Heloise und ihr Paraklet: Ein Kloster nach Mass, zugleich eine Streitschrift gegen die ewige Wiederkehr hermeneutischer Naivität," in *Das Eigene und das Ganze: Zum Individuellen im mittelalterlichen Religiösentum,* ed. Gert Melville and Markus Schürer (Münster: Lit, 2002), 563–619. See also "Kurzes Nachwort" and "Vom Nutzen der Philologie."

31. Von Moos, "Die *Epistolae duorum amantium.*"

32. Anne-Marie Turcan-Verkerk, "Langue et littérature latines du Moyen Âge," *Annuaire de l'École pratique des Hautes Études, Section des sciences historiques et philologiques* 141 (2011), 128–34; Jean-Yves Tilliette, "Rhétorique et sincerité: La lettre d'amour dans le Moyen Âge latin," in *Charmer, convaincre: La rhétorique dans l'histoire,* ed. Jacques Jouanna, Laurent Pernot, and Michel Zink (Paris: Diffusion de Boccard, 2014), 145–48.

33. Étienne Wolff, trans., *La lettre d'amour au Moyen Âge: Textes présentés, traduits du latin et commentés* (Paris: NiL Éditions, 1996), 117–51; *Abelard and Heloise: The Letters and Other Writings,* trans. William Levitan (Indianapolis: Hackett, 2007), 315–28. Despite his title, Levitan is not inclined to accept the attribution.

34. According to Könsgen ("Der Nordstern," 1118), the text was first posted by Werner Robl, an independent scholar, in 2000; it was still online as of 2013.

35. Von Moos, "Die *Epistolae duorum amantium,*" 104–11.

36. Ibid., 67.

37. Francesco Stella, "*Epistolae duorum amantium*: Nuovi paralleli testuali per gli inserti poetici," *Journal of Medieval Latin* 18 (2008), 378.

38. Dronke, *Abelard and Heloise in Medieval Testimonies*, 25.

39. Helmut Plechl and Werner Bergmann, eds., *Die Tegernseer Briefsammlung des 12. Jahrhunderts,* MGH Briefe der deutschen Kaiserzeit 8 (Hanover: Hahnsche Buchhandlung, 2002), 343–66. For facsimiles of the manuscript pages see Jürgen Kühnel, ed., *Dû bist mîn, ih bin dîn: Die lateinischen Liebes- (und Freundschafts-) Briefe des clm 19411. Abbildungen, Text und Übersetzung* (Göppingen: Kümmerle, 1977), 41–47. Peter Dronke edits letters 1–7 with an

English translation in *Medieval Latin and the Rise of European Love-Lyric*, 2 vols. (Oxford: Clarendon, 1965–66), 2:472–82.

40. Martin Camargo, *Ars dictaminis, ars dictandi* (Turnhout: Brepols, 1991), 50; Carol Dana Lanham, *Salutatio Formulas in Latin Letters to 1200: Syntax, Style, and Theory* (Munich: Arbeo-Gesellschaft, 1975), 107.

41. Dieter Schaller, "Zur Textkritik und Beurteilung der sogenannten Tegernseer Liebesbriefe," *Zeitschrift für deutsche Philologie* 101 (1982), 117.

42. Gerald A. Bond, *The Loving Subject: Desire, Eloquence, and Power in Romanesque France* (Philadelphia: University of Pennsylvania Press, 1995); Jaeger, *Ennobling Love*, 82–106; Mews, *Lost Love Letters*, 87–114; Dronke, *Medieval Latin and the Rise of European Love-Lyric*, 1:209–38, and *Women Writers of the Middle Ages*, 84–97.

43. For an overview of Latin poetry by nuns see Jane Stevenson, *Women Latin Poets: Language, Gender, and Authority, from Antiquity to the Eighteenth Century* (Oxford: Oxford University Press, 2005), 108–38.

44. On the relationship between emotional and textual communities, see Barbara H. Rosenwein, *Emotional Communities in the Early Middle Ages* (Ithaca, NY: Cornell University Press, 2006), 25.

Making Love in the Twelfth Century: An Essay in the History of Emotions

1. Anthony Trollope, *He Knew He Was Right* (1869), ed. Robertson Davies (London: Trollope Society, 1994), 179.

2. Fraser Sutherland, "Why Making Love Isn't What It Used to Be," in *Challenging Change: Literary and Linguistic Responses*, ed. Vesna Lopičić and Biljana Mišić Ilić (Newcastle upon Tyne: Cambridge Scholars, 2012), 15–21.

3. The phrase was coined by Ludwig Traube, *Vorlesungen und Abhandlungen*, vol. 2, *Einleitung in die lateinische Philologie des Mittelalters* (Munich: Beck, 1911), 113.

4. See Barbara Newman, *God and the Goddesses: Vision, Poetry, and Belief in the Middle Ages* (Philadelphia: University of Pennsylvania Press, 2003), 138–51.

5. Karen Cherewatuk and Ulrike Wiethaus, eds., *Dear Sister: Medieval Women and the Epistolary Genre* (Philadelphia: University of Pennsylvania Press, 1993); Joan M. Ferrante, *To the Glory of Her Sex: Women's Roles in the Composition of Medieval Texts* (Bloomington: Indiana University Press, 1997), 10–35.

6. Hildegard of Bingen, *Epistolarium*, ed. Lieven Van Acker and Monika Klaes-Hachmöller, 3 vols., CCCM 91–91B (Turnhout: Brepols, 1991–2001); *The Letters of Hildegard of Bingen*, trans. Joseph L. Baird and Radd K. Ehrman, 3 vols. (New York: Oxford University Press, 1994–2004).

7. St. Anselm's correspondence includes six letters from Queen Matilda, the wife of Henry I of England, plus one from the queen to Pope Paschal II—apparently preserved for their political significance. *The Letters of Saint Anselm of Canterbury*, trans. Walter Fröhlich, 3 vols. (Kalamazoo: Cistercian Publications, 1990–94), nos. 242, 317, 320, 323 (to Pope

Paschal), 384, 395, 400; Sally N. Vaughn, *St Anselm and the Handmaidens of God: A Study of Anselm's Correspondence with Women* (Turnhout: Brepols, 2002), 221–41, 246–50.

8. Dieter Schaller, "Probleme der Überlieferung und Verfasserschaft lateinischer Liebesbriefe des hohen Mittelalters," *Mittellateinisches Jahrbuch* 3 (1966): 25–36; Ernstpeter Ruhe, *De Amasio ad Amasiam: Zur Gattungsgeschichte des mittelalterlichen Liebesbriefes* (Munich: Wilhelm Fink, 1975).

9. For the authenticity of the Tegernsee letters, see Peter Dronke, *Medieval Latin and the Rise of European Love-Lyric*, 2 vols. (Oxford: Clarendon, 1965–66), 2:482; Ruhe, *De Amasio ad Amasiam*, 87–90; Dieter Schaller, "Zur Textkritik und Beurteilung der sogenannten Tegernseer Liebesbriefe," *Zeitschrift für deutsche Philologie* 101 (1982): 104–21. Jürgen Kühnel argues otherwise in *Dû bist mîn, ih bin dîn: Die lateinischen Liebes- (und Freundschafts-) Briefe des clm 19411. Abbildungen, Text und Übersetzung* (Göppingen: Kümmerle, 1977), 22–24. Helmut Plechl thinks at least the first seven letters were composed for a formulary: Helmut Plechl and Werner Bergmann, eds., *Die Tegernseer Briefsammlung des 12. Jahrhunderts*, MGH Briefe der deutschen Kaiserzeit 8 (Hanover: Hahnsche Buchhandlung, 2002), xvi, 345–65 (headnotes). On the EDA, see the next chapter on "Frequently Asked Questions."

10. Born in Lavardin near Vendôme, this prominent writer and prelate is also designated as Hildebert of Le Mans (bishop, 1096–1125) or of Tours (archbishop, 1125–33).

11. Hilary of Orléans, *Versus et ludi, Epistolae, Ludus Danielis Belouacensis*, ed. Walther Bulst and M. L. Bulst-Thiele (Leiden: Brill, 1989). Two of Hilary's poems also appear among the *Carmina burana* (nos. 95 and 117); three items are plays, including the famous *Ludus Danielis*.

12. Jean-Yves Tilliette, "Note sur le manuscrit des poèmes de Baudri de Bourgueil (Vatican, Reg. lat. 1351)," *Scriptorium* 37 (1983): 241–45; Baudri de Bourgueil, *Poèmes*, ed. and trans. Jean-Yves Tilliette, 2 vols. (Paris: Les Belles Lettres, 1998–2002), 1:xxxviii–xlv. There was no *editio princeps* until 1926.

13. "Voui Vulcano quod scribsi carmine uano" (I have vowed to Vulcan [i.e., to the fire] what I wrote in vain poetry): Fulcoius of Beauvais, *Epistula* 26.1, "Fvlcoii Belvacensis Epistvlae," ed. Marvin L. Colker, *Traditio* 10 (1954), 267; Thomas C. Moser, Jr., *A Cosmos of Desire: The Medieval Latin Erotic Lyric in English Manuscripts* (Ann Arbor: University of Michigan Press, 2004), 363 n.13.

14. Gerald A. Bond in 1995 called Marbod "the most unjustly ignored theorist and poet of the entire Latin Middle Ages"—a judgment that still holds true. See Bond, *The Loving Subject: Desire, Eloquence, and Power in Romanesque France* (Philadelphia: University of Pennsylvania Press, 1995), 70–98 (quotation, 70); Moser, *A Cosmos of Desire*, 34–46; and Walther Bulst, "Studien zu Marbods *Carmina varia* und *Liber decem capitulorum*," *Nachrichten von der Gesellschaft der Wissenschaften zu Göttingen*, n.s. 4 (1939): 173–241.

15. Marbod of Rennes, *Liber decem capitulorum* 1–4 (ca. 1102), ed. Rosario Leotta (Rome: Herder, 1984), 59–60. On his recantation see below, pp. 66–67.

16. Marbod of Rennes, "Liebesbriefgedichte Marbods," ed. Walther Bulst, in *Liber Floridus: Mittellateinische Studien Paul Lehmann zum 65. Geburtstag*, ed. Bernhard Bischoff and Suso Brechter (St. Ottilien: Eos Verlag der Erzabtei, 1950), 287–301. Two

twelfth-century MSS include some of Marbod's erotic poems: London, British Library, Add. MS 24199 (from Bury St. Edmunds), and Zürich, Zentralbibliothek, MS C 58/275: Moser, *A Cosmos of Desire*, 17, 38. Aside from the poems edited by Bulst, *De lapidibus*, and the *Liber decem capitulorum*, most of Marbod's works must still be sought (along with spuria) in PL 171.

17. "Ad quandam puellam litteratam nomen habentem Laetitiae sed non omen, sub amatoris sui specie (To a certain literate girl, who has the name Letitia but not its substance [gladness], in the guise of her lover). Gerald of Wales, *Symbolum electorum* II.8, in *Giraldi Cambrensis Opera*, vol. 1, ed. J. S. Brewer (London: Longman, 1861), 356–57.

18. "His temporibus florere cepit in Theutonica terra Menegaldus philosophus, divinis et secularibus litteris ultra cohetaneos suos eruditus. Uxor quoque et filiae eius religione florentes multam in scripturis habuere notitiam et discipulos proprios filiae eius predictae docebant." (At this time the philosopher Manegold began to flourish in Germany, learned beyond his contemporaries in divine and secular literature. His wife and daughters, too, flourishing in religious life, had great knowledge of literature; and his aforesaid daughters taught their own students.) Richard of Poitiers, *Chronica*, ed. Georg Waitz, MGH Scriptores 26 (Hanover: Hahn, 1882), 78. I agree with John O. Ward that *scripturis* probably means secular writings: "Women and Latin Rhetoric from Hrotsvit to Hildegard," in *The Changing Tradition: Women in the History of Rhetoric*, ed. Christine M. Sutherland and Rebecca Sutcliffe (Calgary: University of Calgary Press, 1999), 126–27.

19. This clause has puzzled many readers. My interpretation in the light of Ovidian poetics and *ars dictaminis* is influenced by Jean-Yves Tilliette, "Hermès amoureux, ou les métamorphoses de la Chimère: Réflexions sur les *Carmina* 200 et 201 de Baudri de Bourgueil," *Mélanges de l'École Française de Rome* 104 (1992), 151; and Peter von Moos, "Die *Epistolae duorum amantium* und die *säkulare Religion der Liebe*: Methodenkritische Vorüberlegungen zu einem einmaligen Werk mittellateinischer Briefliteratur," *Studi Medievali* 44 (2003), 56–57. For *species* in the sense of a role or persona, see note 17 above.

20. "Interea cum versificandi studio ultra omnem modum meum animum immersissem, ita ut universa divinae paginae seria pro tam ridicula vanitate seponerem, ad hoc ipsum, duce mea levitate, jam veneram, ut ovidiana et bucolicorum dicta praesumerem, et lepores amatorios in specierum distributionibus epistolisque nexilibus affectarem. Oblita igitur mens debiti rigoris, et professionis monasticae pudore rejecto, talibus virulentae hujus licentiae lenociniis laetabatur, hoc solum trutinans, si poetae cuipiam comportari poterat quod curialiter dicebatur." Guibert of Nogent, *De vita sua, sive Monodiae* 1.17; *Autobiographie*, ed. Edmond-René Labande (Paris: Belles Lettres, 1981), 134–35. My translation.

21. For Marbod's letter see Bruce L. Venarde, trans., *Robert of Arbrissel: A Medieval Religious Life* (Washington, DC: Catholic University of America Press, 2003), 88–100. Baudri's comments are from his "First Life of Robert of Arbrissel," 17, in ibid., 15. His language is almost shocking: "Mulieres tamen ab hominibus segregavit, et inter claustrum eas velut *damnavit*" (PL 162: 1052b, emphasis added).

22. Ovid continued to be used for elementary education in grammar and rhetoric. But after the mid-twelfth century we no longer find adult monks—let alone abbots like Baudri of Bourgueil—devoting themselves to the composition of amorous verse. On rhetorical

education, see Ralph J. Hexter, *Ovid and Medieval Schooling: Studies in Medieval School Commentaries on Ovid's* Ars Amatoria, Epistulae ex Ponto, *and* Epistulae Heroidum (Munich: Arbeo-Gesellschaft, 1986); Carol Dana Lanham, "Freshman Composition in the Early Middle Ages: Epistolography and Rhetoric Before the *Ars Dictaminis*," *Viator* 23 (1992): 115–34; Douglas Kelly, "The Medieval Art of Poetry and Prose: The Scope of Instruction and the Uses of Models," in *Medieval Rhetoric: A Casebook*, ed. Scott D. Troyan (New York: Routledge, 2004), 1–24.

23. C. Stephen Jaeger, "Pessimism in the Twelfth-Century 'Renaissance,'" *Speculum* 78 (2003): 1151–83.

24. Schaller, "Probleme der Überlieferung," 32.

25. Peter Dronke, *Women Writers of the Middle Ages: A Critical Study of Texts from Perpetua († 203) to Marguerite Porete († 1310)* (Cambridge: Cambridge University Press, 1984), 85; Gerald A. Bond, "Composing Yourself: Ovid's *Heroïdes*, Baudri of Bourgueil and the Problem of Persona," *Mediaevalia* 13 (1987), 115 n.37, and *The Loving Subject*, 229 n.71; Jane Stevenson, *Women Latin Poets: Language, Gender, and Authority, from Antiquity to the Eighteenth Century* (Oxford: Oxford University Press, 2005), 122. See also Constance S. Wright, "'Vehementer amo': The Amorous Verse Epistles of Baudry of Bourgueil and Constance of Angers," in *The Influence of the Classical World on Medieval Literature, Architecture, Music and Culture*, ed. Fidel Fajardo-Acosta (Lewiston, NY: Edwin Mellen, 1992), 154–66.

26. Tilliette, "Hermès amoureux," 139–44. This is also the position of Otto Schumann, "Baudri von Bourgueil als Dichter," in *Studien zur lateinischen Dichtung des Mittelalters: Ehrengabe für Karl Strecker*, ed. Walter Stach and Hans Walther (Dresden: Wilhelm und Bertha von Baensch Stiftung, 1931), 162–63; and Étienne Wolff, *La lettre d'amour au Moyen Âge: Textes présentés, traduits du latin et commentés* (Paris: NiL éditions, 1996), 83 n.26. F. J. E. Raby is agnostic: *A History of Secular Latin Poetry in the Middle Ages*, 2 vols., 2nd ed. (Oxford: Clarendon, 1957), 1:344 n.1.

27. Katherine Kong, *Lettering the Self in Medieval and Early Modern France* (Cambridge: D. S. Brewer, 2010), 38–54; on authenticity, 28.

28. Stevenson, *Women Latin Poets*, 114.

29. Ferrante, *To the Glory of Her Sex*, 31–34; Stevenson, *Women Latin Poets*, 122–23; Gabriela Signori, "Muriel and the Others . . . or Poems as Pledges of Friendship," in *Friendship in Medieval Europe*, ed. Julian Haseldine (Stroud: Sutton, 1999), 199–212.

30. Jane Stevenson, "Anglo-Latin Women Poets," in *Latin Learning and English Lore: Studies in Anglo-Saxon Literature for Michael Lapidge*, vol. 2, ed. Katherine O'Brien O'Keeffe and Andy Orchard (Toronto: University of Toronto Press, 2005), 95. Signori stands alone in placing Muriel at Le Ronceray, rather than Wilton: "Muriel and the Others," 200–201. Dronke claims only that she was educated there: *Women Writers*, 85. *Inclyta versificatrix* is from an epitaph by Hermann of Tournai.

31. "Dicta sonant hominem, uox muliebris erat." Baudri of Bourgueil, *Carmina* 137.10, 2:46. See also Hildebert of Lavardin, *Carmina minora* 26, ed. A. Brian Scott (Leipzig: Teubner, 1969), 17–18; and Serlo of Bayeux, "Ad Murielem sanctimonialem," in Thomas Wright,

ed., *The Anglo-Latin Satirical Poets and Epigrammatists of the Twelfth Century*, 2 vols. (London: Longman, 1872), 2:233–40.

32. Hilary of Orléans, *Versus et ludi*, nos. 2–5, pp. 25–29.

33. Fulcoius of Beauvais, *Epistulae* 16–17, "Fvlcoii Belvacensis Epistvlae," 251–53.

34. "Versibus applaudit scitque uacare libris. / Haec etiam nouit sua merces esse poetis, / A probitate sua nemo redit uacuus. / Rursus inest illi dictandi copia torrens." (She has an ear for verse and takes an interest in books. / Also, she's well aware that the poet deserves his stipend; / Through her largesse, no poet must leave her court unpaid. / She herself has a lively talent for writing poems.) Baudri of Bourgueil, "Adelae Comitissae," *Carmina* 134.38–41, 2:3, trans. Monika Otter, "Baudri of Bourgueil, 'To Countess Adela,'" *Journal of Medieval Latin* 11 (2001), 67. For more on Adela see Hildebert, *Carmina minora* 10 and 15, pp. 4–5, and Bond, *The Loving Subject*, 129–57.

35. André Boutemy, "Recueil poétique du manuscrit Additional British Museum 24199," *Latomus* 2 (1938), 42–44. This edition is reprinted with a translation in Bond, *The Loving Subject*, 166–69, though the following translation is my own.

36. "O noua relligio uitae discretio sancta / Iam si quod quid sit littera nosse scelus! / Illa uel ille bonus cui cernua semper imago, / Qui, quoniam nil scit, se putat esse bonum. / Esse tamen sanctum cui de nihilo meditari / Vel cui scire nihil contulit esse nihil? / Si capitur sensu deus et capitur ratione, / Plus capiet cui plus iam rationis inest. / Esse bonum non me prohibebit littera multa, / Dat mihi, non prohibet, littera nosse deum. / Credimus et ratione deum cognoscimus esse, / Hoc quoque quod facimus non prohibere deum. / Quod facimus prohibet, uos quod facitis prohibemus. / Clio, fida comes, pellimur, egredere!"

37. "Non est sanctarum mulierum fingere [MS *frangere*] uersus, / Quaerere nec nostrum quis sit Aristotiles. / Ista uetus probitas, nil carmina tempore uestro, / Nil genus aut species rethoricusque color. / Quid seruare modos iuuat, argumenta notare? / Clio, fida comes, pellimur, egredere!"

38. Giles Constable, *The Reformation of the Twelfth Century* (Cambridge: Cambridge University Press, 1996).

39. Constant J. Mews links this poem to Heloise, unconvincingly in my view. The speaker's figurative "exile" (modelled on Ovid's) need not literally refer to Heloise's banishment from Argenteuil, which was unrelated to her learning. Mews, *The Lost Love Letters of Heloise and Abelard: Perceptions of Dialogue in Twelfth-Century France* (New York: Palgrave, 1999), 164–69.

40. John F. Benton, "Philology's Search for Abelard in the *Metamorphosis Goliae*," *Speculum* 50 (1975): 199–217; Peter Dronke, *Abelard and Heloise in Medieval Testimonies* (Glasgow: University of Glasgow Press, 1976), 16–18; David E. Luscombe, "Peter Abelard and the Poets," in *Poetry and Philosophy in the Middle Ages: A Festschrift for Peter Dronke*, ed. John Marenbon (Leiden: Brill, 2001), 155–71.

41. Thomas Stehling, ed. and trans., *Medieval Latin Poems of Male Love and Friendship* (New York: Garland, 1984). No such poems by Fulcoius are extant, though some may have been among the youthful *nugae* that he burned. Both Fulcoius and Marbod wrote verse letters criticizing the homoerotic tendencies of others.

42. C. Stephen Jaeger, *Ennobling Love: In Search of a Lost Sensibility* (Philadelphia: University of Pennsylvania Press, 1999).

43. Boncompagno da Signa, *Rota Veneris*, ed. Friedrich Baethgen (Rome: Regenberg, 1927).

44. Plechl and Bergmann, *Die Tegernseer Briefsammlung*, ix. Dronke conjectures that these letters are "probably contemporary" with those of Heloise, which date from the 1130s. *Medieval Latin and the Rise of European Love-Lyric*, 2:482.

45. Hexter, *Ovid and Medieval Schooling*, 12–13, 143–45; Christine Elisabeth Eder, *Die Schule des Klosters Tegernsee im frühen Mittelalter im Spiegel der Tegernseer Handschriften* (Munich: Arbeo-Gesellschaft, 1972); Peter Dronke, "A Note on *Pamphilus*," *Journal of the Warburg and Courtauld Institutes* 42 (1979): 225–30.

46. One extant source, cited in both collections, is the late eleventh- or early twelfth-century comedy *Ovidius puellarum*. This short play is widely agreed to be French, yet almost all of its fourteen manuscripts (mostly from the fourteenth and fifteenth centuries) come from German lands, as do those of the later comedy *Pamphilus*. Thus Dieter Schaller remarks that "French cultural influence, and/or the enjoyment of fashionable literature from the West, must be considered as background to the Tegernsee letters." "Zur Textkritik und Beurteilung," 110–11.

47. Robert d'Orbigny, *Le conte de Floire et Blanchefleur*, vv. 227–34, 255–61, 265–70, ed. and trans. Jean-Luc Leclanche (Paris: Champion, 2003), 14–16; my English translation of passages here. It is Leclanche who identifies the author and supplies the date; earlier scholarship dated the romance later in the twelfth century.

48. Bond, "Composing Yourself," 113 n.29; Baudri of Bourgueil, *Carmina* 97–98, 1:96–104.

49. Anke Paravicini, ed., *Carmina Ratisponensia* (Heidelberg: Carl Winter, 1979). There is little criticism on these poems, but see Dronke, *Medieval Latin and the Rise of European Love-Lyric*, 1:221–29, 2:422–47 (edition with translations); and Jaeger, *Ennobling Love*, 74–78 and 101–3.

50. Shulamith Shahar, *Childhood in the Middle Ages* (London: Routledge, 1990), 220.

51. John W. Baldwin, "*L'ars amatoria* au XIIe siècle en France: Ovide, Abélard, André le Chapelain et Pierre le Chantre," in *Histoire et société: Mélanges offerts à Georges Duby*, vol. 1, *Le couple, l'ami et le prochain*, ed. Charles M. de la Roncière (Aix-en-Provence: Publications de l'Université de Provence, 1992), 19–29.

52. Cf. Baudri of Bourgueil's poetic defense of Ovid: "Naturam nostram plenam deus egit amoris: / Nos natura docet quod deus hanc docuit. / Si culpatur amor, actor culpetur amoris: / Actor amoris enim criminis actor erit." (God created our nature full of love; Nature teaches us what God first taught her. If love is blamed, the author of love will be blamed, for the author of love will be the author of sin.) *Carmina* 97.51–54, 1:98.

53. Andreas Capellanus, *On Love* (*De amore*), ed. and trans. P. G. Walsh (London: Duckworth, 1982), 30–31 and 286–87.

54. Shahar, *Childhood in the Middle Ages*, 174.

55. This genre was also cultivated by troubadours such as Arnaut de Mareuil (mid-twelfth century). The Occitan *salut d'amor* is a letter-poem in couplets, which follows

dictaminal rules by including a *salutatio, captatio benevolentiae, narratio,* and so forth. Max Schiendorfer, *Mine Sinne di sint Minne: Zürcher Liebesbriefe aus der Zeit des Minnesangs* (Zollikon: Kranich-Verlag, 1988), 67–68.

56. Bernardinus of Bologna, *Introductiones prosaici dictaminis,* in Ruhe, *De Amasio ad Amasiam,* 299.

57. Hexter, *Ovid and Medieval Schooling,* 144–45.

58. Bernard de Meung, *Flores dictaminum,* selections in Ruhe, *De Amasio ad Amasiam,* 300–307. Neither Bernardinus's nor Bernard de Meung's work has been edited in full.

59. Martin Camargo, *Ars dictaminis, ars dictandi* (Turnhout: Brepols, 1991), 50.

60. Boncompagno da Signa, *Rota Veneris,* 12–14.

61. Ibid., 19 (paraphrase).

62. A fine recent study represents Boncompagno as a precursor of Chaucer's Pandarus: Jonathan M. Newman, "Dictators of Venus: Clerical Love Letters and Female Subjection in *Troilus and Criseyde* and the *Rota Veneris,*" *Studies in the Age of Chaucer* 36 (2014): 103–38. See also Jean-Yves Tilliette, "Rhétorique et sincerité: La lettre d'amour dans le Moyen Âge latin," in *Charmer, convaincre: La rhétorique dans l'histoire,* ed. Jacques Jouanna, Laurent Pernot, and Michel Zink (Paris: Diffusion de Boccard, 2014), 133–37.

63. Malcolm Richardson, "The *Ars dictaminis,* the Formulary, and Medieval Epistolary Practice," in *Letter-Writing Manuals and Instruction from Antiquity to the Present: Historical and Bibliographic Studies,* ed. Carol Poster and Linda C. Mitchell (Columbia: University of South Carolina Press, 2007), 52–66; Anne-Marie Turcan-Verkerk, "Langue et littérature latines du Moyen Âge," *Annuaire de l'École pratique des Hautes Études, Section des sciences historiques et philologiques* 141 (2011), 135–46.

64. Ruhe, *De Amasio ad Amasiam,* 89.

65. Von Moos, "Die *Epistolae duorum amantium,*" 33. The Man's seduction poem (no. 113), which I take to be the first letter actually sent, fulfills this purpose; but the *ars dictaminis* deals in prose.

66. John Van Engen, "Letters, Schools, and Written Culture in the Eleventh and Twelfth Centuries," in *Dialektik und Rhetorik im früheren und höhen Mittelalter,* ed. Johannes Fried (Munich: Oldenbourg, 1997), 97–132; Brian Patrick McGuire, *Friendship and Community: The Monastic Experience, 350–1250,* 2nd ed. (Ithaca, NY: Cornell University Press, 2010), 180–230.

67. Vaughn, *St Anselm and the Handmaidens of God,* 225.

68. Stephanie Hollis, "Wilton as a Centre of Learning," in *Writing the Wilton Women: Goscelin's* Legend of Edith *and* Liber confortatorius, ed. Stephanie Hollis (Turnhout: Brepols, 2004), 307–38. The orgy of destruction that marked the Dissolution makes it impossible to assess the standard of learning at such great Saxon nunneries as Wilton, Barking, and Shaftesbury.

69. "Et nulla abbatissa . . . sibi subditas . . . nullatenus ibi *winileodes* scribere vel mittere praesumant." *Capitula regum francorum,* canon 19, MGH Leges, Sectio II (Hanover: Hahn, 1883–97), 63. The tenth-century Italian song "Foebus abierat" is sometimes identified as a *winileoda.*

70. Alison I. Beach, "Voices from a Distant Land: Fragments of a Twelfth-Century Nuns' Letter Collection," *Speculum* 77 (2002), 36.

71. Ibid., 52 (letter 2); my translation.

72. Ibid., 49.

73. See especially Tilliette, "Rhétorique et sincerité."

74. Verlyn Klinkenborg, *Several Short Sentences About Writing* (New York: Random House, 2012), 81–82.

75. Baudri of Bourgueil, *Carmina* 85.39, 1:81; Tilliette, "Hermès amoureux," 128–29.

76. Baudri of Bourgueil, *Carmina* 99.189–90, 1:110, emphasis added.

77. Ibid. 200.75, 2:127, emphasis added; trans. Bond, *The Loving Subject*, 175.

78. Marbod of Rennes, "Ad eandem resipiscentem" 19–20, in "Liebesbriefgedichte Marbods," 293.

79. Sir Philip Sidney, *Astrophil and Stella* 1.14, in *The Norton Anthology of English Literature*, 7th ed. (New York: Norton, 2000), 1:917.

80. "Casta fui, sum casta modo, uolo uiuere casta; / O utinam possim uiuere sponsa Dei! / Non ob id ipsa tamen uestrum detestor amorem: / Seruos sponsa Dei debet amare sui." Baudri of Bourgueil, *Carmina* 201.113–16, 2:133; trans. Bond, *The Loving Subject*, 189.

81. "Sponsa domini mei domina mea est": Hildebert of Lavardin, *Epistola* 6 (PL 171: 149b); "domina mea esse cepisti, Domini mei sponsa effecta": Abelard, letter 5.3, in *The Letter Collection of Peter Abelard and Heloise*, ed. David Luscombe, trans. Betty Radice and rev. David Luscombe (Oxford: Clarendon, 2013), 180. The ultimate source is Jerome: "Dominam quippe debeo uocare sponsam Domini mei." Ep. 22.2 to Eustochium, in *Lettres* (*Epistulae*), ed. Jérôme Labourt, 8 vols. (Paris: Belles Lettres, 1949–), 1:112.

82. "Ei michi si tantum gemitus imitaris amantum / Et si que loqueris, non ea mente geris. / Cum lego que dicis, verbis accendor amicis, / Cum te flere lego, do lacrimas et ego. / Per nimios questus intelligo pectoris estus, / Os quod tanta dolet, vim michi cordis olet. / Sencio quod sentis, o nostre portio mentis, / Cordi cara meo, quicquid habes, habeo. / Quod tibi sit soli vulnus graue, dicere noli, / Sed dicas potius, quod michi sit grauius. / Ardeo non iuste, quia scilicet ardeo plus te, / Aut nec amor tuus est, aut grauior meus est." Marbod of Rennes, "Liebesbriefgedichte Marbods," 294; my translation.

83. C. Stephen Jaeger, "Friendship of Mutual Perfecting in Augustine's *Confessions* and the Failure of Classical *amicitia*," in *Friendship in the Middle Ages and Early Modern Age: Explorations of a Fundamental Ethical Discourse*, ed. Albrecht Classen and Marilyn Sandidge (Berlin: De Gruyter, 2010), 185–200.

84. Von Moos calls the *amabilis concertatio* "one of the most interesting and original thoughts in the whole work": "Die *Epistolae duorum amantium*," 90.

85. Mews, *Lost Love Letters*, 17–19, 24–25, 136–37.

86. Christine Mohrmann, *Études sur le latin des chrétiens*, 3 vols. (Rome: Edizioni di storia e letteratura, 1961–65), 1:90, 2:24, 3:113.

87. "Nonnulli arbitrantur aliud esse dilectionem sive caritatem, aliud amorem. Dicunt enim dilectionem accipiendam esse in bono, amorem in malo." Augustine, *De civitate Dei* 14.7, ed. Bernardus Dombart and Alfonsus Kalb, 2 vols., 5th ed. (Stuttgart: Teubner, 1993), 2:14.

88. Jaeger, *Ennobling Love*, 163.

89. Von Moos, "Die *Epistolae duorum amantium*," 14.

90. Ewald Könsgen, ed., *Epistolae duorum amantium: Briefe Abaelards une Heloises?* (Leiden: Brill, 1974), 89.

91. This poem is the last item in the manuscript, but was surely the first in the exchange. For discussion, see below, pp. 57–58.

92. Von Moos reads no. 45 as an *epistola post factum*, in the terminology of the *ars dictaminis*: "Die *Epistolae duorum amantium*," 15. Sylvain Piron sees evidence of a new, more overtly sexual tone beginning with letters 76–79: *Lettres des deux amants attribuées à Héloïse et Abélard* (Paris: Gallimard, 2005), 13.

93. Constant J. Mews, "Philosophical Themes in the *Epistolae duorum amantium*: The First Letters of Heloise and Abelard," in *Listening to Heloise: The Voice of a Twelfth-Century Woman*, ed. Bonnie Wheeler (New York: St. Martin's Press, 2000), 47.

94. See no. 22 below and Dronke, *Medieval Latin and the Rise of European Love-Lyric*, 1:224–29.

95. Constant J. Mews, "Philosophical Themes in the *Epistolae duorum amantium*," "Bernard of Clairvaux, Peter Abelard and Heloise on the Definition of Love," *Revista Portuguesa de Filosofia* 60 (2004): 633–60, "Cicero and the Boundaries of Friendship in the Twelfth Century," *Viator* 38 (2007): 369–84, "Discussing Love: The *Epistolae duorum amantium* and Abelard's *Sic et Non*," *Journal of Medieval Latin* 19 (2009): 130–47, and "Abelard, Heloise, and Discussion of Love in the Twelfth-Century Schools," in *Rethinking Abelard: A Collection of Critical Essays*, ed. Babette S. Hellemans (Leiden: Brill, 2014), 11–36.

96. Von Moos links the Man's definition with a celebrated passage from Augustine's *De Trinitate* (8.10.14) that defines *amor* as a unitive force, making the lover one with the beloved: "Die *Epistolae duorum amantium*," 82.

97. Sallust, *De coniuratione Catilinae* 20.4.

98. "Est enim amicitia nihil aliud nisi omnium divinarum humanarumque rerum cum benevolentia et caritate consensio." Cicero, *Laelius* (*De amicitia*) 20.

99. Karl F. Morrison, *"I Am You": The Hermeneutics of Empathy in Western Literature, Theology, and Art* (Princeton, NJ: Princeton University Press, 1988). See also Friedrich Ohly, "Du bist mein, ich bin dein—du in mir, ich in dir—ich du, du ich," in *Kritische Bewahrung: Beiträge zur deutschen Philologie; Festschrift für Werner Schröder*, ed. Ernst-Joachim Schmidt (Berlin: E. Schmidt, 1974), 371–415.

100. My analysis is indebted to Nicholas Watson, "Desire for the Past / Afterword," in *Maistresse of My Wit: Medieval Women, Modern Scholars*, ed. Louise D'Arcens and Juanita Feros Ruys (Turnhout: Brepols, 2004), 149–88. See especially 162–64 and 185–86.

101. This poem appears in the edition of Marbod's works and at least two twelfth-century manuscripts, one in Paris, one in Liège; the latter ascribes it to Marbod's friend Gautier. Walther Bulst, ed., *Carmina Leodiensia* (Heidelberg: Carl Winter, 1975), 16, 26; Maurice Delbouille, "Un mystérieux ami de Marbode: Le 'redoutable poète' Gautier," *Le Moyen Âge* 57 (1951), 236–37.

102. "Gaudia nimpharum, violas floresque rosarum, / Lilia candoris miri quoque poma saporis / Parque columbarum, quibus addita mater earum, / Vestes purpureas, quibus

exornata Napeas / Vincere tam possim cultu quam transeo vultu, / Insuper argentum, gem-
mas promittis et aurum. / Omnia promittis, sed nulla tamen mihi mittis. / Si me diligeres et
que promittis haberes, / Res precessissent et verba secuta fuissent. / Ergo vel est fictus nes-
cisque cupidinis ictus / Vel verbis vanis es diues, rebus inanis. / Quod si multarum sis plenus
diuiciarum, / Rusticus es, qui me tua, non te credi[s] amare." Marbod of Rennes, "Liebesbriefgedichte Marbods," 290, my translation.

103. Heloise, letter 2.10, emphasis added, trans. Radice in Luscombe, *Letter Collection*,
132–33.

104. Cf. Heloise's statement in letter 2.10: "God is my witness that if Augustus, emperor of the whole world, thought fit to honour me with marriage and conferred all the earth
on me to possess forever, it would seem to me dearer and more honourable to be called not
his empress [*imperatrix*] but your mistress" (*meretrix*, literally "whore"). Ibid.

105. Jaeger, *Ennobling Love*, 164.

106. Ibid., 159.

107. Jean Leclercq, *Monks and Love in Twelfth-Century France: Psycho-Historical Essays* (Oxford: Clarendon, 1979), 80; Peter Dronke, *Women Writers of the Middle Ages*,
94–95 and review of *Listening to Heloise*, ed. Bonnie Wheeler, in *International Journal of
the Classical Tradition* 8 (2001), 138; Peter Dronke and Giovanni Orlandi, "New Works by
Abelard and Heloise?" *Filologia mediolatina: Studies in Medieval Latin Texts and Their
Transmission* 12 (2005), 145. For Dronke's argument and my response, see comment on no.
84 below.

108. "Qualia sunt que veste tegis? Vix mente quiesco" (no. 113).

109. James A. Brundage, *Law, Sex, and Christian Society in Medieval Europe* (Chicago:
University of Chicago Press, 1987), 154–60, 198–99, 601.

110. Abelard, letter 5.20, in Luscombe, *Letter Collection*, 198–99.

111. Marjorie Curry Woods, "Rape and the Pedagogical Rhetoric of Sexual Violence,"
in *Criticism and Dissent in the Middle Ages*, ed. Rita Copeland (Cambridge: Cambridge
University Press, 1996), 56–86.

112. Augustine, *Confessions* 1.17, trans. R. S. Pine-Coffin (London: Penguin, 1961),
37–38.

113. Marjorie Curry Woods, "Weeping for Dido: Epilogue on a Premodern Rhetorical
Exercise in the Postmodern Classroom," in *Latin Grammar and Rhetoric: From Classical
Theory to Medieval Practice*, ed. Carol Dana Lanham (London: Continuum, 2002), 286. See
also Lanham, "Freshman Composition," and Manfred Kraus, "*Progymnasmata* and Pro-
gymnasmatic Exercises in the Medieval Classroom," in *The Classics in the Medieval and Re-
naissance Classroom: The Role of Ancient Texts in the Arts Curriculum as Revealed by
Surviving Manuscripts and Early Printed Books*, ed. Juanita Feros Ruys, John O. Ward, and
Melanie Heyworth (Turnhout: Brepols, 2013), 175–97.

114. Anne L. Klinck, ed. and trans., *Carmina burana* 126, in *Anthology of Ancient and
Medieval Woman's Song* (New York: Palgrave Macmillan, 2004), 93–94. The poem is sometimes called "Tempus instat floridum" because in the manuscript, an unrelated stanza with
that incipit precedes it.

115. Stevenson, *Women Latin Poets*, 115.

116. Juanita Feros Ruys, "Hearing Mediaeval Voices: Heloise and *Carmina Burana* 126," in *The Poetic and Musical Legacy of Heloise and Abelard*, ed. Marc Stewart and David Wulstan (Ottawa: Institute of Mediaeval Music, 2003), 91–99.

117. "Non multo autem post, puella se concepisse comperit, et cum summa exultatione mihi super hoc ilico scripsit." (Soon afterwards the girl found that she was pregnant, and immediately wrote me a letter full of rejoicing.) Abelard, *Historia calamitatum* 21, in Luscombe, *Letter Collection*, 32–33.

118. "Flava prius Rhenum sua flumina rebar in Histrum / Vertere, quam soli te mihi nolle loqui, / Qua ratione tibi modo sim magis ipsa pudori / Quam prius, omnino dicere non potero. / Venerat hoc ex te, quicquid tibi displicet in me: / Nonne probasti mea? cur modo carpis ea? / Tunc ego gemma fui, tunc flos, tunc lilia campi; / Tunc quoque nulla fuit orbe mei similis. / Illud idem, quod eram, modo sum, nisi virgo; nec umquam / Id fieri potero: quod sine fine fleo. / Hoc ego nocte die fleo, quod non fata tulere / Cum dulci vitam virginitate meam." "Ad fugitivum," 116.26–37, in Jakob Werner, ed., *Beiträge zur Kunde der lateinischen Literatur des Mittelalters aus Handschriften gesammelt*, 2nd ed. (Aarau: Sauerländer, 1905), 45–46.

119. These are not exclusively feminine epithets; the Woman bestows the same praise on the Man just as often (cf. nos. 49, 53, 73, 76, 79, 109).

120. Lawrence Lipking, *Abandoned Women and Poetic Tradition* (Chicago: University of Chicago Press, 1988), xxiii.

121. C. Stephen Jaeger, "The *Epistolae duorum amantium*, Abelard and Heloise: An Annotated Concordance," *Journal of Medieval Latin* 24 (2014), 209–14.

Abelard and Heloise? Some Frequently Asked Questions

1. Jan M. Ziolkowski, "Lost and Not Yet Found: Heloise, Abelard, and the *Epistolae duorum amantium*," *Journal of Medieval Latin* 14 (2004), 190; Sylvain Piron, trans., *Lettres des deux amants attribuées à Héloïse et Abélard* (Paris: Gallimard, 2005), 179.

2. Ewald Könsgen, ed., *Epistolae duorum amantium: Briefe Abaelards und Heloises?* (Leiden: Brill, 1974), 97; Jean Leclercq, *Monks and Love in Twelfth-Century France: Psycho-Historical Essays* (Oxford: Clarendon, 1979), 79.

3. Sylvain Piron dates the love affair and its tragic sequel to ca. 1114–17, Constant Mews and C. Stephen Jaeger to ca. 1115–17, and Ewald Könsgen and M. T. Clanchy to ca. 1117–18. Piron, *Lettres des deux amants*, 17, 27; Constant J. Mews, *The Lost Love Letters of Heloise and Abelard: Perceptions of Dialogue in Twelfth-Century France* (New York: Palgrave, 1999), 146; C. Stephen Jaeger, "The *Epistolae duorum amantium*, Abelard and Heloise: An Annotated Concordance," *Journal of Medieval Latin* 24 (2014), 189; Könsgen, *Epistolae duorum amantium*, 98; M. T. Clanchy, *Abelard: A Medieval Life* (Oxford: Blackwell, 1997), 120.

4. Könsgen, *Epistolae duorum amantium*, 93–94.

5. Gerald A. Bond, "Composing Yourself: Ovid's *Heroïdes*, Baudri of Bourgueil and the Problem of Persona," *Mediaevalia* 13 (1987), 84–87, and *The Loving Subject: Desire, Eloquence, and Power in Romanesque France* (Philadelphia: University of Pennsylvania Press, 1995), 43. On the medieval popularity of Ovid's exile poetry, see Ralph J. Hexter, *Ovid and*

Medieval Schooling: Studies in Medieval School Commentaries on Ovid's Ars Amatoria, Epistulae ex Ponto, *and* Epistulae Heroidum (Munich: Arbeo-Gesellschaft, 1986), 86–97.

6. Könsgen, *Epistolae duorum amantium*, 96–97. The work circulated widely in England and France, though apparently no farther. Its editor, Anselm Hoste, knew of thirteen manuscripts, ten of them before 1300: Aelred of Rievaulx, *Opera omnia*, ed. Anselm Hoste and C. H. Talbot, CCCM 1 (Turnhout: Brepols, 1971). Peter von Moos has proposed seven citations from Aelred, but none are exact. All are either very distant or rooted in an earlier common source, such as the Bible or Cicero. "Die *Epistolae duorum amantium* und die *säkulare Religion der Liebe*: Methodenkritische Vorüberlegungen zu einem einmaligen Werk mittellateinischer Briefliteratur," *Studi Medievali* 44 (2003), 104.

7. Réka Forrai and Sylvain Piron, "The Debate on the *Epistolae duorum amantium*: Current *status quaestionis* and Further Research," 5, online, posted 9 March 2007. Von Moos responds that one would not expect Aristotle to be cited in love letters from any period on grounds of genre: "Vom Nutzen der Philologie für den Umgang mit anonymen Liebesbriefen: Ein Nachwort zu den *Epistolae duorum amantium*," in *Schrift und Liebe in der Kultur des Mittelalters*, ed. Mireille Schnyder (Berlin: Walter de Gruyter, 2008), 46 n.57.

8. For the predictably very different use of allusion in Abelard's theological works, see David Luscombe, "Peter Abelard and the Poets," in *Poetry and Philosophy in the Middle Ages: A Festschrift for Peter Dronke*, ed. John Marenbon (Leiden: Brill, 2001), 155–71.

9. Some of Marbod's works had an enduring popularity, especially his famous lapidary; 125 manuscripts of that work survive, along with medieval translations into five languages. Marbod of Rennes, *De lapidibus*, ed. John M. Riddle (Wiesbaden: Franz Steiner, 1977). But his love poems remained very little known after his lifetime.

10. Bond, *The Loving Subject*, 71; Dieter Schaller, "Probleme der Überlieferung und Verfasserschaft lateinischer Liebesbriefe des hohen Mittelalters," *Mittellateinisches Jahrbuch* 3 (1966), 30–32.

11. Douglas Kelly, "The Medieval Art of Poetry and Prose: The Scope of Instruction and the Uses of Models," in *Medieval Rhetoric: A Casebook*, ed. Scott D. Troyan (New York: Routledge, 2004), 1–24.

12. Von Moos, "Die *Epistolae duorum amantium*," 101.

13. The register can be found in ibid., 104–11.

14. Ibid., 106–8.

15. Ibid., 61–62.

16. Baudri of Dol, "First Life of Robert of Arbrissel," trans. Bruce L. Venarde, in *Robert of Arbrissel: A Medieval Religious Life* (Washington, DC: Catholic University of America Press, 2003), 1–21; on Hersende, 18.

17. Three different obituaries commemorate the death of Hersende, prioress of Fontevraud, on 29 November, 30 November, and 1 December, while the Paraclete necrology records the death on 1 December of *Hersindis mater domine Heloise abbatisse nostre*. Slight discrepancies of this kind are common in medieval obituaries. In addition, the name Heloise (fairly unusual at this time) is attested as an ancestral name in the family of Hersende of Fontevraud. Finally, while Abelard names Heloise's uncle as Fulbert, the Paraclete necrology calls him *Hubertus*, which was also the name of Hersende's father. Werner Robl,

Heloisas Herkunft: Hersindis Mater (Munich: Olzog, 2001), 96–100, with genealogical tree on 105; Constant J. Mews, "Negotiating the Boundaries of Gender in Religious Life: Robert of Arbrissel and Hersende, Abelard and Heloise," *Viator* 37 (2006), 125–29.

18. Karl Polheim, *Die lateinische Reimprosa* (Berlin: Weidmann, 1925), 363–435. Von Moos does not contest this: "Die *Epistolae duorum amantium*," 45–46.

19. Martin Camargo, *Ars dictaminis, ars dictandi* (Turnhout: Brepols, 1991), 35; Tore Janson, *Prose Rhythm in Medieval Latin from the Ninth to the Thirteenth Century* (Stockholm: Almqvist & Wiksell, 1975), 57–59, 80.

20. In an article by Peter Dronke and Giovanni Orlandi, "New Works by Abelard and Heloise?" *Filologia mediolatina: Studies in Medieval Latin Texts and Their Transmission* 12 (2005), 146–77, Orlandi includes mathematical tables and a complete scansion of the EDA. Francesco Stella describes Orlandi's argument as "particularly complex," with inconclusive results that could be interpreted in two opposite senses: "Analisi informatiche dei lessico e individuazione degli autori nelle *Epistolae duorum amantium* (XII secolo)," in *Latin vulgaire—latin tardif VIII: Actes du VIIIe colloque international sur le latin vulgaire et tardif*, ed. Roger Wright (Hildesheim: Olms-Weidmann, 2008), 562. There is another, not very helpful survey of *cursus* in John O. Ward and Neville Chiavaroli, "The Young Heloise and Latin Rhetoric: Some Preliminary Comments on the 'Lost' Love Letters and Their Significance," in *Listening to Heloise: The Voice of a Twelfth-Century Woman*, ed. Bonnie Wheeler (New York: St. Martin's Press, 2000), 78–80.

21. Von Moos, "Die *Epistolae duorum amantium*," 43, 47, statistical table, 103.

22. Dag Norberg, *An Introduction to the Study of Medieval Latin Versification*, trans. Grant C. Roti and Jacqueline de La Chapelle Skubly, ed. Jan Ziolkowski (Washington, DC: Catholic University of America Press, 2004), 33–34, 59–60; Karl Strecker, *Introduction to Medieval Latin*, rev. and trans. Robert B. Palmer, 3rd ed. (Zurich: Weidmann, 1965), 74.

23. Von Moos, "Die *Epistolae duorum amantium*," 19.

24. Constant J. Mews, *Abelard and Heloise* (Oxford: Oxford University Press, 2005), 63. A few English masters are attested as teaching at Paris by the second quarter of the twelfth century, such as Adam of Petit-Pont and Robert of Melun (Abelard's student), but this was rare. I thank William Courtenay for this information.

25. C. Stephen Jaeger, "*Epistolae duorum amantium* and the Ascription to Heloise and Abelard," in *Voices in Dialogue: Reading Women in the Middle Ages*, ed. Linda Olson and Kathryn Kerby-Fulton (Notre Dame, IN: University of Notre Dame Press, 2005), 145–47.

26. See comments on nos. 21 and 53 below.

27. Ward and Chiavaroli, "The Young Heloise," 82.

28. Juanita Feros Ruys, "*Eloquencie vultum depingere*: Eloquence and *Dictamen* in the Love Letters of Heloise and Abelard," in *Rhetoric and Renewal in the Latin West, 1100–1540: Essays in Honour of John O. Ward*, ed. Constant J. Mews, Cary J. Nederman, and Rodney M. Thomson (Turnhout: Brepols, 2003), 103.

29. *Abelard and Heloise: The Letters and Other Writings*, trans. William Levitan (Indianapolis: Hackett, 2007), 324 n.13.

30. Ward and Chiavaroli, "The Young Heloise," 87; Ruys, "*Eloquencie vultum depingere*," 103.

31. For an edition, see Karin Margareta Fredborg, "Abelard on Rhetoric," in Mews, Nederman, and Thomson, *Rhetoric and Renewal in the Latin West*, 55–80.

32. See comment on no. 50 below. All citations from the *Historia calamitatum* (letter 1) and other letters of Abelard and Heloise are taken from *The Letter Collection of Peter Abelard and Heloise*, trans. by Betty Radice, lightly rev. by David Luscombe (Oxford: Clarendon, 2013).

33. Von Moos, "Die *Epistolae duorum amantium*," 57.

34. Giles Constable, "The Authorship of the *Epistolae duorum amantium*: A Reconsideration," in Olson and Kerby-Fulton, *Voices in Dialogue*, 169, 172.

35. Mary Garrison, "'Send More Socks': On Mentality and the Preservation Context of Medieval Letters," in *New Approaches to Medieval Communication*, ed. Marco Mostert (Turnhout: Brepols, 1999), 69–99.

36. Ibid., 73.

37. Ibid., 69.

38. Jaeger, "*Epistolae duorum amantium* and the Ascription," 127–28.

39. Von Moos, "Die *Epistolae duorum amantium*," 27–28.

40. Piron, *Lettres des deux amants*, 190.

41. Von Moos, "Die *Epistolae duorum amantium*," 6–7, 15, 27, 29, 101.

42. Ibid., 34, 100–101.

43. Abelard, *Historia calamitatum* 16, in Luscombe, *Letter Collection*, 26–27.

44. Heloise, letter 2.16 in Luscombe, *Letter Collection*, 140–41.

45. In total length rather than number of letters, it is actually longer, at least if we count the *Historia calamitatum* as part of the exchange. Even omitting Abelard's *Rule*, the intervening letters 2–8 are quite lengthy and, unlike the EDA, unabridged. Perhaps the longest extant exchange between two individuals is that of Hildegard of Bingen and Guibert of Gembloux (twelve letters, many of them very long): Hildegard of Bingen, *Epistolarium*, ed. Lieven Van Acker and Monika Klaes-Hachmöller, 3 vols., CCCM 91–91b (Turnhout: Brepols, 1991–2001), 2:258–71; and Guibert of Gembloux, *Epistolae*, ed. Albert Derolez, 2 vols., CCCM 66–66a (Turnhout: Brepols, 1988–89), 1:216–57. Hildegard's correspondence includes six other exchanges containing five letters or more: with Abbot Manegold of Hirsau (sixteen letters), Frederick Barbarossa (five letters), Pope Eugenius III (five letters), Abbess Hazzecha of Krauftal (five letters), Abbot Ludwig of St. Eucharius in Trier (five letters), and Abbot Berthold of Zwiefalten (five letters). *The Letters of Hildegard of Bingen*, trans. Joseph L. Baird and Radd K. Ehrman, 3 vols. (New York: Oxford University Press, 1994–2004).

46. Könsgen, *Epistolae duorum amantium*, ix–xiv.

47. Ibid., xxviii–xxxi.

48. Von Moos, "Die *Epistolae duorum amantium*," 92–93 n.284.

49. Piron, *Lettres des deux amants*, 178.

50. Anne-Marie Turcan-Verkerk, "Langue et littérature latines du Moyen Âge," *Annuaire de l'École pratique des Hautes Études, Section des sciences historiques et philologiques* 141 (2011), 129.

51. D. E. Luscombe, "Excerpts from the Letter Collection of Heloise and Abelard in Notre Dame (Indiana) MS 30," in *Pascua Mediaevalia: Studies voor Prof. Dr. J. M. De Smet*,

ed. R. Lievens, E. Van Mingroot, and W. Verbeke (Leuven: Universitaire Pers Leuven, 1983), 529–44. See also Carla Bozzolo, "L'Humaniste Gontier Col et la traduction française des *Lettres* d'Abélard et Héloïse," *Romania* 95 (1974): 199–215; Peter Dronke, *Abelard and Heloise in Medieval Testimonies* (Glasgow: University of Glasgow Press, 1976), 55–60; Luscombe, in Abelard and Heloise, *Letter Collection*, lxxxi–c; Sylvain Piron, "La 'collection' des lettres d'Abélard et Héloïse" (review), *Cahiers de civilisation médiévale* 57 (2014): 337–42.

52. Cf. Jean-Yves Tilliette, "Rhétorique et sincerité: La lettre d'amour dans le Moyen Âge latin," in *Charmer, convaincre: La rhétorique dans l'histoire*, ed. Jacques Jouanna, Laurent Pernot, and Michel Zink (Paris: Diffusion de Boccard, 2014), 147.

53. Peter Abelard, "Abelard's Letter of Consolation to a Friend (*Historia Calamitatum*)," ed. J. T. Muckle, *Mediaeval Studies* 12 (1950), 171–72, and *Historia calamitatum*, ed. Jacques Monfrin (Paris: J. Vrin, 1959), 53–59; David E. Luscombe, "From Paris to the Paraclete: The Correspondence of Abelard and Heloise," *Proceedings of the British Academy* 74 (1988): 247–83; Giovanni Orlandi, "Considerazioni sulla trasmissione del testo," in *Epistolario di Abelardo ed Eloisa*, ed. Ileana Pagani (Turin: Unione Tipografico-Editrice Torinese, 2004), 55–66.

54. Piron, "La 'collection' des lettres d'Abélard et Héloïse," 340.

55. Jacques Dalarun, "Nouveaux aperçus sur Abélard, Héloïse et le Paraclet," *Francia* 32 (2005), 32–39. Piron, following Mews, doubts that a lost duplicate copy ever existed: "La 'collection' des lettres d'Abélard et Héloïse," 339; Constant J. Mews, "La bibliothèque du Paraclet du XIIIe siècle à la Révolution," *Studia Monastica* 27 (1985), 40–43.

56. *La vie et les epistres Pierres Abaelart et Heloys sa fame: Traduction du XIIIe siècle attribuée à Jean de Meun*, ed. Eric Hicks (Paris: Champion, 1991).

57. Jean de Meun, in Guillaume de Lorris and Jean de Meun, *Le roman de la rose*, vv. 8759–8832, ed. Daniel Poirion (Paris: Garnier-Flammarion, 1974), 253–54.

58. Luscombe, *Letter Collection*, cii–ciii.

59. Piron, *Lettres des deux amants*, 185. For details see comment on no. 23 below.

60. Cicero, Bernard of Clairvaux, and Petrarch did the same; this was standard practice for the authors of literary letters. Giles Constable, *Letters and Letter-Collections* (Turnhout: Brepols, 1976), 52.

61. Tilliette, "Rhétorique et sincerité," 147.

62. A point well made by Morgan Powell, "Listening to Heloise at the Paraclete: Of Scholarly Diversion and a Woman's 'Conversion,'" in Wheeler, *Listening to Heloise*, 255–86.

63. Helmut Plechl and Werner Bergmann, eds., *Die Tegernseer Briefsammlung des 12. Jahrhunderts*, MGH Briefe der deutschen Kaiserzeit 8 (Hanover: Hahnsche Buchhandlung, 2002), xiv.

64. Peter Dronke, *Medieval Latin and the Rise of European Love-Lyric*, 2 vols. (Oxford: Clarendon, 1965–66), 1:221.

65. Piron, "La 'collection' des lettres d'Abélard et Héloïse," 341; Julia Barrow, Charles S. F. Burnett, and David E. Luscombe, "A Checklist of the Manuscripts Containing the Writings of Peter Abelard and Heloise and Other Works Closely Associated with Abelard and His School," no. 220, in *Revue d'histoire des textes* 14–15 (1984–85), 231.

66. Dalarun, "Nouveaux aperçus," 54.

67. Piron, *Lettres des deux amants*, 210.

68. Von Moos, "Die *Epistolae duorum amantium*," 26–27.

69. Cf. Mews, *Lost Love Letters*, 23–25 and 140–43; Piron, *Lettres des deux amants*, 24–26; Ward and Chiavaroli, "The Young Heloise," 65. Piron speculates that the Man had destined the poem of no. 113 for wider diffusion, so that it was belatedly tacked on after the end of the correspondence.

70. Von Moos, "Die *Epistolae duorum amantium*," 25.

71. I owe this hypothesis to Cathy Sanok; personal conversation, 3 April 2014.

72. In Eco's novel *Baudolino*, his picaresque hero falls in love with Frederick Barbarossa's wife and writes her letters adapted from the EDA. Afraid to send them, yet eager to have a response, he decides to write her replies as well. This packet of letters is copied by one of the writer's school friends, then stolen by a dissolute canon and hidden in the library of Saint-Victor, where "one day someone will will find [them] among the jumble of papers . . . and attribute them to God knows whom." Umberto Eco, *Baudolino* (2000), trans. William Weaver (London: Secker & Warburg, 2002), 84.

73. Piron takes no. 108 to mean that, after discovering the love affair, Fulbert sent Heloise away from Paris for a time and Abelard did not dare follow her. *Lettres des deux amants*, 10–11.

74. Clanchy, *Abelard*, 185.

75. Sylvain Piron, "Heloise's Literary Self-fashioning and the *Epistolae duorum amantium*," in *Strategies of Remembrance: From Pindar to Hölderlin*, ed. Lucie Doležalová (Newcastle upon Tyne: Cambridge Scholars, 2009), 114–25, 151–52. See comment on no. 79 below.

76. Barbara Newman, "Authority, Authenticity, and the Repression of Heloise," in *From Virile Woman to WomanChrist: Studies in Medieval Religion and Literature* (Philadelphia: University of Pennsylvania Press, 1995), 74.

77. I have searched for all these terms in the *Patrologia Latina, Monumenta Germaniae Historica*, and *Library of Latin Texts* databases. *Dulcifer* is used twice by Froumund of Tegernsee (tenth century), and *immarcidus* appears in only two prior texts. The other terms do not occur at all.

78. Stella, "Analisi informatiche," 567.

79. Mews, *Lost Love Letters*, 120–22.

80. On this formula see Hans Walther, "*Quot-tot*: Mittelalterliche Liebesgrüße und Verwandtes," *Zeitschrift für deutsches Altertum und deutsche Literatur* 65 (1928): 257–89.

81. Jaeger, "*Epistolae duorum amantium* and the Ascription," 137–38; Ruys, "*Eloquencie vultum depingere*," 101–4.

82. Baudri de Bourgueil, *Carmina* 103.23, *Poèmes*, ed. and trans. Jean-Yves Tilliette, 2 vols. (Paris: Les Belles Lettres, 1998–2002), 1:113.

83. Camargo, *Ars dictaminis, ars dictandi*, 24–25; Carol Dana Lanham, *Salutatio Formulas in Latin Letters to 1200: Syntax, Style, and Theory* (Munich: Arbeo-Gesellschaft, 1975).

84. If the sender were of higher rank than the recipient, he would place his own name first (e.g., pope to bishop or king to count). But in other circumstances, courtesy requires the recipient to be named first. Salutations like *amans amanti* and *par pari* are exceptional; in such cases the sender may be given priority.

85. Lanham, *Salutatio Formulas*, 10–11, 42–55.

86. The *Aurea gemma* of Henricus Francigena, writing in Pavia ca. 1121–24, says the only verb in a salutation should be an infinitive "for the sake of courtesy or affection": Lanham, *Salutatio Formulas*, 101. Similarly, the anonymous *Rationes dictandi* (1135) remarks, "it is absolutely necessary that we close the salutation itself with infinitives or in some way in which its words are related to the infinitive construction." Translated as "The Principles of Letter-Writing" in James M. Murphy, ed. and trans., *Three Medieval Rhetorical Arts* (Berkeley: University of California Press, 1971), 9.

87. Hugh of Bologna mentions this option in his *Rationes dictandi prosaice* (ca. 1119): Lanham, *Salutatio Formulas*, 103.

88. Von Moos, "Die *Epistolae duorum amantium*," 52–53, citing the *Pomerium Rhetorice* of Bichilino da Spello (1304). Von Moos argues that this "crass violation of the rules" speaks strongly against an early twelfth-century origin, but that does not follow if the later *dictatores* were explicitly theorizing rules (and exceptions to them) that had long been observed in practice.

89. Stella, "Analisi informatiche," 567.

90. Heloise, letter 2.13; see also 2.16 and *Historia calamitatum* 19: "When inspiration [came] to me, it was for writing love songs [*carmina amatoria*], not the secrets of philosophy. A lot of these songs . . . are still popular and sung in many places, particularly by those who enjoy the kind of life I led."

91. Levitan, *Abelard and Heloise*, 58 n.12.

92. Ziolkowski, "Lost and Not Yet Found," 195–96.

93. Jaeger, "*Epistolae duorum amantium* and the Ascription," 136.

94. Stella, "Analisi informatiche," 567.

95. Ibid., 566–67.

96. Ibid., 568. The rare technical terms that led Stella to this conclusion are found only in the Woman's letters, suggesting that she was eager to show off what she had learned from the Man. I deal with this evidence in the commentary below.

97. Ziolkowski, "Lost and Not Yet Found," 186, 188.

98. My account of the decline of leonine verse relies on Joseph Descroix, *De versu leonino* (Lyon: Audin, 1931), 62–65.

99. Hildebert of Lavardin, *Carmina minora*, ed. A. Brian Scott (Leipzig: Teubner, 1969). For end rhyme see "De abbate" (no. 31) and the famous "De sancta Trinitate" (no. 55); for leonine rhyme, several epigrams (no. 6, 10, 12) and "De lapsu mundi" (no. 25). Among his many unrhymed poems are two in honor of learned women: "Ad Murielem litteratam" (no. 26) and "Versus ad Ceciliam abbatissam" (no. 46).

100. Marbod of Rennes, *Liber decem capitulorum* 1.1–4, ed. Rosario Leotta (Rome: Herder, 1984), 59–60.

101. Janet Martin, "Classicism and Style in Latin Literature," in *Renaissance and Renewal in the Twelfth Century*, ed. Robert L. Benson and Giles Constable (Cambridge, MA: Harvard University Press, 1982), 558–59.

102. Gilo of Paris, cited in Norberg, *An Introduction to the Study of Medieval Latin Versification*, 34.

103. This is confirmed by Tore Janson's study of *cursus*, which occurs in 60 percent of all *clausulae* in Abelard's letters to Heloise—a higher percentage than in any of his other works. But this finding, Janson notes, could also mean that Heloise herself did the final editing of those letters. "Schools of Cursus in the Twelfth Century and the Letters of Heloise and Abelard," in *Retorica e poetica tra i secoli XII e XIV*, ed. Claudio Leonardi and Enrico Menestò (Perugia: Regione dell'Umbria, 1988), 191, 195.

104. Mary Martin McLaughlin, "Abelard as Autobiographer: The Motives and Meanings of His 'Story of Calamities,'" *Speculum* 42 (1967): 463–88.

105. "If you are anxious to please me in everything, as you claim, and in this at least would end my torment, or even give me the greatest pleasure, you must rid yourself of [your bitterness against God]. If it persists you can neither please me nor attain bliss with me. Can you bear me to come to this without you—I whom you declare yourself ready to follow to Vulcan's pit? Seek piety in this at least, lest you cut yourself off from me who am hastening, you believe, towards God." Letter 5.16 in Luscombe and Radice, p. 195.

106. Garrison, "'Send More Socks,'" 95.

107. John Van Engen, "Letters, Schools, and Written Culture in the Eleventh and Twelfth Centuries," in *Dialektik und Rhetorik im früheren und hohen Mittelalter*, ed. Johannes Fried (Munich: Oldenbourg, 1997), 106.

108. "Plus quippe lectioni quam sermoni deditus, expositionis insisto planitiem, non eloquentiae compositionem: sensum litterae, non ornatum rhetoricae. Ac fortasse pura minus quam ornata locutio quanto planior fuerit, tanto simplicium intelligentiae commodior erit; et pro qualitate auditorum ipsa inculti sermonis rusticitas quaedam erit ornatus urbanitas, et quoddam condimentum saporis parvularum intelligentia facilis." "Epistola ad Heloissam," *Sermones*, PL 178: 379.

109. Ruys, "*Eloquencie vultum depingere*," 101–2.

110. "Copia uerborum est ubi non est copia sensus" (v. 15); "ratio cuius preminet eloquio" (v. 824); "factis non uerbis sapiencia se profitetur" (v. 57); "factis quisque suis, non dictis glorificatur" (v. 339). *Carmen ad Astralabium*, ed. Juanita Feros Ruys, in *The Repentant Abelard: Family, Gender, and Ethics in Peter Abelard's* Carmen ad Astralabium *and* Planctus, by Juanita Feros Ruys (New York: Palgrave Macmillan, 2014), 94, 132, 96, 109. My translations.

111. Ernst Robert Curtius, *European Literature and the Latin Middle Ages*, trans. Willard R. Trask (Princeton, NJ: Princeton University Press, 1953), 282. On mannerism, see also Martin, "Classicism and Style," 550, 554–55.

112. Mews, *Lost Love Letters*, 130–31, and "Hugh Metel, Heloise, and Peter Abelard: The Letters of an Augustinian Canon and the Challenge of Innovation in Twelfth-Century Lorraine," *Viator* 32 (2001): 59–91.

113. "Fama sonans per inane uolans apud nos sonuit, quae digna sonitu de uobis, nobis intonuit. Foemineum enim sexum uos excessisse nobis notificauit. Quomodo? Dictando, uersificando, noua junctura nota uerba nouando." Hugh Metel, *Epistola* 16, in Mews, "Hugh Metel, Heloise, and Peter Abelard," 89.

114. Dronke notes that *versificare* most often (though not always) meant versifying a preexistent prose text, such as a saint's life: Dronke and Orlandi, "New Works by Abelard

and Heloise?," 129. This was a common practice at the time, so it is likely that she had tried her hand at it. I have translated *dictando* as "composing letters" (cf. *ars dictandi*), but it could also refer more broadly to prose composition.

115. Several scholars have attempted to link Heloise with anonymous poems, e.g. Mews, *Lost Love Letters*, 163–69, on "Laudis honor, probitatis amor," and "Heloise, the Paraclete Liturgy, and Mary Magdalen," in *The Poetic and Musical Legacy of Heloise and Abelard*, ed. Marc Stewart and David Wulstan (Ottawa: Institute of Mediaeval Music, 2003), 100–112. See also Juanita Feros Ruys, "Hearing Mediaeval Voices: Heloise and *Carmina Burana* 126," in the same volume, 91–99. Dronke takes a skeptical look at these claims in Dronke and Orlandi, "New Works by Abelard and Heloise?" On *Carmina burana* 126, see above, pp. 37–38.

116. I have lightly modified Könsgen's punctuation. For a translation see no. 84 below.

117. In keeping with early twelfth-century practice, in scanning *cursus* I consider only the number of weak beats between the two final stresses and after the last stress in a *clausula*. I take no account of the number of syllables in each word, a practice on which late twelfth-century *dictatores* would insist.

118. Polheim, *Die lateinische Reimprosa*.

119. Janson, *Prose Rhythm in Medieval Latin*, 45–48.

120. Alain Boureau, "The Letter-Writing Norm, a Mediaeval Invention," in Roger Chartier, Alain Boureau, and Cécile Dauphin, *Correspondence: Models of Letter-Writing from the Middle Ages to the Nineteenth Century*, trans. Christopher Woodall (Princeton: Princeton University Press, 1997), 38.

121. Janson, *Prose Rhythm*, 72–79; Terence O. Tunberg, "Prose Styles and *Cursus*," in *Medieval Latin: An Introduction and Bibliographical Guide*, ed. F. A. C. Mantello and A. G. Rigg (Washington, DC: Catholic University of America Press, 1996), 114–18.

122. Janson, *Prose Rhythm*, 80; Camargo, *Ars dictaminis, ars dictandi*, 35.

123. Thiofrid of Echternach, *Flores epytaphii sanctorum*, ed. Michele Camillo Ferrari, CCCM 133 (Turnhout: Brepols, 1996); Guibert of Nogent, *De vita sua, sive Monodiae. Autobiographie*, ed. Edmond-René Labande (Paris: Belles Lettres, 1981).

124. Polheim, *Die lateinische Reimprosa*, 56–87.

125. In the late twelfth century, Serlo of Wilton (d. 1181) is still writing highly virtuosic, mannerist leonine verse, while Matthew of Vendôme in his *Ars versificatoria* (early 1170s) complains that such verse has not *venustas* but *ventositas*—windiness, not charm. Martin, "Classicism and Style," 558–60.

126. Janson, *Prose Rhythm*, 37; "Schools of Cursus in the Twelfth Century," 175.

127. Janson, "Schools of Cursus in the Twelfth Century," 180–81.

128. Janson concludes that Abelard disregards *cursus* in his philosophical and theological works, but uses it moderately (favoring the *tardus* and *trispondaicus*) in his letters to Heloise and other correspondents: "Schools of Cursus in the Twelfth Century," 188–91. I have found little evidence that the Man of the EDA took any interest in prose rhythm.

129. Ward and Chiavaroli, "The Young Heloise," 88–90.

130. Christopher Baswell, "Heloise," in *The Cambridge Companion to Medieval Women's Writing*, ed. Carolyn Dinshaw and David Wallace (Cambridge: Cambridge University Press, 2003), 169.

131. Peter Dronke, *Women Writers of the Middle Ages: A Critical Study of Texts from Perpetua (†203) to Marguerite Porete (†1310)* (Cambridge: Cambridge University Press, 1984), 109, 119, 126–27; Michael Calabrese, "Ovid and the Female Voice in the *De Amore* and the *Letters* of Abelard and Heloise," *Modern Philology* 95 (1997): 1–26.

132. Von Moos, "Die *Epistolae duorum amantium*," 99. Von Moos ascribes the phrase "secular religion of love" to Kurt Flasch. In English criticism, C. S. Lewis made a similar argument long ago: *The Allegory of Love: A Study in Medieval Tradition* (London: Oxford University Press, 1936), 39–43.

133. Barbara Newman, "*La mystique courtoise*: Thirteenth-Century Beguines and the Art of Love," in *From Virile Woman to WomanChrist*, 137–67, "Love Divine, All Loves Excelling," in *God and the Goddesses: Vision, Poetry, and Belief in the Middle Ages* (Philadelphia: University of Pennsylvania Press, 2003), 138–89, and "Conversion: The Literary Traditions of Marguerite Porete," in *Medieval Crossover: Reading the Secular Against the Sacred* (Notre Dame, IN: University of Notre Dame Press, 2013), 111–65.

134. Newman, *From Virile Woman to WomanChrist*, 71–72.

135. Bond, *The Loving Subject*, 129–37; Joan M. Ferrante, *To the Glory of Her Sex: Women's Roles in the Composition of Medieval Texts* (Bloomington: Indiana University Press, 1997), 34–35, 96–98.

136. Hildegard of Bingen, *Epistolarium*, nos. 185 and 186, 2:416–19.

137. Jaeger, "*Epistolae duorum amantium* and the Ascription," 149; Ward and Chiavaroli, "The Young Heloise," 58–62, 81–82; Forrai and Piron, "The Debate on the *Epistolae duorum amantium*," 10.

138. "Audiebam tunc temporis, mulierem licet necdum saeculi nexibus expeditam, litteratoriae scientiae quod perrarum est, et studio licet saecularis sapientiae, summam operam dare." *The Letters of Peter the Venerable*, no. 115, ed. Giles Constable, 2 vols. (Cambridge, MA: Harvard University Press, 1967), 1:303.

139. Gabriela Signori, "Muriel and the Others . . . or Poems as Pledges of Friendship," in *Friendship in Medieval Europe*, ed. Julian Haseldine (Stroud: Sutton, 1999), 199–212.

140. Aelred of Rievaulx, "De sanctimoniali de Wattun," PL 195:789–96; trans. John Boswell in *The Kindness of Strangers: The Abandonment of Children in Western Europe from Late Antiquity to the Renaissance* (New York: Pantheon, 1988), 452–58; Giles Constable, "Aelred of Rievaulx and the Nun of Watton: An Episode in the Early History of the Gilbertine Order," in *Medieval Women*, ed. Derek Baker (Oxford: Blackwell, 1978), 205–26; Sarah Salih, *Versions of Virginity in Late Medieval England* (Cambridge: D. S. Brewer, 2001), 152–65.

Letters of Two Lovers

1. Werner Robl, *Heloisas Herkunft: Hersindis Mater* (Munich: Olzog, 2001), 96–100; Constant J. Mews, "Negotiating the Boundaries of Gender in Religious Life: Robert of Arbrissel and Hersende, Abelard and Heloise," *Viator* 37 (2006), 125–29. For alternative speculations on Heloise's family, see Brenda M. Cook, "The Birth of Heloise: New Light on an Old

Mystery" (paper delivered at the Institute of Historical Research, University of London, September 2000), online at http://www.pierre-abelard.com/heloisa_fichiers/Heloise.pdf.

2. Gerald A. Bond, *The Loving Subject: Desire, Eloquence, and Power in Romanesque France* (Philadelphia: University of Pennsylvania Press, 1995), 60–61; Ralph J. Hexter, *Ovid and Medieval Schooling: Studies in Medieval School Commentaries on Ovid's* Ars Amatoria, Epistulae ex Ponto, *and* Epistulae Heroidum (Munich: Arbeo-Gesellschaft, 1986), 137–204.

3. Peter Dronke, *Women Writers of the Middle Ages: A Critical Study of Texts from Perpetua († 203) to Marguerite Porete († 1310)* (Cambridge: Cambridge University Press, 1984), 109, 119, 126–27; Michael Calabrese, "Ovid and the Female Voice in the *De Amore* and the *Letters* of Abelard and Heloise," *Modern Philology* 95 (1997): 1–26.

4. "Nesciui plane nunc vsque, quid esset amare, / Non quia nunc prima sit mens mea lesa sagitta, / Sed quia non tantam est mens mea passa sagittam." (I never truly knew till now what it is to love—Not that my mind is wounded now with its first arrow, But that it never felt before so sharp an arrow.) Marbod of Rennes, "Ad amicam repatriare parantem" 4–6, "Liebesbriefgedichte Marbods," ed. Walther Bulst, in *Liber Floridus: Mittellateinische Studien Paul Lehmann zum 65. Geburtstag*, ed. Bernhard Bischoff and Suso Brechter (St. Ottilien: Eos Verlag der Erzabtei, 1950), 289.

5. "Forma, genus, mores, sapientia, res et honores / Morte ruant subita, sola manent merita." (Beauty, high birth, manners, wisdom, goods, and honors may fall to sudden death; merits alone remain.) Hans Walther, *Proverbia sententiaeque Latinitatis medii aevi*, 9 vols. (Göttingen: Vandenhoeck & Ruprecht, 1963–86), no. 9750. This proverb is widely attested; the leonine verse suggests an origin no later than the eleventh or early twelfth century.

6. "Attamen si sciero me casto amore a te adamandam et pignus pudicicie mee inviolandum, non recuso *laborem vel* amorem." The emphasized words are underlined in the manuscript, probably meant for deletion. Helmut Plechl and Werner Bergmann, eds., *Die Tegernseer Briefsammlung des 12. Jahrhunderts*, MGH Briefe der deutschen Kaiserzeit 8 (Hanover: Hahnsche Buchhandlung, 2002), 348; MS facsimile in Jürgen Kühnel, ed., *Dû bist mîn, ih bin dîn: Die lateinischen Liebes- (und Freundschafts-) Briefe des clm 19411. Abbildungen, Text und Übersetzung* (Göppingen: Kümmerle, 1977), 41.

7. Carol Dana Lanham, *Salutatio Formulas in Latin Letters to 1200: Syntax, Style, and Theory* (Munich: Arbeo-Gesellschaft, 1975), 7–12.

8. Ibid., 25, 71–75.

9. Rachel Fulton, *From Judgment to Passion: Devotion to Christ and the Virgin Mary, 800–1200* (New York: Columbia University Press, 2002), chaps. 4–8; E. Ann Matter, *The Voice of My Beloved: The Song of Songs in Western Medieval Christianity* (Philadelphia: University of Pennsylvania Press, 1990).

10. Bernard of Clairvaux, *Sermones super Cantica canticorum*, in *Sancti Bernardi opera*, ed. Jean Leclercq, C. H. Talbot, and H. M. Rochais, vols. 1–2 (Rome: Editiones cistercienses, 1957–58).

11. Constant Mews, "Religious Thinker: 'A Frail Human Being' on Fiery Life," in *Voice of the Living Light: Hildegard of Bingen and Her World*, ed. Barbara Newman (Berkeley: University of California Press, 1998), 52–69; Victoria Sweet, *Rooted in the Earth, Rooted in the Sky: Hildegard of Bingen and Premodern Medicine* (New York: Routledge, 2006).

12. See for example the anonymous *Rationes dictandi* (1135), trans. as "The Principles of Letter-Writing," in *Three Medieval Rhetorical Arts*, ed. and trans. James J. Murphy (Berkeley: University of California Press, 1971), 7.

13. The Woman writes, "Sicut lassus umbram et siciens desiderat undam, ita te desidero videre." This sentence is paralleled in letter 13 from the Admont nuns' register: "Sicut sitiens aquam et sicut estuans desiderat umbram, sic nos desideramus uidere faciem uestram." The parallel suggests that nuns, like monks, must have studied formularies and drawn on the same biblical register to express the same sentiments. Alison I. Beach, "Voices from a Distant Land: Fragments of a Twelfth-Century Nuns' Letter Collection," *Speculum* 77 (2002), 52.

14. Baudri of Bourgueil, *Carmina* 6.12–14, *Poèmes,* ed. and trans. Jean-Yves Tilliette, 2 vols. (Paris: Belles Lettres, 1998–2002), 1:14; this trans. Thomas Stehling, ed., *Medieval Latin Poems of Male Love and Friendship* (New York: Garland, 1984), 47. The Woman quotes this poem directly in no. 49.

15. "Deus, cui omne cor patet, et omnis voluntas loquitur, et quem nullum latet secretum, purifica per infusionem sancti Spiritus cogitationes cordis nostri, ut perfecte te diligere, te digne laudare mereamur." The Collect for Purity, found in the eleventh-century Leofric Missal, the Sarum Missal, and many later service books, derives from Alcuin's votive Mass "De gratia sancti Spiritus postulanda," in his *Liber sacramentorum* (PL 101: 446b).

16. "Non constat verbis dilectio sed benefactis." Anke Paravicini, ed., *Carmina Ratisponensia* 65.1 (Heidelberg: Carl Winter, 1979), 43.

17. "Factis non uerbis sapiencia se profitetur"; "factaque sint uerbis anteferenda tibi." *Carmen ad Astralabium*, vv. 57, 822, ed. Juanita Feros Ruys, in *The Repentant Abelard: Family, Gender, and Ethics in Peter Abelard's* Carmen ad Astralabium *and* Planctus, by Juanita Feros Ruys (New York: Palgrave Macmillan, 2014), 96, 132; cf. Ruys, "*Eloquencie vultum depingere:* Eloquence and *Dictamen* in the Love Letters of Heloise and Abelard," in *Rhetoric and Renewal in the Latin West, 1100–1540: Essays in Honour of John O. Ward*, ed. Constant J. Mews, Cary J. Nederman, and Rodney M. Thomson (Turnhout: Brepols, 2003), 102.

18. Richard H. Rouse and Mary A. Rouse, "Wax Tablets," *Language and Communication* 9 (1989): 175–91; Bond, *The Loving Subject*, 54.

19. "Quemadmodum Caesar a vobis exigit impressionem imaginis suae, sic et Deus, ut quemadmodum illi redditur nummus, sic Deo anima lumine vultus ejus illustrata atque signata." Rabanus Maurus, *Commentarium in Matthaeum* 22 (PL 107: 1059b), citing Augustine, *Enarrationes in Psalmos* 4.8 (PL 36: 81).

20. Fulton, *From Judgment to Passion*, 256. For more on medieval seals see Brigitte Bedos-Rezak, *When Ego Was Imago: Signs of Identity in the Middle Ages* (Leiden: Brill, 2011).

21. Peter Abelard, *Theologia "Scholarium"* 2.112–13, ed. E. M. Buytaert and C. J. Mews, in *Petri Abaelardi Opera theologica* III, CCCM 13 (Turnhout: Brepols, 1987), 462–64.

22. C. Stephen Jaeger, *Ennobling Love: In Search of a Lost Sensibility* (Philadelphia: University of Pennsylvania Press, 1999), 160–70, arguing for continuity with the letters of Heloise.

23. In his *Praecepta dictaminum*, an *ars dictandi* contemporary with these letters (ca. 1115), Adalbertus Samaritanus says that if an equal writes to an equal (*par pari*), either name can be given first *iuxta placitum scriptoris*. Lanham, *Salutatio Formulas*, 98. See also Sylvain Piron, "Héloïse et Abélard: L'éthique amoureuse des *Epistolae duorum amantium*," in

Histoires de l'amour, fragilités et interdits, du Kâmasûtra à nos jours, ed. Jocelyne Dakhlia, Arlette Farge, Christiane Klapisch-Zuber, and Alessandro Stella (Paris: Bayard, 2011), 89–90.

24. Bernart de Ventadorn, "Tant ai mo cor ple de joya," in R. T. Hill and T. G. Bergin, eds., *Anthology of the Provençal Troubadours*, 2 vols., 2nd ed. (New Haven, CT: Yale University Press, 1973), 1:42–43; Cercamon, "Puois nostre temps comens'a brunezir," in William D. Paden and Frances Freeman Paden, trans., *Troubadour Poems from the South of France* (Cambridge: D. S. Brewer, 2007), 50–51; Raimbaut d'Aurenga, "Ar resplan la flors enversa," in Paden and Paden, *Troubadour Poems*, 64–65. As Rüdiger Schnell points out, this motif links vernacular courtly lyrics with Latin texts like the EDA, rooted in monastic literature—over against clerical or goliardic songs like the *Carmina burana. Causa amoris: Liebeskonzeption und Liebesdarstellung in der mittelalterlichen Literatur* (Bern: Francke, 1985), 319.

25. See for example Hildefons of Toledo, *De itinere deserti*, c. 46: "Est quoque candidum lilium flos virginum, rosae purpurantis sanguinis martyrum" (PL 96: 181d).

26. The versified Carolingian *Vita Eligii* gives St. Eligius an "unwithered, evergreen crown of paradise" (*vernans... corona paradisi inmarcida*). MGH Poetae 4, no. 149, v. 387, in Karl Strecker, ed., *Vita Eligii* (Hanover: Hahn, 1914), 801.

27. "Sapienti sat!" Walther, *Proverbia sententiaeque*, no. 27522.

28. P. G. Walsh, ed. and trans., *Love Lyrics from the Carmina Burana* (Chapel Hill: University of North Carolina Press, 1993), 192–93.

29. Ludwig Ehrenthal, *Studien zu den Liedern der Vaganten* (Bromberg: n.p., 1891), 5–8; Philip S. Allen, *Medieval Latin Lyrics* (Chicago: University of Chicago Press, 1931), 107–9; Peter Dronke, *Medieval Latin and the Rise of European Love-Lyric*, 2 vols. (Oxford: Clarendon, 1965–66), 1:313–18.

30. Abelard, *Historia calamitatum* 29; Dronke, *Medieval Latin and the Rise of European Love-Lyric*, 1:315–16. But compare his more skeptical remarks in Peter Dronke and Giovanni Orlandi, "New Works by Abelard and Heloise?" *Filologia mediolatina: Studies in Medieval Latin Texts and Their Transmission* 12 (2005), 140–41.

31. C. Stephen Jaeger, "*Epistolae duorum amantium* and the Ascription to Heloise and Abelard," in *Voices in Dialogue: Reading Women in the Middle Ages*, ed. Linda Olson and Kathryn Kerby-Fulton (Notre Dame, IN: University of Notre Dame Press, 2005), 159 n.102.

32. Chiavaroli and Mews translate the phrase as "the being which she is"—grammatically possible, but unlikely. Constant J. Mews and Neville Chiavaroli, *The Lost Love Letters of Heloise and Abelard: Perceptions of Dialogue in Twelfth-Century France* (New York: Palgrave, 1999), 203.

33. "Fateor namque, quia id appellarem verum esse, si in tui presentia possem continuatim esse.... Fac ergo, ut valeam apprehendere verum esse, quod non alias procedit nisi de tuo esse, mecum esse." Plechl and Bergmann, *Die Tegernseer Briefsammlung*, 362. Cf. Anne-Marie Turcan-Verkerk, "Langue et littérature latines du Moyen Âge," *Annuaire de l'Ecole pratique des Hautes Études, Section des sciences historiques et philologiques* 141 (2011), 131.

34. Bruno uses *aequipollenter* twenty-four times in his *Expositio in Psalmos* and *Expositio in Epistolas Pauli*; it occurs thirty-five times in pseudo-Bede's *De libro Psalmorum* (PL 93: 477–1098). A. B. Kraebel, "Prophecy and Poetry in the Psalms-Commentaries of St. Bruno

and the Pre-scholastics," *Sacris Erudiri* 50 (2011): 413–59, and "Commentary and Poetry in the Medieval School of Reims, *c.* 883–1100," in *Encountering Scripture in Overlapping Cultures: Judaism, Christianity, and Islam*, ed. Mordechai Cohen and Adele Berlin (Cambridge: Cambridge University Press, forthcoming).

35. Peter Damian, *Collectanea in Vetus Testamentum*, c. 16 (PL 145: 1048b); Rupert of Deutz, *De Trinitate et operibus ejus, In Genesim* 8.22 (PL 167: 509b); Peter Lombard, *Commentaria in Psalmos* 120 (PL 191: 1140c).

36. Andrew Marvell, "To His Coy Mistress," 1–2.

37. Friedrich Ohly, "*Cor amantis non angustum*: Vom Wohnen im Herzen," in *Schriften zur mittelalterlichen Bedeutungsforschung* (Darmstadt: Wissenschaftliche Buchgesellschaft, 1977), 128–55.

38. On the theology of coinherence (*perichoresis*), see Catherine Mowry LaCugna, *God for Us: The Trinity and Christian Life* (New York: HarperCollins, 1991), 270–78; Barbara Newman, "Indwelling: A Meditation on Empathy, Pregnancy, and the Virgin Mary," in *Studies on Medieval Empathies*, ed. Karl F. Morrison and Rudolph M. Bell (Turnhout: Brepols, 2013), 189–212.

39. Quintilian, *Institutio oratoria* 3.7.28; Cassiodorus, *Institutiones* 2.2.3. In his *Interpretationes Vergilianae* (ca. 400), Tiberius Claudius Donatus characterized the *Aeneid* as a *laudatio* for Aeneas and Augustus. He represents Virgil's task as an exceptionally difficult one; the reader must "notice first who it is that he has undertaken to praise . . ., what a huge job and what a dangerous work he has begun." Trans. Ineke Sluiter in Rita Copeland and Ineke Sluiter, eds., *Medieval Grammar and Rhetoric: Language Arts and Literary Theory, AD 300–1475* (Oxford: Oxford University Press, 2009), 143–44.

40. C. Stephen Jaeger, "The *Epistolae duorum amantium*, Abelard and Heloise: An Annotated Concordance," *Journal of Medieval Latin* 24 (2014), 209–14.

41. Sylvain Piron, trans., *Lettres des deux amants attribuées à Héloïse et Abélard* (Paris: Gallimard, 2005), 48 n.2 and 185.

42. Augustine's view is typical: "The flesh therefore is set in the wife's place, just as the spirit sometimes is in the husband's. Why? Because he rules and she is ruled; he ought to command and she to serve. . . . What is worse than a home where the woman has authority over the man? But a household is rightly ordered when the man rules and the woman obeys." *In Joannis evangelium tractatus CXXIV* 2.14 (PL 35: 1395); Eva Cescutti, "Lieben auf Lateinisch—Emotion oder rhetorische Codierung? Zu den *Epistolae Duorum Amantium* 24 und 25," in *Funktionsräume, Wahrnehmungsräume, Gefühlsräume: Mittelalterliche Lebensformen zwischen Kloster und Hof*, ed. Christina Lutter (Oldenbourg: Böhlau, 2011), 87.

43. Constant J. Mews, "Bernard of Clairvaux, Peter Abelard and Heloise on the Definition of Love," *Revista Portuguesa de Filosofia* 60 (2004): 633–60, and "Abelard, Heloise, and Discussion of Love in the Twelfth-Century Schools," in *Rethinking Abelard: A Collection of Critical Essays*, ed. Babette S. Hellemans (Leiden: Brill, 2014), 11–36.

44. William of St Thierry, *The Nature and Dignity of Love*, prologue, trans. Thomas X. Davis (Kalamazoo, MI: Cistercian Publications, 1981), 47.

45. Barbara Newman, *God and the Goddesses: Vision, Poetry, and Belief in the Middle Ages* (Philadelphia: University of Pennsylvania Press, 2003), 142–43.

46. "Amor est delectatio cordis alicuius ad aliquid propter aliquid." Hugh of Saint-Victor, *De substantia dilectionis* 5, ed. Roger Baron, in *Six opuscules spirituels*, Sources chrétiennes 155 (Paris: Cerf, 1969), 86; trans. Vanessa Butterfield in Hugh Feiss, ed., *On Love: A Selection of Works of Hugh, Adam, Achard, Richard, and Godfrey of St Victor* (Turnhout: Brepols, 2011), 144.

47. Constant J. Mews, *Abelard and Heloise* (Oxford: Oxford University Press, 2005), 67–68 and 81–83. For a critique of Mews's reading see John Marenbon, "Lost Love Letters? A Controversy in Retrospect," *International Journal of the Classical Tradition* 15 (2008), 273–75. Mews responds in "Between Authenticity and Interpretation: On *The Letter Collection of Peter Abelard and Heloise* and the *Epistolae duorum amantium*," a review in *Tijdschrift voor Filosofie* 76 (2014): 823–42. For an impartial account of Abelard's early teachers and the debate over universals, see *The Letter Collection of Peter Abelard and Heloise*, ed. David Luscombe, trans. Betty Radice and rev. David Luscombe (Oxford: Clarendon, 2013), 519–27.

48. "Quanta autem vis amicitiae sit, ex hoc intellegi maxime potest, quod ex infinita societate generis humani, quam conciliavit ipsa natura, ita contracta res est et adducta in angustum ut omnis caritas aut inter duos aut inter paucos iungeretur." Cicero, *Laelius* (*De amicitia*) 20, in *De senectute, De amicitia, De divinatione*, with trans. by W. A. Falconer, Loeb Classical Library (Cambridge, MA: Harvard University Press, 1964).

49. Peter Abelard, *Sic et non: A Critical Edition*, 138.21, ed. Blanche B. Boyer and Richard McKeon (Chicago: University of Chicago Press, 1976–77), 473; Constant J. Mews, "Discussing Love: The *Epistolae duorum amantium* and Abelard's *Sic et non*," *Journal of Medieval Latin* 19 (2009), 135–39.

50. "Est enim amicitia nihil aliud nisi omnium divinarum humanarumque rerum cum benevolentia et caritate consensio." Cicero, *Laelius* 20.

51. "Caritas uero est amor honestus, qui ad eum uidelicet finem dirigitur ad quem oportet. . . . Amor uero est bona erga alterum propter ipsum uoluntas, qua uidelicet optamus ut eo modo se habeat quo se habere bonum ei esse credimus." Abelard, *Theologia "Scholarium"* 1.2, in *Opera theologica* III, 319; Mews, "Abelard, Heloise, and Discussion of Love," 13–15.

52. On Eva Cescutti's reading, the Woman is trying to "correct" the inverted gender hierarchy expressed in the Man's previous greeting (no. 24). "Lieben auf Lateinisch," 90–91.

53. Anselm of Canterbury, *Cur Deus Homo*, in *Opera omnia*, 6 vols., ed. F. S. Schmitt (Edinburgh: Thomas Nelson, 1946–61), 2:37–133.

54. Elizabeth M. Makowski, "The Conjugal Debt and Medieval Canon Law," *Journal of Medieval History* 3 (1977): 99–114; Julie Ann Smith, "*Debitum obedientie*: Heloise and Abelard on Governance at the Paraclete," *Parergon* 25 (2008): 1–23; Sally Livingston, "'Consider, I Beg You, What You Owe Me': Heloise and the Economics of Relationship," in *Women and Wealth in Late Medieval Europe*, ed. Theresa Earenfight (New York: Palgrave Macmillan, 2010), 51–65.

55. Abelard, *Sic et non* 138.7, p. 471; Mews, "Abelard, Heloise, and Discussion of Love," 28; Piron, *Lettres des deux amants*, 202; Marenbon, "Lost Love Letters?" 275.

56. Aelred of Rievaulx, *Spiritual Friendship* 2.19, trans. Mary Eugenia Laker (Kalamazoo, MI: Cistercian Publications, 1977), 74.

57. "Abessalom, pater pacis": Jerome, *De nominibus Hebraicis* (PL 23: 815). Cf. Angelomus of Luxeuil, *Enarrationes in libros Regum* 2.13 (PL 115: 367d): "Absalom pater pacis, sive patris pax interpretatur." The second interpretation, cited by Isidore of Seville *per antiphrasin*, was more common: *Etymologiae* 7.6.67 (PL 82: 279c).

58. Isidore records that the king had three names, Solomon (*pacificus*), Idida (*dilectus et amabilis Domino*), and Coheleth (*ecclesiastes*, a public speaker): *Etymologiae* 7.6.65 (PL 82: 279c). The Mews-Chiavaroli reading *Ididia* is in error.

59. "Rhythmus in Odonem regem," stanza 6, MGH Poetae latini 4:1 (Berlin: Weidmann, 1899), 138.

60. Peter Abelard, "Planctus Israel super Sanson," ed. and trans. Juanita Feros Ruys, in Ruys, *The Repentant Abelard*, 251–53, 262–63; Peter Dronke, *Poetic Individuality in the Middle Ages: New Departures in Poetry, 1000–1150* (Oxford: Clarendon, 1970), 119–45.

61. Jaeger, "The *Epistolae duorum amantium*, Abelard and Heloise," 218–19.

62. Jaeger, "*Epistolae duorum amantium* and the Ascription," 130. Sylvain Piron thinks the Man is referring not to this letter but to his previous one, apologizing for its coldness: *Lettres des deux amants*, 59 n.2.

63. Peter von Moos, "Kurzes Nachwort zu einer langen Geschichte mit missbrauchten Liebesbriefen: *Epistolae duorum amantium*," in *Abaelard und Heloise: Gesammelte Studien zum Mittelalter*, vol. 1, ed. Gert Melville (Münster: Lit, 2005), 290.

64. Giles Constable, "The Authorship of the *Epistolae duorum amantium*: A Reconsideration," in Olson and Kerby-Fulton, *Voices in Dialogue*, 171; Von Moos, "Kurzes Nachwort," 289.

65. "Ad hujus imperfecti hominis ignominiae cumulum vero pertinet, quod in sigillo, quo fetidas illas litteras sigillasti, imaginem duo capita habentem, unum viri, alterum mulieris, ipse formasti." Roscelin of Compiègne, "Epistola ad Abaelardum" (PL 178: 372a). See also Mews, "Negotiating the Boundaries," 115, 141–42.

66. Könsgen prints *bene facta* as two words, but in light of the rare allusion to Catullus, the Woman probably intended *benefacta priora*. Birger Munk Olsen notes only a single fragment of Catullus (in Paris, BNF MS lat. 8071) copied before 1200: *L'étude des auteurs classiques latins aux XIe et XIIe siècles*, 3 vols. (Paris: Éditions du Centre National de la Recherche Scientifique, 1982–87), 1:88.

67. Jaeger, "*Epistolae duorum amantium* and the Ascription," 136.

68. Paul Gerhard Schmidt and Hans Walther, *Proverbia sententiaeque Latinitatis medii et recentioris aevi*, 3 vols. (Göttingen: Vandenhoeck & Ruprecht, 1982–86), 1:762. The same line appears in an early sixteenth-century miscellany from Trier (Stadtbibliothek, Hs. 804), where it can hardly be quoted from the *Epistolae*: "Wissenschaftliche Miscellanea," *Westdeutsche Zeitschrift für Geschichte und Kunst* 1.6 (June 1882), 42.

69. Abelard, *Sic et non*, prologue, 98; *Commentaria in Epistolam Pauli ad Romanos* 4.13.10, in *Opera theologica* I, ed. E. M. Buytaert, CCCM 11 (Turnhout: Brepols, 1969), 293. In the latter he cites an alternative form of the maxim: "Habe caritatem et fac quidquid uis."

70. Giles Constable, *"Love and Do What You Will": The Medieval History of an Augustinian Precept* (Kalamazoo, MI: Medieval Institute Publications, 1999), 8–12.

71. Mary Carruthers, *The Experience of Beauty in the Middle Ages* (Oxford: Oxford University Press, 2013), 88–89.

72. "Parcius elimans alias Natura puellas, / distulit in dotes esse benigna tuas. / In te fudit opes, et opus mirabile cernens, / est mirata suas hoc potuisse manus." (Gracious Nature, polishing other girls more sparingly, has spent her essence in your gifts. In you she poured out her riches, and on beholding the marvelous work, she was amazed that her hands could have done this.) Hildebert, *Carmina minora* 46.7–10, ed. A. Brian Scott (Leipzig: Teubner, 1969), 37.

73. Peter von Moos agrees: "Die *Epistolae duorum amantium* und die *säkulare Religion der Liebe*: Methodenkritische Vorüberlegungen zu einem einmaligen Werk mittellateinischer Briefliteratur," *Studi Medievali* 44 (2003), 15.

74. Gerard Brault, "Chrétien de Troyes' *Lancelot:* The Eye and the Heart," *Bulletin bibliographique de la Société internationale arthurienne* 24 (1973): 142–53; Begoña Aguiriano, "Le Coeur dans Chrétien," in *Le "Cuer" au Moyen Âge (Réalité et Sénéfiance)* (Aix-en-Provence: Centre Universitaire d'Études et de Recherches Médiévales d'Aix, 1991), 11–25; Joseph Duggan, *The Romances of Chrétien de Troyes* (New Haven, CT: Yale University Press, 2001), 136–39.

75. Sylvain Piron, "Heloise's Literary Self-fashioning and the *Epistolae duorum amantium*," in *Strategies of Remembrance: From Pindar to Hölderlin*, ed. Lucie Doležalová (Newcastle upon Tyne: Cambridge Scholars, 2009), 152.

76. Ewald Könsgen, "'Der Nordstern scheint auf den Pol': Baudolinos Liebesbriefe an Beatrix, die Kaiserin—oder *Ex epistolis duorum amantium*," in *Nova de veteribus: Mittel- und neulateinische Studien für Paul Gerhard Schmidt*, ed. Andreas Bihrer and Elisabeth Stein (Munich: K. G. Saur, 2004), 1115.

77. I disagree with Juanita Feros Ruys, who takes this letter seriously as Heloise's attempt to follow Abelard's directives on writing in a plainer style. Ruys, "*Eloquencie vultum depingere*"; see above, pp. 48–49.

78. Mews, *Lost Love Letters*, 25; Jaeger, "*Epistolae duorum amantium* and the Ascription," 126.

79. Jaeger, "*Epistolae duorum amantium* and the Ascription," 139.

80. Martin Camargo, "Where's the Brief? The *Ars dictaminis* and Reading/Writing Between the Lines," in *The Late Medieval Epistle*, ed. Carol Poster and Richard Utz (Evanston, IL: Northwestern University Press, 1996), 9.

81. Piron, *Lettres des deux amants*, 68 n.1.

82. I have been able to find just one more usage. In his translation of a Greek version of the Marian miracle of Theophilus, Paulus Diaconus writes, "Quid mihi profuit . . . superciliositas vani huius seculi?" Eutychianus, "Miraculum S. Marie de Theophilo penitente," trans. Paulus Diaconus, in Robert Petsch, ed., *Theophilus: Mittelniederdeutsches Drama in drei Fassungen* (Heidelberg: Carl Winter, 1908), 4.

83. Mews, *Lost Love Letters*, 136–37.

84. Christine Mohrmann, *Études sur le latin des chrétiens*, 3 vols. (Rome: Edizioni di storia e letteratura, 1961–65), 1:90 and 2:24. Early Christians used both *caritas* and *dilectio* (but not *amor*) to translate the Greek *agape*.

85. "Veni sancte Spiritus" is usually ascribed to Stephen Langton, archbishop of Canterbury (ca. 1150–1228), which would make it too late to be cited here. But Margot Fassler

suggests that it may have been an earlier twelfth-century piece, given that it was already in wide circulation by the late twelfth century (personal communication, 12 September 2014). The sequence appears in four eleventh-century manuscripts from St. Gall, though in each case it has been inserted by a later hand. All published discussions still seem to rely on John Julian, *A Dictionary of Hymnology, Setting Forth the Origin and History of Christian Hymns of All Ages and Nations* (New York: Scribner, 1892), 1212–15.

86. "Fama sonans per inane uolans apud nos sonuit, quae digna sonitu de uobis, nobis intonuit. Foemineum enim sexum uos excessisse nobis notificauit. Quomodo? Dictando, uersificando, noua iunctura nota uerba nouando. Et quod excellentius omnibus est his, muliebrem mollitiem exuperasti, et in uirile robur indurasti." My translation; I have deleted a comma after *iunctura*. Hugh Metel, *Epistola* 16, ed. Constant J. Mews, in "Hugh Metel, Heloise, and Peter Abelard: The Letters of an Augustinian Canon and the Challenge of Innovation in Twelfth-Century Lorraine," *Viator* 32 (2001), 89.

87. *The Letters of Peter the Venerable*, 115, ed. Giles Constable, 2 vols. (Cambridge, MA: Harvard University Press, 1967), 1:303–4; trans. Betty Radice in *The Letters of Abelard and Heloise*, rev. M. T. Clanchy (London: Penguin, 2003), 217–18.

88. Mews, *Lost Love Letters*, 129–30, 350 n.51; Peter Dronke, review of *Listening to Heloise*, ed. Bonnie Wheeler, in *International Journal of the Classical Tradition* 8 (2001), 136. Albert (d. 1280) uses *scibilitas* in two of his works, the *Metaphysica* and *Summa theologiae*. Llull (d. 1315) is especially partial to the term, which he employs thirty-three times. Rejecting any connection between the Woman and Abelard, Jan M. Ziolkowski argues that "the formation *scibilitas* could occur naturally to a Latin-user engaged in philosophizing in almost any period": "Lost and Not Yet Found: Heloise, Abelard, and the *Epistolae duorum amantium*," *Journal of Medieval Latin* 14 (2004), 185. Dronke makes the same point. Yet *scibilitas* remains extremely rare, and the Woman is hardly "philosophizing" in this letter.

89. John Marenbon objects that Abelard uses *scibilitas* in a passive sense (the capacity to be known), whereas the Woman uses it actively (the capacity to know), so she cannot have learned it from him: "Lost Love Letters?" 276. But this objection is surely beside the point because the Woman was not doing epistemology at all. She was writing in a highly rhetorical vein, with a nod to one of her teacher's pet ideas. Cf. Jaeger, "The *Epistolae duorum amantium*, Abelard and Heloise," 195–96, n.28.

90. Mews, *Lost Love Letters*, 130.

91. Abelard, *Dialectica* 1.2.3, ed. L. M. de Rijk, 2nd ed. (Assen: Van Gorcum, 1970), 85, and *Logica "Ingredientibus,"* in *Peter Abaelards philosophische Schriften*, ed. Bernhard Geyer (Münster: Aschendorff, 1919–33), 1:214. Each of these works survives in a single manuscript, as Dronke notes: review of *Listening to Heloise*, 136. This makes it all the more likely that the Woman acquired the term orally.

92. *Abelard and Heloise: The Letters and Other Writings*, trans. William Levitan (Indianapolis: Hackett, 2007), xix–xxiv. Both Abelard and Heloise quote Seneca's *Epistulae ad Lucilium* in their monastic letters.

93. A fictional lady laments that her lover has forsaken her for a new love: "Satis mihi contraria promittebam, sed incassum sibi promittit quispiam quod est sortis in alea constitutum." (I used to promise myself that could never happen, but a person promises herself in

vain something that depends on a throw of the dice.) Bernard de Meung, *Flores dictaminum*, no. 6, in Ernstpeter Ruhe, *De Amasio ad Amasiam: Zur Gattungsgeschichte des mittelalter-lichen Liebesbriefes* (Munich: Wilhelm Fink, 1975), 304.

94. Von Moos describes no. 66 as a "panegyric poem on the arrival of *a* new teacher." He claims that it, like no. 73, is "perhaps [a] student production inserted later" into a corre-spondence where it does not belong: "Die *Epistolae duorum amantium*," 19. I can see no rea-son for this conjecture other than to eliminate a pointer to Abelard and Heloise.

95. Jaeger, "*Epistolae duorum amantium* and the Ascription," 134–36.

96. Luscombe, *Letter Collection*, 10–11; Jaeger, "*Epistolae duorum amantium* and the Ascription," 146–47; Constant J. Mews, "William of Champeaux, the Foundation of Saint-Victor (Easter, 1111), and the Evolution of Abelard's Early Career," in *Arts du langage et théologie aux confins des XIe–XIIe siècles: Textes, maîtres, débats*, ed. Irène Rosier-Catach (Turnhout: Brepols, 2011), 83–104; Anne Grondeux, "Guillaume de Champeaux, Joscelin de Soissons, Abélard et Gosvin d'Anchin: Étude d'un milieu intellectuel," in Rosier-Catach, *Arts du langage et théologie*, 3–43.

97. In other searches I have found a few more occurrences: in Gerald of Wales' *Specu-lum ecclesie*, a verse life of St. Catherine from Winchester ("Sepius in sexu fragili," probably later twelfth century), and a late medieval chronicle of the bishops of Eichstätt. Marbod's epitaph for Anselm is the only one of these passages the Woman could have known.

98. This famous hymn, once credited to Bernard of Clairvaux, is now ascribed to an English Cistercian. It probably belongs to the later twelfth century.

99. *Lost Love Letters*, 250–51. Chiavaroli and Mews insert a comma that I find mislead-ing: "dum studiosa mei laboris tempora, in te funditus perpendam neglecta." Könsgen has no comma, but a line to set off the rhyming clauses: "dum studiosa mei laboris tempora | in te funditus perpendam neglecta." *Epistolae duorum amantium*, 40.

100. Cf. Piron's translation: "les soupirs de mon coeur s'accroissent encore lorsque je mesure les heures studieuses des efforts que je t'ai consacrés sans que tu en aies tenu compte." *Lettres des deux amants*, 87–88. Von Moos sees rather an erotic allusion. The Woman consid-ers that her tireless labor of love for the Man has been wasted because of his long absence, as she can no longer lie at his side (*collaterari*). "Die *Epistolae duorum amantium*," 19–20, n.58.

101. Dronke, *Women Writers of the Middle Ages*, 141–42.

102. Barbara Newman, "Liminalities: Literate Women in the Long Twelfth Century," in *European Transformations: The Long Twelfth Century*, ed. Thomas F. X. Noble and John Van Engen (Notre Dame, IN: University of Notre Dame Press, 2012), 375.

103. C. Stephen Jaeger, "Friendship of Mutual Perfecting in Augustine's *Confessions* and the Failure of Classical *amicitia*," in *Friendship in the Middle Ages and Early Modern Age: Explorations of a Fundamental Ethical Discourse*, ed. Albrecht Classen and Marilyn Sandidge (Berlin: De Gruyter, 2010), 185–200, and "The *Epistolae Duorum Amantium*, Abelard and Heloise," 200–201.

104. "Si sola in facie videt homo, quia solus Deus intuetur cor, miror, nec satis mirari possum, quomodo, qua ratione, sic tuam atque meam ad invicem dilectionem pensare et distinguere potuisti.... Forte verum est quod dicis, minus scilicet a me amari te quam me diligis; sed certe certus sum certum non esse tibi.... Sed quanto in te,—tibi, pater, dico—,

maior est caritas, tanto minus contemnenda est a te nostra possibilitas, quia etsi plus diligis, quoniam plus vales, non tamen plus diligis quam vales. Nos autem, etsi minus diligimus quam debemus, diligimus tamen quantum valemus." Bernard of Clairvaux, *Epistola* 85.1, 4, in *Sancti Bernardi opera*, vol. 7 (1974), 220–22. See also Von Moos, "Die *Epistolae duorum amantium*," 92–95.

105. Walsh, *Love Lyrics from the Carmina Burana*, no. 29, stanza 24, p. 104.

106. Stehling, *Medieval Latin Poems of Male Love and Friendship*, xxvii.

107. On this poem and its context see C. Stephen Jaeger, *The Envy of Angels: Cathedral Schools and Social Ideals in Medieval Europe, 950–1200* (Philadelphia: University of Pennsylvania Press, 1994), 66–74 and 149–51.

108. "Quot caelum retinet stellas, quot terra lapillos, / Quot saltus ramos, folia, aut quot pontus harenas, / Quot pluviae stillas, quot fundunt nubila guttas, / Quot fluvius pisces vel sunt quot in orbe volucres, / Quot flores prati vel quot sunt gramina campi, / Tot tibi praestantes det virtus trina salutes." Notker Balbulus II.141, in *Notker der Dichter und seine geistige Welt*, ed. Wolfram von den Steinen, 2 vols. (Bern: Francke, 1948). See also Hans Walther, "*Quot-tot*: Mittelalterliche Liebesgrüße und Verwandtes," *Zeitschrift für deutsches Altertum und deutsche Literatur* 65 (1928): 257–89.

109. Poem XLIII, v. 137, in Karl Strecker, ed., *Die Tegernseer Briefsammlung*, MGH Epistolae selectae III (Berlin: Weidmann, 1925), 125–34; also in Walther Bulst, ed., *Die ältere Wormser Briefsammlung*, MGH Briefe der deutschen Kaiserzeit 3 (Weimar: Böhlau, 1949), 119–27, and PL 141: 1303b–8c. In the PL the poem is titled "Apologia pro schola Wirtzburgensi ejusque magistro adversus quemdam calumniatorem" and wrongly ascribed to Froumund of Tegernsee.

110. "Hebet sidus" is a song sometimes ascribed to Abelard (see no. 20 above), but *iuvenilis flos* occurs there in its more typical sense of "youthful bloom."

111. Dronke cites this use of *vetus* as an argument against ascribing the *Epistolae* to Abelard and Heloise, taking the Man to mean something like "although you're no spring chicken, to me you are ever young." *Women Writers of the Middle Ages*, 94, and review of *Listening to Heloise*, 138. In context, however, this is not a comment about age; rather, the Man is protesting that he has not grown bored with the Woman's love. In no. 50 he calls her a *puella*.

112. Bond, *The Loving Subject*, 49.

113. Baudri of Bourgueil, *Carmina* 200.79–80.

114. Constant J. Mews, "Philosophical Themes in the *Epistolae duorum amantium*: The First Letters of Heloise and Abelard," in *Listening to Heloise: The Voice of a Twelfth-Century Woman*, ed. Bonnie Wheeler (New York: St. Martin's Press, 2000), 42–44.

115. Von Moos, "Die *Epistolae duorum amantium*," 86 n.261.

116. Karl F. Morrison, *"I Am You": The Hermeneutics of Empathy in Western Literature, Theology, and Art* (Princeton, NJ: Princeton University Press, 1988). See also Friedrich Ohly, "Du bist mein, ich bin dein—du in mir, ich in dir—ich du, du ich," in *Kritische Bewahrung: Beiträge zur deutschen Philologie; Festschrift für Werner Schröder*, ed. Ernst-Joachim Schmidt (Berlin: E. Schmidt, 1974), 371–415.

117. In an unedited love letter (no. 219) from the twelfth-century Donaueschingen collection, *nauta* (sailor) and *navis* (ship) are euphemisms for penis and vulva. Dieter Schaller,

"Probleme der Überlieferung und Verfasserschaft lateinischer Liebesbriefe des hohen Mittelalters," *Mittellateinisches Jahrbuch* 3 (1966), 36 n.63.

118. "Dehortatio supradicte puelle a nuptiis," cited by Abelard, *Historia calamitatum* 24–26, in Luscombe, *Letter Collection*, 34–43.

119. Jaeger, "The *Epistolae duorum amantium*, Abelard and Heloise," 203–4; Piron, "Heloise's Literary Self-fashioning," 151–52.

120. Dronke compares the famous lines to *Carmina burana* 145a, a brief lyric in Middle High German: "Were diu werlt alle min / von deme mere unze an den Rin, / des wolt ih mih darben / daz chunich [*or* diu chunegin] von Engellant / lege an minem armen!" (If the world were all mine, from the sea to the Rhine, I would give it all up—if the King [or Queen] of England were to lie in my arms!) Dronke, *Women Writers of the Middle Ages*, 97. But I see little resemblance between this lyric and letter 82. The Woman says she wants nothing but what her lover gives her, while the singer offers a high price for a lover that singer *cannot* have.

121. Jaeger, "*Epistolae duorum amantium* and the Ascription," 137. For other readings see Dronke, *Women Writers of the Middle Ages*, 96–97; Mews, *Lost Love Letters*, 112; John O. Ward and Neville Chiavaroli, "The Young Heloise and Latin Rhetoric: Some Preliminary Comments on the 'Lost' Love Letters and Their Significance," in Wheeler, *Listening to Heloise*, 93.

122. Dronke, review of *Listening to Heloise*, 137. Even here, seven of the fourteen lines have internal rhyme.

123. "Non facerem tanti thesauros Octauiani / Quam placuisse tibi, sicut habetur ibi." (I would not consider the treasures of Octavian so great as I would to have given you pleasure, as it is said [in your letter].) Marbod of Rennes, "Rescriptum ad amicam" 5–6, in "Liebesbriefgedichte Marbods," 290. As with the *Carmina burana*, the parallel is distant.

124. Piron, *Lettres des deux amants*, 98 n.1.

125. *Rhetorica ad Herennium* 4.25.34, ed. and trans. Harry Caplan, Loeb Classical Library (Cambridge, MA: Harvard University Press, 1954), 314; Quintilian, *Institutio oratoria* 9.3.54; Jean-Yves Tilliette, "Rhétorique et sincerité: La lettre d'amour dans le Moyen Âge latin," in *Charmer, convaincre: La rhétorique dans l'histoire*, ed. Jacques Jouanna, Laurent Pernot, and Michel Zink (Paris: Diffusion de Boccard, 2014), 140–41.

126. Augustine, *De civitate Dei* 22.30, ed. Bernardus Dombart and Alfonsus Kalb, 2 vols., 5th ed. (Stuttgart: Teubner, 1993), 2:635.

127. "Ecce quod concupivi iam video, quod speravi iam teneo; illi sum iuncta in celis quem in terris posita tota devotione dilexi" (PL 17: 819–20). Cf. *Vita S. Agnetis* 2.11: "Ecce iam quod credidi, video; quod speravi, iam teneo; quod concupivi, complector." *Acta Sanctorum*, 1st ed. (Antwerp: Société des Bollandistes, 1643), 21 January, 2:353. These verses are also found among the prayers of St. Anselm.

128. Sarah McNamer, *Affective Meditation and the Invention of Medieval Compassion* (Philadelphia: University of Pennsylvania Press, 2010), 76. See also René Metz, *La consécration des vierges dans l'Église romaine: Étude d'histoire de la liturgie* (Paris: Presses universitaires de France, 1954), 308. The earliest extant rite to include this antiphon for the consecration of virgins is the pontifical of William Durandus (late thirteenth century), though it could have figured earlier in some local uses.

129. Chrysogonus Waddell, "*Epithalamica:* An Easter Sequence by Peter Abelard," *Musical Quarterly* 72 (1986), 251.

130. Mews, *Lost Love Letters*, 171–72; David Wulstan, "*Novi modulaminis melos:* The Music of Heloise and Abelard," *Plainsong and Medieval Music* 11 (2002): 1–23, and "Heloise at Argenteuil and the Paraclete," in *The Poetic and Musical Legacy of Heloise and Abelard*, ed. Marc Stewart and David Wulstan (Ottawa: Institute of Mediaeval Music, 2003), 67–90.

131. Dronke and Orlandi, "New Works by Abelard and Heloise?" 126–29.

132. Dronke, *Women Writers of the Middle Ages*, 94–95, and review of *Listening to Heloise*, 138; Dronke and Orlandi, "New Works by Abelard and Heloise?" 145. Cf. Jean Leclercq, *Monks and Love in Twelfth-Century France: Psycho-Historical Essays* (Oxford: Clarendon, 1979), 80.

133. Von Moos, "Die *Epistolae duorum amantium*," 22 n.71.

134. Piron suggests it could have been a letter of dedication for Abelard's lost commentary on Ezekiel: *Lettres des deux amants*, 99 n.4.

135. Gregor Lieberz, ed., *Ovidius puellarum (De nuncio sagaci)* 2 (Frankfurt: Peter Lang, 1980), 40. Unfortunately, the date of this comedy is uncertain (any time between the late eleventh century and 1159, when John of Salisbury quotes it); otherwise it would give the EDA a firm *terminus post quem*. See Dronke, review of *Listening to Heloise*, 137, and "A Note on *Pamphilus*," *Journal of the Warburg and Courtauld Institutes* 42 (1979), 229; von Moos, "Kurzes Nachwort," 291–92. Lieberz brackets the question.

136. Ritva Johnson, ed., *Tropes du propre de la Messe I: Cycle de Noël* (Stockholm: Almqvist & Wiksell, 1975), 121; Johann Drumbl, *Quem quaeritis: Teatro sacro dell'alto Medioevo* (Rome: Bulzoni, 1981), 277.

137. Waddell, "*Epithalamica:* An Easter Sequence."

138. Gerard Manley Hopkins, "The Candle Indoors," v. 14.

139. Lanham, *Salutatio Formulas*, 102–3; "Principles of Letter-Writing" (*Rationes dictandi*), 12, 20.

140. Walther, *Proverbia sententiaeque*, no. 16903.

141. *Historia calamitatum* 24–27; Heloise, letter 2.10–12. But see comment on no. 79 and note 119 above.

142. Walther, *Proverbia sententiaeque*, no. 9555.

143. Von Moos, "Die *Epistolae duorum amantium*," 26.

144. I cannot agree with Piron, who takes the poem to mean that after Fulbert discovered the affair, he sent Heloise away from Paris for a time and Abelard didn't dare follow her—though nothing is said of this in the *Historia calamitatum*. This letter would then celebrate her return. *Lettres des deux amants*, 10–11.

145. C. Stephen Jaeger, *The Origins of Courtliness: Civilizing Trends and the Formation of Courtly Ideals, 939–1210* (Philadelphia: University of Pennsylvania Press, 1985); see also *The Envy of Angels*.

146. On this passage, which poses some textual difficulties, see comment, Tegernsee letter 3.

Love Letters from Tegernsee

1. The manuscript is newly foliated for the Plechl and Bergmann edition; older citations give page numbers.

2. Peter Dronke adopts an old assertion by C. H. Haskins that letters 1-7 are Italian, but Haskins cites the Tegernsee manuscript and gives no evidence for their putative Italian origin. Dronke, "Women's Love Letters from Tegernsee," in *Medieval Letters: Between Fiction and Document,* ed. Christian Høgel and Elisabetta Bartoli (Turnhout: Brepols, 2015), 227–29; Charles Homer Haskins, "The Life of Mediaeval Students as Illustrated by Their Letters," in *Studies in Mediaeval Culture* (Oxford: Clarendon, 1929), 31. It is hard to see how (or why) the Tegernsee monks would have acquired a collection of Italian women's letters.

3. The love letters are printed as an appendix to the main collection. Facsimiles of the relevant MS pages can be found in the flawed edition of Jürgen Kühnel, *Dû bist mîn, ih bin dîn: Die lateinischen Liebes- (und Freundschafts-) Briefe des clm 19411. Abbildungen, Text und Übersetzung* (Göppingen: Kümmerle, 1977). Letters 1–7 were edited by Peter Dronke, with translations, in *Medieval Latin and the Rise of European Love-Lyric,* 2 vols. (Oxford: Clarendon, 1965–66), 2:472–82. He has a new edition and translation of Letters 8–10 in an article that appeared as this volume was going to press: "Women's Love Letters from Tegernsee," 215–45.

4. Étienne Wolff, trans., *La lettre d'amour au Moyen Âge* (Paris: NiL Éditions, 1996), 93–116.

5. Ernstpeter Ruhe, *De Amasio ad Amasiam: Zur Gattungsgeschichte des mittelalterlichen Liebesbriefes* (Munich: Wilhelm Fink, 1975), 89.

6. Facsimile in Kühnel, *Dû bist mîn, ih bin dîn,* 41. I have expanded all abbreviations.

7. Wolff translates, "je ne refuse pas l'amour, tant qu'il est sans douleur. En effet on ne peut parler d'amour, quand de lui résulte une très grande peine": *La lettre d'amour,* 98. Kühnel reads, "dann weise ich deine Liebe nicht zurück; sofern sie nämlich ohne Schmerz sein mag. [Denn] das kann nicht Liebe heißen, woraus größtes Leid entsteht": *Dû bist mîn, ih bin dîn,* 55.

8. "I do not refuse you the hardship, or the love.—If it exists without pain, it cannot be called love, to which the greatest hardship belongs." Dronke, *Medieval Latin and the Rise of European Love-Lyric,* 2:475.

9. For this term see Judith M. Bennett, "'Lesbian-Like' and the Social History of Lesbianisms," *Journal of the History of Sexuality* 9 (2000): 1–24.

10. I disagree with the translations of Dronke ("most dearly dear, most sweetly sweet one") and Wolff ("si chèrement chérie, si doucement douce"). Dronke, *Medieval Latin and the Rise of European Love-Lyric,* 2:477; Wolff, *La lettre d'amour,* 99.

11. Wolff reads, "Ta douce perle et le couvent de jeunes filles te saluent": *La lettre d'amour,* 101. Kühnel has the same: "Es grüßt dich die köstliche Perle und der Konvent der Fräulein." *Dû bist mîn, ih bin dîn,* 61. Dronke's translation is also untenable: "It is a greeting to you, my precious pearl, and to the cloisters of your companions." *Medieval Latin and the Rise of European Love-Lyric,* 2:477.

12. Dronke, *Medieval Latin and the Rise of European Love-Lyric*, 2:482; see also "Women's Love Letters from Tegernsee," 229.

13. "[E]ine sonst völlig unbekannte Spezies in die Gattungsgeschichte": Ruhe, *De Amasio ad Amasiam*, 388. Dronke notes that several German scholars have "blinded themselves" to the female love relationships revealed in letters 5–7: "Women's Love Letters from Tegernsee," 227.

14. Dieter Schaller, "Zur Textkritik und Beurteilung der sogenannten Tegernseer Liebesbriefe," *Zeitschrift für deutsche Philologie* 101 (1982), 118.

15. Alcuin, *Epistolae* 10 and 193, ed. Ernst Dümmler, MGH Epistolae IV.2 (Berlin: Weidmann, 1895), 36 and 319; Schaller, "Zur Textkritik und Beurteilung," 117.

16. Plechl, in Plechl and Bergmann, *Die Tegernseer Briefsammlung*, 356.

17. *Altercatio Phyllidis et Florae* (*Carmina burana* 92), ed. and trans. P. G. Walsh, *Love Lyrics from the Carmina Burana* (Chapel Hill: University of North Carolina Press, 1993), 101–25; Andreas Capellanus, *On Love* (*De amore*) 1.6, ed. and trans. P. G. Walsh (London: Duckworth, 1982), 182–89; Paul Pascal, ed. and with commentary, *Concilium Romarici Montis (The Council of Remiremont)* (Bryn Mawr, PA: Thomas Library, Bryn Mawr College, 1993), online at http://faculty.georgetown.edu/jod/remiremont.html.

18. Dronke, "Women's Love Letters from Tegernsee," 217.

19. The German lines were first published independently of the letter in Karl Lachmann and Moriz Haupt, eds., *Des Minnesangs Frühling* (Leipzig: Hirzel, 1857), and have remained there in many successive editions.

20. Cf. the model salutations from Bernardinus of Bologna and Bernard de Meung (ca. 1150–1200) in Ruhe, *De Amasio de Amasiam*, 299, 301.

21. "Amicitia, de qua summus philosophus Cicero loquitur in suo libro: 'Amicitia omnes humanas res excellit, dissociata congregat, congregata conseruat et conseruata in melius augmentat.'" Emma Falque Rey, ed., *Historia Compostellana* 3.51, CCCM 70 (Turnhout: Brepols, 1988), 521; Plechl and Bergmann, *Die Tegernseer Briefsammlung*, 362.

22. Ritva Johnson, ed., *Tropes du propre de la Messe I: Cycle de Noël* (Stockholm: Almqvist & Wiksell, 1975), 121; Johann Drumbl, *Quem quaeritis: Teatro sacro dell'alto Medioevo* (Rome: Bulzoni, 1981), 277.

23. Ryszard Ganszyniec, "Zu den Tegernseer Liebesbriefen," *Zeitschrift für deutsches Altertum und deutsche Literatur* 63 (1926): 23–24.

24. Jan M. Ziolkowski, ed., *Obscenity: Social Control and Artistic Creation in the European Middle Ages* (Leiden: Brill, 1998); Larry Scanlon, "Sex and Sexuality," in *The Oxford Handbook of Medieval Latin Literature*, ed. Ralph Hexter and David Townsend (Oxford: Oxford University Press, 2012), 447–64; Thomas Stehling, ed. and trans., *Medieval Latin Poems of Male Love and Friendship* (New York: Garland, 1984).

25. Dronke translates "to her self, herself," which is yet another possibility because the pronouns *sibi se* are not gender-specific. "Women's Love Letters from Tegernsee," 241.

26. "Omnis re vera meretrix est dicta chimera: / Parte leo prima, medio caper, anguis ad ima. / Est leo per fastus, capra sordibus, anguis ob astus." (Every harlot is truly called a chimera: lion in front, goat in the middle, snake in the tail. She is a lion in haughtiness, a she-goat in filth, a snake for her cunning.) Anonymous verse cited in Ganszyniec, "Zu den Tegernseer Liebesbriefen," 24. See also Regensburg Songs, nos. 2 and 4, and Jean-Yves Tilliette, "Hermès

amoureux, ou les métamorphoses de la Chimère: Réflexions sur les *Carmina* 200 et 201 de Baudri de Bourgueil," *Mélanges de l'École Française de Rome* 104 (1992), 153–54.

From the Regensburg Songs

1. *Eupolemius*, ed. and trans. Jan M. Ziolkowski, in Sextus Amarcius, *Satires*, trans. Ronald E. Pepin (Cambridge, MA: Harvard University Press, 2011). This late eleventh-century epic may be by the same poet, an anonymous German monk, who used the pseudonym Sextus Amarcius.

2. On that poem, see C. Stephen Jaeger, *Ennobling Love: In Search of a Lost Sensibility* (Philadelphia: University of Pennsylvania Press, 1999), 102–3 and 225–26 (trans.).

3. Peter Dronke, *Medieval Latin and the Rise of European Love-Lyric*, 2 vols. (Oxford: Clarendon, 1965–66), 2:440.

Bibliography

Abbreviations

CCCM   Corpus christianorum: Continuatio mediaeualis (Turnhout: Brepols, 1966–)
CCSL   Corpus christianorum: Series latina (Turnhout: Brepols, 1953–)
Loeb   Loeb Classical Library (Cambridge, MA: Harvard University Press, 1912–)
MGH   Monumenta Germaniae Historica (1826–)
PL   *Patrologiae latinae: Cursus completus* (Paris: J.-P. Migne, 1841–55) with searchable database by Chadwyck-Healey

Editions

Könsgen, Ewald, ed. *Epistolae duorum amantium: Briefe Abaelards und Heloises?* Leiden: Brill, 1974.

Kühnel, Jürgen, ed. *Dû bist mîn, ih bin dîn: Die lateinischen Liebes- (und Freundschafts-) Briefe des clm 19411. Abbildungen, Text und Übersetzung.* Göppingen: Kümmerle, 1977.

Paravicini, Anke, ed. *Carmina Ratisponensia.* Heidelberg: Carl Winter, 1979.

Plechl, Helmut, and Werner Bergmann, eds. *Die Tegernseer Briefsammlung des 12. Jahrhunderts.* MGH Briefe der deutschen Kaiserzeit 8. Hanover: Hahnsche Buchhandlung, 2002.

Translations

Ballanti, Graziella, trans. *Un epistolario d'amore del XII secolo (Abelardo e Eloisa?).* Rome: Edizioni Anicia, 1988.

Cescutti, Eva, and Philipp Steger, trans. *Und wärst du doch bei mir, Ex epistolis duorum amantium: Eine mittelalterliche Liebesgeschichte in Briefen.* Zurich: Manesse, 2005.

Mews, Constant J. *The Lost Love Letters of Heloise and Abelard: Perceptions of Dialogue in Twelfth-Century France,* with a translation by Neville Chiavaroli and Constant J. Mews. New York: Palgrave, 1999.

Piron, Sylvain, trans. *Lettres des deux amants attribuées à Héloïse et Abélard.* Paris: Gallimard, 2005.

Wolff, Étienne, trans. *La lettre d'amour au Moyen Âge: Textes présentés, traduits du latin et commentés.* Paris: NiL Éditions, 1996.

Other Primary Sources

Abelard, Peter. "Abelard's Letter of Consolation to a Friend (*Historia Calamitatum*)," ed. J. T. Muckle. *Mediaeval Studies* 12 (1950): 163–213.

———. *Carmen ad Astralabium*, ed. and trans. Juanita Feros Ruys. In *The Repentant Abelard: Family, Gender, and Ethics in Peter Abelard's* Carmen ad Astralabium *and* Planctus, by Juanita Feros Ruys, 93–242. New York: Palgrave Macmillan, 2014.

———. *Commentaria in Epistolam Pauli ad Romanos*. In *Petri Abaelardi Opera theologica* I, ed. E. M. Buytaert. CCCM 11. Turnhout: Brepols, 1969.

———. *Dialectica*, ed. L. M. De Rijk, 2nd ed. Assen: Van Gorcum, 1970.

———. *Historia calamitatum*, ed. Jacques Monfrin. Paris: J. Vrin, 1959.

———. *Logica "Ingredientibus."* In *Peter Abaelards philosophische Schriften*, ed. Bernhard Geyer, vol. 1. Münster: Aschendorff, 1919–33.

———. *Planctus*, ed. and trans. Juanita Feros Ruys. In *The Repentant Abelard: Family, Gender, and Ethics in Peter Abelard's* Carmen ad Astralabium *and* Planctus, by Juanita Feros Ruys, 245–94. New York: Palgrave Macmillan, 2014.

———. *Sermones ad virgines Paraclitenses*. PL 178: 379–607.

———. *Sic et Non: A Critical Edition*, ed. Blanche B. Boyer and Richard McKeon. Chicago: University of Chicago Press, 1976–77.

———. *Theologia "Scholarium."* In *Petri Abaelardi Opera theologica* III, ed. E. M. Buytaert and C. J. Mews, 309–549. CCCM 13. Turnhout: Brepols, 1987.

Abelard, Peter, and Heloise. *Abelard and Heloise: The Letters and Other Writings*, trans. William Levitan. Indianapolis: Hackett, 2007.

———. *Abélard et Héloïse: Correspondance*, ed. and trans. Paul Zumthor. Paris: Union Générale d'Éditions, 1979.

———. *The Letter Collection of Peter Abelard and Heloise*, ed. David Luscombe, trans. Betty Radice and rev. David Luscombe. Oxford: Clarendon, 2013.

———. *The Letters of Abelard and Heloise*, trans. Betty Radice, rev. M. T. Clanchy. London: Penguin, 2003.

———. "The Personal Letters Between Abelard and Heloise: Introduction, Authenticity and Text," ed. J. T. Muckle. *Mediaeval Studies* 15 (1953): 47–94.

———. *La Vie et les epistres Pierres Abaelart et Heloys sa fame: Traduction du XIIIe siècle attribuée à Jean de Meun*, ed. Eric Hicks. Paris: Champion, 1991.

Adso of Montier-en-Der. *Vita S. Frodoberti*. PL 137: 601–20.

Aelred of Rievaulx. "De sanctimoniali de Wattun." PL 195: 789–96.

———. *Spiritual Friendship*, trans. Mary Eugenia Laker. Kalamazoo, MI: Cistercian Publications, 1977.

Alberic of Monte Cassino. *Flowers of Rhetoric*, trans. Joseph L. Miller. In *Readings in Medieval Rhetoric*, ed. Joseph L. Miller, Michael H. Prosser, and Thomas W. Benson, 131–61. Bloomington: Indiana University Press, 1973.

Alcuin. *Carmina*, ed. Ernst Dümmler. MGH Poetae latini medii aevi I. Berlin: Weidmann, 1881.

———. *De ratione animae: Elegiacum carmen*. PL 101: 647–48.

———. *Epistolae*, ed. Ernst Dümmler. MGH Epistolae IV.2. Berlin: Weidmann, 1895.

————. *Liber sacramentorum.* PL 101: 445–66.

Ambrose. *De Joseph.* PL 14: 641–72.

————. *De officiis ministrorum.* PL 16: 23–184.

Analecta hymnica Medii Aevii, ed. Clemens Blume and Guido Maria Dreves, 55 vols. Leipzig; repr. New York: Johnson Reprint, 1886–1922.

Andreas Capellanus. *On Love* (*De amore*), ed. and trans. P. G. Walsh. London: Duckworth, 1982.

Angelomus of Luxeuil. *Enarrationes in libros Regum.* PL 115: 243–552.

Anselm of Canterbury. *Cur Deus Homo.* In *Opera omnia,* 6 vols., ed. F. S. Schmitt, 2:37–133. Edinburgh: Thomas Nelson, 1946–61.

————. *The Letters of Saint Anselm of Canterbury,* trans. Walter Fröhlich, 3 vols. Kalamazoo, MI: Cistercian Publications, 1990–94.

Augustine of Hippo. *Confessions,* trans. R. S. Pine-Coffin. London: Penguin, 1961.

————. *Contra Faustum Manichaeum.* PL 42: 207–518.

————. *De civitate Dei,* ed. Bernardus Dombart and Alfonsus Kalb, 2 vols., 5th ed. Stuttgart: Teubner, 1993.

————. *De Trinitate.* PL 42: 819–1098.

————. *Enarrationes in Psalmos.* PL 36: 67–1968.

————. *Epistolae.* PL 33.

————. *In Epistolam Joannis ad Parthos.* PL 35: 1977–2062.

————. *In Joannis evangelium tractatus CXXIV.* PL 35: 1379–1976.

Baudri de Bourgueil. *Poèmes* (*Carmina*), ed. and trans. Jean-Yves Tilliette, 2 vols. Paris: Belles Lettres, 1998–2002.

————. "To Countess Adela," trans. Monika Otter. *Journal of Medieval Latin* 11 (2001): 60–141.

————. *Vita B. Roberti de Arbrissello.* PL 162: 1043–58.

Bede, Venerable. *De natura rerum.* PL 90: 187–278.

Bernard of Clairvaux. *Sancti Bernardi opera,* ed. Jean Leclercq, C. H. Talbot, and H. M. Rochais, 8 vols. Rome: Editiones cistercienses, 1957–77.

Berno of Reichenau. *Epistolae,* ed. Franz Josef Schmale. *Die Briefe des Abtes Bern von Reichenau.* Stuttgart: Kohlhammer, 1961.

Boethius. *Commentarii in librum Aristotelis Peri hermeneias,* ed. Charles Meiser, 2 vols. Leipzig: Teubner, 1877-80.

————. *De institutione arithmetica,* ed. Henry Oosthout and John Schilling. CCSL 94A. Turnhout: Brepols, 1999.

————. *The Theological Tractates* and *The Consolation of Philosophy,* with trans. by H. F. Stewart, E. K. Rand, and S. J. Tester. Loeb, 1978.

Boncompagno da Signa. *Rota Veneris,* ed. Friedrich Baethgen. Rome: Regenberg, 1927.

Boutemy, André, ed. "Recueil poétique du manuscrit Additional British Museum 24199." *Latomus* 2 (1938): 30–52.

Bulst, Walther, ed. *Carmina Leodiensia.* Heidelberg: Carl Winter, 1975.

————. *Die ältere Wormser Briefsammlung.* MGH Briefe der deutschen Kaiserzeit 3. Weimar: Böhlau, 1949.

Capitula regum francorum. MGH Leges, Sectio II. Hanover: Hahn, 1883–97.

Cassian. *Collationes.* PL 49: 477–1328.

Cassiodorus. *Institutiones divinarum et saecularium litterarum*, ed. R. A. B. Mynors, trans. Wolfgang Bürsgens, 2 vols. Freiburg im Breisgau: Herder, 2003.

———. *Variae.* PL 69: 501–880.

Catullus. *Carmina.* In *Catullus, Tibullus, and Pervigilium Veneris*, with trans. by F. W. Cornish, rev. G. P. Goold, 2nd ed. Loeb, 1988.

Cicero. *De inventione, De optimo genere oratorum* and *Topica*, with trans. by H. M. Hubbell. Loeb, 1968.

———. *De officiis*, with trans. by Walter Miller. Loeb, 1968.

———. *De oratore*, with trans. by E. W. Sutton and H. Rackham, 2 vols. Loeb, 1976–77.

———. *De senectute, De amicitia, De divinatione*, with trans. by W. A. Falconer. Loeb, 1964.

———. *Disputationes Tusculanae. Tusculan Disputations*, with trans. by J. E. King. Loeb, 1966.

———. *Epistulae ad familiares. Letters to Friends*, with trans. by D. R. Shackleton Bailey, 3 vols. Loeb, 2001.

Copeland, Rita, and Ineke Sluiter, ed. and trans. *Medieval Grammar and Rhetoric: Language Arts and Literary Theory, AD 300–1475.* Oxford: Oxford University Press, 2009.

De Pyramo. Three pseudo-Ovidian poems. In *Pseudo-Antike Literatur des Mittelalters*, ed. Paul Lehmann, 35–63. Leipzig: Teubner, 1927.

Eco, Umberto. *Baudolino*, trans. William Weaver. London: Secker & Warburg, 2002.

Feiss, Hugh, ed. *On Love: A Selection of Works of Hugh, Adam, Achard, Richard, and Godfrey of St Victor.* Turnhout: Brepols, 2011.

Fulcoius of Beauvais. *De nuptiis Christi et Ecclesiae libri septem*, ed. Sister Mary I. J. Rousseau. Washington, DC: Catholic University of America Press, 1960.

———. "Fvlcoii Belvacensis Epistvlae," ed. Marvin L. Colker. *Traditio* 10 (1954): 191–273.

Fulgentius. *Mythologiarum libri tres.* Library of Latin Texts, series A. Turnhout: Brepols, 2005. Online ed.

Gerald of Wales. *Giraldi Cambrensis Opera*, vol. 1, ed. J. S. Brewer. London: Longman, 1861.

Gregory I, Pope. *Homiliae in evangelia.* PL 76: 1075–1312.

———. *Regula pastoralis.* PL 77: 13–128.

Gregory of Tours. *Historia Francorum.* PL 71: 159–572.

Guibert of Gembloux. *Epistolae*, ed. Albert Derolez, 2 vols. CCCM 66–66a. Turnhout: Brepols, 1988–89.

Guibert of Nogent. *De vita sua, sive Monodiae. Autobiographie*, ed. Edmond-René Labande. Paris: Belles Lettres, 1981.

———. *Tropologiae in prophetas Osee et Amos ac Lamentationes Jeremiae.* PL 156: 337–487.

Guillaume de Lorris and Jean de Meun. *Le roman de la rose*, ed. Daniel Poirion. Paris: Garnier-Flammarion, 1974.

Hilary of Orléans. *Versus et ludi, Epistolae, Ludus Danielis Belouacensis*, ed. Walther Bulst and M. L. Bulst-Thiele. Leiden: Brill, 1989.

Hildebert of Lavardin. *Carmen in libros Regum.* PL 171: 1239-64.

———. *Carmina minora*, ed. A. Brian Scott. Leipzig: Teubner, 1969.

———. *Carmina miscellanea.* PL 171: 1381–1458.

———. *Historia de Mahumete.* PL 171: 1343–66.

Hildefons of Toledo. *De itinere deserti*. PL 96: 171–92.

Hildegard of Bingen. *Epistolarium*, ed. Lieven Van Acker and Monika Klaes-Hachmöller, 3 vols. CCCM 91–91B. Turnhout: Brepols, 1991–2001.

———. *The Letters of Hildegard of Bingen*, trans. Joseph L. Baird and Radd K. Ehrman, 3 vols. New York: Oxford University Press, 1994–2004.

Hill, R. T., and T. G. Bergin, eds. *Anthology of the Provençal Troubadours*, 2 vols., 2nd ed. New Haven, CT: Yale University Press, 1973.

Horace. *Carmina: The Odes of Horace*, with trans. by Len Krisak. Manchester: Carcanet, 2006.

———. *Epodes,* ed. David Mankin. Cambridge: Cambridge University Press, 1995.

———. *Satires, Epistles,* and *Ars poetica*, with trans. by H. Rushton Fairclough. Loeb, 1991.

Hugh of Saint-Victor. *Adnotatiunculae in Threnos Jeremiae*. PL 175: 255–322.

———. *De substantia dilectionis*. In *Six opuscules spirituels*, ed. Roger Baron. Sources chrétiennes 155. Paris: Cerf, 1969.

———. *Soliloquium de arrha animae*. PL 176: 951–70.

Hugh Primas. *The Arundel Lyrics: The Poems of Hugh Primas*, ed. and trans. Christopher J. McDonough. Cambridge, MA: Harvard University Press, 2010.

Isidore of Seville. *Etymologiae*. PL 82: 73–728.

Jerome. *Commentaria in Ezechielem*. PL 25: 15–490.

———. *De nominibus Hebraicis*. PL 23: 771–858.

———. *Lettres* (*Epistulae*), ed. Jérôme Labourt, 8 vols. Paris: Belles Lettres, 1949– .

Johnson, Ritva, ed. *Tropes du propre de la Messe I: Cycle de Noël*. Stockholm: Almqvist & Wiksell, 1975.

Juvenal. *Satires*. In *Juvenal and Persius*, ed. and trans. Susanna Morton Braund. Loeb, 2004.

Klinck, Anne L., ed. and trans. *Anthology of Ancient and Medieval Woman's Song*. New York: Palgrave Macmillan, 2004.

Lachmann, Karl, and Moriz Haupt, eds. *Des Minnesangs Frühling*. Leipzig: Hirzel, 1857.

Lehmann, Paul, ed. *Pseudo-antike Literatur des Mittelalters*. Leipzig: Teubner, 1927.

Lieberz, Gregor, ed. *Ovidius puellarum* (*De nuncio sagaci*). Frankfurt: Peter Lang, 1980.

Lucan. *De bello civili* (*Pharsalia*), with trans. by J. D. Duff. Loeb, 1962.

Marbod of Rennes. *Carmina varia*, series 1 and 2. PL 171: 1647–86 and 1717–36.

———. *De lapidibus*, ed. John M. Riddle. Wiesbaden: Franz Steiner, 1977.

———. *Liber decem capitulorum*, ed. Rosario Leotta. Rome: Herder, 1984.

———. "Liebesbriefgedichte Marbods," ed. Walther Bulst. In *Liber Floridus: Mittellateinische Studien Paul Lehmann zum 65. Geburtstag*, ed. Bernhard Bischoff and Suso Brechter, 287–301. St. Ottilien: Eos Verlag der Erzabtei, 1950.

———. *Vita B. Maurilii*. PL 171: 1635–48.

———. *Vita S. Thaisidis*. PL 171: 1629–34.

Martial. *Epigrams*, ed. and trans. D. R. Shackleton Bailey, 3 vols. Loeb, 1993.

Missale Romanum (*Ordo Missae in cantu*). Solesmes: Abbaye Saint-Pierre, 1975.

Murphy, James J., ed. and trans. *Three Medieval Rhetorical Arts*. Berkeley: University of California Press, 1971.

Nigellus Wireker (Nigel de Longchamps). *Speculum stultorum*, ed. John H. Mozley and Robert R. Raymo. Berkeley: University of California Press, 1960.

Notker Balbulus. *Notker der Dichter und seine geistige Welt*, ed. Wolfram von den Steinen, 2 vols. Bern: Francke, 1948.

d'Orbigny, Robert. *Le conte de Floire et Blanchefleur*, ed. and trans. Jean-Luc Leclanche. Paris: Champion, 2003.

Otloh of St. Emmeram. *De doctrina spirituali*. PL 146: 263–300.

Ovid. *Ars amatoria* and *Remedia amoris*. In *The Art of Love, and Other Poems*, with trans. by J. H. Mozley. Loeb, 1969.

———. *Fasti*, with trans. by Sir James George Frazer, rev. G. P. Goold, 2nd ed. Loeb, 1989.

———. *Heroïdes* and *Amores*, with trans. by Grant Showerman. Loeb, 1971.

———. *Metamorphoses*, with trans. by Frank Justus Miller, 2 vols. Loeb, 1976–77.

———. *Tristia* and *Ex Ponto*, with trans. by Arthur Leslie Wheeler, rev. G. P. Goold, 2nd ed. Loeb, 1988.

Paden, William D., and Frances Freeman Paden, trans. *Troubadour Poems from the South of France*. Cambridge: D. S. Brewer, 2007.

Pascal, Paul, ed. *Concilium Romarici Montis* (*The Council of Remiremont*), with commentary. Bryn Mawr, PA: Thomas Library, Bryn Mawr College, 1993.

Paulinus of Nola. *Poemata*. PL 61: 438–710.

Persius. *Satires*. In *Juvenal and Persius*, ed. and trans. Susanna Morton Braund. Loeb, 2004.

Peter Damian. *Collectanea in Vetus Testamentum*. PL 145: 985–1184.

———. *Epistolae*. PL 144: 205–498.

Peter Lombard. *Commentaria in Psalmos*. PL 191: 35–1296.

Peter the Venerable. *The Letters of Peter the Venerable*, ed. Giles Constable, 2 vols. Cambridge, MA: Harvard University Press, 1967.

Petsch, Robert, ed. *Theophilus: Mittelniederdeutsches Drama in drei Fassungen*. Heidelberg: Carl Winter, 1908.

Plautus. *Persa* (*The Persian*) and *Stichus*. In *Plautus*, ed. and trans. Wolfgang de Melo, 5 vols. Loeb, 2011– .

Prudentius. *Liber Cathemerinon, Apotheosis, Hamartigenia, Psychomachia*, and *Contra orationem Symmachi I*, with trans. by H. J. Thomson. Loeb, 1949.

Quintilian. *Institutio oratoria*, with trans. by H. E. Butler, 4 vols. Loeb, 1961–66.

Rabanus Maurus. *Commentarium in Matthaeum*. PL 107: 727–1156.

———. *Liber de computo*. PL 107: 669–728.

Rey, Emma Falque, ed. *Historia Compostellana*. CCCM 70. Turnhout: Brepols, 1988.

Rhetorica ad Herennium, ed. and trans. Harry Caplan. Loeb, 1954.

"Rhythmus in Odonem Regem," ed. Paul von Winterfeld. MGH Poetae latini 4:1 (Berlin: Weidmann, 1899), 137–38.

Richard of Poitiers. *Chronica*, ed. Georg Waitz. MGH Scriptores 26. Hanover: Hahn, 1882.

Roscelin of Compiègne. "Epistola ad Abaelardum." PL 178: 357–72.

Rupert of Deutz. *De Trinitate et operibus ejus*. PL 167: 199–1827.

Ruricius of Limoges. *Epistolarum libri II*, ed. Bruno Krusch. MGH Auctores antiquissimi 8 (Berlin: Weidmann, 1887), 299–350.

Sallust. *De coniuratione Catilinae*. In *The War with Catiline* and *The War with Jugurtha*, with trans. by J. C. Rolfe and John T. Ramsey. Loeb, 2013.

Schmidt, Paul Gerhard, and Hans Walther. *Proverbia sententiaeque Latinitatis medii et recentioris aevi*, 3 vols. Göttingen: Vandenhoeck & Ruprecht, 1982–86.

Seneca. *Ad Lucilium epistulae morales*, ed. and trans. Richard M. Gummere, 3 vols. Loeb, 1962–67.

Sextus Amarcius. *Satires*, trans. Ronald E. Pepin, with *Eupolemius*, ed. and trans. Jan M. Ziolkowski. Cambridge, MA: Harvard University Press, 2011.

Statius. *Silvae* and *Thebaid*. In *Statius*, ed. and trans. D. R. Shackleton Bailey, 3 vols. Loeb, 2003.

Stehling, Thomas, ed. and trans. *Medieval Latin Poems of Male Love and Friendship*. New York: Garland, 1984.

Strecker, Karl, ed. *Die Tegernseer Briefsammlung*. MGH Epistolae selectae III. Berlin: Weidmann, 1925.

———. *Vita Eligii*. MGH Poetae latini medii aevi IV, 787–806. Hanover: Hahnsche Buchhandlung, 1914.

Symmachus. *Epistolae*. PL 18: 145–406.

Terence. *Andria (The Woman of Andros)*, *Eunuchus (The Eunuch)*, *Heauton Timorumenos (The Self-Tormentor)*, *Hecyra (The Mother-in-Law)*, and *Phormio*. In *Terence*, ed. and trans. John Barsby, 2 vols. Loeb, 2001.

Thiofrid of Echternach. *Flores epytaphii sanctorum*, ed. Michele Camillo Ferrari. CCCM 133. Turnhout: Brepols, 1996.

Trollope, Anthony. *He Knew He Was Right*, ed. Robertson Davies. 1869; London: Trollope Society, 1994.

Venarde, Bruce L., trans. *Robert of Arbrissel: A Medieval Religious Life*. Washington, DC: Catholic University of America Press, 2003.

Virgil. *Aeneid*, *Eclogues*, and *Georgics*. In *Virgil*, with trans. by H. Rushton Fairclough, rev. ed., 2 vols. Loeb, 1999–2000.

Vita S. Agnetis. *Acta Sanctorum*, 21 January, vol. 2. Antwerp: Société des Bollandistes, 1643.

Walahfrid Strabo. *Carmina*, ed. Ernst Dümmler. MGH Poetae latini medii aevi II. Berlin: Weidmann, 1884.

Walsh, P. G., ed. and trans. *Love Lyrics from the Carmina Burana*. Chapel Hill: University of North Carolina Press, 1993.

Walther, Hans. *Proverbia sententiaeque Latinitatis medii aevi*, 9 vols. Göttingen: Vandenhoeck & Ruprecht, 1963–86.

Werner, Jakob, ed. *Beiträge zur Kunde der lateinischen Literatur des Mittelalters aus Handschriften gesammelt*, 2nd ed. Aarau: Sauerländer, 1905.

William of Saint-Thierry. *The Nature and Dignity of Love*, trans. Thomas X. Davis. Kalamazoo, MI: Cistercian Publications, 1981.

"Wissenschaftliche Miscellanea." *Westdeutsche Zeitschrift für Geschichte und Kunst* 1.6 (June 1882): 42–44.

Wright, Thomas, ed. *The Anglo-Latin Satirical Poets and Epigrammatists of the Twelfth Century*, 2 vols. London: Longman, 1872.

Secondary Sources

Aguiriano, Begoña. "Le Coeur dans Chrétien." In *Le "Cuer" au Moyen Âge (Réalité et Séné-fiance)*, 11–25. Aix-en-Provence: Centre Universitaire d'Études et de Recherches Mé-diévales d'Aix, 1991.

Allen, Philip S. *Medieval Latin Lyrics*. Chicago: University of Chicago Press, 1931.

Baldwin, John W. "L'*ars amatoria* au XIIe siècle en France: Ovide, Abélard, André le Chapelain et Pierre le Chantre." In *Le Couple, l'ami et le prochain*, vol. 1 of *Histoire et Société: Mélanges offertes à Georges Duby*, ed. Charles M. de la Roncière, 19–29. Aix-en-Provence: Presses Universitaires de Provence, 1992.

Barrow, Julia, Charles S. F. Burnett, and David Luscombe. "A Checklist of the Manuscripts Containing the Writings of Peter Abelard and Heloise and Other Works Closely Asso-ciated with Abelard and His School." *Revue d'histoire des textes* 14–15 (1984–85): 183–302.

Baswell, Christopher. "Heloise." In *The Cambridge Companion to Medieval Women's Writ-ing*, ed. Carolyn Dinshaw and David Wallace, 161–71. Cambridge: Cambridge Univer-sity Press, 2003.

Beach, Alison I. "Voices from a Distant Land: Fragments of a Twelfth-Century Nuns' Let-ter Collection." *Speculum* 77 (2002): 34–54.

Bedos-Rezak, Brigitte. *When Ego Was Imago: Signs of Identity in the Middle Ages*. Leiden: Brill, 2011.

Bennett, Judith M. "'Lesbian-Like' and the Social History of Lesbianisms." *Journal of the History of Sexuality* 9 (2000): 1–24.

Benton, John F. "Fraud, Fiction and Borrowing in the Correspondence of Abelard and Hel-oise." In *Pierre Abélard—Pierre le Vénérable: Les courants philosophiques, littéraires et artistiques en Occident au milieu du XIIe siècle*, ed. René Louis and Jean Jolivet, 469–506. Paris: Éditions du Centre National de la Recherche Scientifique, 1975.

———. "Philology's Search for Abelard in the *Metamorphosis Goliae*." *Speculum* 50 (1975): 199–217.

———. "A Reconsideration of the Authenticity of the Correspondence of Abelard and Hel-oise." In *Petrus Abaelardus (1079–1142): Person, Werk und Wirkung*, ed. Rudolf Tho-mas, Jean Jolivet, David E. Luscombe, and Lambertus M. de Rijk, 41–52. Trier: Paulinus-Verlag, 1980.

Bond, Gerald A. "Composing Yourself: Ovid's *Heroïdes*, Baudri of Bourgueil and the Prob-lem of Persona." *Mediaevalia* 13 (1987): 83–117.

———. *The Loving Subject: Desire, Eloquence, and Power in Romanesque France*. Philadel-phia: University of Pennsylvania Press, 1995.

Boswell, John. *The Kindness of Strangers: The Abandonment of Children in Western Europe from Late Antiquity to the Renaissance*. New York: Pantheon, 1988.

Boureau, Alain. "The Letter-Writing Norm, a Mediaeval Invention." In Roger Chartier, Alain Boureau, and Cécile Dauphin, *Correspondence: Models of Letter-Writing from the Middle Ages to the Nineteenth Century*, trans. Christopher Woodall, 24–58. Prince-ton, NJ: Princeton University Press, 1997.

Bozzolo, Carla. "L'Humaniste Gontier Col et la traduction française des *Lettres* d'Abélard et Héloïse." *Romania* 95 (1974): 199–215.

Brault, Gerard. "Chrétien de Troyes' *Lancelot*: The Eye and the Heart." *Bulletin bibliographique de la Société internationale arthurienne* 24 (1973): 142–53.

Brundage, James A. *Law, Sex, and Christian Society in Medieval Europe*. Chicago: University of Chicago Press, 1987.

Bulst, Walther. "Studien zu Marbods *Carmina varia* und *Liber decem capitulorum*." *Nachrichten von der Gesellschaft der Wissenschaften zu Göttingen*, n.s. 4 (1939): 173–241.

Calabrese, Michael. "Ovid and the Female Voice in the *De Amore* and the *Letters* of Abelard and Heloise." *Modern Philology* 95 (1997): 1–26.

Camargo, Martin. *Ars dictaminis, ars dictandi*. Turnhout: Brepols, 1991.

———. "Where's the Brief? The *Ars dictaminis* and Reading/Writing Between the Lines." In *The Late Medieval Epistle*, ed. Carol Poster and Richard Utz, 1–18. Evanston, IL: Northwestern University Press, 1996.

Carruthers, Mary. *The Experience of Beauty in the Middle Ages*. Oxford: Oxford University Press, 2013.

Cescutti, Eva. "Lieben auf Lateinisch—Emotion oder rhetorische Codierung? Zu den *Epistolae Duorum Amantium* 24 und 25." In *Funktionsräume, Wahrnehmungsräume, Gefühlsräume: Mittelalterliche Lebensformen zwischen Kloster und Hof*, ed. Christina Lutter, 81–94. Oldenbourg: Böhlau, 2011.

Charrier, Charlotte. *Héloïse dans l'histoire et dans la légende*. Paris: Champion, 1933.

Cherewatuk, Karen, and Ulrike Wiethaus, eds. *Dear Sister: Medieval Women and the Epistolary Genre*. Philadelphia: University of Pennsylvania Press, 1993.

Clanchy, M. T. *Abelard: A Medieval Life*. Oxford: Blackwell, 1997.

Constable, Giles. "Aelred of Rievaulx and the Nun of Watton: An Episode in the Early History of the Gilbertine Order." In *Medieval Women*, ed. Derek Baker, 205–26. Oxford: Blackwell, 1978.

———. "The Authorship of the *Epistolae duorum amantium*: A Reconsideration." In *Voices in Dialogue: Reading Women in the Middle Ages*, ed. Linda Olson and Kathryn Kerby-Fulton, 167–78. Notre Dame, IN: University of Notre Dame Press, 2005.

———. *Letters and Letter Collections*. Turnhout: Brepols, 1976.

———. *"Love and Do What You Will": The Medieval History of an Augustinian Precept*. Kalamazoo, MI: Medieval Institute Publications, 1999.

———. *The Reformation of the Twelfth Century*. Cambridge: Cambridge University Press, 1996.

Cook, Brenda M. "The Birth of Heloise: New Light on an Old Mystery." Paper delivered at the Institute of Historical Research, University of London, September 2000. Online at http://www.pierre-abelard.com/heloisa_fichiers/Heloise.pdf.

Curtius, Ernst Robert. *European Literature and the Latin Middle Ages*, trans. Willard R. Trask. Princeton, NJ: Princeton University Press, 1953.

Dalarun, Jacques. "Nouveaux aperçus sur Abélard, Héloïse et le Paraclet." *Francia* 32 (2005): 19–66.

Delbouille, Maurice. "Un mystérieux ami de Marbode: le 'redoutable poète' Gautier." *Le Moyen Âge* 57 (1951): 205–40.

Descroix, J. *De versu leonino*. Lyon: Audin, 1931.

Dronke, Peter. *Abelard and Heloise in Medieval Testimonies*. Glasgow: University of Glasgow Press, 1976.

———. "Heloise's *Problemata* and *Letters*: Some Questions of Form and Content." In *Petrus Abaelardus (1079–1142): Person, Werk und Wirkung*, ed. Rudolf Thomas, Jean Jolivet, David E. Luscombe, and Lambertus M. de Rijk, 53–73. Trier: Paulinus-Verlag, 1980.

———. *Medieval Latin and the Rise of European Love-Lyric*, 2 vols. Oxford: Clarendon, 1965–66.

———. "A Note on *Pamphilus*." *Journal of the Warburg and Courtauld Institutes* 42 (1979): 225–30.

———. *Poetic Individuality in the Middle Ages: New Departures in Poetry, 1000–1150*. Oxford: Clarendon, 1970.

———. Review of *Listening to Heloise*, ed. Bonnie Wheeler. *International Journal of the Classical Tradition* 8 (2001): 134–39.

———. *Women Writers of the Middle Ages: A Critical Study of Texts from Perpetua († 203) to Marguerite Porete († 1310)*. Cambridge: Cambridge University Press, 1984.

———. "Women's Love Letters from Tegernsee." In *Medieval Letters: Between Fiction and Document*, ed. Christian Høgel and Elisabetta Bartoli, 215–45. Turnhout: Brepols, 2015.

Dronke, Peter, and Giovanni Orlandi. "New Works by Abelard and Heloise?" *Filologia mediolatina: Studies in Medieval Latin Texts and Their Transmission* 12 (2005): 123–77.

Drumbl, Johann. *Quem quaeritis: Teatro sacro dell'alto Medioevo*. Rome: Bulzoni, 1981.

Duby, Georges. *Dames du XIIe siècle*, vol. 1: *Héloïse, Aliénor, Iseut et quelques autres*. Paris: Gallimard, 1995.

Duggan, Joseph. *The Romances of Chrétien de Troyes*. New Haven, CT: Yale University Press, 2001.

Eder, Christine Elisabeth. *Die Schule des Klosters Tegernsee im frühen Mittelalter im Spiegel der Tegernseer Handschriften*. Munich: Arbeo-Gesellschaft, 1972.

Ehrenthal, Ludwig. *Studien zu den Liedern der Vaganten*. Bromberg: n.p., 1891.

Ferrante, Joan M. *To the Glory of Her Sex: Women's Roles in the Composition of Medieval Texts*. Bloomington: Indiana University Press, 1997.

Forrai, Réka, and Sylvain Piron. "The Debate on the *Epistolae duorum amantium*: Current *status quaestionis* and Further Research." 9 March 2007. Online at http://www.tdtc.unisi.it/digimed/files/Piron-status%20quaestionis.pdf.

Fraioli, Deborah. "The Importance of Satire in Jerome's *Adversus Jovinianum* as an Argument Against the Authenticity of the *Historia calamitatum*." In *Fälschungen im Mittelalter*, Part 5: *Fingierte Briefe, Frömmigkeit und Fälschung, Realienfälschungen*, MGH Scriptores 33, 167–200. Hanover: Hahnsche Buchhandlung, 1988.

Fredborg, Karin Margareta. "Abelard on Rhetoric." In *Rhetoric and Renewal in the Latin West, 1100–1540: Essays in Honour of John O. Ward*, ed. Constant J. Mews, Cary J. Nederman, and Rodney M. Thomson, 55–80. Turnhout: Brepols, 2003.

Fulton, Rachel. *From Judgment to Passion: Devotion to Christ and the Virgin Mary, 800–1200*. New York: Columbia University Press, 2002.

Ganszyniec, Ryszard. "Zu den Tegernseer Liebesbriefen." *Zeitschrift für deutsches Altertum und deutsche Literatur* 63 (1926): 23–24.

Garrison, Mary. "'Send More Socks': On Mentality and the Preservation Context of Medieval Letters." In *New Approaches to Medieval Communication*, ed. Marco Mostert, 69–99. Turnhout: Brepols, 1999.

Grondeux, Anne. "Guillaume de Champeaux, Joscelin de Soissons, Abélard et Gosvin d'Anchin: Étude d'un milieu intellectuel." In *Arts du langage et théologie aux confins des XIe–XIIe siècles: Textes, maîtres, débats*, ed. Irène Rosier-Catach, 3–43. Turnhout: Brepols, 2011.

Haskins, Charles Homer. "The Life of Mediaeval Students as Illustrated by Their Letters." In *Studies in Mediaeval Culture*, 1–35. Oxford: Clarendon, 1929.

Hexter, Ralph J. *Ovid and Medieval Schooling: Studies in Medieval School Commentaries on Ovid's* Ars Amatoria, Epistulae ex Ponto, *and* Epistulae Heroidum. Munich: Arbeo-Gesellschaft, 1986.

Hollis, Stephanie. "Wilton as a Centre of Learning." In *Writing the Wilton Women: Goscelin's* Legend of Edith *and* Liber confortatorius, ed. Stephanie Hollis, 307–38. Turnhout: Brepols, 2004.

Jaeger, C. Stephen. *Ennobling Love: In Search of a Lost Sensibility.* Philadelphia: University of Pennsylvania Press, 1999.

———. *The Envy of Angels: Cathedral Schools and Social Ideals in Medieval Europe, 950–1200.* Philadelphia: University of Pennsylvania Press, 1994.

———. "The *Epistolae duorum amantium*, Abelard and Heloise: An Annotated Concordance." *Journal of Medieval Latin* 24 (2014): 185–224.

———. "*Epistolae duorum amantium* and the Ascription to Heloise and Abelard." In *Voices in Dialogue: Reading Women in the Middle Ages*, ed. Linda Olson and Kathryn Kerby-Fulton, 125–66. Notre Dame, IN: University of Notre Dame Press, 2005.

———. "Friendship of Mutual Perfecting in Augustine's *Confessions* and the Failure of Classical *amicitia*." In *Friendship in the Middle Ages and Early Modern Age: Explorations of a Fundamental Ethical Discourse*, ed. Albrecht Classen and Marilyn Sandidge, 185–200. Berlin: De Gruyter, 2010.

———. *The Origins of Courtliness: Civilizing Trends and the Formation of Courtly Ideals, 939–1210.* Philadelphia: University of Pennsylvania Press, 1985.

———. "Pessimism in the Twelfth-Century 'Renaissance.'" *Speculum* 78 (2003): 1151–83.

———. "A Reply to Giles Constable." In *Voices in Dialogue: Reading Women in the Middle Ages*, ed. Linda Olson and Kathryn Kerby-Fulton, 179–86. Notre Dame, IN: University of Notre Dame Press, 2005.

Janson, Tore. *Prose Rhythm in Medieval Latin from the Ninth to the Thirteenth Century.* Stockholm: Almqvist & Wiksell, 1975.

———. "Schools of Cursus in the Twelfth Century and the Letters of Heloise and Abelard." In *Retorica e poetica tra i secoli XII e XIV*, ed. Claudio Leonardi and Enrico Menestò, 171–200. Perugia: Regione dell'Umbria, 1988.

Julian, John. *A Dictionary of Hymnology, Setting Forth the Origin and History of Christian Hymns of All Ages and Nations.* New York: Scribner, 1892.

Kamuf, Peggy. *Fictions of Feminine Desire: Disclosures of Heloise*. Lincoln: University of Nebraska Press, 1982.

Kaufmann, Linda S. *Discourses of Desire: Gender, Genre, and Epistolary Fictions*. Ithaca, NY: Cornell University Press, 1986.

Kelly, Douglas. "The Medieval Art of Poetry and Prose: The Scope of Instruction and the Uses of Models." In *Medieval Rhetoric: A Casebook*, ed. Scott D. Troyan, 1–24. New York: Routledge, 2004.

Klinkenborg, Verlyn. *Several Short Sentences About Writing*. New York: Random House, 2012.

Kong, Katherine. *Lettering the Self in Medieval and Early Modern France*. Cambridge: D. S. Brewer, 2010.

Könsgen, Ewald. "'Der Nordstern scheint auf den Pol': Baudolinos Liebesbriefe an Beatrix, die Kaiserin—oder *Ex epistolis duorum amantium*." In *Nova de veteribus: Mittel- und neulateinische Studien für Paul Gerhard Schmidt*, ed. Andreas Bihrer and Elisabeth Stein, 1113–21. Munich: K. G. Saur, 2004.

Kraebel, A. B. "Commentary and Poetry in the Medieval School of Reims, *c.* 883–1100." In *Encountering Scripture in Overlapping Cultures: Judaism, Christianity, and Islam*, ed. Mordechai Cohen and Adele Berlin. Cambridge: Cambridge University Press, forthcoming.

———. "Prophecy and Poetry in the Psalms-Commentaries of St. Bruno and the Pre-scholastics." *Sacris Erudiri* 50 (2011): 413–59.

Kraus, Manfred. "*Progymnasmata* and Progymnasmatic Exercises in the Medieval Classroom." In *The Classics in the Medieval and Renaissance Classroom: The Role of Ancient Texts in the Arts Curriculum as Revealed by Surviving Manuscripts and Early Printed Books*, ed. Juanita Feros Ruys, John O. Ward, and Melanie Heyworth, 175–97. Turnhout: Brepols, 2013.

LaCugna, Catherine Mowry. *God for Us: The Trinity and Christian Life*. New York: HarperCollins, 1991.

Lanham, Carol Dana. "Freshman Composition in the Early Middle Ages: Epistolography and Rhetoric Before the *Ars Dictaminis*." *Viator* 23 (1992): 115–34.

———. *Salutatio Formulas in Latin Letters to 1200: Syntax, Style, and Theory*. Munich: Arbeo-Gesellschaft, 1975.

Leclercq, Jean. *Monks and Love in Twelfth-Century France: Psycho-Historical Essays*. Oxford: Clarendon, 1979.

Lewis, C. S. *The Allegory of Love: A Study in Medieval Tradition*. London: Oxford University Press, 1936.

Lipking, Lawrence. *Abandoned Women and Poetic Tradition*. Chicago: University of Chicago Press, 1988.

Livingston, Sally. "'Consider, I Beg You, What You Owe Me': Heloise and the Economics of Relationship." In *Women and Wealth in Late Medieval Europe*, ed. Theresa Earenfight, 51–65. New York: Palgrave Macmillan, 2010.

Luscombe, David E. "Excerpts from the Letter Collection of Heloise and Abelard in Notre Dame (Indiana) MS 30." In *Pascua Mediaevalia: Studies voor Prof. Dr. J. M. De Smet*, ed. R. Lievens, E. Van Mingroot, and W. Verbeke, 529–44. Leuven: Universitaire Pers Leuven, 1983.

———. "From Paris to the Paraclete: The Correspondence of Abelard and Heloise." *Proceedings of the British Academy* 74 (1988): 247–83.

———. "The Letters of Heloise and Abelard Since 'Cluny 1972.'" In *Petrus Abaelardus (1079–1142): Person, Werk und Wirkung*, ed. Rudolf Thomas, Jean Jolivet, David E. Luscombe, and Lambertus M. de Rijk, 23–31. Trier: Paulinus-Verlag, 1980.

———. "Peter Abelard and the Poets." In *Poetry and Philosophy in the Middle Ages: A Festschrift for Peter Dronke*, ed. John Marenbon, 155–71. Leiden: Brill, 2001.

Makowski, Elizabeth M. "The Conjugal Debt and Medieval Canon Law." *Journal of Medieval History* 3 (1977): 99–114.

Marenbon, John. "Authenticity Revisited." In *Listening to Heloise: The Voice of a Twelfth-Century Woman*, ed. Bonnie Wheeler, 19–33. New York: St. Martin's Press, 2000.

———. "Lost Love Letters? A Controversy in Retrospect." *International Journal of the Classical Tradition* 15 (2008): 267–80.

Martin, Janet. "Classicism and Style in Latin Literature." In *Renaissance and Renewal in the Twelfth Century*, ed. Robert L. Benson and Giles Constable, 537–68. Cambridge, MA: Harvard University Press, 1982.

Matter, E. Ann. *The Voice of My Beloved: The Song of Songs in Western Medieval Christianity.* Philadelphia: University of Pennsylvania Press, 1990.

McGuire, Brian Patrick. *Friendship and Community: The Monastic Experience, 350–1250*, 2nd ed. Ithaca, NY: Cornell University Press, 2010.

McLaughlin, Mary Martin. "Abelard as Autobiographer: The Motives and Meanings of His 'Story of Calamities.'" *Speculum* 42 (1967): 463–88.

McNamer, Sarah. *Affective Meditation and the Invention of Medieval Compassion.* Philadelphia: University of Pennsylvania Press, 2010.

Metz, René. *La consécration des vierges dans l'Église romaine: Étude d'histoire de la liturgie.* Paris: Presses Universitaires de France, 1954.

Mews, Constant J. *Abelard and Heloise.* Oxford: Oxford University Press, 2005.

———. "Abelard, Heloise, and Discussion of Love in the Twelfth-Century Schools." In *Rethinking Abelard: A Collection of Critical Essays*, ed. Babette S. Hellemans, 11–36. Leiden: Brill, 2014.

———. "Bernard of Clairvaux, Peter Abelard and Heloise on the Definition of Love." *Revista Portuguesa de Filosofia* 60 (2004): 633–60.

———. "Between Authenticity and Interpretation: On *The Letter Collection of Peter Abelard and Heloise* and the *Epistolae duorum amantium*." *Tijdschrift voor Filosofie* 76 (2014): 823–42.

———. "La bibliothèque du Paraclet du XIIIe siècle à la Révolution." *Studia Monastica* 27 (1985): 31–67.

———. "Cicero and the Boundaries of Friendship in the Twelfth Century." *Viator* 38 (2007): 369–84.

———. "Discussing Love: The *Epistolae duorum amantium* and Abelard's *Sic et Non*." *Journal of Medieval Latin* 19 (2009): 130–47.

———. "Heloise, the Paraclete Liturgy, and Mary Magdalene." In *The Poetic and Musical Legacy of Heloise and Abelard*, ed. Marc Stewart and David Wulstan, 100–112. Ottawa: Institute of Mediaeval Music, 2003.

———. "Hugh Metel, Heloise, and Peter Abelard: The Letters of an Augustinian Canon and the Challenge of Innovation in Twelfth-Century Lorraine." *Viator* 32 (2001): 59–91.

———. "Negotiating the Boundaries of Gender in Religious Life: Robert of Arbrissel and Hersende, Abelard and Heloise." *Viator* 37 (2006): 113–48.

———. "Philosophical Themes in the *Epistolae duorum amantium:* The First Letters of Heloise and Abelard." In *Listening to Heloise: The Voice of a Twelfth-Century Woman*, ed. Bonnie Wheeler, 35–52. New York: St. Martin's Press, 2000.

———. "Religious Thinker: 'A Frail Human Being' on Fiery Life." In *Voice of the Living Light: Hildegard of Bingen and Her World*, ed. Barbara Newman, 52–69. Berkeley: University of California Press, 1998.

———. "William of Champeaux, the Foundation of Saint-Victor (Easter, 1111), and the Evolution of Abelard's Early Career." In *Arts du langage et théologie aux confins des XIe-XIIe siècles: Textes, maîtres, débats*, ed. Irène Rosier-Catach, 83–104. Turnhout: Brepols, 2011.

Mohrmann, Christine. *Études sur le latin des chrétiens*, 3 vols. Rome: Edizioni di storia e letteratura, 1961–65.

Morrison, Karl F. *"I Am You": The Hermeneutics of Empathy in Western Literature, Theology, and Art*. Princeton, NJ: Princeton University Press, 1988.

Moser, Thomas C., Jr. *A Cosmos of Desire: The Medieval Latin Erotic Lyric in English Manuscripts*. Ann Arbor: University of Michigan Press, 2004.

Newman, Barbara. "Authority, Authenticity, and the Repression of Heloise." *Journal of Medieval and Renaissance Studies* 22 (1992): 121–57.

———. *From Virile Woman to WomanChrist: Studies in Medieval Religion and Literature*. Philadelphia: University of Pennsylvania Press, 1995.

———. *God and the Goddesses: Vision, Poetry, and Belief in the Middle Ages*. Philadelphia: University of Pennsylvania Press, 2003.

———. "Indwelling: A Meditation on Empathy, Pregnancy, and the Virgin Mary." In *Studies on Medieval Empathies*, ed. Karl F. Morrison and Rudolph M. Bell, 189–212. Turnhout: Brepols, 2013.

———. "Liminalities: Literate Women in the Long Twelfth Century." In *European Transformations: The Long Twelfth Century*, ed. Thomas F. X. Noble and John Van Engen, 354–402. Notre Dame, IN: University of Notre Dame Press, 2012.

———. *Medieval Crossover: Reading the Secular Against the Sacred*. Notre Dame, IN: University of Notre Dame Press, 2013.

Newman, Jonathan M. "Dictators of Venus: Clerical Love Letters and Female Subjection in *Troilus and Criseyde* and the *Rota Veneris*." *Studies in the Age of Chaucer* 36 (2014): 103–38.

Norberg, Dag. *An Introduction to the Study of Medieval Latin Versification*, trans. Grant C. Roti and Jacqueline de La Chapelle Skubly, ed. Jan Ziolkowski. Washington, DC: Catholic University of America Press, 2004.

Ohly, Friedrich. "*Cor amantis non angustum*: Vom Wohnen im Herzen." In *Schriften zur mittelalterlichen Bedeutungsforschung*, 128–55. Darmstadt: Wissenschaftliche Buchgesellschaft, 1977.

———. "Du bist mein, ich bin dein—du in mir, ich in dir—ich du, du ich." In *Kritische Bewahrung: Beiträge zur deutschen Philologie; Festschrift für Werner Schröder*, ed. Ernst-Joachim Schmidt, 371–415. Berlin: E. Schmidt, 1974.

Olsen, Birger Munk. *L'étude des auteurs classiques latins aux XIe et XIIe siècles*, 3 vols. Paris: Éditions du Centre National de la Recherche Scientifique, 1982–87.

Orlandi, Giovanni. "Considerazioni sulla trasmissione del testo." In *Epistolario di Abelardo ed Eloisa*, ed. Ileana Pagani, 55–66. Turin: Unione Tipografico-Editrice Torinese, 2004.

Piron, Sylvain. "La 'collection' des lettres d'Abélard et Héloïse." Review of *The Letter Collection of Peter Abelard and Heloise*, ed. David Luscombe. *Cahiers de civilisation médiévale* 57 (2014): 337–42.

———. "Héloïse et Abélard: L'éthique amoureuse des *Epistolae duorum amantium*." In *Histoires de l'amour, fragilités et interdits, du Kâmasûtra à nos jours*, ed. Jocelyne Dakhlia, Arlette Farge, Christiane Klapisch-Zuber, and Alessandro Stella, 71–94. Paris: Bayard, 2011.

———. "Heloise's Literary Self-fashioning and the *Epistolae duorum amantium*." In *Strategies of Remembrance: From Pindar to Hölderlin*, ed. Lucie Doležalová, 103–62. Newcastle upon Tyne: Cambridge Scholars, 2009.

Polheim, Karl. *Die lateinische Reimprosa*. Berlin: Weidmann, 1925.

Powell, Morgan. "Listening to Heloise at the Paraclete: Of Scholarly Diversion and a Woman's 'Conversion.'" In *Listening to Heloise: The Voice of a Twelfth-Century Woman*, ed. Bonnie Wheeler, 255–86. New York: St. Martin's Press, 2000.

Raby, F. J. E. *A History of Secular Latin Poetry in the Middle Ages*, 2 vols., 2nd ed. Oxford: Clarendon, 1957.

Richardson, Malcolm. "The *Ars dictaminis*, the Formulary, and Medieval Epistolary Practice." In *Letter-Writing Manuals and Instruction from Antiquity to the Present: Historical and Bibliographic Studies*, ed. Carol Poster and Linda C. Mitchell, 52–66. Columbia: University of South Carolina Press, 2007.

Robertson, D. W., Jr. *Abelard and Heloise*. New York: Dial Press, 1972.

Robl, Werner. *Heloisas Herkunft: Hersindis Mater*. Munich: Olzog, 2001.

Rosenwein, Barbara H. *Emotional Communities in the Early Middle Ages*. Ithaca, NY: Cornell University Press, 2006.

Rouse, Richard H., and Mary A. Rouse. "Wax Tablets." *Language and Communication* 9 (1989): 175–91.

Ruhe, Ernstpeter. *De Amasio ad Amasiam: Zur Gattungsgeschichte des mittelalterlichen Liebesbriefes*. Munich: Wilhelm Fink, 1975.

Ruys, Juanita Feros. "*Eloquencie vultum depingere*: Eloquence and *Dictamen* in the Love Letters of Heloise and Abelard." In *Rhetoric and Renewal in the Latin West, 1100–1540: Essays in Honour of John O. Ward*, ed. Constant J. Mews, Cary J. Nederman, and Rodney M. Thomson, 99–112. Turnhout: Brepols, 2003.

———. "Hearing Mediaeval Voices: Heloise and *Carmina Burana* 126." In *The Poetic and Musical Legacy of Heloise and Abelard*, ed. Marc Stewart and David Wulstan, 91–99. Ottawa: Institute of Mediaeval Music, 2003.

———. *The Repentant Abelard: Family, Gender, and Ethics in Peter Abelard's* Carmen ad Astralabium *and* Planctus. New York: Palgrave Macmillan, 2014.

Salih, Sarah. *Versions of Virginity in Late Medieval England.* Cambridge: D. S. Brewer, 2001.

Scanlon, Larry. "Sex and Sexuality." In *The Oxford Handbook of Medieval Latin Literature*, ed. Ralph Hexter and David Townsend, 447–64. Oxford: Oxford University Press, 2012.

Schaller, Dieter. "Probleme der Überlieferung und Verfasserschaft lateinischer Liebesbriefe des hohen Mittelalters." *Mittellateinisches Jahrbuch* 3 (1966): 25–36.

———. "Zur Textkritik und Beurteilung der sogenannten Tegernseer Liebesbriefe." *Zeitschrift für deutsche Philologie* 101 (1982): 104–21.

Schiendorfer, Max. *Mine Sinne di sint Minne: Zürcher Liebesbriefe aus der Zeit des Minnesangs.* Zollikon: Kranich-Verlag, 1988.

Schmeidler, Bernhard. "Bemerkungen zum Corpus der Briefe der hl. Hildegard von Bingen." In *Corona Quernea: Festgabe Karl Strecker*, 335–66. Leipzig: Hiersemann, 1941.

———. "Der Briefwechsel zwischen Abälard und Heloise als eine literarische Fiktion Abälards." *Zeitschrift für Kirchengeschichte* 54 (1935): 323–38.

Schnell, Rüdiger. *Causa amoris: Liebeskonzeption und Liebesdarstellung in der mittelalterlichen Literatur.* Bern: Francke, 1985.

Schumann, Otto. "Baudri von Bourgueil als Dichter." In *Studien zur lateinischen Dichtung des Mittelalters: Ehrengabe für Karl Strecker*, ed. Walter Stach and Hans Walther, 158–70. Dresden: Wilhelm und Bertha von Baensch Stiftung, 1931.

Shahar, Shulamith. *Childhood in the Middle Ages.* London: Routledge, 1990.

Signori, Gabriela. "Muriel and the Others . . . or Poems as Pledges of Friendship." In *Friendship in Medieval Europe*, ed. Julian Haseldine, 199–212. Stroud: Sutton, 1999.

Silvestre, Hubert. "Die Liebesgeschichte zwischen Abaelard und Heloise: Der Anteil des Romans." In *Fälschungen im Mittelalter*, Part 5: *Fingierte Briefe, Frömmigkeit und Fälschung, Realienfälschungen*, MGH Scriptores 33, 121–65. Hanover: Hahnsche Buchhandlung, 1988.

———. "Réflexions sur la thèse de J. F. Benton relative au dossier 'Abélard-Héloïse.'" *Recherches de théologie ancienne et médiévale* 44 (1977): 211–16.

Smith, Julie Ann. "*Debitum obedientie*: Heloise and Abelard on Governance at the Paraclete." *Parergon* 25 (2008): 1–23.

Stella, Francesco. "Analisi informatiche dei lessico e individuazione degli autori nelle *Epistolae duorum amantium* (XII secolo)." In *Latin vulgaire—latin tardif VIII: Actes du VIIIe colloque international sur le latin vulgaire et tardif*, ed. Roger Wright, 560–69. Hildesheim: Olms-Weidmann, 2008.

———. "*Epistolae duorum amantium*: Nuovi paralleli testuali per gli inserti poetici." *Journal of Medieval Latin* 18 (2008): 374–97.

Stevenson, Jane. "Anglo-Latin Women Poets." In *Latin Learning and English Lore: Studies in Anglo-Saxon Literature for Michael Lapidge*, ed. Katherine O'Brien O'Keeffe and Andy Orchard, 2 vols., 2:86–107. Toronto: University of Toronto Press, 2005.

———. *Women Latin Poets: Language, Gender, and Authority from Antiquity to the Eighteenth Century*. Oxford: Oxford University Press, 2005.

Strecker, Karl. *Introduction to Medieval Latin*, rev. and trans. Robert B. Palmer, 3rd ed. Zurich: Weidmann, 1965.

Sutherland, Fraser. "Why Making Love Isn't What It Used to Be." In *Challenging Change: Literary and Linguistic Responses*, ed. Vesna Lopičić and Biljana Mišić Ilić, 15–21. Newcastle upon Tyne: Cambridge Scholars, 2012.

Sweet, Victoria. *Rooted in the Earth, Rooted in the Sky: Hildegard of Bingen and Premodern Medicine*. New York: Routledge, 2006.

Tilliette, Jean-Yves. "Hermès amoureux, ou les métamorphoses de la Chimère: Réflexions sur les *Carmina* 200 et 201 de Baudri de Bourgueil." *Mélanges de l'École Française de Rome* 104 (1992): 121–61.

———. "Note sur le manuscrit des poèmes de Baudri de Bourgueil (Vatican, Reg. lat. 1351)." *Scriptorium* 37 (1983): 241–45.

———. "Rhétorique et sincerité: La lettre d'amour dans le Moyen Âge latin." In *Charmer, convaincre: La rhétorique dans l'histoire*, ed. Jacques Jouanna, Laurent Pernot, and Michel Zink, 129–48. Paris: Diffusion de Boccard, 2014.

Traube, Ludwig. *Vorlesungen und Abhandlungen*, vol. 2, *Einleitung in die lateinische Philologie des Mittelalters*. Munich: Beck, 1911.

Tunberg, Terence O. "Prose Styles and *Cursus*." In *Medieval Latin: An Introduction and Bibliographical Guide*, ed. F. A. C. Mantello and A. G. Rigg, 111–21. Washington, DC: Catholic University of America Press, 1996.

Turcan-Verkerk, Anne-Marie. "Langue et littérature latines du Moyen Âge." *Annuaire de l'École pratique des Hautes Études, Section des sciences historiques et philologiques* 141 (2011): 128–47.

Van Engen, John. "Letters, Schools, and Written Culture in the Eleventh and Twelfth Centuries." In *Dialektik und Rhetorik im früheren und hohen Mittelalter*, ed. Johannes Fried, 97–132. Munich: Oldenbourg, 1997.

Vaughn, Sally N. *St Anselm and the Handmaidens of God: A Study of Anselm's Correspondence with Women*. Turnhout: Brepols, 2002.

Von Moos, Peter. "Abaelard, Heloise und ihr Paraklet: Ein Kloster nach Mass, zugleich eine Streitschrift gegen die ewige Wiederkehr hermeneutischer Naivität." In *Das Eigene und das Ganze: Zum Individuellen im mittelalterlichen Religiösentum*, ed. Gert Melville and Markus Schürer, 563–619. Münster: Lit, 2002.

———. "Die *Epistolae duorum amantium* und die *säkulare Religion der Liebe*: Methodenkritische Vorüberlegungen zu einem einmaligen Werk mittellateinischer Briefliteratur." *Studi Medievali* 44 (2003): 1–115.

———. "Kurzes Nachwort zu einer langen Geschichte mit missbrauchten Liebesbriefen: *Epistolae duorum amantium*." In *Abaelard und Heloise: Gesammelte Studien zum Mittelalter*, vol. 1, ed. Gert Melville, 282–92. Münster: Lit, 2005.

———. *Mittelalterforschung und Ideologiekritik: Der Gelehrtenstreit um Héloise*. Munich: Wilhelm Fink, 1974.

———. "Le silence d'Héloïse et les idéologies modernes." In *Pierre Abélard—Pierre le Vénérable: Les courants philosophiques, littéraires et artistiques en Occident au milieu du XIIe siècle*, ed. René Louis and Jean Jolivet, 425–68. Paris: Éditions du Centre National de la Recherche Scientifique, 1975.

———. "Vom Nutzen der Philologie für den Umgang mit anonymen Liebesbriefen. Ein Nachwort zu den *Epistolae duorum amantium*." In *Schrift und Liebe in der Kultur des Mittelalters*, ed. Mireille Schnyder, 23–47. Berlin: Walter De Gruyter, 2008.

Waddell, Chrysogonus. "*Epithalamica*: An Easter Sequence by Peter Abelard." *Musical Quarterly* 72 (1986): 239–71.

Walther, Hans. "*Quot-tot*: Mittelalterliche Liebesgrüße und Verwandtes." *Zeitschrift für deutsches Altertum und deutsche Literatur* 65 (1928): 257–89.

Ward, John O. "Women and Latin Rhetoric from Hrotsvit to Hildegard." In *The Changing Tradition: Women in the History of Rhetoric*, ed. Christine M. Sutherland and Rebecca Sutcliffe, 121–32. Calgary: University of Calgary Press, 1999.

Ward, John O., and Neville Chiavaroli. "The Young Heloise and Latin Rhetoric: Some Preliminary Comments on the 'Lost' Love Letters and Their Significance." In *Listening to Heloise: The Voice of a Twelfth-Century Woman*, ed. Bonnie Wheeler, 53–119. New York: St. Martin's Press, 2000.

Watson, Nicholas. "Desire for the Past / Afterword." In *Maistresse of My Wit: Medieval Women, Modern Scholars*, ed. Louse D'Arcens and Juanita Feros Ruys, 149–88. Turnhout: Brepols, 2004.

Woods, Marjorie Curry. "Rape and the Pedagogical Rhetoric of Sexual Violence." In *Criticism and Dissent in the Middle Ages*, ed. Rita Copeland, 56–86. Cambridge: Cambridge University Press, 1996.

———. "Weeping for Dido: Epilogue on a Premodern Rhetorical Exercise in the Postmodern Classroom." In *Latin Grammar and Rhetoric: From Classical Theory to Medieval Practice*, ed. Carol Dana Lanham, 284–94. London: Continuum, 2002.

Wright, Constance S. "'Vehementer amo': The Amorous Verse Epistles of Baudry of Bourgueil and Constance of Angers." In *The Influence of the Classical World on Medieval Literature, Architecture, Music and Culture*, ed. Fidel Fajardo-Acosta, 154–66. Lewiston, NY: Edwin Mellen, 1992.

Wulstan, David. "Heloise at Argenteuil and the Paraclete." In *The Poetic and Musical Legacy of Heloise and Abelard*, ed. Marc Stewart and David Wulstan, 67–90. Ottawa: Institute of Mediaeval Music, 2003.

———. "*Novi modulaminis melos*: The Music of Heloise and Abelard." *Plainsong and Medieval Music* 11 (2002): 1–23.

Ziolkowski, Jan M. "Lost and Not Yet Found: Heloise, Abelard, and the *Epistolae duorum amantium*." *Journal of Medieval Latin* 14 (2004): 171–202.

———, ed. *Obscenity: Social Control and Artistic Creation in the European Middle Ages*. Leiden: Brill, 1998.

General Index

Abelard, Peter, character of, 61, 113, 144, 164–65, 185; definition of love, 117–18, 327 n.51; devotion to Paraclete, 151; epitaphs of, 155, 298; love affair of, 23, 59–60, 67, 83, 106, 110, 144, 161, 191, 198, 225, 318 n.73, 334 n.144; manuscripts of, 54–56, 101, 330 n.91; poetic style of, 65; prose style of, 68–69, 314 n.8; seal of, 132–33; students of, 5, 44, 55, 107, 315 n.24; teaching career of, 116–17, 147, 169–70, 286
—works of: biblical commentaries, 136, 185; Boethius commentary, 49; *Carmen ad Astralabium*, 64, 68, 98–99, 320 n.110; *Dialectica*, 67, 155–56; *Epithalamica*, 197, 199; "Hebet sidus," 94, 105–6, 332 n.110; *Historia calamitatum*, xiii, 49, 52, 54–60, et passim; *Hymnarius Paraclitensis*, 65; letters to Heloise, 4, 22, 52–55, 67, 164, 320 n.105; list of, 297; lost songs, 65, 297; *Planctus*, 64, 125; *Problemata Heloissae*, 176; rule for the Paraclete, 54, 176; sermons, 320 n.108; *Sic et non*, 121, 136, 176; *Theologia "scholarium,"* 102, 117
Absalom, 124–25, 328 n.57
Adalbertus Samaritanus, 229, 324 n.23
Adam of Petit-Pont, 315 n.24
Adela, countess of Blois, 8, 21, 76, 307 n.34
Admont, nuns of, 17–18, 96, 290, 324 n.13
Adso of Montier-en-Der, 225, 289
Aelred of Rievaulx, 3, 43, 45, 121, 146, 314 n.6
Agnes, St., 197, 333 n.127
Alan of Lille, 44, 46, 216
Alberic of Monte Cassino, 229
Albertus Magnus, 155, 330 n.88
Alcuin, 44, 98, 141, 159, 170, 241–42, 289, 324 n.15
Altercatio Phyllidis et Florae, 180
Ambrose, St., 122, 152, 289
Amicus et Amelius, 3
Andreas Capellanus, 3, 14–15, 25, 29, 43
Angers, xvi, 5, 8, 39, 47
Anna Karenina, 35

Anselm of Canterbury, 333 n.127; *Cur Deus Homo*, 34, 120; letters of, 4, 16, 53, 303 n.7
Anselm of Laon, 45, 69, 185; epitaph of, 170
Argenteuil, 56, 106, 144, 307 n.39
Aristotle, 314 n.7; *De interpretatione*, 254; *Nicomachean Ethics*, 30, 43–44
Arnaut de Mareuil, 308 n.55
Arno of Salzburg, 241
Ars dictaminis, xv, 4, 34; and epistolary fiction, 46–47, 51–52; and prose style, 48–49; conventions of, 63–64, 89, 121–22, 148, 212; manuals of, 14–15, 229; of nuns, 16, 25, 39–40, 76, 92, 236
Astralabe, 60, 298
Augustine, St., 44, 53, 176, 289; *Confessions*, 24, 37, 204; *Contra Faustum*, 148; *De civitate Dei*, 174, 197; *De Trinitate*, 241–42, 311 n.96; *Epistolae*, 93; on gender, 326 n.42; on love, 116, 136, 311 n.96

Baldwin of Ford, 216
Ballanti, Graziella, xiv, 302 n.26
Barking Abbey, 309 n.68
Baudri of Bourgueil, xvi, 6, 29, 38, 40, 287; and Adela of Blois, 76, 307 n.34; and EDA, 27, 45, 84, 289; and Ovidian revival, 7–8, 12, 25, 43, 305 n.22, 308 n.52; and Robert of Arbrissel, 45–46, 305 n.21; career of, 5, 44; cited in EDA, 85, 89, 106, 114, 118, 122, 133, 148, 156, 171, 182–83, 188, 194, 202, 204; letter-poem to Constance, 7–8, 20–22, 187; manuscript of, 5; poetry of, 10–12, 21, 97, 181, 308 n.52
Beach, Alison, 17
Beaugendre, Antoine, 5
Bede, 110, 289
Benedictines, 18
Benton, John, xi–xii, 300 n.10
Berengar, 55, 107, 298
Bergen, 50
Bergmann, Werner, 229, 250
Bernard de Meung, 10, 14–15, 39, 166, 309 n.58, 331 n.93, 336 n.20

Index of Latin Terms

Acknowledgments

I am delighted to acknowledge the support of the Andrew W. Mellon Foundation, generous benefactor of medieval studies at Northwestern University, for the research leave that enabled me to complete this project. It has been a great pleasure to collaborate once again with Jerry Singerman, editor extraordinaire at the University of Pennsylvania Press.

Like all students of medieval Latin poetry, I am deeply in the debt of Peter Dronke. It has been a special privilege to return to my old teacher's classic, *Medieval Latin and the Rise of European Love-Lyric*, and make some of his material accessible to a new generation with the help of new editions. C. Stephen Jaeger, Constant Mews, and Sylvain Piron have inspired me in their several ways, all generously allowing me to see prepublication copies of their work. In addition, Stephen Jaeger offered invaluable guidance as a press reader, as did a second, anonymous reviewer. Barbara Rosenwein helpfully vetted my essay on the history of emotions. I am grateful to Jan Ziolkowski, John Marenbon, and Peter von Moos, despite our disagreements, for insisting on a new rigor in the study of the *Epistolae duorum amantium*. William Courtenay, Margot Fassler, Andrew Kraebel, Constant Mews, and Catherine Sanok kindly answered my questions and made helpful suggestions on various points. Richard Kieckhefer, a better Latinist than I, spent many delightful hours puzzling with me over tricky bits of prose and ambiguous verse (with the help of our cat Hyperbole, whose insight into the rhetoric of the *Epistolae* has been invaluable). If I have never dedicated a book to my beloved husband before, it is only because I was waiting for this one.